CHRISTOLOGY

Christology

Hans Schwarz

WILLIAM B. EERDMANS PUBLISHING COMPANY
GRAND RAPIDS, MICHIGAN / CAMBRIDGE, U.K.

© 1998 Wm. B. Eerdmans Publishing Co.
255 Jefferson Ave. S.E., Grand Rapids, Michigan 49503 /
P.O. Box 163, Cambridge CB3 9PU U.K.

Printed in the United States of America

03 02 01 00 99 98   7 6 5 4 3 2 1

Library of Congress Cataloging-in-Publication Data

Schwarz, Hans, 1939-
    Christology / Hans Schwarz.
      p.   cm.
    Includes bibliographical references and index.
    ISBN 0-8028-4463-4 (pbk. : alk. paper)
    1. Jesus Christ — Person and offices. I. Title.
BT202.S378 1998
   232 — dc21   98-29921
                                    CIP

Contents

Preface   viii

Abbreviations   xi

Introduction   1

PART I:
IN SEARCH OF THE HISTORICAL JESUS

Chapter 1: The Quest for Jesus   7

  1. Jesus in the Eyes of Modern Reason   8

    a. The Jesus of the Enlightenment   8

    b. Jesus in the Nineteenth Century   17

    c. Jesus according to the Social Gospel   34

  2. A New Look at the Sources   39

    a. The Limits of Rational Inquiry   39

    b. Analyzing the Synoptic Material   42

    c. The New Quest for the Historical Jesus   48

    d. The Continued Quest   51

  3. The Third Wave   60

    a. A Non-eschatological Jesus   62

    b. An Eschatological but Nonapocalyptic Jesus   64

    c. Jesus in Context   67

PART II:
THE BIBLICAL TESTIMONY
AND ITS ASSESSMENT THROUGH HISTORY

Chapter 2: The History of Jesus 75

1. The Life and Destiny of Jesus 77
   a. *Date and Place of His Birth* 77
   b. *Jesus' Descent* 81
   c. *Jesus and John the Baptist* 86
   d. *Duration and Extent of Jesus' Public Ministry* 91
   e. *Trial and Death* 92
   f. *The Empty Tomb and the Epiphanies of the Resurrected One* 97

2. The Proclamation of Jesus 99
   a. *Jesus and the Law* 99
   b. *Announcing the Kingdom* 102
   c. *A Different Messiah* 105

Chapter 3: Jesus the Christ 113

1. Centrality of the Resurrection 114

2. The Witness of the Synoptics 118
   a. *The Markan Witness* 119
   b. *The Matthean Witness* 120
   c. *The Lukan Witness* 122

3. The Johannine Witness 125

4. The Pauline Witness 129

Chapter 4: Stations of Christological Reflection 137

1. The Early Church 137

2. Medieval Trends 160

3. The Reformation Emphasis 168

4. The Modern Era 175

PART III:
THE RELEVANCE OF JESUS CHRIST FOR TODAY

Chapter 5: The Human Face of God   203

    1. Bridging the Ugly, Broad Ditch   203

    2. The Jewishness of Jesus   209

    3. Jesus As Word and Deed   218

    4. Jesus' Self-Awareness   223

Excursus: Incarnation, Preexistence, and Virgin Birth   230

Chapter 6: Cross and Resurrection   241

    1. Jesus' Self-Interpretation of His Death (Eucharist)   242

    2. The Salvational Significance of Jesus' Death   249

    3. The Enigmatic Character of Christ's Resurrection   260

    4. The Turning Point of the Resurrection   268

    5. Christus or Christa?   277

Chapter 7: Christ's Presence and Future   289

    1. Descent and Ascension of Christ   290

    2. No Other Name?   299

    3. The Kingdom and the Church   311

    4. The Return of Christ   324

    Subject Index   337

    Name Index   342

    Scripture Reference Index   347

Preface

Books on the historical Jesus abound in both the scholarly market and the popular press. After the old quest for the historical Jesus of the nineteenth century and the short-lived new quest of the late 1950s and early 1960s, a third quest of the historical Jesus is on the way. Like the first two quests, it, too, is a quest pursued mainly by scholars teaching not in denominational seminaries or renowned graduate schools but in the departments of religious studies of secular universities. It comes then as no surprise that the interdisciplinary quest for the historical Jesus using insights from the history of religions, cultural anthropology, and the social sciences is gaining increasing attention. This also means that the old consensus that Jesus was an eschatological prophet who proclaimed the imminent end of the world is rapidly disappearing. In its place a new Jesus emerges, a teacher of subversive wisdom, a charismatic "holy man," or even a Jewish Cynic peasant. Yet what does this mean for the Christ of faith in whom Christians believe and whom the church proclaims as Lord and Savior? Does not such scholarship pull away the rock on which the Christian faith rests? Do we have to admit that the Jesus whom we adore and to whom we pray is a pious construct?

Of course, we can simply ignore contemporary scholarship and brush it off as the result of godless secular education or as the attempt of the left-wing popular press to throw mud on decent people. Indeed, some of the questions asked in religious studies departments concerning Jesus would rarely be on the agenda in a mainline denominational seminary. Some publishing houses know how to drum up sensationalism. The best thing is to bring out a provocative title and — simultaneously — a rejoinder, in order to cash in on both sides of the argument. Yet all things considered, it would be ill-fitting for Christians to bury their heads in the sand like ostriches. As early Christian history has shown us, Christians did not shun the world but asserted their faith in the midst of it, venturing from Palestine through the bustling and booming cities around the Mediterranean all the way to the capital of the Roman Empire and far beyond. Following the Pauline admonition "Test everything; hold fast to what is good" (1 Thess. 5:21), we cannot ignore contemporary Jesus research and its possible effects on the Christian faith. Yet being heirs of a nearly two-thousand-year-old history, just speaking of the Christian era, and another one thousand plus years taking into account the whole Judeo-Christian tradition, it would be unreasonable simply to concentrate on the last ten or fifteen years, exciting and thought provoking as they may be. Putting contemporary issues into a larger perspective not only relativizes them but also shows us that some ideas claimed as novel are in fact resurgences of earlier themes. For instance, the recent debate about Jesus' resurrection reminds us of the claims made by Reimarus at the height of the Enlightenment era. Therefore we cannot cling to the Christ of faith unless we are informed by history: the history of Jesus that is discernible in the New Testament documents, the history of christological reflection based on these documents, and the history of research leading us from the christological assertions back to their foundations in Scripture. Of course, access to the Christian faith is possible without the encumbrance of historical reflection. The Christian faith, however, is not an ideology, holding on to its tenets stubbornly and defiantly without listening to anything or anybody, but a discerning and thinking faith. It is good practice to give good reasons why one believes what one believes. While historical reflections on the search for the historical Jesus and on the biblical testimony in its assessment through history must necessarily concentrate on the essentials, the main points and persons, they should not be abbreviated to such an extent that their significance is hardly discernible. Moreover, they cannot be a pursuit in themselves but must lead up to the all-decisive question of what the relevance of Jesus Christ is for today. Pursuit of the historical Jesus and the Christ of faith can never be an endeavor for its own sake if it is not to lose its significance as theology, that is, as a word of and about God. It is my hope that I have tried to steer this middle course by presenting a solid historical and biblical introduction to the Christ of faith and an exposition of the relevance of this faith for today.

Since this exposition has been in the works for a number of years, it is difficult to remember everyone who was involved in the preparation of this text. Among many others who remain unnamed, I would like to thank my New Testament colleague Charles Sigel from Lutheran Theological Southern Seminary in Columbia, South Carolina, with whom I discussed some of the New Testament angles of this christology. Many thanks also go to my graduate research assistant David C. Ratke, who improved my English and also gave me many hints on how to present some sections much more precisely than I had originally planned. Finally, I want to thank Hildegard Ferme, who unfailingly typed up one draft after another and together with David Ratke also helped with the indexes.

Regensburg, June 1997   HANS SCHWARZ

Abbreviations

ACW   *Ancient Christian Writers*, ed. Johannes Quasten and Joseph C. Plumpe. Westminster, MD: Newman Press, 1946-.

ANF   *Ante-Nicene Fathers*, ed. Alexander Roberts and James Donaldson. 10 vols. Grand Rapids: Eerdmans, reprint of 1884-86 edition.

BC   *The Book of Concord*, ed. Theodore G. Tappert. Philadelphia: Fortress Press, 1959.

CD   *Church Dogmatics*, by Karl Barth. Ed. Geoffrey W. Bromiley and Thomas F. Torrance. Trans. Geoffrey W. Bromiley. Edinburgh: T. & T. Clark, 1936-62.

CR   *Corpus Reformatorum*, ed. W. Baum, E. Cunitz, and E. Reuss. Braunschweig: Schwetschke, 1863.

FaCH   *Fathers of the Church*, ed. Ludwig Schopp and R. J. Defarrari. New York: Cima Publishing Company and Fathers of the Church, Inc., 1949-.

LW   *Luther's Works, American Edition.* Vols. 1-30, ed. Jaroslav Pelikan. St. Louis: Concordia Publishing House, 1955-67. Vols. 31-55, ed. Helmut T. Lehmann. Philadelphia: Fortress Press, 1955-67.

NPNF   *Nicene and Post-Nicene Fathers of the Christian Church*, ed. Philip Schaff. Grand Rapids: Eerdmans, 1983 reprint edition.

PG   *Patrologia graeca.* Vols. 1-161, ed. J. P. Migne. Paris: 1876-91.

RAC   *Reallexikon für die Antike und Christentum.*

TDOT   *Theological Dictionary of the Old Testament*, ed. G. Johannes

Botterweck, Helmer Ringgren, and Heinz-Josef Fabry.
Trans. John T. Willis et al. Grand Rapids: Eerdmans, 1977-.

TDNT   *Theological Dictionary of the New Testament,* ed. Gerhard Kittel and Gerhard Friedrich. Trans. Geoffrey W. Bromiley. 10 vols. Grand Rapids: Eerdmans, 1964-76.

TRE   *Theologische Realenzyklopädie.* Vols. 1-. Ed. Gerhard Krause and Gerhard Müller. Berlin and New York: Walter de Gruyter, 1977-.

WA   *D. Martin Luthers Werke: Kritische Gesamtausgabe.* Vols. 1-. Weimar: Hermann Böhlau, 1883-.

Introduction

Who was and who is Jesus of Nazareth? Questions like these have been posed since the beginning of the Christian faith, because none of the founders of the major world religions has been as much contested in his message and person as Jesus of Nazareth. There is little debate about whether Mohammed ever lived or what he taught. It is commonly accepted that he regarded himself as Allah's prophet and that he made known to the people Allah's revelation, which, he claimed, was given to him through an angel. We also know approximately when Buddha lived, who his parents were, and what the major tenets of his teaching were. But with Jesus the story is different. Occasionally some people still claim that he never lived and that the New Testament is a fictitious composition. But even among the vast majority of scholars who agree on Jesus' historicity there is no consensus on the significance of Jesus or on the content of his teaching.

The reason for this dilemma is twofold: First, while the Muslim religion stresses obedience and Buddhism emphasizes contemplation, the Christian faith invites understanding. When Philip was summoned to join a court official of Queen Candace and heard the official reading the scroll of the prophet Isaiah, he did not ask him in Buddhist fashion whether he had the right insight nor in the vein of a good Muslim whether he had obeyed all the precepts of the prophet. His question instead was "Do you understand what you are reading?" (Acts 8:30). The Christian faith invites discerning reflection. Yet this reflection can be carried so far that the object of reflection disintegrates.

The second reason for our dilemma is that Jesus can be regarded as the founder of the Christian faith only in a very limited sense. While

1

during his lifetime he had only a modest following, after his death a rapidly growing community emerged that considered him, in one sense or another, to be the Christ. Rudolf Bultmann (1884-1976) rightly claimed: "He who formerly had been the *bearer* of the message was drawn into it and became its essential *content. The proclaimer became the proclaimed* —but the central question is: In what sense?"[1]

The question then arises whether Jesus is actually part of the Christian faith or only its presupposition. Again, Bultmann was right when he asserted that "*the message of Jesus* is a presupposition for the theology of the New Testament rather than a part of that theology itself."[2] Without the message of Jesus, there would be no New Testament theology, and, conversely, New Testament theology is a reflection upon Jesus rather than just a collection of his sayings. Even the Gospels do not present a strict biographical account of his life and teachings. How history and theological reflection are intertwined becomes immediately evident when we look at the beginning of the Gospels. Mark, for instance, opens his account with the sentence: "The beginning of the good news of Jesus Christ, the Son of God" (Mark 1:1). Similarly, Matthew starts with the announcement: "An account of the genealogy of Jesus the Messiah" (Matt. 1:1). Only Luke seems to take a different path when he claims that he attempted "to write an orderly account" (Luke 1:3). Yet the intention of his account is neither biographical nor historical but seeks rather "to know the truth [of the faith]" (1:4). We have no document that exists exclusively for the purpose of narrating the story of Jesus.

Skeptical minds might conclude that the reason for the lack of biographical interest is that the mission of Jesus ended in failure. At the end of Jesus' life stood the cross. Why should anybody want to tell about a person who did not succeed unless one has a morbid fascination with negativity and failure? Such reasoning, however, finds no backing in the biblical sources. We remember that two of the Synoptic writers introduce their Gospel as that of Jesus Christ or of Jesus the Messiah. The recognition of Jesus as the Christ led to a neglect of the human person of Jesus and an attempt to demonstrate his Christ-like attributes. Skeptics could object that the move to recognize Jesus as the Christ was the great

1. Rudolf Bultmann, *Theology of the New Testament*, trans. Kendrick Grobel (New York: Charles Scribner's, 1954), 1:33.
2. Bultmann, *Theology of the New Testament*, 1:3.

2

cover-up by which his early followers sought to ignore the fact that his mission had failed. Confronted with this situation there are two possibilities.

In the first place we could simply ignore this objection and continue to proclaim Jesus as the Christ, a claim the church has made for nearly two thousand years. Such an approach would ignore the charge of the skeptic and erect a sign of faith in a doubting world. But it would neither attempt to persuade the growing number of skeptics nor endeavor to engage them in dialogue. Moreover, our unwillingness to listen to their charges could be interpreted as a sign of acquiescence. The other avenue open to us, and the one which is pursued in the following pages, is to ascertain, as far as this is still possible, whether the confession of Jesus as Christ rests on the proclamation, person, and destiny of Jesus of Nazareth. In other words, we want to show that faith in Jesus as Lord and Savior is not a deception; and if faith is not a logical consequence, at least it is a legitimate possibility based upon the Christ event.

The second option which confronts us deals with the issue of continuity. To what extent is there continuity between Jesus of Nazareth and the Christ who is portrayed in the biblical documents, and further to what extent is there continuity between the biblical Christ and the Christ of the dogma of the church, such as the trinitarian and christological dogma? Once we have ascertained this kind of continuity, at least in outline, provided it ever existed, we can move on to ask what significance Christ has for us today.

In all these pursuits we must keep in mind that our purpose is not to produce an exegetical or historical study. Though we must delve into both areas, detailed knowledge of them cannot be reproduced here. Yet before we venture into our project, we must at least briefly review the main results of the search already completed. After all, Albert Schweitzer (1875-1965) claimed that the search for Jesus ended with a big question mark. Perhaps he was correct that we cannot establish any continuity between Jesus Christ, the focus of the Christian faith, and the Jesus of history. Therefore it is even more necessary to give careful attention both to the results of the search for the Jesus of history and its presuppositions.

Part I
In Search of
the Historical Jesus

Every reflection on Christ is ultimately nourished by the New Testament documents. Even those who see in Jesus Christ an especially gifted teacher must reconfirm their ideas in the New Testament sources. Small wonder that the New Testament has a long history of interpretation as far as the historical Jesus is concerned and is itself part of this interpretation process.

1. The Quest for Jesus

In his famous study *The Quest for the Historical Jesus: A Critical Study of Its Progress from Reimarus to Wrede* (1906), Albert Schweitzer defined very perceptively the emergence of autonomous reason as the historical starting point for the inquiry into the historical Jesus. Until the Reformation, the New Testament served as the basis for the dogma of the church. The quest for the "historical" Jesus was identical with the quest for Jesus Christ. The emphasis, especially in the Lutheran Reformation, was on the salvific accomplishment of Christ and not on his person or his words. This is evident from Luther's explanation of the second article of the Apostles' Creed, where he immediately focuses on what Christ has done for us, saying: "I believe that Jesus Christ . . . is my Lord, who has redeemed me."[1] Similarly, Philipp Melanchthon (1497-1560) declared in his *Loci communes* of 1521: "This is to know Christ, to wit, to know his benefits and not as they [i.e., the Scholastics] teach to perceive his natures and the mode of his incarnation."[2] Through the development of an increasingly critically historical consciousness the distinction was then made between the Jesus of history and the Christ of the New Testament. The quest for Jesus was the result of autonomous reason which wanted to investigate the history leading up to the formation of the New Testament and which sensed a difference between that which is recorded in these documents and the actual course of history. Since

---

1. Martin Luther, *The Small Catechism,* in *BC,* 345.
2. *The Loci Communes of Philip Melanchthon,* trans. Charles Leander Hill, intro. E. E. Flack (Boston: Meador, 1944), 68.

reason was thought to be the reliable guide in historical matters, this first phase was characterized by a rationalistic interpretation of Jesus.

1. Jesus in the Eyes of Modern Reason

The Christian faith cannot be fathomed without the help of reason. The decisive question, however, is what weight reason should receive. Is it serving faith, is it opposed to faith, or is it a distant observer? The rationalistic interpretation of Jesus was initially characterized by a critical animosity of reason to the New Testament documents that only gradually changed to a more constructive approach. This initial hostility was the fault not only of the investigators, but to a large measure also of the theological and ecclesiastical establishment, which, like any tradition of long order, did not welcome new approaches to its subject matter. The first part of the pilgrimage largely coincided with the Enlightenment of the eighteenth century and is characterized by Reimarus at the beginning and Semler at the end.

a. The Jesus of the Enlightenment

Hermann Samuel Reimarus (1694-1768) served for most of his life as professor of oriental languages at the Gymnasium Johanneum in Hamburg. During his lifetime he was a locally respected scholar and teacher, neither internationally famous nor original in his thoughts. Reimarus influenced more than anybody else the approach to the scriptural documents during the Enlightenment. There exists a close similarity between his views and those of the English Deists such as Anthony Collins (1676-1729), John Tolland (1670-1722), or even Thomas Woolston (1669-1733). Woolston, for example, severely attacked the credibility of the New Testament in his *Six Discourses on the Miracles of Our Saviour* (1727-30). Most interesting was his treatment of Christ's resurrection. He attempted to show that the guards at the tomb and the sealed entrance do not exclude a fraudulent removal of the corpse but almost presuppose it. Since the seal was removed without the knowledge of the authorities, fraud is nearly proven. The Gospel even admits that the soldiers were open to bribery.

The epiphanies of the resurrected one are interpreted with similar skepticism. The reports of the four Gospels are said to show such discrepancies that they must be tales of "old superstitious women." Then Woolston explains the resurrection in a mystical-allegorical way as a spiritual one. Perhaps Reimarus was familiar with the writings of the English Deists, or at least their fate. Not only had Woolston drawn the ire of literary enemies, but the political authorities had indicted him for his blasphemy and he eventually died in prison.

Reimarus, however, was not a Deist. He was known as a pious and devout Christian, and he attended church services and participated in the Lord's Supper. Yet amid his studies, doubts about the reliability of the biblical documents arose in him. He entrusted them to his pen, hoping to find evidence to remove these doubts. But his doubts grew and finally were documented in the rather sizable manuscript, *Apology or Treatise in Defense of the Reasonable Worship of God*, of which one part is entitled *The Goal of Jesus and His Disciples.* Since he knew that they would, at the least, receive criticism, he showed his writings only to a few trusted friends.[3] Reimarus and his ideas gained prominence only posthumously, when Gotthold Ephraim Lessing (1729-81) obtained permission from Reimarus's children to publish a few "fragments" of the *Apology* between 1774 and 1778. Altogether Lessing chose six essays or fragments, claiming that he had found them in Wolfenbüttel Library without knowing who their author was. The last and most important of the essays was entitled *The Goal of Jesus and His Disciples,* which Lessing published in a heavily edited version in 1778. It was uncertain until 1814, the year when Reimarus's son gave a copy of the *Apology* to the library of the University of Göttingen, who the real author was, though some had suspected Reimarus's authorship as early as 1777.

Reimarus was an Enlightenment Rationalist, and as a Rationalist he attempted wherever possible to base ideas, ideals, and beliefs in reason. Revelation was supplanted by reason. Reimarus never doubted the historicity of Jesus, but he did come to the Scriptures with certain questions and presuppositions. The first question he asked was, "What did Jesus

---

3. In fact only three original copies of this manuscript have survived, at least one of them written by Reimarus himself. For more on the origin of the *Apology* and the influence of others on Reimarus see Charles H. Talbert, ed., *Reimarus: Fragments,* trans. Ralph S. Fraser (Philadelphia: Fortress, 1970), esp. 1-43, and Hermann Samuel Reimarus, *The Goal of Jesus and His Disciples,* trans. George W. Buchanan (Leiden: E. J. Brill, 1970), 1-32.

himself hold in his teaching and action to be the purpose of his ministry?"[4] The second question with which Reimarus was concerned was: Is the Christian faith "reasonable"?

To answer these questions Reimarus set out a method by which he could discern what Jesus really taught. He wanted to separate completely what the apostles set forth in their own writings from what Jesus himself taught during his own lifetime. His conclusion or answer to the first question of how Jesus saw the purpose of his own teaching and activity was that the whole content of Jesus' proclamation could be reduced to the summons, "Repent, for the Kingdom of Heaven has come near" (Matt. 3:2). "Both the Kingdom of Heaven and conversion belong together, because the Kingdom of Heaven is the goal and conversion is a means or a preparation for this Kingdom of Heaven."[5] Jesus was born a Jew and wanted to remain one. He did not want to abolish the Jewish religion and in its stead reveal new articles of faith and introduce new mysteries; rather, Jesus' intention was directed toward a change of mind, sincere love of God and one's neighbor, patience, gentleness, self-denial, and the suppression of all evil desire — in short, conversion. Jesus did not want to revise the Jewish faith; rather, he wanted to renew it.

If this was the faith of Jesus, or how Jesus understood the purpose of his teaching and activity, then what is the relationship of Jesus' faith to the Christian faith? Reimarus set out to investigate the biblical roots of fundamental Christian articles of faith. He investigated the understanding of heaven, the dogma of Trinity, and the work of salvation through Jesus as the Son of God and as God-man.

With respect to Jesus' identity, Reimarus concluded that, in the New Testament, for the Jews and in Jesus' own words, "son of God" points to a man loved by God in a special way. While it is not a unique attribute, it denotes an individual who is distinguished from others by some form of superiority or degree of perfection. Reimarus conceded that "Jesus appropriated for himself all those superiorities which came from the designations of an exceptional prophet, king, and beloved of God and were in conformity with the opinions of the Jews at that time concerning the Messiah." But he is quick to add that "this all still remained within

4. Reimarus, *The Goal of Jesus*, 36.
5. Reimarus, *The Goal of Jesus*, 38.

the limits of humanity."[6] Though Jesus certainly knew that he was the Messiah, he was not divine. Reimarus then went on to equate the Son of God and the Son of Man and correctly suggested that Jesus preferred to call himself the Son of Man, which, in Reimarus's view, pointed to Jesus' own humility.

Once Reimarus had "solved" the mystery of Jesus' divinity, he investigated the notion of the triune God. The key passage for the Trinity is Jesus' baptism, when the Spirit descends from heaven in the form of a dove. Reimarus found it strange that only Jesus saw the Spirit, not the bystanders. He surmised it was perhaps a vision in which Jesus was presented with extraordinary spiritual gifts from heaven. "So only one godly person is left in the vision, namely the One that calls from heaven."[7] If Jesus himself wanted to present this strange teaching, completely unknown to Jews, of three different persons in one divine essence, he would not have kept silent about this until after his resurrection. Even the frequent mentioning of the unity of the Father and the Son — for example, "I and the Father are one" (John 10:30) — means nothing but the unity of disposition and will. Jesus loved his Father and acted according to his will. This unity foreshadowed what Schleiermacher nearly a century later called "the feeling of absolute dependence." Reimarus concluded that in the New Testament being "one" means nothing but an agreement or a unity of disposition. So when Jesus said, "I and the Father are one," he did not intend to make himself God or one with the divine essence. He just wanted to express the powerful kind of love he had toward the Father and the Father had toward him.

With regard to the sacraments, Reimarus wondered why baptism was not explicitly introduced in the New Testament (unlike the Eucharist), and why only one Evangelist connected it with a triune formula. Yet this triune formula only expressed what should have been evident, that someone who is baptized should become a child of God, follow the Messiah, and experience the fullness of spiritual gifts. In other words, Reimarus again spiritualized and allegorized the reference to the Trinity in order to stay within a this-worldly reference system. Neither did the Last Supper introduce anything new, according to Reimarus. It did not lead to the Eucharist but was a memorial symbol signifying that Jesus'

6. Reimarus, *The Goal of Jesus*, 51.
7. Reimarus, *The Goal of Jesus*, 57.

11

life and body had been given for his disciples. He did not abolish the Passover but confirmed it through his own sacrifice.

The resurrection and the parousia were particularly troubling and objectionable to Reimarus. He thought it significant that the only accounts of resurrection appearances were those of the disciples of Jesus, to whom he did not attach much credibility. Furthermore, the Sanhedrin and other leading Jews in Jerusalem were silent on this issue. Reimarus trusted the High Council of Jerusalem more than the disciples, and the High Council claimed that the disciples came secretly during the night, stole the corpse, and went around saying he had risen. Even the accounts of the resurrection are fraught with inconsistencies. For instance, it is impossible to understand how Jesus could have spoken clearly during his lifetime of his death and of his resurrection after three days and the disciples speak and act as if they heard nothing of it. "They wrap up the corpse and try to preserve it with many spices to protect it from foulness and decomposition."[8] They assumed that Jesus was dead and would remain dead, as other people remained dead who had died before him. Reimarus concluded that the Christian faith was founded on a deliberate fraud. Even the Old Testament references that are supposed to substantiate Jesus' resurrection often point in the opposite direction.

Closely related to the contradictions of the resurrection are the problems of the claim that "Jesus after his ascension to heaven would soon come again in greater power and glory from above and then would begin his glorious kingdom."[9] "Now if the apostles would have said at that time that there would still be another seventeen, eighteen, or more, centuries before Christ would come again from the clouds of heaven to begin his kingdom, people would only have laughed at them. People would have believed that by postponing the fulfillment of the promise until after so many men and generations had passed, they were only trying to conceal their own embarrassment and that of their Master."[10]

The delay of the parousia together with the rejection of the resurrection were Reimarus's two main objections to the Christian faith. Even the miracles, suspect as they were, could not support the faltering basis of the Christian faith. Why would the disciples, however, resort to a

8. Reimarus, *The Goal of Jesus*, 81.
9. Reimarus, *The Goal of Jesus*, 104.
10. Reimarus, *The Goal of Jesus*, 106.

deliberate fraud? Again Reimarus had a plausible answer: secular exaltation and advantages. The poor fishermen followed Jesus hoping that they would play a prominent role in his kingdom. Already during his lifetime they had quarreled about the seats of honor they would occupy. When Jesus died and their hopes collapsed, they were initially haunted by anxiety and fear that they would also be persecuted. But things remained quiet and they wondered what they should do now. Going back to their previous menial labor would have meant hardship and dangers. But it would also have meant insult because their hopes had been greatly reduced from their exalted views. They remembered that they had a relatively easy life following their teacher, and he was not labeled "an eater and a wine guzzler" for nothing. So they "opened up for themselves a new way through a bold invention."[11] Reimarus even suggests that the disciples waited fifty days before they publicly announced his resurrection. By then his body was so decomposed that nobody could have recognized him if anyone had found the stolen corpse.

Reimarus concluded that since the new system which the disciples developed depends on things they did not know before and omits things which were essential to Jesus' history, their new system is not in agreement with history. History was conformed to their new system. In other words, the Christian faith, the new system developed by the disciples, is largely a literary device and void of historical undergirding. While the disciples regarded Jesus until his death as the secular savior of Israel, in the new system they saw him as the spiritual deliverer of all people. This shift depended very heavily on the claim that Jesus rose from the dead and ascended into heaven; the shift depended on the resurrection. Why did the disciples reinterpret and revise the teaching and activity of Jesus?

With respect to the resurrection, Reimarus asserted that the shift from Jesus as a secular Messiah to Jesus as the Savior of all humanity is that the first notion was rendered useless through his suffering and death. As we have already noted, Reimarus said that Jesus did not intend to institute anything new in the Jewish religion; the change had to come with the disciples. Reimarus suggested that until his death the disciples thought Jesus was a secular, powerful savior of the people of Israel. Only when their hope collapsed on account of his (uneventful) death "did the apostles build the system of a spiritual suffering savior of the whole

---

11. Reimarus, *The Goal of Jesus*, 129.

13

human race."[12] Since the Gospel writers wrote their stories of Jesus' teaching and action long after his death, they changed the stories to conform to their new understanding of Jesus. They even acknowledged that initially they had understood him incorrectly. Reimarus admits, however, that the Gospel writers still left, "accidentally and by human carelessness, a few remnants of the old system."[13] This gives us a chance to perceive the difference between the original proclamation and the changes that were introduced by the disciples.

The construct that Reimarus offered is certainly not entirely unfounded. The sacraments, the two-nature christology, the doctrine of the Trinity, and so on were not taught by Jesus of Nazareth. Reimarus's objections have appeared, in one form or another, throughout the centuries. The immense furor at the time of the publication of the fragments was not caused because Reimarus had disclaimed the historicity of certain events. It was caused rather by Reimarus's attempt to explain the transition from Jesus of Nazareth to Jesus the Christ by assuming a deliberate fraud. While this thesis was wrong, we should not overlook Reimarus's achievements. He showed that there is a difference between the Jesus of history and the biblical Christ. He also perceived correctly that the Gospels were written under the impression of the Easter event and therefore were not biographies in the strict sense of the term. They were written to facilitate the proclamation of Jesus Christ. He also noticed that the resurrection and parousia of our Lord are central to the Christian faith. Yet he failed to realize that these central points of the Christian faith did indeed imply a reality effected by history.

Gotthold Ephraim Lessing (1729-81), who published the "fragments" when he served as librarian at Wolfenbüttel, had a very different outlook from that of Reimarus. This becomes clear when he juxtaposed "the accidental truths of history" to the "necessary truths of reason."[14] Important for him was not history but reason. Christ was "the first *reliable, practical* teacher of the immortality of the soul."[15] Christ was reliable

---

12. Reimarus, *The Goal of Jesus*, 80.

13. Reimarus, *The Goal of Jesus*, 81.

14. *On the Proof of the Spirit and of the Power*, in *Lessing's Theological Writings*, trans. Henry Chadwick (London: Adam & Charles Black, 1956), 53. For the ambiguity of the metaphor see Gordon E. Michalson Jr., *Lessing's 'Ugly Ditch': A Study of Theology and History* (University Park, Pa.: Pennsylvania State University, 1985), 1ff.

15. For the following and for the quotation see Gotthold Ephraim Lessing, *The Education of the Human Race* 58, in *Lessing's Theological Writings*, 92.

because of the prophecies he fulfilled, the miracles he achieved, and his revival after death. Yet Lessing was unconvinced that these "proofs" were still valid. Once these proofs were useful for recognizing and accepting the truth of Jesus' teachings, but they in the age of reason they were no longer necessary. Previously the doctrine of immortality was received immediately through God's revelation, but now it could also be derived from reason in an immediate way. Eventually Scripture would no longer be necessary in educating humanity.

In his posthumously published fragment *The Religion of Christ* (1780), Lessing draws, similarly to Reimarus, a distinction between the Christian religion and the religion of Christ. The Christian religion is the religion which assumes as true that Jesus was more than a human being and thus makes him "the object of its worship."[16] Since reason questions that he was more than a human being, it is inconceivable that the religion of Christ and the Christian religion can focus on the same person. While the religion of Christ is very clearly presented in the Gospels, the Christian religion is so ambiguous that it is difficult to find two people who agree as to its content. Undoubtedly Lessing preferred the religion of Christ, the religion that Christ realized and practiced as a human being and that every human being should and can share with him. In other words, Lessing advocated a religion of reason common to all humanity that has its prime example in Jesus. Jesus then becomes the example and advocate of the true (natural) religion.

Johann Salomon Semler (1725-91), professor of theology at Halle, was one of many who reacted against Reimarus. Semler's approach is especially interesting, since he wrote a four-volume treatise, *A Free Investigation of the Canon* (1771-75), in which he claimed that the word of God and Holy Scripture are not identical. He called for a free investigation of the historical circumstances under which every book of the canon had been written and of its permanent value for further religious development.[17] Semler proposed a rigorously historical perspective on the Bible. Yet he did not want to act destructively. He was convinced that

---

16. Gotthold Ephraim Lessing, *The Religion of Christ* 4, in *Lessing's Theological Writings,* 106.

17. See for further details Werner Georg Kümmel, *The New Testament: The History of the Investigation of Its Problems,* trans. S. McLean Gilmour and Howard C. Kee (New York: Abingdon, 1972), 63ff.

such a procedure would not impede true Christian religion or interfere with its power and spiritually beneficial efficiency.

Helpful for this kind of approach and for reconciling biblical criticism with the Christian faith was the theory of accommodation, which dates back to the Greek fathers and which had gained renewed attention toward the close of the eighteenth century.[18] Semler assumed that there are certain figurative ways of speech and religious concepts in which Jesus and his disciples accommodated themselves to a certain degree to the traditional religious concepts of their audience. Semler saw his assumption substantiated by Jesus talking directly to his disciples, while speaking in parables to other people. Even to his disciples he did not always communicate the blunt truth. Semler also surmised that the Evangelists differed in their Gospels because they wanted to accommodate their message to the religious and ethnic background of their respective audiences. Paul even explicitly mentioned that he wanted to be a Jew to the Jews and a Greek to the Greeks (1 Cor. 9:20).

When he came to the message of Jesus, Semler claimed that Jesus' advocacy of the near advent of the parousia was an accommodation to Jewish apocalyptic expectations. Yet in stark contrast to Jewish particularism, Jesus himself proclaimed the presence of salvation and of the kingdom. He did not advocate a visible, political kingdom, but an invisible, eternal, and spiritual kingdom that is open to all and can be realized in the hearts of all people. Though Semler discarded any manifest futurist eschatology in terms of a cataclysmic catastrophe, he advocated that individuals would meet their judge and Lord in the beyond. With this emphasis on the interiorization of the Christian faith, Semler rejected the rationalism of Lessing.

Semler charged that Lessing's work could only discredit serious theology. While this was true, Semler's approach had its own shortcomings and dangers. Certainly we must distinguish between Jesus and the conceptual background out of which he came, but it is also true that the kingdom of God was at the center of Jesus' proclamation. To completely disregard the historical background as an accommodation or as picturesque language is too simple. Here we must heed Bultmann's caution

18. For Semler's theory of accommodation see Gottfried Hornig, *Die Anfänge der historisch-kritischen Theologie: Johann Salomo Semlers Schriftverständnis und seine Stellung zu Luther* (Göttingen: Vandenhoeck & Ruprecht, 1961), 211-36, esp. 222.

that the task of the theologian is not to discard but to interpret. Yet the imaginations of both Lessing and Semler were captivated by christology and not some theistic or deistic doctrine of God. This seems to be the great difference between English Deism and German biblical criticism. The Reformation catchwords of *sola Scriptura* (Scripture alone) and *solus Christus* (Christ alone) continued to work in scholars who had long ago discarded the *sola fide* (faith alone) of the Reformers. In England, however, the scholastic tradition of the Cambridge Platonists and of other philosophical minds was much too persuasive to allow for such christocentric investigations.

b. Jesus in the Nineteenth Century

The nineteenth century marks the high point of the search for the life of Jesus. Albert Schweitzer was right when he claimed, "The greatest achievement of German theology is the critical investigation of the life of Jesus. What was accomplished here has laid down the conditions and determined the course of the religious thinking of the future."[19] The nineteenth century did more than any other to promulgate research into the life of Jesus. Part of this may have been due to greater awareness of the different sources contained within the New Testament. Another reason for the increase of interest in the historical Jesus was Romanticism and its interest in antiquity. Alongside Rome and Greece the Holy Land figured prominently; a natural curiosity emerged about the "founder" of the Christian religion.

Friedrich Schleiermacher (1768-1834) was the first theologian to lecture publicly on the life of Jesus.[20] Books on the life of Jesus had already been published, but the life of Jesus had not become a distinct part of academic studies. Schleiermacher attempted to perceive Jesus in the context of his time and in his own right. He was convinced that we can have a firm faith only if we can ascertain its ground. "If the person of Christ is not to be retained, then Christianity as such must be given

19. Albert Schweitzer, *The Quest of the Historical Jesus: A Critical Survey of Its Progress from Reimarus to Wrede,* trans. W. Montgomery, 2d ed. (London: A. & C. Black, 1922), 1.

20. So Jack Verheyden in his introduction to Friedrich Schleiermacher, *The Life of Jesus,* trans. Jack Verheyden (Philadelphia: Fortress, 1975), xi.

up and only what is true for itself about it must remain."[21] With this caution in mind, and knowing that he could not present a detailed bibliography, Schleiermacher attempted to sketch out Jesus' life and ministry. He knew that some historical details could not be definitively ascertained, for instance, whether Jesus was born in Nazareth or in Bethlehem. But for faith this uncertainty was of no consequence. Even such an important issue as the virginal conception of Jesus was carefully circumvented, since "faith has no interest in this because the indwelling of the divine can depend not on the lack of human conception but only on the absence of the sinful."[22]

Schleiermacher recognized that one of the problems of historical investigation is the practical necessity of conceiving of Christ in purely human terms, while faith associates a divine action with him. Yet he claims that "it has always tacitly been admitted that it is possible for both the divine and the human to exist in an individual Christian, and the question resolves itself into the problem of accounting for the same conjunction in the instance of the person of Christ."[23] Jesus knew about his Messiahship through the claims made by others and through the confirmation of it in his self-consciousness. This self-consciousness gradually developed in him until it assumed definite form in being in full relationship with the Father's will. When Schleiermacher considered Jesus' activities, he asserted that he was not an activist with a plan, but "his influential activity was the pure communication of himself."[24] Central to him was the idea of the kingdom of God which arose out of his self-consciousness and his perception of sin.

Schleiermacher did not perceive Jesus' baptism as the starting point of his mission, since such an emphasis on baptism would either lead to a Gnostic identification of Jesus with the world or to the rationalistic idea that he was first made aware of his vocation at baptism. Both of these notions have no backing in Scripture. Jesus' baptism was, in part, "a symbolic aspect of his proclamation and in part the recognition of the Baptist and of the relation of the Baptist's mission to his own."[25] In

21. Schleiermacher, *The Life of Jesus*, 22.
22. Schleiermacher, *The Life of Jesus*, 56.
23. Schleiermacher, *The Life of Jesus*, 87.
24. Schleiermacher, *The Life of Jesus*, 123.
25. Schleiermacher, *The Life of Jesus*, 136.

other words, it was not a baptism for the forgiveness of Jesus' sins, but to acknowledge John as his forerunner.

Schleiermacher distinguished between an inner and an outer dimension of Jesus' public life. The outer dimension is specified by locality and external relationships (including the miracles) since they deal with specific occasions, while the inner is concerned with the teaching of Christ and the founding of a community. In his attempt to pinpoint the locality of Jesus' public ministry, Schleiermacher noticed the discrepancy between the different Gospels. Thus it is difficult to establish an itinerary of Jesus or definite places of residency. Schleiermacher also noted that miracles make up a large portion of Jesus' ministry. A true recognition of Jesus might be confirmed by the miracles which Jesus performed, but never based on their performance.[26] Furthermore, Schleiermacher realized that the distinction between the natural and the supernatural did not exist at Jesus' time and therefore should not be applied to the discussion of Jesus' miracles.[27] Jesus performed healing miracles only incidentally and occasionally. Schleiermacher did not quickly discard the factuality of miracles. He cautioned, however, that they must be carefully examined, and he drew analogies to them from today's experiences whenever feasible. Thus he limited Christ's miracles to the extent that they can be understood in human terms and that Christ made use of his wonder-working power in a way that was in conformity with his office.

Schleiermacher saw no need to distinguish between the teaching *of* Christ and the teaching *about* Christ. This is not surprising since he held the Gospel of John (which carefully weaves together both aspects) to be older than the Synoptics. He also found his position substantiated by the fact that everything relating to the kingdom of God, a central focus of Jesus' teachings, is also about Christ. The centrality of the kingdom of God in Jesus' teachings seems to have started with Schleiermacher, though it was not foreign to Reimarus either.[28] But Schleiermacher introduced another distinction: between what Christ himself taught and what he took over from tradition. Though Schleiermacher conceded that Jesus adopted con-

---

26. Friedrich Schleiermacher, *The Christian Faith* §103, ed. H. R. Mackintosh and J. S. Stewart (New York: Harper, 1963), 2:450.

27. Schleiermacher, *The Life of Jesus*, 194.

28. Verheyden, in Schleiermacher, *The Life of Jesus*, 235 n. 29.

cepts from tradition, such as the Messianic idea, he contended that this often occurred polemically. Since the idea of the kingdom cannot be separated from that of the Son of God, Christ's teaching was about his person and his mission. Everything else developed from this.

With respect to Christ's death and resurrection, it is interesting to note that Schleiermacher argued quite differently from Reimarus. For the latter, the story of the guard at the tomb was an invention to support the Sanhedrin's claim that the body was stolen. But for Schleiermacher this story did not lead to this conclusion. Jesus was indeed resurrected. Yet strangely enough, the resurrection was not a prominent theme in Schleiermacher's theology. He stated in *The Christian Faith:* "The facts of the Resurrection and the Ascension of Christ, and the prediction of His Return to Judgment cannot be laid down as properly constituent parts of the doctrine of His Person."[29] His extensive discussion of the resurrection and ascension indicates that he held that the resurrection of Christ did indeed occur. Contrary to Albert Schweitzer, Schleiermacher thought of Christ's death as an actual death.[30] In his resurrection Christ continued his work as he had done before, though he considered his resurrection to be only temporary, concluding with his ascension. The ascension, which Schleiermacher accepted as something incomprehensible, marks the end of Jesus' second life on earth. Although Schleiermacher showed Jesus to be in continuity with the covenant history of the Old Testament, he completely ignored the eschatological aspects of Jesus' life and work. Perhaps this resulted from his endeavor to show the complete humanity of Jesus. At the same time, however, he consistently referred to him as Christ and not as Jesus. Schleiermacher's historical interest aside, it is more a dogmatic Christ who is presented to us than a Jesus of history, as Schweitzer rightly noted.[31]

The Christ that Schleiermacher discovered was the fulfillment of the Old Testament covenant. *"What the men of God of the old covenant wished and expressed as their hopes and as divine promises was fulfilled in Christ,"* was Schleiermacher's conclusion.[32] Christ's teaching about his person and his

29. Schleiermacher, *The Christian Faith* §99, 2:417.

30. For discussion and details see Verheyden, in Schleiermacher, *The Life of Jesus,* 456-57 n. 60.

31. Schweitzer, *Quest of the Historical Jesus,* 67.

32. Schweitzer, *Quest of the Historical Jesus,* 252.

mission came together. In his person and mission Christ was totally dependent on God. "He could do nothing of himself, but must always look to the Father. In other words, his consciousness of God never failed him, and apart from it he amounted to nothing."[33] *"He attributes everything to the constancy of his relationship to God, to the constant, uninterrupted vitality of his consciousness of God."*[34] There was a constant divine communication between Jesus and his Father. Christ's teaching about God reflects that dependence. He showed that God is love. Out of love for the Son, God loves those whom Christ loves. This love is the foundation for the fellowship of the individual believer of Christ with him and the fellowship of believers among themselves. Schleiermacher realized that Christ's aspirations were not of a political nature. He stated that the kingdom of God was opposed to the world and saw this opposition in analogy to the struggle of the spirit against the flesh.

David Friedrich Strauss (1808-74) addressed the issue of the historical Christ in a series of books beginning with his two-volume *Life of Jesus* in 1835. If Schleiermacher's christology was based on the Christ *event*, then Strauss's christology was based on the Christ *idea*. His critical approach was much more radical than that of Schleiermacher. The birth, infancy, and childhood narratives were declared to be without historical value and largely mythical. Strauss did concede that Jesus came under the influence of John the Baptist, whose proclamation of the coming Messianic kingdom he continued once John had been imprisoned. In contrast to many twentieth-century New Testament scholars, such as Rudolf Bultmann, Strauss also declared: "Jesus held and expressed the conviction that he was the Messiah; this is an indisputable fact."[35] Jesus also thought that he would visibly make his second advent on the clouds of heaven as the Messianic Son of Man and terminate the existing dispensation. At first Jesus thought the Messianic glory would soon arrive, but later he came to realize that his suffering and death were a necessary part of his Messianic mission. In the *New Life of Jesus* Strauss went a step further and ascribed these apocalyptic predictions to the early church rather than to Jesus himself. With regard to the resurrection

---

33. Schweitzer, *Quest of the Historical Jesus*, 263.
34. Schweitzer, *Quest of the Historical Jesus*, 265.
35. David Friedrich Strauss, *The Life of Jesus Critically Examined* §62, ed. Peter C. Hodgson, trans. George Eliot (Philadelphia: Fortress, 1972), 284.

Strauss posed the following dilemma in *Life of Jesus:* "Either Jesus was not really dead, or he did not really rise again."[36] While according to Strauss reason favored the first option, he was convinced that historical evidence must lead to the latter. The reports of the empty tomb were legendary, and the appearances of the resurrected Christ were subjective visions or hallucinations engendered by the enthusiasm of the disciples. The ascension, too, is declared to be myth.

Of what significance could such a demythologized Jesus still be? Strauss had been deeply influenced by Hegel. While the followers of Hegel contended that in Jesus we encounter in one sentient historical individual the embodiment of the idea of the unity of the divine with the human, Strauss took this idea one step further and asserted that this unity could not be restricted to one individual. He asked: "Is not the idea of the unity of the divine and human natures a real one in a far higher sense, when I regard the whole race of mankind as its realization, than when I single out one man as such a realization?"[37] In other words, the incarnation is taking place in the whole of humanity instead of only in Jesus. Admittedly, given the subjective religious needs of the ancient world, Strauss argued, the idea of the unity between God and humanity could only be perceived in the concrete figure of an individual, but today this is no longer necessary. The idea of humanity as one with God "has become a spiritual and divine idea, which has its confirmation no longer in history but in philosophy."[38] Here Lessing's old question of how an accidental event in history (e.g., Jesus' life and work) could ever attain the status of necessary truth of reason is answered in the negative. We do not need history but philosophy. It was with this in his arsenal that Strauss attacked Schleiermacher. As noted above, Schleiermacher grounded his christology in the Christ event. But Strauss argued that the historicity of this event was not verifiable and thus could not be critically substantiated. Indeed, it no longer needed to be substantiated since the foundation of christology lay elsewhere — in humanity as a whole and in the idea of the divine-human union. Strauss could then state that the differences between the authors of the New Testament and modern reason could not be overcome: "the New Testament authors have an

36. Strauss, *Life of Jesus,* 736.
37. Strauss, *Life of Jesus,* 780.
38. Strauss, *Life of Jesus,* 780-81.

idea of the person and of the life of Jesus which cannot be harmonized with our concepts of human life and the laws of nature."[39] Small wonder that the book was never well received. Strauss never did find a widespread audience receptive to his ideas even after toning down his arguments in a third edition.

The conflict which Strauss sensed here and under which he personally suffered was the one between the emerging causal-mechanistic worldview and the dynamic worldview of Jesus' own time. Strauss does not want to make any compromises between these two exclusive worldviews. According to his estimate Schleiermacher was a supernaturalist in christology and a rationalist in criticism and exegesis. Such a position was unacceptable for Strauss. Strauss did not yet want to abandon the divine or supernatural completely. He maintained the union between the divine and the human, not in a single human being, but in humanity as a whole.

A few years later in *Der alte und der neue Glaube* (The Old Faith and the New Faith) (1872), Strauss went beyond a universalistic symbiosis. He answered the question: "Are we still Christians?" with a flat "No."[40] The question of whether we are still religious, he contended, can only be answered in the affirmative even if we do not believe in God but convey the same piety to the universe which was once conveyed to God. In posing the question: "How we do understand the world?" he appealed to Darwin's theory of evolution. In his last question: "How do we order our lives?" he referred to middle-class intellectual morality. With this approach both theology and the Hegelian dialectic were finally abandoned in favor of bourgeois materialism. How did Hegel become so dangerous?

In *The Positivity of the Christian Religion* (1795-96), Georg Wilhelm Friedrich Hegel (1770-1831) attempted to answer the question of how the religion of Jesus was transformed into the positive Christian religion.[41] He presented Jesus as the teacher of a purely moral religion.

39. David Friedrich Strauss, *The Christ of Faith and the Jesus of History: A Critique of Schleiermacher's Life of Jesus,* trans. and ed. Leander E. Keck (Philadelphia: Fortress, 1977), 159.

40. David Friedrich Strauss, *Der alte und der neue Glaube: Ein Bekenntnis,* 12th-14th ed. (Bonn: Emil Strauss, 1895), 61.

41. For a good treatment of the different phases in Hegel's understanding of the Christian faith, see Bernard M. G. Reardon, *Hegel's Philosophy of Religion* (New York: Barnes & Noble, 1977).

Miracles and other signs were not intended to be the bases of doctrines but rather the means by which morally deaf people were awakened. Many people considered Jesus to be the Messiah who would soon show himself in his glory. Jesus did not contradict these hopes, "but he tried to lead their messianic hopes into the moral realm and dated his appearance in his glory at a time after his death."[42] Jesus' teaching, Hegel stated, "requires an unconditional and disinterested obedience to the will of God and the moral law and makes this obedience a condition of God's favor and the hope of salvation."[43] The mission of Jesus was an attempt to introduce a positive morality, but this mission was essentially a failure since the Jews, who were accustomed to servility, did not want to accept his attempt to introduce freedom and morality into their religious life. Jesus proclaimed a kingdom of God which had already come, which is made real by faith, and in which everyone is a citizen.[44] The coming of the kingdom did not play a significant role in Jesus' message.

In *The Spirit of Christianity and Its Fate* (1798-99) Hegel conceded:

> [The] idea of a Kingdom of God completes and comprises the whole of the [Christian] religion as Jesus founded it. . . . In the Kingdom of God what is common to all is life in God. This is not the common character which a concept expresses, but is love, a living bond which unites the believers; it is the feeling of unity of life, a feeling in which all oppositions . . . are annulled.[45]

Hegel certainly recognized the unifying factor of the kingdom but failed to discern its eschatological quality. Similarly, he carefully delineated the divine quality of Jesus. Hegel demonstrated that the divinity which Jesus claimed was not peculiar to him alone, shaping a unique individuality. All the children of God could be animated by the Holy Spirit and share in the divine life. "All thought of a difference in essence between Jesus and those in whom faith in him has become life, in whom the divine is present, must be eliminated. When Jesus speaks of himself so often as

42. Georg Wilhelm Friedrich Hegel, *The Positivity of the Christian Religion* (§8), trans. T. M. Knox, in G. W. F. Hegel, *Early Theological Writings* (Chicago: University of Chicago, 1948), 77.

43. Hegel, *Positivity of the Christian Religion* (§15), 85.

44. Hegel, *Positivity of the Christian Religion* (§3), 180.

45. G. W. F. Hegel, *The Spirit of Christianity and Its Fate* (§iv), trans. T. M. Knox, in G. W. F. Hegel, *Early Theological Writings*, 278.

of a pre-eminent nature, this is to contrast himself with the Jews."[46] The ontological uniqueness of the God-man Jesus is almost entirely eliminated. Small wonder that someone less interested in following the Christian tradition might get the notion that Jesus was in no way preeminent but that the divinity he symbolized was essentially shared by all. The change from Hegel to Strauss, though not a necessary one, is at least plausible.

In Hegel's 1821 *Lectures on the Philosophy of Religion,* the heritage of the Enlightenment is largely overcome. Unlike Schleiermacher, Hegel still did not pay much attention to the mission of Jesus as narrated in the Gospels. More important was the total significance of Christ as it is confessed and embodied in the spiritual community, the church. In the church the dogma of Christ receives its fullest expression and thus Hegel declares, in adherence to orthodoxy, that the Son "is also God and has the entire fullness of divine nature within itself."[47] God had to appear in the world in a single human being *"in order for his divine-human unity to become certain for man."*[48] The finitude of the world and the frailty of human nature are incompatible with this divine-human unity. In other words, Jesus as truly human and truly divine shows that the unity of God and humanity is attainable. There is also a unity of Jesus' life and teaching, since in Jesus "the divine Idea is portrayed in [the whole of] his life and destiny, which are integrated by his teaching."[49] The most outstanding and comprehensive facet in Jesus' teaching is love, which culminated in Christ's sacrificial death, "the highest love."[50] His death was salvific because "God cannot be satisfied by something else, only by himself."[51] God died, so to speak, and Christ was raised up to the right hand of God. God put death to death and rose again to life, thus reversing the cosmic order. Finitude was put to death in Christ's death, the finite and evil were destroyed, and the world was reconciled.[52] From here it

46. Hegel, *The Spirit of Christianity* (§iv), 268.

47. Georg Wilhelm Friedrich Hegel, *The Christian Religion: Lectures on the Philosophy of Religion,* part 3, *The Revelatory, Consummate, Absolute Religion,* ed. and trans. Peter Hodgson (Missoula, Mont.: Scholars, 1979), 180.

48. Hegel, *Christian Religion: Lectures,* 3:181.

49. Hegel, *Christian Religion: Lectures,* 3:184.

50. Hegel, *Christian Religion: Lectures,* 3:202.

51. Hegel, *Christian Religion: Lectures,* 3:209-10.

52. Hegel, *Christian Religion: Lectures,* 3:219.

was an easy step to the necessary recognition of the triune God. While Hegel himself was able to assert the logic of the Spirit's movement into a specific human being and from there into all humanity and back to itself, many others felt less guided by the Christian tradition and advocated Christ the symbol rather than the singular reality of the historical Jesus. This became obvious not only in Strauss but in many other proponents of classical liberal theology. /

In the nineteenth century proper we find many works which attempted to present a historical account of the life of Jesus. Some authors leaned toward pure fiction, while others felt more responsibility to the New Testament sources. For instance, Ernst Renan (1823-92) presented a novel-like description of Jesus and his work, while Bruno Bauer (1809-82) denied that Jesus was even a historical figure. Among these numerous authors Albrecht Ritschl (1822-89) stands out as a representative figure who had a significant impact on theology in general and whose influence has been felt far into the twentieth century.[53] Ritschl did not write a life of Jesus, but in his monumental work *The Christian Doctrine of Justification and Reconciliation* (1870-74) he entitled a section "The Doctrine of Christ's Person and Life-Work." Here he stated:

> Beyond all doubt Jesus was conscious of a new and hitherto unknown relation to God, and said so to His disciples; and His aim was to bring His disciples into the same attitude toward the world as His own and to the same estimate of themselves that under these conditions He might enlist them in the world-wide mission of the Kingdom of God, which He knew to be not only His own business, but theirs.[54]

The aim of Jesus' life was the union of people in the kingdom of God. "Jesus is the bearer of the perfect spiritual religion, which consists in mutual fellowship with God, the Author of the world and its final goal."[55] This mutual fellowship with God implied the union of humanity through love or the realization of the kingdom of God. By the example of Jesus' life humans are called to dedicate themselves to an ethical

---

53. For the lasting influence of Ritschl on Barth, Bultmann, and others, see the significant study by James Richmond, *Albrecht Ritschl: A Reappraisal* (London: Collins, 1978).

54. Albrecht Ritschl, *The Christian Doctrine of Justification and Reconciliation: The Positive Development of the Doctrine,* trans. H. R. Mackintosh and A. B. Macaulay (New York: Charles Scribner's, 1900), 386.

55. Ritschl, *Christian Doctrine of Justification and Reconciliation,* 414.

vocation.[56] This assessment of the aim of Jesus' life reflected many of the values of Ritschl and his contemporaries. For instance, Ritschl wrote that Jesus "adopted a neutral attitude toward all the other interests of human society, toward law and State, industry and science."[57] This "modern" interpretation is also apparent when he asserted that the disciples were received into the same relation to God in which Christ stood to his Father. Though Ritschl acknowledged that Jesus was the "Revealer of God in the full sense," Jesus seems to have been of the same kind as we are.[58] His death was not one of substitutionary punishment but "the highest proof of faithfulness to His vocation."[59] Since Christ's vocation rules supreme, neither his apocalyptic proclamation nor his resurrection received any attention. Though Ritschl's theological system was consistently christological, with Christ being the revealer of God's purpose representing the kingdom of God and being the founder of the kingdom, his christology, though in continuous dialogue with the Reformation tradition, lacked the dynamism of the living Lord. Jesus' proclamation resulted primarily in an ethical religion not so very different from that espoused by Kant.[60]

Nonetheless Jesus was not just a significant human being who lived his vocation to the very end. In his *Lectures in Dogmatics* (1881/82) Ritschl asserted that "one can only attribute saving significance to Christ's death if one knows Christ as the resurrected one. But the resurrection must also be understood as the goal of Christ's whole active life, insofar as the dying in obedience attests to the power and value of this life."[61] In other words, without the resurrection Christ's life would be incomplete and without salvific value. Yet Ritschl refrained from attempting to prove the facticity of the resurrection; rather, it is a truth of faith that is often tacitly presupposed when one speaks about Christ. He spoke about Christian hope similarly. Though in many ways the future hope is con-

56. Ritschl, *Christian Doctrine of Justification and Reconciliation*, 446.
57. Ritschl, *Christian Doctrine of Justification and Reconciliation*, 447.
58. Ritschl, *Christian Doctrine of Justification and Reconciliation*, 455.
59. Ritschl, *Christian Doctrine of Justification and Reconciliation*, 477.
60. See §5 of Albrecht Ritschl's *Instruction in the Christian Religion* in Albert Temple Swing, *The Theology of Albrecht Ritschl*, together with *Instruction in the Christian Religion*, trans. Alice Mead Swing (London: Longmans, Green, and Co., 1901), 174-75.
61. Rolf Schäfer, *Ritschl: Grundlinien eines fast verschollenen dogmatischen Systems* (Tübingen: J. C. B. Mohr, 1968), 186-206, quotation on p. 198, my trans.

trary to the present it cannot be entirely discontinuous with the present but will entail the completion of the kingdom of God in which we presently stand and are actively involved. Ritschl was even convinced that not all people will reach the goal of eternal bliss. Yet he did not indulge in a travelogue eschatology but admitted that our perceptions and even that of the New Testament documents are unclear at this point.[62] While the validity of many of Ritschl's tenets must be recognized, it is clear that he was not yet cognizant of the all-pervasive nature of eschatology, apart from which Jesus and his proclamation cannot be adequately understood. It is also not without significance that, similar to Schleiermacher, he usually referred to Christ and not to Jesus, perhaps indicating the more dogmatic emphasis of his inquiry. In Harnack, the eminent historian and theologian who stood at the theological changing of the guard from liberal theology to neoorthodoxy, we observe a similar neglect of the eschatological dimension of Jesus' message.

In the winter semester of 1899-1900 Adolf von Harnack, the great church historian, gave a series of lectures at Berlin for nearly six hundred university students on the topic "What Is Christianity?" Rudolf Bultmann rightly called the ensuing book "a theological-historical document of the greatest importance. . . . Every theologian who would be clear about the present situation in theology and its origins should be familiar with it."[63] Harnack contended that while Strauss thought he had almost completely destroyed the historical credibility of the Gospels, two generations of historical criticism succeeded in restoring their credibility insofar as its main outline was concerned.[64] The biblical materials

> *offer us a plain picture of Jesus' teaching, in regard both to its main features and to its individual application; in the second place they tell us how his life issued in the service of his vocation; and in the third place, they describe to us the impression which he made upon his disciples, and which they transmitted.*[65]

Harnack was also much more open to the factuality of Jesus' miracles. In his opinion science again allowed for the feasibility of many of them:

---

62. Schäfer, *Ritschl*, 202.
63. Adolf von Harnack, *What Is Christianity?* trans. Thomas Bailey Saunders (Philadelphia: Fortress, 1986), vii.
64. Harnack, *What Is Christianity?* 20.
65. Harnack, *What Is Christianity?* 31.

"in our present state of knowledge we have become more careful, more hesitating in our judgment in regard to the stories of the miraculous which we have received from antiquity."[66]

Harnack portrayed Jesus as a very reasonable man; at times there were hints of the Romantic, but overall Jesus was not so very different from the liberal Protestants of the end of nineteenth century. Jesus was not part of a separatist ascetic community, his life and his discourses stood in relation to the Greek spirit, and, Harnack says, he was "possessed of a quite uniform, collected demeanour, with everything directed to one goal."[67] There were three main points to Jesus' message:

- First, the kingdom of God and its coming.
- Second, God the Father and the infinite value of the human soul.
- Third, the higher righteousness and the commandment of love.[68]

This means that Jesus is not even in the center of the gospel. Any doubts about what Harnack meant are vanquished by his comment that *"the gospel, as Jesus proclaimed it, has to do with the Father only and not with the Son."*[69] Jesus' function is similar to that of John the Baptist in Grünewald's painting of the Isenheim Altar. He points to God and restores our trust in God. Jesus knew God as the Father and as his father: "Jesus is convinced that he knows God but in a way in which no one knew Him before, and he knows that it is his vocation to communicate this knowledge of God to others by word and by deed — and with it the knowledge that men are God's children."[70]

Harnack was convinced that Jesus was not just an ordinary human being. Jesus knew himself to be the Messiah and acted accordingly. Since the Messiah, Jesus' influence extends into our age: "The certainty of the

---

66. Harnack, *What Is Christianity?* 28.

67. Harnack, *What Is Christianity?* 35-36.

68. Harnack, *What Is Christianity?* 51. Harnack also summarized the gospel thus: "In the combination of these ideas — God the Father, Providence, the position of men as God's children, the infinite value of the human soul — the whole Gospel is expressed." See Harnack, *What Is Christianity?* 68.

69. Harnack, *What Is Christianity?* 144.

70. Harnack, *What Is Christianity?* 128. With this statement he anticipates the program of the Social Gospel Movement, namely the recognition of the "Fatherhood of God" and therefore the acknowledgment of human solidarity in the "brotherhood of men."

29

resurrection and of a life eternal which is bound up with the grave in Joseph's garden has not perished and on the conviction that *Jesus lives* we still base those hopes of citizenship in an Eternal City which make our earthly life worth living and tolerable."[71] Harnack did not go on to prove the facticity of the resurrection, since for him it was a matter of faith and indeed is the bedrock of the Christian faith.

Though Harnack recognized the central role of the theme of the kingdom of God in Jesus' teaching and ministry, he did not develop a sense of eschatological realism. He asserted that Jesus simply shared the same apocalyptic eschatology as his contemporaries.[72] Jesus grew into it and retained it. The other view, however, that the kingdom does not come with outward signs but is already here, was actually his own. Eschatology is spiritualized, and the kingdom of God is "a still and mighty power in the hearts of men."[73]

Though Harnack recognized the eschatological context of Jesus and his proclamation, in an effort to show the singularity of Jesus he overlooked the fact that Jesus was the decisive center of this context. In classical liberal fashion Harnack distinguished between those things that we can no longer believe and those that we still believe, labeling the former as nonessential elements in Jesus' message, while the latter contained for him the actual core of Jesus' message. Here Albert Schweitzer, though realizing the essentially eschatological character of Jesus and his message, shared with Harnack the same limitation.

In 1901 Albert Schweitzer, the famous Bach interpreter, doctor in tropical Africa, and New Testament scholar, published a book with the title *The Mystery of the Kingdom of God: The Secret of Jesus' Messiahship and Passion*, in which he attempted to portray a life of Jesus. This booklet contained enough dynamite for conservatives and liberals alike to shatter many of their cherished thoughts. His entire approach was somewhat unorthodox. He began not at the beginning of Jesus' life but in the middle. Schweitzer asked, similarly to Strauss: Did Jesus regard himself as the Messiah? If so, why did he not act like the Messiah? If Jesus did not

---

71. Harnack, *What Is Christianity?* 162.

72. The idea of the kingdom of God and of the devil and of a last eschatological battle in which the devil is defeated is a Jewish apocalyptic view inherited by Jesus. See Harnack, *What Is Christianity?* 54.

73. Harnack, *What Is Christianity?* 54.

think he was the Messiah, how did he come to be regarded as the Messiah?[74] The point was that Jesus either really took himself to be the Messiah or this dignity was first ascribed to him by the early church. Unlike Strauss, Schweitzer did not opt for a literary solution. Like Harnack, he was convinced that Jesus knew himself to be the Messiah. But unlike both Strauss and Harnack, Schweitzer took eschatology to be the key to understanding Jesus. The secret of Jesus' identity was disclosed to him at his baptism — he was the one whom God has chosen to be the Messiah. Now Jesus' task was to suffer and labor for the kingdom of God as the "unrecognised and hidden Messiah."[75] Jesus was an eschatological — even apocalyptic — figure like John the Baptist. They shared a similar message: repent and attain righteousness, because the kingdom of God is close at hand. Unlike John, Jesus performed miracles. But Jesus' life and activity was a disappointment. His preaching did not yield much success despite his best efforts, and the coming of the kingdom was delayed. One of the signs of the coming kingdom was the discovery that John the Baptist was Elijah reincarnate. The final blow was the beheading of John. With that and the realization that the kingdom was not immediately at hand, Jesus realized that he too had to suffer death. Thus he turned with his disciples to Jerusalem and claimed to be the Messiah. The Jewish authorities, who had always been suspicious of him, accused him of blasphemy and put him to death. He died, but nothing happened. This was the first significant attempt to explain Jesus' mission as founded on an idea that had proved to be wrong. Nonetheless Schweitzer saw heroic qualities in Jesus and stated that his intent was *"to depict the figure of Jesus in its overwhelming heroic greatness and to impress it upon the modern age and upon the modern theology."*[76]

A different reception greeted Schweitzer's 1906 book, *The Quest of the Historical Jesus: A Critical Study of Its Progress from Reimarus to Wrede.* It was the first massive and conscientious attempt to assess the value of the numerous investigations into the life of Jesus. Each generation (rationalism, liberalism, modern theology, etc.), Schweitzer argued, tore down the picture of Jesus erected in the preceding generation and started to

74. Albert Schweitzer, *The Mystery of the Kingdom of God: The Secret of Jesus' Messiahship and Passion,* trans. Walter Lowrie (New York: Macmillan, 1950), viii.

75. Schweitzer, *Mystery of the Kingdom,* 160-61.

76. Schweitzer, *Mystery of the Kingdom,* 174.

build its own without realizing that this new edifice reflected its own aspirations and desires more than the Jesus who had actually walked on this earth. Though these biographies reflected utmost sincerity, they were without value for our faith. "The abiding and eternal in Jesus is absolutely independent of historical knowledge and can only be understood by contact with His spirit which is still at work in the world. . . . Jesus as a concrete historical personality remains a stranger to our time."[77] Schweitzer did not give up in despair, since it is Jesus' spirit that is important; but this spirit is only accessible if we conceive of Jesus as an eschatological figure. Therefore the two people mentioned in Schweitzer's title, Reimarus and William Wrede, circumscribe his program. Reimarus provided an eschatological picture of Jesus, though he disclaimed its historical truthfulness. Wrede (1859-1906) showed that a non-eschatological view of Jesus was untenable. Schweitzer again proposed the alternative which he had already advanced in *The Mystery of the Kingdom of God*:

> There is, on the one hand, the eschatological solution, which at one stroke raises the Markian account as it stands, with all its disconnectedness and inconsistencies, into genuine history; and there is, on the other hand, the literary solution, which regards the incongruous dogmatic element as interpolated by the earlier Evangelist into the tradition and therefore strikes out the Messianic claim altogether from the historical life of Jesus. *Tertium non datur.*[78]

Once again Schweitzer took a clear stand for a thoroughgoing eschatological interpretation of Jesus. He declared that Jesus' ethics were interim ethics aimed at the preparation for the kingdom of God, but since the kingdom had not come when Jesus expected it, our ethics cannot be derived from Jesus' ethics. Jesus' demand of world denial and perfection of personality is still valid for us, although it is in contrast to our ethics of reason. We need more persons like Jesus. His enthusiasm and heroism are important for us, because they were derived from choosing the kingdom of God and from faith in this kingdom, which was only strengthened by his encounter with obstacles.

---

77. Schweitzer, *Quest of the Historical Jesus,* 399.
78. Schweitzer, *Quest of the Historical Jesus,* 335.

In the knowledge that He is the coming Son of Man [Jesus] lays hold of the wheel of the world to set it moving on that last revolution which is to bring all ordinary history to a close. It refuses to turn, and He throws Himself upon it. Then it does turn; and crushes Him. Instead of bringing in the eschatological conditions, He has destroyed them. The wheel rolls onward, and the mangled body of the one immeasurable great Man, who was strong enough to think of Himself as the spiritual ruler of mankind and to bend history to His purpose, is still hanging upon it. That is His victory and His reign.[79]

It is relatively unimportant for Schweitzer that Jesus was actually deceived in his eschatological expectations. All-decisive was Jesus' attitude toward both history and the obstacles he had to overcome in accomplishing his goal.

The Quest of the Historical Jesus caused an immense uproar. Liberal Protestantism could tolerate Schweitzer's portrayal of Jesus as a deceived religious fanatic but not the idea that his ethics were mere interim ethics. Regardless of how critical Protestant liberalism had been toward the Jesus of the New Testament, it cherished his ethical ideals. Now Schweitzer had declared quite rightly that it was impossible to separate Jesus' ethics from his eschatological proclamation. The attempt of liberal theology to eliminate the eschatological dimension of Jesus' proclamation and to confine itself to the "timeless" validity of his ethical teachings could no longer be founded in the historical Jesus. Conservative scholars also reacted, arguing that Schweitzer fell into the very trap he had pointed out, namely that each scholar had projected his own image of Jesus in the attempt to write a life of Jesus. They argued that the true historical Jesus could not be found strictly by historical investigation but only through faith. In England, Schweitzer found acclaim. F. C. Burkitt (1864-1935), a leading New Testament scholar, immediately translated *The Quest of the Historical Jesus* and attached a preface to it. William Sanday (1843-1920), another prominent figure in British New Testament

---

79. Schweitzer, *Quest of the Historical Jesus*, 368-69. In a posthumously published manuscript, *The Kingdom of God and Primitive Christianity* (1950-51), ed. Ulrich Neuenschwander, trans. L. A. Garrard (New York: Seabury 1968), 123, Schweitzer continued this same line, saying that Jesus eventually concluded that through his death the kingdom of God would be ushered in. Schweitzer consistently maintained that Jesus was a "heroic failure."

scholarship, initially praised Schweitzer's books, but then realized the radical attitude behind them and quickly changed his mind.

Schweitzer's study marked a breakthrough in life of Jesus research. He recognized the eschatological dimensions of Jesus and his ministry. He attempted to undergird Jesus with an immovable bedrock and rid the historical Jesus from the constantly changing results of historical research, claiming that "Jesus means something to our world because a mighty spiritual force streams forth from him and flows through our time also. This fact can neither be shaken nor confirmed by historical discovery. It is the solid foundation of Christianity."[80] While we cannot lay our hands on Jesus as a historical reality, his spirit is still alive and active among us. The foundation of the Christian faith is essentially spiritual (and not historical) and therefore timeless. Schweitzer held fast to one of the basic tenets of liberal theology, the timelessness of Jesus.

c. Jesus according to the Social Gospel

Before we embark on decidedly twentieth-century contributions to the study on the historical Jesus, we must at least mention the Social Gospel Movement. This is timely, since some late-twentieth-century variations which depict Jesus as a revolutionary or a social activist bear remarkable resemblance to the Jesus of the Social Gospel of more than half a century earlier. The foundations of the Social Gospel were laid in the 1870s and 1880s, climaxed in the 1890s, and gradually declined in the aftermath of World War I. In many ways it was a genuinely American phenomenon, responding to the rapid industrialization and the inpouring of hundreds of thousands of immigrants. It had its affinity in the increased social consciousness of British theology and was influenced by German liberal theology.

Shailer Mathews (1863-1941), for many years professor of New Testament history and interpretation and later dean at the Divinity School of the University of Chicago, is representative of the Social Gospel interpretation of Jesus. The central category of his 1897 book, *The Social Teachings of Jesus: An Essay in Christian Sociology*, is the idea of the kingdom. Under this rubric he covered topics such as the silence of Jesus in regard to politics, the interest of Jesus in economic life, his

80. Schweitzer, *Quest of the Historical Jesus*, 397.

doctrine of equality, the doctrine of nonresistance, and the transformation of society in general. Economics and politics were important and recurring themes in *The Social Teachings of Jesus.*[81] Mathews did not play favorites; he asserted that Jesus "was neither socialist nor individualist. . . . He calls the poor man to sacrifice as well as the rich man. He was the Son of Man not the son of a class of men."[82] The kingdom was neither a merely political kingdom, nor a theocratic state, nor a subjective state of the individual, nor exclusively eschatological. The kingdom was a concrete reality and not an idea, and furthermore, "this reality was not to be left as an unattainable ideal, but was to be progressively realized, perhaps evolved."[83] Indeed, the theme of an evolutionary progression of the kingdom is prominent in Shailer's interpretation of the historical Jesus. The evolutionary progression of the kingdom of God was an ideal by which humanity related to God as sons and daughters and therefore to each other as sisters and brothers.[84] This relationship of humanity with God and with one another is the propelling force of social amelioration and will usher in the kingdom. But the kingdom will not be brought about by our own efforts. At one point, we do not know when, the growth of the kingdom will be supplemented by a divine cataclysm. Then the new social order will triumph and offenders of this order will be isolated. "Individual and institutional life will no longer testify to the reign of even an enlightened selfishness. The world will, by virtue of man's endeavor and God's regenerating power, have been transformed into the kingdom."[85] The kingdom is the result of our cooperation with God as his sons and daughters and as brothers and sisters among ourselves.

Mathews revised and expanded the themes of *The Social Teachings of Jesus* in *Jesus on Social Institutions* (1928), using the frame of the "revolutionary spirit" that he developed as a consequence of his research on the French Revolution. He discerned the revolutionary expectations of

81. Mathews stated that "inevitably Jesus touched upon economics" and that "wealth must be used for the establishment of the ideal social order whose life is that of brothers — the kingdom of God." See Shailer Mathews, *The Social Teachings of Jesus: An Essay in Christian Sociology* (New York: Macmillan, 1902), 134, 144.

82. Mathews, *Social Teachings of Jesus,* 156-57.

83. Mathews, *Social Teachings of Jesus,* 53.

84. The famous slogan of the Social Gospel Movement is "the fatherhood of God and the brotherhood of man." For more see Mathews, *Social Teachings of Jesus,* 54.

85. Mathews, *Social Teachings of Jesus,* 228-29.

Jesus' time and the general mood of instability. Jesus was portrayed as an agitator. But he was not just any kind of agitator; he was not an agitator primarily of social change or one who discussed morals in general. He was an agitator with the Messianic-revolutionary point of view who had "adopted what might be called revolutionary technique, and, like John, formed his group *(ecclesia)* of sympathizers."[86] His teaching was intended for the active soul and is carried on by the church. True disciples of Jesus are "those who possess something of the revolutionary attitude."[87] Yet a revolutionary spirit does not imply violence, bloodshed, and war. On the contrary, it is the realization "that God is love and that brotherliness rather than coercion is the true basis for human relations."[88] The revolutionary spirit recognizes the truth of Jesus' teaching that "goodwill is a practicable basis upon which to build human society."[89] The weakness of Mathews's presentation is that he overlooked or neglected the immensity of human depravity and the inbreaking of the kingdom of God. Mathews's eschatology is more an evolutionary process resulting in human and global betterment than a radical reordering of the cosmos.

Other representatives of the Social Gospel Movement, such as Washington Gladden (1836-1918), Henry Churchill King (1858-1934), and Francis Greenwood Peabody (1847-1936), portray Jesus similarly. Jesus' basic conviction was that love is at the heart of the world and that God is the eternal principle of love; other important convictions were the value of life, the solidarity of the human family, the necessity for the strong to stand up for the weak, and the absolute worth of any human individual. They also asserted that Jesus did not share the eschatological ideas of his age. The coming of the kingdom was to be a gradual process. People on earth will bring about the kingdom and usher in the ideal social order in which people will relate to God as sons and daughters and to each other as brothers and sisters. The Sermon on the Mount is the gospel in brief. The greatest of all possible good is the reign of God, that is, the dominion of love, in individuals and in society.

It should not be assumed that representatives of the Social Gospel intended to use Jesus for their own purposes. They were aware of the

---

86. Mathews, *Social Teachings of Jesus,* 40.
87. Mathews, *Social Teachings of Jesus,* 82.
88. Mathews, *Social Teachings of Jesus,* 39.
89. Mathews, *Social Teachings of Jesus,* 154.

danger of portraying Jesus in their own image; Peabody explicitly stated: "No modern interpretation of the Gospel is more superficial and unhistorical than the conversion of its teaching into a call for social agitation or a program of economic revolution."[90] In the Social Gospel the kingdom of God does not break into the world mechanistically nor does Jesus become a new lawmaker; the emphasis was on social dynamics and the spirit which Jesus engenders. The primary characteristic of the kingdom is spiritual power; it is its first mark.[91] Through the power of Jesus' personality the kingdom of God is to be established and ruled. The coming of the kingdom is not a mechanical process but a spiritual adventure. Peabody did not want to displace communion with God with the service of people to each other, or revelation with revolution. He asked for the dedication of the will to a practical loyalty which may open a way to the religious vision which lies beyond. Thus Peabody called for that which we today call Christo-praxis instead of a summons to mere orthodoxy. In *Jesus Christ and the Social Question* (1900) Peabody added a new twist to the Social Gospel treatment of the historical Jesus.[92] Since Jesus did not give up regardless of the mounting difficulties, Peabody asserted that Jesus "is the most unfaltering of optimists."[93] This optimistic assessment of Jesus was not uncommon among the representatives of the Social Gospel Movement; we find it again in Walter Rauschenbusch, the most prominent speaker of the group.

Walter Rauschenbusch (1861-1918), educated both in Germany and the United States, taught German and later church history at Rochester Theological Seminary after having served as the pastor of an inner-city parish in New York City. His experiences in Hell's Kitchen, the area covered by his parish, were the basis of his theology, which was com-

90. Francis Greenwood Peabody, *The Social Teaching of Jesus Christ* (Philadelphia: University of Pennsylvania Press, 1924), 21. That Peabody did not leave out concern for the individual is evident in the title of his Lyman Beecher Lectures of 1904 at Yale University, *Jesus and the Christian Character: An Examination of the Teaching of Jesus in Its Relation to Some of the Moral Problems of Personal Life* (New York: Hodder & Stoughton, 1905).

91. Peabody, *Social Teaching,* 35.

92. Peabody, *Jesus Christ and the Social Question: An Examination of the Teaching of Jesus and Its Relation to Some of the Problems of Modern Social Life* (New York: Macmillan, 1915).

93. Peabody, *Jesus Christ and the Social Question,* 300. Peabody must certainly have been aware of *The Quest of the Historical Jesus* in which Schweitzer made the same point.

prehensively laid out in *A Theology of the Social Gospel.*[94] A central thesis was that the doctrine of kingdom of God "is itself the social gospel."[95] The kingdom is not a transcendent idea, but offers a teleological dimension: "the social gospel tries to see the progress of the Kingdom of God in the flow of history; not only in the doings of the Church, but in the clash of economic forces and social classes."[96] Rauschenbusch admitted that the Social Gospel was less concerned with christological and trinitarian ideas and more concerned about "how the divine life of Christ can get control of human society."[97] Individualistic piety is rejected in favor of a more communal approach. Important for one's own piety is the discovery of the real personality of Jesus who would set a great historical process in motion. "It was by virtue of his personality that he became the initiator of the Kingdom."[98] In Jesus the human and the divine element attained a unity, and he became the actual revelation of God.

Rauschenbush maintained, like other Social Gospel thinkers, that Jesus was not a pessimist. Jesus experienced God in a new way by virtue of his God-consciousness and was optimistically engaged with the world. But Rauschenbusch even went a step further, claiming that Jesus was neither an ascetic nor an apocalyptic. He was sure that "the professional theologians of Europe, who all belong by kinship and sympathy to the bourgeois classes and are constitutionally incapacitated for understanding any revolutionary ideas, past or present, have overemphasized the ascetic and eschatological elements in the teachings of Jesus."[99] Rauschenbusch, in contrast, saw democratic elements in Jesus' teaching.[100] Here the young and optimistic heartbeat of America is heard. In the midst of immense social problems and injustices, hope for a better

94. *A Theology of the Social Gospel* (New York: Macmillan, 1922) was originally presented as a series of lectures at Yale. A year previous to the Yale lectures Rauschenbusch's *The Social Principles of Jesus* (New York: YWCA, 1916) was published, of which the YMCA distributed twenty thousand copies in the first year.

95. Rauschenbusch, *Theology of the Social Gospel*, 131.

96. Rauschenbusch, *Theology of the Social Gospel*, 146.

97. Rauschenbusch, *Theology of the Social Gospel*, 148.

98. Rauschenbusch, *Theology of the Social Gospel*, 151.

99. Rauschenbusch, *Theology of the Social Gospel*, 158.

100. Rauschenbusch characterized Jesus' teachings as "anticipations of the fraternal ethics of democracy and prophecies of social common sense," 158.

world this side of heaven is enunciated which sought its verification in Jesus' teachings. However, while this-worldly expectations are instrumental in sensitizing the church to social issues, they show little appreciation for the eschatological message of Jesus. This message rested dormant until the dawn of neo-Reformation theology.

2. A New Look at the Sources

The twentieth century does not herald an essentially new approach to the understanding of Jesus, unless one focuses on the fact that Jesus was now seen within the context of apocalyptic. In this respect, twentieth-century theology is inspired by the eschatological message and figure of Jesus, who lived and taught in the context of Jewish apocalyptic. Yet at the same time a new questioning of the validity of historical research arose. While the late nineteenth century and the early twentieth century were known for solid historical research, climaxing in the claim of Ernst Troeltsch (1865-1923) that every figure and movement of the past must be interpreted within the matrix of a causal nexus, now scholars began to question whether such a thoroughly this-worldly reference system could do justice to Jesus the Christ, the center of the Christian faith.

a. The Limits of Rational Inquiry

In 1892 Martin Kähler (1835-1912), professor of systematic theology at the University of Halle, gave a lecture to a group of pastors entitled "The So-called Historical Jesus and the Historic Biblical Christ." In this lecture Kähler claimed that "*the historical Jesus of modern authors conceals from us the living Christ. The Jesus of the 'Life-of-Jesus' movement is merely a modern example of human creativity . . . far removed from the real Christ.*"[101] Furthermore there are no reliable and adequate extant sources for a "Life of Jesus."[102] An unbiased picture of Jesus is impossible, since it is always colored by our presuppositions. While Albert Schweitzer would have agreed with that skeptically sounding position,

---

101. Martin Kähler, *The So-called Historical Jesus and the Historic Biblical Christ*, trans. and ed. Carl E. Braaten (Philadelphia: Fortress, 1964), 43.

102. Kähler, *So-called Historical Jesus*, 48.

Kähler continued: the *"real Christ is the Christ who is preached."*[103] Faith is independent of both christological dogma and the uncertain and tentative statements of historical research.[104] Faith is grounded neither in the subjective realms of life of Jesus research nor in the authority of dogma. Kähler concluded that we do not believe in Christ because of the Bible but we believe in the Bible because of Christ. Jesus Christ is the biblical Christ as he is mediated to us through the Bible. The biblical and historical Christ is the revealed Christ in his salvific action. Instead of grounding faith in the ever-changing results of historical Jesus research, the Christian faith is grounded in the whole biblical Christ.

This bold approach seems to extricate the Christian proclamation from the strictures of historical criticism. Rudolf Bultmann (1884-1976) followed this way of thinking in stating that he was not interested in "Christ after the flesh," nor in the personality of Jesus, nor even in the teaching of Jesus. He flatly stated in an article on christology: "I often have the impression that my conservative New Testament colleagues feel very uncomfortable. . . . I calmly let the fire burn, for I see that what is consumed is only the fanciful portraits of Life-of-Jesus theology, and that means nothing other than 'Christ after the flesh himself'. . . . But the 'Christ after the flesh' is no concern of ours. How things looked in the heart of Jesus I do not know and do not want to know."[105]

He later elaborated on his approach, claiming that it would not even matter if Jesus was not the originator of the Jesus tradition but someone else.[106] Neither is the personality of Jesus decisive — we know precious little about him. Nor is the timeless value of his teachings decisive — by looking for that we would remove him from the context of history. Important only is "what he *purposed*, and hence to what in his purpose as part of history makes a present demand on us."[107] Bultmann did not want to look at history objectively but rather to be drawn into a personal encounter with history. Such an existential interpretation of the New Testament message or kerygma did not need to distinguish between that

103. Kähler, *So-called Historical Jesus*, 66.
104. Kähler, *So-called Historical Jesus*, 72-73.
105. Rudolf Bultmann, "On the Question of Christology," in *Faith and Understanding*, ed. Robert W. Funk, trans. Louise Pettibone Smith (New York: Harper, 1969), 132.
106. Rudolf Bultmann, *Jesus and the Word*, trans. Louise Pettibone Smith and Erminie Huntress Lantero (New York: Charles Scribner's, 1958), 14.
107. Bultmann, *Jesus and the Word*, 8.

which can be traced to the historical Jesus and is therefore reliable and that which was later added and should have been discarded. The entire New Testament could again be appreciated as leading us to an encounter with the kerygmatic Christ, the Christ who became alive in the proclamation.

This new turn was hailed by many as a major breakthrough, especially since historically guided theological research had largely focused on philological issues, editing the New Testament sources with ever more precise details yet with preciously little attention to the existential message of the text. Karl Barth (1886-1968), pursuing for a short time the same concerns as did Bultmann, remarked in his epoch-making commentary on Romans: "The Word ought to be exposed in the words."[108] Critical historians should not leave us with blocks of merely historical and accidental concepts but uncover the relationship between the words and the Word. They must penetrate to the point where one is not just confronted with the enigma of the document but with the enigmatic character of the envisioned thing itself. The text must become alive so that the barrier breaks down between the first century and our century and we listen to what is said not then and there but here and now. Barth confessed that "my whole energy of interpreting has been expended in an endeavour to see through and beyond history into the spirit of the Bible, which is the Eternal Spirit. . . . If we rightly understand ourselves, our problems are the problems of Paul; and if we be enlightened by the brightness of his answers, those answers must be ours."[109]

Barth attempted to bridge the ugly broad ditch of history of which Lessing spoke, and he did not want to restrict himself to a timeless truth, as von Harnack had advocated. The word of God, speaking to us through the biblical documents, is the same as it has always been, but it is nevertheless also new because it meets us in our concrete situation of today. While Barth succeeded in expounding on the whole biblical Christ in his monumental *Church Dogmatics,* Bultmann employed existential analysis and in turn reduced the whole biblical Christ to the thatness of the

108. For the following see Karl Barth, *The Epistle to the Romans,* trans. from the 6th ed. by Edwyn C. Hoskyns (London: Oxford University, 1933), 8, in his preface to the 2nd ed.

109. Barth, *Epistle to the Romans,* 1 (preface to the 1st ed.).

Christ event. He actualized the existential impact of the message to such an extent that its historical anchor was felt to be irrelevant. With this disinterest in the historical Jesus the stage was set for a concentrated analysis of the Synoptic material, this time not in order to establish a foundation on which to erect a new life of Jesus but to see what kind of materials we have in the New Testament and what gave rise to them or, stated in a more technical way, what was their *Sitz im Leben.*

b. Analyzing the Synoptic Material

It is sometimes amazing that major breakthroughs are achieved almost simultaneously by several people working independently. For instance, the discovery of the form-critical method and its seminal application to the Synoptic material occurred within two years. In 1919 Karl Ludwig Schmidt (1891-1956) wrote *Rahmen der Geschichte Jesu* [The Frame of the Story of Jesus], the same year Martin Dibelius (1883-1947) published *From Tradition to Gospel,* and two years later Rudolf Bultmann's *The History of the Synoptic Tradition* appeared. These authors recognized that the historical dilemma of establishing a reliable life of Jesus is foremost a literary problem. In turning to the creative milieu out of which the Gospels originated, these theologians asked whether those items which look like topographical or chronological references in the Gospels can really be taken as such.

In general, form critics maintain that only occasionally do various accidentally retained motifs say something about the chronological or topographical peculiarity of a certain event. The oldest Jesus tradition was made up of pericopes consisting of individual scenes and sayings that had been handed down in the Christian community without definite chronological or topographical reference points. Apart from the passion narrative (which contains more "original" data), what looks to us like chronological or topographical information is usually just the so-called form which was later added to the "pictures." From the rest of the material we can deduce only a fragmentary itinerary of Jesus. The Christian community was primarily interested in Jesus as an object of faith, and thus the transhistorical and picturelike remnants of events were emphasized. The Christian community had no interest in the actual itinerary of Jesus as such, and since the Christian community had no interest, it has been irrevocably lost. Schmidt stated that

42

only occasionally can we determine the time or locus of a story more precisely on account of internal considerations. But in general, we do not obtain a life of Jesus in the sense of an evolving life-history, no chronological plan of the story of Jesus, just individual stories, pericopes which are placed into a frame.[110]

The framework in the Gospels is the work of later authors, namely the Evangelists, who arranged the stories or sayings according to rather simple criteria. Sometimes several parables or discussions were lumped together, and sometimes stereotypical editorial means such as "and," "he went to Capernaum," or "they came from the synagogue" were employed to connect the individual stories. A "purely" historical witness to Jesus never existed; "whatever was told of Jesus' words and deeds was always a testimony of faith as formulated for preaching and exhortation in order to convert unbelievers and confirm the faithful."[111]

Rudolf Bultmann also endeavored to uncover the history of the individual units of the tradition, beginning with the origin of that tradition through its various stages of transformation until it found its literary fixation in the Gospels. By reconstructing the origin and history of the individual pieces through inter-Synoptic comparison, he claimed that one can detect the relatively strict rules of growth and change and even illuminate some pieces of the preliterary tradition.[112] Underlying the attempt to decipher and trace certain forms was the conviction that the literature emerging from the Christian community spoke to a certain situation out of which it originated. This *Sitz im Leben* (life setting) was thought to be indicative of certain literary forms.

Yet Bultmann did not want to deal solely with the Christian community. He also wanted to determine the historical reliability of New Testament sayings and stories about Jesus: Do they lead back to Jesus or not? In his impressive analysis of the Synoptic material, there

---

110. Karl Ludwig Schmidt, *Der Rahmen der Geschichte Jesu: Literarkritische Untersuchungen zur ältesten Jesusüberlieferung* (Berlin: Trowitzsch, 1919), 317.

111. Martin Dibelius, *From Tradition to Gospel*, trans. Bertram Lee Woolf (Cambridge: James Clarke, 1971), 295. See also Martin Dibelius, *Gospel Criticism and Christology* (London: Ivor Nicholson & Watson, 1935), where he deals extensively with the problem of unearthing material about Jesus of Nazareth (66-85), and reiterates that the oldest tradition is "closely connected with preaching" (70).

112. Rudolf Bultmann, *The History of the Synoptic Tradition*, trans. John Marsh, rev. ed. (New York: Harper, 1968), 5.

is preciously little of which he unambiguously asserted dates back to the Jesus of history. He still assumed that he was continuing the conviction of Martin Kähler that, compared with modern critical historical research, the biblical sources are not historical documents in the modern sense. Kähler and Bultmann were correct in this conclusion and therefore could rightly abandon their interest in Jesus of Nazareth. They no longer doubted, as some nineteenth-century radicals did, that Jesus gave rise to the gospel tradition. Their main focus was not on some followers of Jesus who remembered something about their leader, contrary to what many scholars had naively proposed in the nineteenth century, but on the community of the resurrected Lord. This community believed in Jesus as the crucified and resurrected one, and believing in him they proclaimed him in literary forms which exemplified his significance for salvation and for the life of the community. It is no wonder that the growth of the materials, now being attributed to the community, needed no longer to be seen as an aberration from the simple faith of Jesus, contrary to what liberal theology had claimed. It was rightly seen as the consequent development of this faith in their Lord.

The form-critical approach, in its emphasis on the tradition of the literary unit, however, ignored the fact that the Evangelists were not disinterested editors and treated their available material from a certain perspective. This deficiency was thereby corrected in a subsequent period of exegesis, called redaction criticism. Redaction critics (the most prominent of whom are Hans Conzelmann, Krister Stendahl, and Willi Marxsen) gave attention to the frame and the slant which stood behind the arrangements peculiar to each Gospel. The questions which were addressed were: What led the Evangelists to select the materials they chose? What were their intentions in their unique arrangements of the material? Does this portray something of their own theology or is it purely accidental? While form criticism was still moved by the search for the historical Jesus (though in the guise of looking for the primary materials and their earliest form), redaction criticism now turned to the so-called frame of the secondary materials. While theologians in the first period asked for the origin of the proclamation or kerygma, in the second period theologians asked how the kerygma became the object matter of theological reflection.

Hans Conzelmann (1915-89), for instance, asked, "In what sense then can Luke be described as a 'historian'"?[113] In other words, what did Luke have in mind when he wrote his account the way he did? With this question in mind it is apparent that Luke realized the difference between his own time and the time of Jesus and perceived them as different epochs in the broad course of salvation history, each having its own particular characteristics. Conzelmann asserted that Luke portrayed salvation history in three steps: the first, the time of Israel which ended with the death of John the Baptist; the second, the time of Jesus' activity, meaning primarily his activities starting with his ministry in Galilee; and the third, the time since the enthronement of the Lord — the time of the church. The church is persecuted in the world, but with the help of the Spirit she can withstand this persecution. In retrospect, the Christian community knows that it is under divine protection and therefore is confident that the gospel will prevail against all opposition until the end of time. The German title of Conzelmann's investigation therefore bears the fitting title *Die Mitte der Zeit* ("The Center of Time"), since Jesus' activity is the pivotal point of time from which we gain our strength during the present time of trials. Conzelmann's masterly work showed that the Evangelists were receivers of the *kerygma*, who used it in a Christian way to give an account of their faith. Comparing the Lukan story to the confession of the Apostles' Creed is not farfetched. Yet behind this story and not in its center, redaction criticism tells us, looms the one who ultimately gave rise to it, Jesus of Nazareth.

Krister Stendahl, in his suggestive study *The School of St. Matthew* (1954), saw a stronger line of connection between Jesus of Nazareth and the Gospels. He questioned the assertion of Dibelius and other form critics that the *Sitz im Leben* of the Gospel material was the preaching within and without the Christian community.[114] He admitted that the preaching activity was obviously one of the factors which influenced the Gospel material. But if the Gospel sections were in constant circulation for homiletic purposes, why do they survive only in nonhomiletic form? The actual facts about the Jesus story were not proclaimed in sermons, except that he died and was resurrected, but were referred to as well

---

113. Hans Conzelmann, *The Theology of St. Luke*, trans. Geoffrey Buswell (Philadelphia: Fortress, 1982), 12.

114. For the following see Krister Stendahl, *The School of St. Matthew and Its Use of the Old Testament* (Philadelphia: Fortress, 1968), 15-19.

known. Furthermore, the activity of preaching cannot provide a concrete milieu for the selection and composition of the different parts of the Gospels.

After these rather severe criticisms, Krister Stendahl showed that behind the Gospel of Matthew stood a school. He agreed with the suggestion that the author of Matthew might have been a converted rabbi.[115] Such a rabbi was never entirely alone but worked and lived in a community. If the term *hyperētai tou logou* in Luke 1:2 is translated as "instructors," then the most concrete *Sitz im Leben* of the Gospel material is the school. Stendahl suggested that in Judaism "the synagogue was an undefined combination of a house of worship and a school," thus providing various ways in which homiletic themes could be expounded. He claimed that analogously the Matthean school must be understood as a school for teachers and church leaders, "and for this reason the literary work of that school assumes the form of a manual for teaching and administration within the church."[116] Though he did not want to advance a strictly evolutionary model, he concluded that "there may therefore be an unbroken line from the School of Jesus via the 'teaching of the Apostles,' the 'ways' of Paul, the basic teaching of Mark and to other *hyperētai tou logou,* and the more mature School of John to the rather elaborate School of Matthew with its ingenious interpretation of the O.T. as the crown of its scholarship."[117] This means that for Stendahl the New Testament Gospels stand in direct succession to what Jesus taught and did. In contrast to Conzelmann, Stendahl did not stay with the Evangelist but went right back to Jesus.

I should mention Willi Marxsen who, in his study *Mark the Evangelist* (1956), polemicized against a strictly form-critical approach that attempts to bypass the Evangelists in analyzing the Synoptic tradition.[118] He claimed that both form history and redaction history must be taken up. In his analysis of the Markan account, Marxsen concluded that Mark oriented his Gospel to Galilee and the awaited impending return of the Lord there.[119] This was the motive for arranging the Gospel in its par-

115. See Stendahl, *School of St. Matthew,* 30-33.
116. Stendahl, *School of St. Matthew,* 33.
117. Stendahl, *School of St. Matthew,* 34.
118. Willi Marxsen, *Mark the Evangelist: Studies on the Redaction History of the Gospel,* trans. James Boyce et al. (Nashville: Abingdon, 1969), 21.
119. See Marxsen, *Mark the Evangelist,* 209-10, for the following.

ticular shape. Because the Lord did not return in Galilee, it was soon
outdated. A different ending had to be added by later copyists, and
consequently the Markan account received a different character and
became similar to the Matthean and Lukan accounts. But, Marxsen
stated, such a timely and soon-outmoded account "that addresses the
concrete community of its time" is actually what a good "sermon" is
about.[120] The early Christian community understood the "gospel" to be
the salvific proclamation and representation of the Lord which occurs
in its midst. To that end Mark wrote his Gospel. As Marxsen asserted,
Mark occupied a "central position." In this respect, he is a "thoroughly
unique theologian, he occupies a position between Paul and the anonymous tradition on the one hand, and the later evangelists on the other."[121]
Marxsen made no attempt to penetrate beyond Mark and his tradition;
he was content to elucidate the plot of the Evangelist.

A more recent method applied to the New Testament sources, a
structuralist or narrative approach, is even less interested in uncovering
the oldest stratum. Attempting to see the New Testament as literature,
it includes both the material and the reader in the exegetical process.
The text is considered as "the expression of a human who, beginning
with certain innate linguistic capacity, has accommodated to his mental
system symbolic capacity and historical and existential levels of meaning,
extending on to life and to God."[122] Behind the surface structures of the
text stand abstract narrative structures. These narrative structures may
be operative both in the production of the narrative and in the reading
process. To obtain the complete effect of the "language event" in the
present, both text and reader must be considered. While historically
minded or sometimes even historically obsessed exegesis may have made
the ugly broad ditch between text and reader too wide, structural analysis
wants to bridge it by drawing author and reader together. "The text is
not a screen to be penetrated but a fabric to be unfolded."[123] The
structural method is more a method of reading than of interpretation. It
does not extricate only one meaning but sets forth all possible meanings,

120. Marxsen, *Mark the Evangelist,* 148 n. 102.

121. Marxsen, *Mark the Evangelist,* 216.

122. Edgar V. McKnight, *Meaning in Texts: The Historical Shaping of a Narrative Hermeneutics* (Philadelphia: Fortress, 1978), 272.

123. Alain Blancy, "Supplemental Theses," in *Structuralism and Biblical Hermeneutics: A Collection of Essays,* ed. and trans. Alfred M. Johnson (Pittsburgh: Pickwick, 1979), 180.

with the effect that the text is always open to several meanings. While this method certainly allows some New Testament materials to gain new light, it does not establish the connection between the Jesus of history and the resultant kerygma. Yet why should such a connection even be necessary? Is not the Christian faith founded on exactly what its name says, faith as trust? The proponents of the new quest for the historical Jesus give a partial answer to these questions.

c. The New Quest for the Historical Jesus

Rudolf Bultmann not only had exegetical reasons to confine himself to a form-critical approach and leave the question of the connection between the historical Jesus and the New Testament tradition unanswered. Bultmann rightly saw that the historical Jesus is not the object matter of our faith, and therefore it was theologically unwarranted to search for the Jesus of history. Only Jesus the Christ who addresses us in the kerygma is the focus of our faith. But then Bultmann maintains that we are not allowed to penetrate behind the kerygma and ask whether its portrayal of Christ is correct.[124] The Christ of the kerygma is not a historical person who could be in continuity with the historical Jesus. Only the kerygma is a historical phenomenon and can be in continuity with the historical Jesus. It was sufficient for Paul that Jesus existed and was crucified. More than that we need not know, since we can ascertain that there indeed is a continuity between Jesus and the Christian kerygma. The historical Jesus stands behind the kerygma: that is enough. It is impossible to find out whether there is an agreement in content between what Jesus said and did and what the kerygma claims he said and did.[125] Such an agreement, however, is not needed, since both the kerygma and Jesus of Nazareth understand human existence alike, calling for a break with the past and a turning to the future of God. Since Christ is present only in the Christian kerygma, Christian faith also implies faith in the church which treasures and proclaims the kerygma.[126]

---

124. See for the following Rudolf Bultmann, *Das Verhältnis der Christusbotschaft zum historischen Jesus* (Heidelberg: Carl Winter, 1960), 7ff.

125. Bultmann, *Das Verhältnis der Christusbotschaft*, 14.

126. Bultmann, *Das Verhältnis der Christusbotschaft*, 26. It is strange that as a self-avowedly "Lutheran" theologian Bultmann would call for faith in the church as the bearer of the kerygma.

Bultmann sees only a formal analogy between the historical Jesus and the kerygma, or, at best, a coincidence of intentions. While it might be possible to agree with this minimalist position, it is difficult to agree with Bultmann's assertion that Christians must trust the church as the bearer of the kerygma. Too often the church in its attempt to preserve the kerygma has domesticated it and only revolt against ecclesial authorities has released the kerygma to its original intention. Almost invariably these revolts have accorded Scripture a higher authority than they did the church. In due course one is always referred to Scripture as the one and only authority.

Ernst Käsemann pointed out, in his noteworthy essay "The Problem of the Historical Jesus" (1954), that for two hundred years critical historical research attempted to extricate itself from the dogmatic strictures of ecclesial authorities and now at the conclusion of our endeavors we realize that we cannot cast off our reliance on dogma and the Christian tradition.[127] In this situation a new search for the historical Jesus is needed, a search which goes beyond the ecclesial authorities and its tradition and attempts to elucidate what had actually happened so that the kerygma gains new credibility. Käsemann is well aware that because we know hardly anything about Jesus' development, a life of Jesus in the traditional sense is no longer possible. Nonetheless he is convinced that the Synoptics thought that they offered us the "authentic tradition about Jesus."[128] Already in the earliest accounts history was fused with assessments of Jesus' significance. We can only know about Jesus through the proclaiming interpretation of the Christian community, the kerygma. In its Easter faith the community did not, nor did it want to, distinguish between the earthly and the exalted Jesus.

Käsemann claims that we need to ask about the Jesus of history for three reasons. The first is that, as Bultmann emphasized, the singularity of the salvific event in Jesus, the *that* of Jesus, was important. Second, God's self-disclosure occurred in space and time. It has an incarnational quality. It took place within history. We concern ourselves with Jesus of Nazareth for this reason.[129] And third, the question of the historical Jesus

127. See Ernst Käsemann, "The Problem of the Historical Jesus," in *Essays on New Testament Themes,* trans. W. J. Montague (Naperville, Ill.: Alec R. Allenson, 1964), 17.

128. Käsemann, "Problem of the Historical Jesus," 22.

129. Käsemann, "Problem of the Historical Jesus," 32.

is the question of the continuity between Jesus and us.[130] Unfortunately, apart from the parables, there are very few formal criteria with which we can ascertain the original material of Jesus. But for any thorough historian there are still pieces of the Synoptic tradition which must be acknowledged as authentic. This material is primarily found in the proclamation of Jesus and the accounts of his actions and destiny. After Käsemann's eloquent summon, the quest for the historical Jesus was resumed by many students of Bultmann.

Ernst Fuchs, in "The Quest for the Historical Jesus" (1956), dealt with the parables as a means of investigating Jesus' self-understanding. He asserted that "*Jesus' conduct* was itself the real framework of his proclamation."[131] In this way, "Jesus validates the will of God in exactly the same way as a man must do if he were in God's place." God's will is exemplified by Jesus' own conduct. This implies that Jesus' conduct provided the actual context of his proclamation. Consequently, if both conduct and speech point in the same direction we have in all probability an original saying of Jesus. Jesus lived as one who dared to act as if he stood in God's place. This then leads to the question of whether his conduct was proper or presumptuous. Jesus anticipated this question and called for a decision to accept him as the Christ. This call for a decision had already been noted by Bultmann when he wrote in his *Theology of the New Testament:* "Jesus' call to decision implies a christology."[132] Yet Bultmann never developed this indirect christology.

Most scholars today take the route of an indirect christology, making conclusions about Jesus' identity on the basis of his message and conduct. The criteria for discovering what Jesus actually did and said need not be left to subjective preference but can be ascertained with some degree of probability. Herbert Braun, one of the most radical students of Bultmann, rejects the idea that the researchers' predilections must color the outcome. He claims that research into the historical Jesus is a craft which

130. Käsemann stated that "the question of the historical Jesus is, in its legitimate form, the question of the continuity of the Gospel within the discontinuity of the times and within the variation of the kerygma." "Problem of the Historical Jesus," 46.

131. Ernst Fuchs, "The Quest for the Historical Jesus," in *Studies of the Historical Jesus,* trans. Andrew Scobie (Naperville, Ill.: Alec R. Allenson, 1964), 21, for this and the following quotations.

132. Rudolf Bultmann, *Theology of the New Testament,* trans. Kendrick Grobel (New York: Charles Scribner's, 1951), 1:43.

demands "care and sensitivity."[133] For instance, if a saying is formulated in Jewish form but its content cannot be derived from Jewish or Qumranic sources (and indeed contradicts such thinking), then most likely it can be traced to Jesus. Yet if it is so Jewish that it contradicts things that Jesus repeatedly said and did, we may assume that it is not from Jesus. Proceeding in this way, Braun asserts originality for quite a few items of Jesus' proclamation and his actions. He even suggests that it is likely that, according to the worldview of his time, Jesus healed sick people; he did indeed free them from the demons which cause sickness.[134]

The new quest does not have sources available that were not accessible beforehand. It also does not treat its sources less critically than Bultmann did. For that matter it should not be overlooked that Bultmann himself wrote a book on Jesus of Nazareth. But while for him the person of Jesus was of no significance, it was now felt that one could be legitimately interested in the continuity between the Christian kerygma and Jesus' own self-understanding; indeed, there is even a theological necessity to do so. If Jesus understood himself in a radically different way from the way the Christian kerygma understood him, then there is no continuity between him and the kerygma. Without being anchored in history the latter is a dogmatic construct or, one could even say, it is a Gnostic myth.[135] Thus this new or continued quest for the historical Jesus is not interested in providing us with a life of Jesus. It knows very well that it cannot give us such a life, but it wants to ascertain the basic features of the life, the proclamation, and destiny of Jesus to show that there is indeed a continuity between the Christian faith and the Jesus of history.

d. The Continued Quest

Though Rudolf Bultmann and his followers were quite influential in the twentieth century, especially in Germany, there were always scholars who had never given up the quest for the historical Jesus. We can geographically divide them into a German group, a Scandinavian group,

---

133. Herbert Braun, *Jesus of Nazareth: The Man and His Time*, trans. Everett R. Kalin (Philadelphia: Fortress, 1979), 23.

134. So Braun, *Jesus of Nazareth*, 28.

135. See the seminal book by James M. Robinson, *A New Quest for the Historical Jesus* (Naperville, Ill.: Alec R. Allenson, 1959), 91.

and a Anglo-American group. Most prominent among the Germans were Joachim Jeremias and Ethelbert Stauffer. Joachim Jeremias was in a unique position, since he had lived in Palestine for a long time and was intimately familiar with Palestinian customs and the Hebrew and Aramaic spoken in Jesus' time. He confronted the neglect of the historical Jesus with the claim that "at no time had there been in early Christendom a kerygma without a Didache."[136] Missionary preaching *(kērygma)* had always been supplemented with instruction *(didachē)* of the congregation. This means that the kerygma always points beyond itself to the history through which it was engendered.

In dealing with the sources, Jeremias wants to go beyond the criterion of dissimilarity, a method by which one discerns the oldest tradition by eliminating everything which can be traced back to Jewish or Hellenistic parallels.[137] Jeremias cautions that this principle relies too much on the assumption of originality. When this principle is applied in every instance where Jesus used available material, then all of this material would be eliminated. Thus we arrive at a dangerous reduction of that which can be attributed to Jesus. Jeremias himself prefers linguistic and stylistic criteria, asking where we find something that sounds like Jesus had spoken it. He points to Aramaisms, to the avoidance of God's name, antithetical (Semitic) parallelisms, and so on. With this kind of method, Jeremias wants to penetrate to the *ipsissima vox* (the very voice) of Jesus' original sayings. Yet he, too, does not entirely abandon the criterion of dissimilarity, claiming that Jesus' parables were unique and that they belonged to "the bedrock of the tradition about him."[138] According to Jeremias, the same is true with Jesus' mention of the *basileia tou theou* ("kingdom of God"), which has no parallel among his contemporaries, the affirmative "Amen" at the beginning of a saying, and the *abba* (colloquial, "father") in addressing God. Especially by analyzing the Aramaic language still noticeable behind the Gospel text of the Greek New Testament, Jeremias can unearth a treasure of sayings which must be attributed to Jesus.

While Jeremias focused on the text of the New Testament, Ethelbert

---

136. Joachim Jeremias, *Das Problem des historischen Jesus* (Stuttgart: Calwer, 1960), 15.

137. See for the following Joachim Jeremias, *New Testament Theology: The Proclamation of Jesus,* trans. John Bowden (New York: Charles Scribner's, 1971), 2.

138. Jeremias, *New Testament Theology,* 30.

Stauffer concentrated on the context of the New Testament. He was convinced that, with the help of still neglected sources, we can discern which materials in the New Testament tradition reliably portray a Jesus who actually lived. The first category of sources are of an indirect nature, such as contemporary testimonies to the conditions, events, and persons who in some way or other are connected to the history of Jesus.[139] For instance, unearthing the then-valid Jewish and Roman legal provisions can explain and/or correct many details about Jesus' trial as reported in the Gospels. The second category of sources are those found in Jewish antiquity which allude to Jesus or even mention him explicitly. Though they are often of a polemical nature, they provide valuable contrasting material over against the accounts in the Synoptics. For instance, if the Jew Celsus tells of a Roman soldier who impregnated Mary, we might have another witness to the fact that Joseph was not the biological father of Jesus. Finally, there is a third group of texts which provide valuable insights, the literature of late Jewish apocalypticism. This body of literature, including the Qumran writings, shows that Jesus was intimately familiar with apocalyptic thought forms, an insight which may help us better understand major facets of his proclamation. Altogether these materials will not allow us to write a biography of Jesus analogous to the nineteenth-century tradition, but they do give us clues for the history of Jesus. When one reads Stauffer's treatise on Jesus, one wonders, however, his many new insights notwithstanding, whether he is not sometimes inclined to return to a romantic biographical narrative which overextends the limits of his material.[140]

Harald Riesenfeld and Birger Gerhardsson are the most prominent of the Scandinavian scholars active in the quest for the historical Jesus. At the Congress on the Four Gospels held in London in 1957, the Swedish New Testament scholar Riesenfeld presented a paper entitled "The Gospel Tradition and Its Beginnings" in which he attacked head-on the form-critical approach and proposed a noteworthy alternative. Against the claim made by form critics that the Synoptic material was composed in the earliest Christian community, he countered that "the

139. See for the following Ethelbert Stauffer, *Jesus and His Story,* trans. Richard and Clara Winston (New York: Alfred A. Knopf, 1960), viii-xiii.

140. James M. Robinson in *A New Quest for the Historical Jesus,* 14, calls him not unjustifiably "an extremist who clearly went too far."

very existence of such an anonymous creative generation in primitive Christianity presupposes . . . a truly miraculous and incredible factor in the history of the Gospel tradition."[141] And he went on to assert that "mission preaching was not the *Sitz im Leben* of the Gospel tradition."[142] Riesenfeld attempted to show that the Gospel tradition belongs to a category of its own and therefore has its own *Sitz im Leben*. The *Sitz im Leben* of the Gospel tradition was neither mission preaching nor communal instruction. However, mission preaching pointed and led to the Gospel tradition. Riesenfeld found it significant that "the original New Testament designation for the Gospel tradition was not *euangelion*—this word stands for missionary appeal—but *logos* and *logos theou*—terms which correspond with the names current in Judaism for 'Holy Scripture.'"[143] The words and deeds of Jesus were considered holy, as in the Old Testament, and the tradition of this precious material was entrusted to special persons. Riesenfeld regarded Jesus as a teacher or rabbi. "It is evident that Jesus did not preach indiscriminately nor continually, but that he imposed certain limitations on his preaching as he did in the case of his miracles. And what was essential to his message he taught his disciples, that is, he made them learn it by heart."[144] One cannot discount that Jesus reckoned with the recital of the Gospel tradition in the epoch between his death and his parousia. Furthermore, if he regarded himself in some way or other as the Messiah, we need not be surprised that "Jesus was conscious of himself as the bearer of revelation, as the bringer of the new law and as a teacher."[145] That is, once one considers Jesus in the context of the Old Testament and of Judaism, one can easily explain many facets of the origin of the Gospel tradition.

The bold strokes with which Riesenfeld sketched the origin of the Gospel tradition were drawn out in detail by Birger Gerhardsson, especially in his book *Memory and Manuscript: Oral Tradition and Written Transmission in Rabbinic Judaism and Early Christianity*. Gerhardsson picks up on Rudolf Bultmann's comment: "It can hardly be doubted that Jesus did teach

141. Harald Riesenfeld, *The Gospel Tradition and Its Beginnings*, 2d ed. (London: A. R. Mowbray, 1961), 9.

142. Riesenfeld, *Gospel Tradition*, 13.

143. Riesenfeld, *Gospel Tradition*, 22.

144. Riesenfeld, *Gospel Tradition*, 26.

145. Riesenfeld, *Gospel Tradition*, 28-29.

as a Rabbi, gather disciples and engage in disputations."[146] Investigating the traditioning process in rabbinic Judaism, he concludes: "It is not possible historically to understand the origin of early Christian tradition by beginning with the *preaching* of the primitive Church. Such procedure is both unhistorical and theologically dubious."[147] Though Jesus taught through word and deed, his ministry not only fulfilled a pedagogical function. Yet the emerging church saw his whole life as a teaching mission. Gerhardsson claimed that with Jesus we must distinguish between text and interpretation, just as we would with Jewish and Hellenistic teachers. "If he taught, he must have required his disciples to memorize."[148] He suggested that the exposition of the parables' interpretation may have been derived from Jesus' own interpretive exposition of the parables. Gerhardsson stated that, against the background of the Jewish milieu, the early Christian apostles were compelled to present their message as an eyewitness account to that which they had seen and heard, which then was supported by scriptural quotations. Thus in the early Christian kerygma both eyewitness accounts and Scripture were present.

Gerhardsson's main criticism of the form-critical approach was that it is not sufficiently historical. It does not convincingly show how the Gospel tradition could have originated, given the Jewish milieu of Palestine and elsewhere at the time of the New Testament. In turn, he claimed that in the light of the ancient Jewish method of teaching it seems entirely reasonable that Jesus presented sayings two or more times in an effort to impress them upon the minds of his hearers. "If Jesus created *meshalim* [parables] during his public ministry, it is reasonable to assume that his disciples preserved these texts right from the beginning. They must have fixed them in their memories, pondered them, and discussed them. Otherwise, they were not his disciples."[149] Gerhardsson's contextual approach, which has affinities to Stendahl's and Stauffer's positions, has certain merits and can provide insights into one aspect of Jesus' life and mission, since Jesus was a rabbi and teacher.

---

146. Bultmann, *The History of Synoptic Tradition*, 50; cf. Birger Gerhardsson, *Memory and Manuscript: Oral Tradition and Written Transmission in Rabbinic Judaism and Early Christianity* (Lund: C. W. K. Gleerup, 1961), 12.

147. Gerhardsson, *Memory and Manuscript*, 324.

148. Gerhardsson, *Memory and Manuscript*, 328.

149. Gerhardsson, *The Origins of the Gospel Tradition* (Philadelphia: Fortress, 1979), 72.

The Anglo-Saxon approach, which was not as unified as the Scandinavian, proceeded along various lines and is represented by scholars such as T. W. Manson, W. D. Davies, Vincent Taylor, and C. H. Dodd.

Charles H. Dodd admitted that the Gospels are indeed religious documents and bear witness to the faith of the church. But in contrast to form criticism, he also asserted that they are historical documents and that their authors had an interest in historical facts. Consequently, "the attempt to make a sharp division between fact and interpretation and set them over against one another is misguided."[150] He also saw this reflected in historical scholarship, since for the serious historian, as opposed to the mere chronicler, "the interest and meaning which an event bore for those who felt its impact is a part of the event."[151] This sentiment is widely accepted in secular historiography. Since in the New Testament the facts are communicated with the intention of bringing out as forcibly as possible the meaning which the authors believed to be their true meaning, there is no strict biography of Jesus available. Yet we obtain a lively picture "of the *kind* of thing that Jesus did, the *kind* of attitude which his actions revealed, the *kind* of relations in which he stood with various types of people he encountered and the causes of friction between him and the religious leaders."[152] This means we do not obtain a photograph of Jesus but rather a reliable painting.

In his research Dodd concerned himself extensively with John, the Fourth Gospel, showing that it was by far not as exclusively nonhistorical and theological as many German scholars had claimed. In a way similar to that of the Synoptics, it reflected an Aramaic background (the language which Jesus spoke) and provided valuable additions and corrections to the Synoptics. "It transmitted a credible account of an early ministry of Jesus . . . [and] preserved a considerable body of topographical information, indicating at least certain steps in the itinerary of Jesus and some of the scenes of his work."[153] The late bishop John A. T. Robinson, a student of Dodd, was similarly convinced that John gives us a much more detailed topographical and chronological framework of Jesus' ministry than the

---

150. Charles H. Dodd, *The Founder of Christianity* (London: Macmillan, 1970), 27.
151. Dodd, *Founder of Christianity,* 27-28.
152. Dodd, *Founder of Christianity,* 36.
153. Charles H. Dodd, *Historical Tradition in the Fourth Gospel* (Cambridge: University Press, 1963), 429.

synoptics.[154] He also stated that "it is surely evident that the early Christians had an interest in the historical story for its own sake,"[155] a claim that we have also heard from Harald Riesenfeld.

In a 1943 lecture Thomas W. Manson claimed, in opposition to the form critics, that Mark did not just contain patchwork but respectable historical material on the life and ministry of Jesus.[156] Much earlier Manson proposed four motifs at work to compile a record of Jesus' teachings in the New Testament material. First, there was the pastoral work of the churches, that is, to find out from the acts and words of Jesus what his will and his spirit were for the lives of the people. Second, there was the personal interest of the disciples in their master, "who pondered his sayings in their hearts, not with an eye to the future needs of the Church, but simply because they had known the author of them and loved him."[157] Third, such teaching had apologetic value in the Gentile world, where, especially for the better educated, missionary preaching alone did not suffice but had to be supplemented by the sayings and deeds of Jesus to demonstrate the value of the new religion. And fourth, the Palestine community needed to defend itself against Jewish misrepresentation. One had to refer to Jesus to show that this interpretation of the law uncovered its actual intention. The teachings of Jesus were also important as propaganda among Jewish scholars who might show some sympathy toward Christianity.

Manson was convinced that the tradition concerning Jesus' teaching rested on a broader basis than we commonly imagine. Thus "the Church's task in meeting the problems which arose in its own life and in its relations with Jewish authorities was not of creating words of Jesus applicable to these situations but rather that of selecting what was relevant from the available mass of reminiscences."[158] This, of course, was a clear refutation of the form critics, who saw the creativity not so much with Jesus, but with the early Christian community. Whether one can

154. See John A. T. Robinson's remarkable book, *Can We Trust the New Testament?* (Grand Rapids: Eerdmans, 1977), 116.

155. Robinson, *Can We Trust the New Testament?* 115.

156. See Thomas W. Manson, "The Life of Jesus: A Study of the Available Materials" (1943), in *Studies in the Gospels and Epistles,* ed. Matthew Black (Manchester: Manchester University Press, 1962), 26.

157. Thomas W. Manson, *The Sayings of Jesus* (London: SCM, 1964 [1937]), 10.

158. Manson, *Sayings of Jesus,* 13.

opt for Manson or for the form critics is perhaps futile to decide since the truth is most likely somewhere in the middle. Yet there cannot be much doubt that the original body of tradition contained much more material than what is included in the four Gospels, since the Gospels preserved a rather deliberate selection (cf. John 20:31-32).

Vincent Taylor, in *The Life and Ministry of Jesus* (1954), picked up on the distinction between the Jesus of history and the Christ of faith, claiming that "we cannot see the Jesus of history if we close our eyes to the Christ of faith; we do not see the Christ of faith except in the light of the Jesus of history."[159] In other words, we must consider both the inferences drawn from the sources and to what extent they cohere with the religious and theological aspects of his person. We simply cannot proclaim Christ unless we know of Jesus. Yet in dealing with Jesus, the dangers of distortion are as great as the problems of understatement. Modern and critical study of the Gospel tradition has revealed that it is trustworthy "provided we do not make impossible demands upon it."[160] We will not be able to know the last detail about Jesus with ultimate accuracy, and many items will remain unsolved, but "within their limitations, the Gospels, while always subject to literary and historical criticism, are a reliable guide to the study of the mind and purpose of Jesus and to the turning points of his ministry in Galilee and Jerusalem."[161] Moreover, "the Fourth Gospel, along with the interpretative element in it, supplies independent tradition of great value to the historian."

A similar line is pursued by William D. Davies, a student of Dodd, whose inaugural lecture at Union Theological Seminary in New York was suggestively entitled "A Quest to Be Resumed in New Testament Studies" (1959). Davies did not want simply to continue the old quest but to resume it "on a new level."[162] He did not want to bypass the valid insights of form criticism. He assured his audience that one could not recover the intention of Jesus and his understanding of existence, as Bultmann and many of his followers had wanted, without attempting to uncover what Jesus said and did. "The Kerygma revolves around Him,

---

159. Vincent Taylor, *The Life and Ministry of Jesus* (London: Macmillan, 1961), 36.

160. Taylor, *Life and Ministry of Jesus*, 33.

161. Taylor, *Life and Ministry of Jesus*, 27 for this and the following quote.

162. William D. Davies, "A Quest to Be Resumed in New Testament Studies," in *Christian Origins and Judaism* (Philadelphia: Westminster, 1962), 16.

and we therefore want to assume that the Kerygma itself implies that if Jesus, the Christ, be not taken seriously as a 'fact' in history, He is in a real sense a contradiction in terms."[163] Because Jesus was a human being, the humanness of this being must be unearthed if the kerygmatic Christ is not to become a lifeless construct. Therefore Davies emphatically asserts: "The quest of the historical Jesus must go on."[164]

Having traveled through more than two centuries of research, we have finally arrived at the last quarter century. Regardless of all the diverse opinions we have heard, there is no reason for despair. Clearly no biblical scholar is naive enough to believe that an accurate biographical sketch of Jesus is still possible. In fact, it never was possible, and where it was attempted it resulted in an imaginary construct. Yet a critical look at the sources available did not end in the negative. After the initial shock over the fact that we have no unbiased sources, we gradually realized that all sources gathered and established by humans are biased. With this admission we can, however, attempt to reconstruct history, always knowing that it is a reconstruction and not the actual history itself. Both from the new quest and from the continued quest we heard that such pursuit must be continued, not simply for the love of the Lord of the Christian community, though that dare not be excluded. The main point in the pursuit of the quest for the historical Jesus was put forth by Vincent Taylor when he stated: "Christology cannot be effectively studied unless we can give an intelligible account of the life and ministry of Jesus as they are revealed in the gospels."[165] If we limit ourselves in christology to Christ, we confine our faith and the resultant Christian theology to something which we claim has no precedent. Christ would become a docetic Christ, and faith would be indistinguishable from credulity. Since the proper name Jesus "refers to a historical figure of the public past and not to a private myth or meaning-syndrome, the door is open to inquiry concerning him to whom Christians give allegiance."[166]

Both Rudolf Bultmann and Hans Conzelmann (in many ways his closest follower) dealt in their New Testament theologies with the histori-

---

163. Davies, "A Quest to be Resumed," 10. Cf. also Leander Keck, *A Future for the Historical Jesus: A Place for Jesus in Preaching and Theology* (Nashville: Abingdon, 1971), 25, who thinks along similar lines.

164. Davies, "A Quest to Be Resumed," 10.

165. Taylor, *Life and Ministry of Jesus*, v.

166. Keck, *A Future for the Historical Jesus*, 39.

cal Jesus. Bultmann clearly designated Jesus as a presupposition of New Testament christology, while Conzelmann appears to connect Jesus closer to the Synoptic kerygma.[167] Yet Conzelmann has precious little to say about Jesus. While such reticence may be called for if one is confined to what one can be absolutely certain about Jesus, one wonders what the result of such modesty would be in the case of Socrates or Plato. Could we ever quote them as authorities? While it is true that Jesus is not an authority for us — here lies also the limitation of securing the *ipsissima vox* of Jesus — the living Christ remains mere rhetoric unless he is in continuity with the Jesus of history. Therefore W. D. Davies correctly claims: "As long as the Jesus of History was a significant factor in the interpretation of the Faith of the New Testament, the works and words of Jesus themselves provided a context for the Kerygma which was religiously and ethically enriching. But once the Kerygma was materially divorced from these, it could now become to some extent an empty shell, or . . . a skeleton with no flesh."[168] Such reduction leaves the kerygma concerning the living Christ without much vigor and also cuts off other vital functions of the Christian tradition. For instance, today many people appeal to Jesus as a model for action and belief. Yet what sense do these appeals make if there is nothing that can legitimize these appeals? Similarly, Jesus is often invoked in sermons, and inferences are made from his life and ministry. But again, what justification do these references have unless we are willing and able to give historical warrants for their content? Unless we are able and willing to arrive in good conscience at a likely or a most likely outline of the life and destiny of Jesus, we will end up with a docetic and anemic Christ and jeopardize the credibility of the kerygma.

3. The Third Wave

In the preface to his book *Jesus in Contemporary Scholarship,* Marcus J. Borg wrote, "A third quest of the historical Jesus is underway, replacing the

---

167. Bultmann, *Theology of the New Testament,* 3. His first chapter is entitled "The Message of Jesus" (3-32). Hans Conzelmann, *An Outline of the Theology of the New Testament,* trans. John Bowden (New York: Harper, 1969), 127, asks concerning the Synoptic tradition "What does it tell us about Jesus himself?"

168. Davies, "A Quest to Be Resumed," 9.

old quest of the nineteenth century and the short-lived 'new quest' of the late 1950's and early 1960's."[169] Indeed, there has been a resurgence of new books on the historical Jesus, some of which were the result of added media attention and lacked solid scholarship. The lively debate of whether the Qumran manuscripts should still remain entrusted to the editors to whom they had originally been assigned or be handed over to scholars who will publish them in a relatively short time span led to rumors that the reason that the Dead Sea Scrolls had not yet been published was that their publication would undermine the Christian faith.[170] German translations of the books by Robert H. Eisenman and Michael O. Wise, *The Dead Sea Scrolls Uncovered: The First Complete Translation and Interpretation of Fifty Key Documents Withheld for Over Thirty-Five Years,* and by Michael Baigent and Richard Leigh, *The Dead Sea Scrolls Deception,* quickly became best-sellers for Bertelsmann, the largest book club in Europe.[171] Bertelsmann simultaneously offered a rejoinder by the New Testament scholars Otto Betz and Rainer Riesner, *Jesus, Qumran und der Vatikan: Klarstellungen.*[172] Betz and Riesner refuted the charge that the Vatican had anything significant to do with the delay of the scholarly publications of the Qumran manuscripts. They also attacked the claim that Jesus must be seen in direct line with the Qumran community.

The other noteworthy event was the Jesus Seminar, founded and led by Robert Funk. Funk was concerned that scholars make their research readily available to the general public, and therefore the Seminar made frequent use of press releases and news conferences. The purpose of the Seminar was "to assess the degree of scholarly consensus about the histori-

169. Marcus J. Borg, *Jesus in Contemporary Scholarship* (Valley Forge, Pa.: Trinity, 1994), ix.

170. For the following see James H. Charlesworth, *Jesus and the Dead Sea Scrolls* (New York: Doubleday, 1992), 4, who refers to the theses by R. H. Eisenman and the more outlandish claims by Barbara Thiering, *Jesus and the Riddle of the Dead Sea Scrolls: Unlocking the Secrets of His Life Story* (San Francisco: Harper, 1992), that Jesus "was born at Qumran and did not die on the cross but spent the remainder of his life in an Essene monastery."

171. Robert H. Eisenman and Michael O. Wise, *The Dead Sea Scrolls Uncovered: The First Complete Translation and Interpretation of Fifty Key Documents Withheld for Over Thirty-Five Years* (Rockport, Mass.: Element, 1992); Michael Baigent and Richard Leigh, *Dead Sea Scrolls Deception* (London: Cape, 1991).

172. Otto Betz and Rainer Riesner, *Jesus, Qumran und der Vatikan: Klarstellungen,* rev. ed. (Freiburg: Herder, 1993); Engl. trans. published as *Jesus, Qumran, and the Vatican: Clarifications,* trans. John Bowden (New York: Crossroad, 1994).

cal authenticity of each of the sayings attributed to Jesus in the New Testament and other early Christian documents written before the year 300."[173] The consensus is reached by a vote and the result is then expressed with the colors red, pink, gray, or black, indicating a higher or lower degree of historical probability. As in other critical research, parables and aphorisms are seen as the bedrock of the Jesus tradition. This time, however, Jesus emerged as a "wisdom teacher." After concentrating exclusively on the sayings of Jesus the group now ventures to determine the authenticity of actions attributed to Jesus, such as his miraculous healings.

The most noteworthy features of the third wave are that the scholars are mainly from North America and that many of them work within the mind-set of secular academia. This secular environment yields corresponding results: First, the old consensus that Jesus was an eschatological prophet who proclaimed the imminent end of the world has disappeared.[174] Second, there is a new understanding of Jesus as teacher, especially as a teacher of subversive wisdom. And third, studies of the social world of Jesus have become central. While we do not want to review the more than forty scholarly books on Jesus that were published between 1980 and 1988, it is important to highlight some aspects that have come to the fore in recent research.

a. A Noneschatological Jesus

Marcus J. Borg, professor of religion and culture at Oregon State University and a member of the Jesus Seminar who, by his own admission, is "a committed Christian deeply involved in the life of the church," has advanced a noneschatological interpretation of Jesus.[175] This interpretation is based primarily on three factors:[176] First, the sayings regarding the coming of the "Son of man" do not date back to the historical Jesus and therefore cannot substantiate an eschatological claim. Second, the understanding of the kingdom of God as portraying the imminent end of the world is without basis in the kingdom texts. Third, Borg has the

---

173. Borg, *Jesus in Contemporary Scholarship*, 162.

174. These three points are brought out by Borg, *Jesus in Contemporary Scholarship*, 7-10.

175. Borg, *Jesus in Contemporary Scholarship*, 161.

176. Borg, *Jesus in Contemporary Scholarship*, 51.

conviction that the kingdom of God does not need to be conceived in the framework of the temporal paradigm of the present/future.

It is not surprising that he disclaims the authenticity of the coming Son of man sayings, since this had already been done by Rudolf Bultmann and his followers. What is new in his argument, however, is the claim that the "Son of man" was not an apocalyptic title in Judaism.[177] His second claim goes together with the first one. Since the kingdom of God and the coming Son of man represent two different traditions, one cannot transfer the imminence associated with the coming Son of man to the kingdom of God sayings. Moreover, by themselves the kingdom of God sayings do not have the element of imminence in them. The only apparent exception would be Mark 9:1: "Truly I tell you, there are some standing here who will not taste death until they see that the kingdom of God has come with power." Yet Borg feels that this verse is not without its problems. "It is not clear that the coming of the kingdom in power refers to the end of the world; the verse permits a number of interpretations and is sometimes viewed as inauthentic."[178] Borg goes even one step further stating that "Jesus did not emphasize a future act of God (the end of the world), but emphasized the present kingly power of God and invited his hearers to 'enter' it and have their lives shaped by it."[179] The kingdom of God concept is pulled entirely into the present and has no end-time significance whatsoever.

Borg may be correct that the expectation of an imminent future event as central to Jesus' own (eschatological) expectation "now seems to have become a minority position in North American Jesus scholarship." Nonetheless this does not necessitate a shift toward a noneschatological interpretation of Jesus.[180] Conservative scholars, regardless of their geographic origin, have never accepted the thesis that Jesus was deceived in his expectation of the imminent coming of the kingdom. They rejected both the deception theory and the imminence of the kingdom. Yet for many other scholars as well, the first Christian com-

177. Borg, *Jesus in Contemporary Scholarship*, 52. He bases his claim on the research of Norman Perrin, *Rediscovering the Teaching of Jesus* (London: SCM, 1967), 173-74 and 260, and others, who stated that there never had been an apocalyptic concept of the Son of man.

178. Borg, *Jesus in Contemporary Scholarship*, 54.

179. Borg, *Jesus in Contemporary Scholarship*, 57.

180. Borg, *Jesus in Contemporary Scholarship*, 74.

munity's hypothesized disappointment about the delay of the parousia cannot be substantiated in historical documents. Borg himself does not want to abandon the eschatological dimension completely. Since for him this dimension is missing in the Jesus of history, it unfolds within the post-Easter experience. Therefore he reasons: "The 'coming Son of man' sayings express the church's expectation of Jesus' return, of his 'second coming.' The expectation of the imminent end of the world thus originates with the church's expectation of Jesus' return as Son of man. The belief in the imminent end of the world is best understood as a post-Easter development."[181] There is no continuity between the Jesus of history and the coming Son of man. Whatever emerged at Easter is not a clarification but an addition to the Jesus of history. We should notice, however, that even Robert Funk emphasized that "methodology is not an indifferent net; it catches only what it is designed to catch.[182] A noneschatological Jesus set apart from the eschatologically minded Christian community is not the only possibility.

b. An Eschatological but Nonapocalyptic Jesus

After careful methodological and historical consideration, Ben Witherington comes to the conclusion that "Jesus saw himself as not merely announcing but bringing about the eschatological blessings promised in the Isaiah prophecies. Unlike John, Jesus apparently did not expect a coming one, a successor. He himself was bringing the final eschatological message and work of God for God's people Israel."[183] Witherington is aware that eschatology is often loosely defined. Therefore he understands it as a study of the events and things that conclude human history, or at least bring that history to a climax. He suggests that this term can also be legitimately used "to refer to events that have to do with a messianic age that precedes 'the end of the world,' an age that in the relevant Jewish literature can last for a considerable period of time before the 'end of the world'."[184] He objects to Borg's attempt to reconstruct a

---

181. Borg, *Jesus in Contemporary Scholarship*, 58.
182. Robert Funk, "Beyond Criticism in Quest of Literacy: The Parable of the Leaven," in *Interpretation* 25 (1971): 151.
183. Ben Witherington III, *The Christology of Jesus* (Minneapolis: Fortress, 1990), 54.
184. Witherington, *Christology of Jesus*, 193.

noneschatological Jesus. Such a reconstruction is doomed to failure, because numerous eschatological sayings of Jesus that refer not just to the future coming of the kingdom of God or of the Son of man must be dismissed as inauthentic. Likewise many parables must be similarly dismissed, since they talk about a future judgment.[185]

At the same time Witherington does not agree that Jesus was an apocalypticist, if by apocalypse one means a certain type of literature with a narrative framework, in which revelation is mediated by an otherworldly being to a human recipient, disclosing a transcendent reality which is both temporal and spatial. It is temporal insofar as it envisages eschatological salvation; and spatial insofar as it involves another supernatural world. Witherington assures us that Jesus never produced an apocalypse nor did he use the sort of narrative framework that can "broadly speaking, be called apocalyptic, nor did he speak of visions or things that were happening in heaven or were hidden behind the visible tapestry of history."[186] Of course, Jesus' teaching contained some apocalyptic elements and images, but his main concern was what was happening to human lives during and through his ministry in the early first century. Witherington also contradicts Borg by saying that no texts speak about the entering of the kingdom of God during Jesus' ministry. "All the entrance texts refer to a future entrance, although how distant in the future is not said."[187]

Witherington would also contradict Borg's claim that the coming Son of man sayings are inauthentic. For instance, with reference to Mark 14:62 Witherington concludes: "The implication of this text is not only that Jesus is to be identified with the coming Son of man, but also that those who judge him now will be judged by him later—the kind of reversal of which Jesus apparently spoke on more than one occasion (cf. Lk. 12:8-9)."[188] Therefore he concludes that Jesus seemed to have a Messianic or transcendent self-understanding. While there were others during Jesus' time who perceived themselves as the Messiah of Israel, Jesus deliberately distanced himself from that form of expectation. He was no political revolutionary but expressed his self-understanding using

185. See Witherington, *Christology of Jesus*, 192, where he carefully elaborates on these points.
186. Witherington, *Christology of Jesus*, 193.
187. Witherington, *Christology of Jesus*, 206.
188. Witherington, *Christology of Jesus*, 261.

the Son of man terminology analogous to Daniel 7. However, this self-concept was also shaped by other Old Testament sources. Witherington concurs with Raymond Brown, who writes: *"Jesus knew his own identity* which involved the unique relationship to God that we call the divinity of the Son. Christians of a later period were able to formulate Jesus' identity as 'true God and true man.'"[189]

James H. Charlesworth, intimately familiar with the Dead Sea Scrolls and other extracanonical literature, does not want to present what Jesus said in a positivistic fashion but rather seeks to discern what Jesus intended to communicate.[190] He starts with a portrait of Jesus which, according to him, is widely accepted by many New Testament specialists:

> Jesus had some relationship with John the Baptizer, who certainly baptized him. He began his public ministry in or near Capernaum and took the initiative in calling men and women to follow him.
>
> He did select a special group, the twelve, and this action seems to indicate some revolutionary purpose to "restore Israel." He performed healings and probably also exorcisms. He was an itinerant preacher who proclaimed the nearness (even presence at times) of God's kingdom. He insisted that God is a loving Father; his favorite word for God was not the ineffable and common Jewish name for God, Yahweh, which according to our sources he never used. He customarily called God *"Abba,"* the Aramaic noun which for him denoted a beloved and intimate Father. He also taught his disciples in the Lord's Prayer, to call God by this unsophisticated term of endearment.[191]

Also Charlesworth is not hesitant to deduce a certain self-understanding of Jesus. According to him, Jesus sees himself in line with the prophets of the Old Testament, but also links himself with the great martyrs.[192] It is also evident for him "that Jesus thought of himself as God's son. . . . This term and title denoted a function that was to be performed with the will, power, and grace of God."[193] Yet Charlesworth refuses to speculate further on the precise meaning of the sonship in the

---

189. Raymond E. Brown, "Did Jesus Know He Was God?" in *Biblical Theology Bulletin* 15 (1985): 77-78.

190. So Charlesworth, *Jesus and the Dead Sea Scrolls*, 7.

191. Charlesworth, *Jesus and the Dead Sea Scrolls*, 151.

192. Charlesworth, *Jesus and the Dead Sea Scrolls*, 158.

193. Charlesworth, *Jesus and the Dead Sea Scrolls*, 160.

mind of Jesus. It is sufficient to him to see it in line with Psalm 2, namely that Jesus was specially chosen by God.

c. Jesus in Context

While Charlesworth sees Jesus primarily in the context of Qumran and of intertestamental literature, some other authors quite deliberately try to determine what can be known about Jesus through insights drawn from cultural and social anthropology, medical anthropology, the sociology of colonial protest movements, the dynamics and structure of pre-industrial peasant societies, and so on. For instance, Richard A. Horsley and John S. Hanson caution us that "the Zealots proper did not originate as a group until almost forty years after the career of Jesus" and that while there is little evidence for Jewish expectations of a Messiah or a prophet, popular movements often gathered around a king or prophet.[194] A similar sentiment is stated by Charlesworth, who wrote that "Jewish messianology does not flow majestically into Christian christology."[195] These insights necessitate a more differentiating approach to the issue of the historical Jesus. Yet multidimensional studies can shed new light on the historical Jesus. For instance,

> [S]tudy of Jewish social banditry may shed some light on the way in which Jesus was arrested (as if a brigand, Mk. 14:48) and on the crucifixion scene, in which Jesus was crucified with two brigands (not thieves, Mk. 15:27). More importantly, the occurrence of banditry illustrates the disintegrating social conditions in which Jesus' words and actions would have found a resonant response.[196]

Gerd Theissen, who has also attempted a contextual approach to the historical Jesus, comes to the conclusion that this kind of research can only make an indirect contribution to the issue of the historical Jesus.[197] In his

194. Richard A. Horsley and John S. Hanson, *Bandits, Prophets, and Messiahs: Popular Movements at the Time of Jesus* (San Francisco: Harper, 1988), 256.

195. James H. Charlesworth, "From Jewish Messianology to Christian Christology: Some Caveats and Perspectives," in *Judaisms and Their Messiahs at the Turn of the Christian Era*, ed. Jacob Neusner et al. (Cambridge: Cambridge University Press, 1987), 255.

196. Horsley and Hanson, *Bandits, Prophets, and Messiahs*, 256.

197. Gerd Theissen, *Lokalkolorit und Zeitgeschichte in den Evangelien* (Göttingen: Vandenhoeck & Ruprecht, 1989), 15.

book *The Shadow of the Galilean* he weds together various strands of historical source material in poetic form through a "narrative exegesis."[198] Nearly analogous to Albert Schweitzer's conclusion at the end of *The Quest of the Historical Jesus,* that of Gerd Theissen recovers only "footprints" of Jesus: anecdotes, narratives, traditions, and rumors, while "he himself remained elusive."[199] But all of this neatly fits together in Theissen's book. Illumined through its historical context, the book sketches out a historically reliable portrait of Jesus and his time.

John Dominic Crossan pursued a more direct approach to the historical Jesus in a book about which Marcus Borg said: "It could be the most important book on the historical Jesus since Albert Schweitzer's *Quest of the Historical Jesus* at the beginning of this century."[200] After laying out the different contextual facets that made up Palestine at the time of Jesus, Crossan establishes four layers of the Jesus tradition, which correspond to the following periods: A.D. 30-60, A.D. 60-80, A.D. 80-120, and A.D. 120-150. He goes beyond the present Gospel of Mark to an earlier layer in which he places the source Q, early Thomas, the genuine letters of Paul, a miracle collection, and a few other sources. What emerges of the historical Jesus is

> *a peasant Jewish Cynic.* His peasant village was close enough to a Greco-Roman city like Sepphoris that sight and knowledge of Cynicism are neither inexplicable nor unlikely. But his work was among the farms and villages of Lower Galilee. His strategy, implicitly for himself and explicitly for his followers, was the combination of *free healing and common eating,* a religious and economic egalitarianism that negated alike and at once the hierarchical and patronal normalcies of Jewish religion and Roman power.[201]

Jesus was a Jewish cynic peasant with an alternative social vision. He practiced healing outside of recognized religious authority and enjoyed meal fellowship with his peasant clients. "Miracle and parable, healing and eating were calculated to force individuals into unmediated physical

198. Gerd Theissen, *Der Schatten des Galiläers: Historische Jesusforschung in erzählender Form* (Munich: Christian Kaiser, 1986), 33.

199. Theissen, *Der Schatten des Galiläers,* 181.

200. Borg, *Jesus in Contemporary Scholarship,* 33.

201. John Dominic Crossan, *The Historical Jesus: The Life of a Mediterranean Jewish Peasant* (Edinburgh: T. & T. Clark, 1991), 421-22, for this and the following quotation.

and spiritual contact with God and unmediated physical and spiritual contact with one another. He announced, in other words, the brokerless kingdom of God." Jesus was neither a bandit leader nor a Messianic claimant; he was neither a millennial prophet nor a nonviolent protester. In him came together two rather disparate elements, "healer and Cynic, magic and meal."[202] "The kingdom of which Jesus spoke was a sapiential kingdom, not an apocalyptic kingdom."[203] Such a Jesus is hardly the Jesus of the Johannine Gospel and even less the Christ of early Christendom. Therefore Crossan sees a dialectic between Jesus and Christ. Nonetheless he feels that there is no contradiction between the historical Jesus and the later Christ who was defined as wholly God and wholly man, since in so doing he was again understood as the "unmediated presence of the divine to the human."[204] Yet Crossan is not so sure that there was no ultimate betrayal "in the move from Christ to Constantine."

Crossan rightly concedes that the historical Jesus here on earth is a scholarly reconstruction. He also rightly admits that a noncommitted, objective, dispassionate historical study like nineteenth-century research attempted is impossible to achieve. Scholars will always confront us with divergent historical Jesuses. When Crossan continues, however, to draw a parallel between the reconstruction of the historical Jesus and the reconstruction of the original text of the New Testament, he seems to go too far. Certainly there are disputed readings in the New Testament. Yet different textual readings of particular passages do not yield appreciably different texts so that there would be distinctly different historical Jesuses, one according to Crossan and another according to Charlesworth, to name just two recent New Testament scholars. Of course, we "can reconstruct only fragments of a mosaic, the faint outline of a faded fresco that allows for many interpretations."[205] This rather modest result, which always has to be kept in mind, should not lead to historical pessimism. In comparison to many shadowy figures of ancient history, such as Thales of Milet, Apollonius of Tyana, or Hillel, it is surprising how much we actually do know about Jesus.

202. Crossan, *The Historical Jesus,* 421.

203. This is the summary of Crossan's results according to Borg, *Jesus in Contemporary Scholarship,* 36.

204. Crossan, *The Historical Jesus,* 424, for this and the following quotation.

205. John P. Meier, "The Historical Jesus: Rethinking Some Concepts," in *Theological Studies* 51 (1990): 19.

John P. Meier is certainly correct when he asserts that "the proper object of Christian faith is not and cannot be an idea or scholarly reconstruction, however reliable. The object of Christian faith is a living person, Jesus Christ, who fully entered into a true human existence on earth in the first century A.D."[206] As Paul made unmistakably clear, Christians do not believe or put their trust in an earthly Jesus, however impressively he might be portrayed, but only in the resurrected Christ. What then are some of the insights gained by the seemingly never-ending study of the historical Jesus? At least four points should be noted:

1. The Christian faith is not an ideology that some people dreamed up but took its origin with one particular person. This person was born on this earth in a specific geographical region at a particular time in human history. He lived there, suffered, and died. In contrast to other founders of major world religions, he is both the subject and the object of the Christian faith.

2. In pointing us to the sources of the Christian faith, we are continuously reminded that Jesus is not a projection of our own imaginations or longings, be it an Arian Christ, an androgynic Christus/a, or a black Jesus. Jesus was a first-century Jew, a person truly human.

3. While one is often tempted to turn to the Bible as an answer book for all of life's questions, research in the historical Jesus makes us aware that Jesus was remarkably silent on many of the burning social and political issues of his day. He was also silent on many of our hot issues, from genetics to atomic energy, from capital punishment to family planning. Research into the historical Jesus always issues a caution against coopting Jesus for sanctioning our own predilections.

4. Research into the historical Jesus finally reminds us that Jesus is not just the *pantocrator,* the trans-earthly ruler of this world who sits at the right hand of the Father. He was also once one among us.

Any responsible study of christology is "indissolubly linked with the particularity of Jesus' own life, teachings, death, and resurrection."[207] If

---

206. Meier, "The Historical Jesus," 22.

207. So rightly Charlesworth, "From Jewish Messianology to Christian Christology," 254, who also raises the possibility of the subsequently mentioned connection.

we do not make this kind of connection, then christology, however dogmatically correct it may be, remains docetic and is in danger of furthering a myth. Therefore the legitimacy of the continuity must be examined between Jesus' own self-understanding and intentionality and what later came to be known as the church's christology. If there is no theologically perceivable continuity between the two, we are not proclaiming a living Christ who can make a claim on our lives today. Only someone who once lived can live again.

Part II
The Biblical Testimony and
Its Assessment through History

2. The History of Jesus

When I now venture to ascertain what can be known about Jesus of Nazareth, I will not follow a kerygmatic approach since a kerygmatic Christology sooner or later must be anchored in history if it is not to become fideistic. For the same reason I will also not pursue a dogmatic Christology. The dogma has no binding value unless it is derived from the source of the Christian dogma, Jesus of Nazareth. It has also become clear that we have no direct access to the Jesus of history. All the relevant documents, whether Christian or not, are written from a peculiar perspective of faith. But how do we get behind these documents to that which gave rise to them? One could apply the criterion of dissimilarity and look for the "uniqueness" of Jesus. So whatever is without parallel in either Judaism or Christianity and is clearly anchored in the biblical tradition must come from Jesus. While such material might point to sources that are no longer or not yet available to us, it is a weak criterion by which to establish what dates back to Jesus. Every historical figure is colored by the time in which he or she lived. By excluding this material we might get more a distortion of Jesus than Jesus himself. Yet it would be overreacting to establish a contextual Jesus who remains virtually indistinguishable from his context. With a "Mediterranean peasant" or a "bandit leader" standing behind the New Testament tradition we would be at a loss to account for the rise of this tradition and the attraction of the Christian faith in its formative stages.

When we compare the Gospels with Greco-Roman biographical literature of that time, we notice, however, that they are not exceptional. "Except for biographical satires, most Graeco-Roman biographies are didactic in intent. A life story is narrated in order to make a moral point and to inspire the reader to imitation."[1] The Evangelists were similarly concerned to show that Jesus' life and death were in conformity with God's will as contained in the Scriptures. The supernatural character of Jesus' life also finds its parallels in such biographies since, in contrast to modern biographies, there was an openness to the miraculous. Christian apologists such as Justin Martyr saw these affinities and claimed that the pagan parallels to the virgin birth of Jesus, his miracles, and his resurrection and ascension were inventions of the devil.[2] It is virtually impossible to obtain biographies from antiquity that meet our contemporary standards of metaphysical neutrality and historical objectivity. In attempting to reconstruct the life and person of Jesus of Nazareth there is very little which we can ascertain with absolute certainty. There exists a high degree of probability that many items date back to the Jesus of history and most items seem to be true to Jesus' life and mission. But they could just as well fit the description of many other people of that time. This becomes especially evident when we consider the Jewishness of Jesus. Since Jesus was a Jew, his life and his teaching had Jewish parallels and they in turn can be used to illuminate his life story. But we must take heed that we do not construct a Jewish life of Jesus that is primarily based on his affinity to Judaism and speculates from there what he said and did without being sure that he indeed acted this way. The same holds for the trial of Jesus. As has been argued by Ethelbert Stauffer and others, knowledge of the Jewish law allows us to reconstruct the trial of Jesus.[3] But is this then the trial that actually took place? Rudolf Bultmann was right when he claimed that the miracle stories in the Gospels follow a certain pattern that has parallels in Greco-Roman literature.[4] But when he concluded that this affinity discounted the historicity of the biblical accounts, he went beyond what can be legitimately concluded. He did not ask whether patterns that effectively narrate these stories are limited, and therefore his inference invalidates the historical skepticism which he advocated. Keeping all these caveats

1. So rightly Schuyler Brown, *The Origins of Christianity: A Historical Introduction to the New Testament* (Oxford: Oxford University Press, 1984), 42.

2. Justin Martyr, *Dialogue with Trypho* 69, in *ANF* 1:233.

3. Ethelbert Stauffer, *Jesus and His Story*, trans. Richard and Clara Winston (New York: Alfred A. Knopf, 1960), viii-ix.

4. Rudolf Bultmann, *The History of the Synoptic Tradition*, trans. John Marsh, rev. ed. (New York: Harper, 1968), 220-21.

in mind, I will start my own inquiry by first attempting to arrive at a chronology of the life of Jesus.

1. *The Life and Destiny of Jesus*

Since there is hardly any doubt that Jesus of Nazareth was a historical figure, he must have had a beginning and an end in time. There are two items demanding careful scrutiny concerning the date of Jesus' birth: the star and the census. The Gospel according to Matthew tells us: "Wise men from the East came to Jerusalem asking, 'Where is the child who has been born king of the Jews? For we have observed his star in its rising and have come to pay him homage'" (Matt. 2:2). Then we read in Luke about a census:

> In those days a decree went out from Emperor Augustus that all the world should be registered. This was the first registration and was taken while Quirinius was governor of Syria. All went to their towns to be registered. Joseph also went from the town of Nazareth in Galilee to Judea, to the city of David called Bethlehem, because he descended from the house and family of David. He went to be registered with Mary, to whom he was engaged and who was expecting a child. While they were there, the time came for her to deliver her child. And she gave birth to her firstborn son and wrapped him in bands of cloth, and laid him in a manger, because there was no place for them in the inn. (Luke 2:1-7)

a. Date and Place of His Birth

Our Christian division of time, before and after Christ, naturally was not introduced at the time when Jesus was born. The Romans counted the years *ab urbe condita* (since the foundation of the city [of Rome]). Centuries later, a monk named Dionysius Exiguus in A.D. 525 introduced our familiar division into B.C. and A.D. to show that with Jesus a new epoch had started. Dionysius was far from accurate in counting back to the time of Jesus' birth. Matthew 2:1 tells us that Herod (the Great) was still king when Jesus was born. Since he died in April, 4 B.C., we may assume that Jesus must have been born before that.

The slaying of the children in Bethlehem as related in Matthew 2:16

77

reminds us of the slaying of all the male children in connection with the birth of Moses.[5] The star, however, points to the oracle of Balaam, one of the oldest messianic references in the Old Testament: "A star shall come out of Jacob, and a scepter shall rise out of Israel" (Num. 24:17). That the heavens were indeed watched very closely is shown by the incident when, because of certain prophecies foretold by the stars, astrologers from Persia in the company of King Tiridates of Armenia came to Rome in A.D. 66 to pay homage to Nero as king of the universe.[6] The names of the (three) wise men whom tradition elevated to kings in the fifth or sixth century point to the East too. But in the Bible they appear nameless and are not numbered. While tradition magnified Matthew's story, this does not necessarily imply that it is devoid of any historical remembrances.

In 1603 Johannes Kepler attempted to calculate what kind of sidereal phenomenon could have attracted the curiosity of the magi and noticed in 7 B.C. the conjunction (coming into line) of Jupiter and Saturn, a phenomenon which occurred three times in that year.[7] This conjunction then was joined in February 6 B.C. by Mars, so that the three bright bodies formed a triangle in the twilight sky. Jupiter was regarded as the star of the ruler of the universe, and Saturn stood for the Amorites of the Syria-Palestine region. Moreover, the three planets met in the zodiacal sign of the Pisces, "sometimes associated with the last days and with the Hebrews."[8] This great conjunction of the three planets, according to Kepler, takes place only once every 805 years. Furthermore, Chinese astronomic records show that an important comet was seen in 5 B.C. While this may not be of great significance, since comets are usually considered to be forebears of ill-fortune, it is also interesting that the same records indicate for the year 4 B.C. an unusual star, either a comet or a nova. Such a nova might have also been the bright star which later faded into the background. This nova would not have allowed for sufficient time, if Jesus was to be born during the rule of Herod. An earlier date, perhaps 7 or 6 B.C., would be more likely.

5. Cf. Josephus, *Jewish Antiquities* 2.205-15, in *Josephus*, with an English trans., ed. H. St.-J. Thackeray, vol. 4 (London: William Heinemann, 1930), 253-57.

6. So Eduard Schweizer, *The Good News according to Matthew*, trans. D. E. Green (London: SPCK, 1976), 37, who assumes that these analogies prompted the formation of this story.

7. Jack Finegan, *Jesus, History, and You* (Richmond, Va.: John Knox, 1964), 23.

8. Raymond Brown, *The Birth of the Messiah: A Commentary on the Infancy Narratives in Matthew and Luke* (Garden City, N.Y.: Doubleday, 1977), 172-73.

Since it was widely believed in the Greco-Roman era that magi and astrologers possessed the ability to recognize the signs of the times and to foretell events of world importance (including the rise of kings), and since unusual heavenly portents were often associated with the ascendance of new rulers, one might be tempted to dismiss the episode of the magi as a pious legend, as many exegetes do. "The story of the star and the magi from the east seeking a king would not have been foreign to the ancients.... One cannot, however, altogether exclude the possibility of some historical basis."[9]

This story and the date 7 or 6 B.C. would also corroborate another phenomenon, the census related in Luke 2:1-5. But Raymond Brown cautions us that "this information is dubious at almost every score."[10] His major objection is that "the one and only census conducted while Quirinius was legate in Syria affected only Judea, not Galilee, and took place in A.D. 6-7, more than 10 years after the death of Herod the Great." Josephus, a first-century Jewish historian, reported that under Quirinius an account was taken of the people's possessions and this prompted Judas the Galilean to an uprising.[11] The context for this is the reign of Augustus, in whom many Romans put high hopes. As early as 27 B.C. he received his name Augustus, that is, the one who deserves adoration.[12] This was also the year in which he started to reform his empire, especially with regard to assessing his holdings. In Gaul this led to bloody resistance around 9 B.C. We also have a document from Gaius Vibius Maximus, governor of Egypt, dating from A.D. 104, in which he mentions that people should "return to their domestic hearths, that they may also accomplish the customary dispensation of enrollment."[13] Such enrollment, called *apographa*, took place every fourteen years. All people were required to

9. William D. Davies and Dale C. Allison, *A Critical and Exegetical Commentary on the Gospel according to Saint Matthew* (Edinburgh: T. & T. Clark, 1988), 1:233 and 235, who adduce extensive analogous material from antiquity.

10. Brown, *Birth of the Messiah*, 413, for this and the following quotation.

11. Josephus, *Jewish Antiquities* 18.1, in *The Life and Works of Flavius Josephus*, trans. William Whiston, intro. H. Stebbing (New York: Holt, Rinehart and Winston, n.d.), 529-30.

12. For the following see the enlightening comments by Walter Grundmann, *Das Evangelium nach Lukas*, 2nd ed. (Berlin: Evangelische Verlagsanstalt, n.d.), 76ff.

13. According to Adolf Deissmann, *Light from the Ancient East: The New Testament Illustrated by Recently Discovered Texts from the Graeco-Roman World*, trans. Lionel R. M. Strachan (New York: George H. Doran, 1927), 271.

return to their place of residence to be assessed. It is interesting that Luke uses the same word *apographa* as does Gaius Vibius Maximus, while Josephus uses the term *apotimesis*. It seems that there were two acts connected with the census, the assessment, at which time everything one owned was catalogued, and then the actual payment, at which time the taxes were levied. Most likely Luke and Josephus were talking about two phases of the same process that were separated by several years, especially since this was a first assessment in Syria.

When Luke mentions in this connection Publius Sulpicius Quirinius, we have again an inscription which connects Quirinius with a census and an insurrection, perhaps as a result of this census. Quirinius had been active in Palestine since 12 B.C. in a variety of ways. Tertullian tells us "that at this very time a census had been taken in Judea by Sentius Saturinus."[14] He was governor of Syria from 9-6 B.C. and presumably worked with Quirinius, whom Luke calls "governor." This period again coincides with the rule of Herod. Though the king was called "Friend of Caesar" *(Amicus Caesaris)* and "Ally of the People of Rome" *(Socius populi Romani)*, his reign was not unchallenged.[15] His subjects had to pledge allegiance to the Romans in 8 B.C., and most likely soon afterwards the census was started in his own territory. This was the time when Joseph journeyed to Bethlehem with his fiancé Mary. Thus both Matthew and Luke seem to indicate for this journey a date prior to the death of Herod, most likely around 7 B.C.

When we now ask whether Jesus was born in Bethlehem, we again have only the infancy narratives in Matthew and Luke to give us

14. Tertullian, *The Five Books against Marcion* 4.19, in *ANF* 3:378.
15. Ethelbert Stauffer, *Jesus and His Story*, 31; cf. also Brown, *Birth of the Messiah*, 413, who claims that Luke mistakenly exchanged two troubled endings of Herodian reigns, that of Herod the Great in 4 B.C., when the Jews protested against the giving of Judea to his son Archelaus, and the end of Archelaus in 6 A.D., when they revolted against the census by Quirinius. The weakness of Brown's assessment is that this argument is primarily based on Josephus's report of an *apotimesis*, while Luke clearly talks about an *apographa*; as Grundmann has shown, Josephus is not always to be trusted blindly in his historical statements. The only problem remaining would be that Luke calls Quirinius "governor," while we know that actually Saturinus was governor of Syria. Yet when we look closely, we see that Luke uses the term *hēgemoneuein*, i.e., "being in a position of leadership," instead of *hēgemōn*, which could be translated as "governor." Even this inconsistency disappears.

information about the birthplace. One might infer from Luke 2:4-11 that Jesus had to be born in Bethlehem, the city of David, to underscore his Davidic line of descent. Yet such reasoning seems unlikely. In the Gospel of Matthew the story of the magi does not connect Bethlehem with a Davidic descent. To substantiate Bethlehem as the birthplace of Jesus, it refers to the Messianic prediction of Micah 5:2: "But you, O Bethlehem of Ephrathah, who are one of the little clans of Judah, from you shall come forth for me one who is to rule in Israel" (Mic. 5:2; cf. Matt. 2:6). It is also important that the later Jewish polemics attacked Jesus' messiahship but not his birth in Bethlehem. They would have surely rejected Bethlehem, too, unless there was historical evidence for it.[16] Yet Origen tells us that after Jesus' birth Jewish scholars suppressed the expectation that the Messiah would be born at Bethlehem, a fact which again would support this city as Jesus' birthplace.[17]

There is positive evidence, however, that Galilee was Jesus' native region and Nazareth his hometown. Mark 6:1 mentions Jesus coming to his hometown, and Luke 4:16 is even more specific: "He came to Nazareth, where he had been brought up." Even if we had only the Gospel of Mark, we would assume that Jesus was born in Nazareth, though Mark does not explicitly say so (cf. Mark 1:16). John leaves the issue completely open as to whether we should opt for Bethlehem or for Nazareth, while Matthew and Luke point to Bethlehem. Of course, Bethlehem could always be a theological construct. But it is not simply tradition that gives us cause to favor Bethlehem.[18]

b. Jesus' Descent

In both the Matthean and Lukan genealogies (Matt. 1 and Luke 2:4), we read that Joseph is of Davidic descent. At the same time, both Gospels tell us that Jesus is born of the *virgin* Mary. While the genealogy in Matthew traces Jesus' lineage back to Abraham, Luke 3:23-38 traces his lineage to Adam and finally to God. Yet there are evident discrepancies

---

16. Brown, *Birth of the Messiah,* 514.

17. Origen, *Against Celsus* 1.51, in *ANF* 4:418.

18. Contrast with Hans Conzelmann, *Jesus,* trans. J. Raymond Lord (Philadelphia: Fortress, 1973), 26-27.

in both genealogies.[19] While Luke may have had more interest in asserting that Jesus was the Son of God, Matthew, by contrast, endeavored to show that Jesus was of Davidic descent.

Certainly family trees were important in Jesus' time. Ever since the return from the Babylonian exile, one had to prove that there were no mixed marriages (i.e., marriages with a Gentile) in one's ancestry in order to exercise rights as a citizen. If a girl wished to marry into a priest's family, she had to produce her genealogy extending back five generations.[20] Especially numerous were references to the tribe of Judah and the line of David. Eusebius, following Hegesippus, reports that after the capture of Jerusalem the Emperor Vespasian issued an order that "all descendants of David should be ferreted out."[21] Again from the same source he quotes that Emperor Domitian "ordered the execution of all who were of David's line."[22] And finally under Emperor Trajan, Symeon, son of Clopas, was charged with "being a descendant of David and a Christian," which resulted in his execution.[23] At Jesus' time and well beyond we hear of descendants of David's line.

Next to the descendants from the tribe of Judah came those of Benjamin. We hear, for instance, that Paul is "an Israelite, a descendant of Abraham, a member of the tribe of Benjamin" (Rom. 11:1; cf. Phil. 3:5). If Jesus was born of the virgin Mary and if Joseph was of Davidic descent, it might sound strange that a claim would be established that Jesus was of Davidic descent. Such a claim would seem to contradict his being born by a virgin. This dilemma presents itself in a different light when we read in the Babylonian Talmud: "The family of the father is regarded [as the proper] family [but] the family of the mother is not regarded [as the proper] family."[24] This means that if Joseph is the biological father of Jesus he naturally passes his Davidic lineage to his

19. For details see Brown, *Birth of the Messiah*, 57-93.

20. Joachim Jeremias, *Jerusalem in the Time of Jesus: An Investigation into Economic and Social Conditions during the New Testament Period*, trans. F. H. and C. H. Cave (Philadelphia: Fortress, 1969), 275-76.

21. Eusebius, *The History of the Church from Christ to Constantine* 3.12, trans. G. A. Williamson (Minneapolis: Augsburg, 1975), 124.

22. Eusebius, 3.19-20, 126.

23. Eusebius, 3.32, 142.

24. *The Babylonian Talmud: Seder Nezikin* (Baba Bathra 109b), ed. I. Epstein (London: Soncino, 1935), 452.

son. But if he were not the biological father, the same would be true, provided that he legitimized Jesus. Indeed, the latter seems to have occurred. Joseph accepted Mary and the child to whom she gave birth.

Nevertheless, the Davidic descent could also be a theological construct of the Christian community, arising out of the desire to show that Jesus was the Messiah. The Messiah was supposed to be from David's line; hence the emphasis on the Davidic origin of Jesus. Yet there are several factors which counter this kind of reasoning. One, while it is true that there was a strong tendency to announce that the Messiah would come from David, this was by no means a unanimous opinion. For instance, Bar Kochba was hailed as a Messianic figure even though he was not of Davidic origin.[25] Then there was also some speculation that the Messiah would be one of unknown origin who would suddenly be revealed. Last, but not least, in the Qumran community and perhaps even noticeably in the Gospel of John, there was the hope for the coming of a Messiah from Aaron, that is, an anointed high priest of Levitical ancestry. Second, relatives of Jesus were still known among the first-generation Christians. Some were also persecuted by the Romans because of their Davidic descent. If Jesus had not been of Davidic descent, hostile Jews or even Christian Davidids would certainly have not hesitated to expose the claim of a Davidic descent as a theological construct, especially since such lineage did not give them an automatic leadership position in the church. Third, the New Testament references to the Davidic ancestry of Jesus are not restricted to Matthew and Luke but occur throughout the New Testament. For instance, Paul writes of Jesus Christ, "who was descended from David according to the flesh" (Rom. 1:3), and Jesus himself implies his Davidic ancestry (Mark 12:35ff.). There are no Jewish polemics, however, against the Davidic descent of Jesus. But other points at which an alternate claim could logically be established, such as his "resurrection" or his "virginal conception," were attacked by Jewish writers. So we can assume with a very high degree of certainty that Jesus was indeed of Davidic descent.

The other claim, usually going with Jesus' Davidic lineage, that he was virginally conceived, is much more difficult to establish. The birth narratives in Matthew and Luke vary considerably, but their genealogies

25. See for the following and for details Brown, *Birth of the Messiah,* 507-8; cf. also Stauffer, *Jesus and His Story,* 14-15.

trace Jesus' Davidic descent through Joseph without denoting Joseph as having begotten Jesus. Presupposed here are the Jewish marriage customs as we know them from rabbinic sources. First comes a formal exchange of consent before witnesses (Mal. 2:14).[26] This is usually translated as betrothal or "engagement" (Luke 2:5). It is a covenant, a legally ratified marriage which gave the young man rights over the girl. She is now his wife (*gynē:* Matt. 1:20), and any disloyalty at this time would constitute adultery. Yet the wife still lived for another year with her family. Then came the second step, in which the groom would take his bride home (Matt. 25:1-13) and would assume her support. Both Matthew and Luke indicate that Joseph is between these two steps. When he found out that Mary was pregnant, he considered this adulterous behavior and contemplated divorcing her (Matt. 1:19). Luke, however, does not mention Joseph's reaction. Both Matthew and Luke affirm that the pregnancy is through or of the Holy Spirit.

It must be stated again that our intensely modern historical mind-set is foreign to the understanding of history within the New Testament. It strikes us as a strange lapse into rationalism to suggest "that the 'catalyst' for the notion [of the virginal conception] might have been that Jesus was born prematurely (i.e., too early after Joseph and Mary came to live together — cf. Mt. 1:18)."[27] Matthew and Luke do not present the virginal conception as a symbol; rather, "both of them regarded the virginal conception as historical."[28] Yet their main intent in mentioning the virginal conception was theological or rather christological, assuring the full humanity of Jesus while at the same time indicating that his coming was a special creative act of God. They had no biological interest in the virgin birth. A similar intention, though without mentioning the virgin birth, is voiced by Paul when he writes: "When the fullness of time had come, God sent forth his Son, born of a woman, born under the law" (Gal. 4:4).

When we look beyond the birth narratives we find no further mention of the virginal conception. Only the reference to "the son of Mary" (Mark 6:3; cf. Matt. 13:55, in which this is changed to the "carpenter's son," and in

---

26. See for the following Raymond E. Brown et al., eds., *Mary in the New Testament: A Collaborative Assessment by Protestant and Roman-Catholic Scholars* (Philadelphia: Fortress, 1978), 83-84.

27. Brown, *Mary in the New Testament,* 291.

28. So rightly Brown, *Birth of the Messiah,* 517.

Luke 4:22 we read "Joseph's son") could indicate that his father was unknown.[29] Even when his father had already died he would still be called his father's son. Of course, there could be non-Christian catalytic influences responsible for the story of the virgin birth, since many important figures were allegedly born of a virgin even if their parents were well known. Yet in the Near Eastern and Hellenistic context there is always a sexual element present, a divine marriage, for instance, in which a divine male in human or other form impregnates a woman. But in the New Testament we read of the nonsexual virginal conception of Jesus.[30] Nor does Judaism give us any close parallels to the virginal conception of Jesus.

How was the incident of the virginal conception handed down to the Christian church? It is unlikely that the story comes from Joseph, since after the infancy narratives he fades out of the picture. To assume that there was a family tradition is not convincing either. There is a strong indication that Jesus' brothers did not believe in him during his ministry (cf. Mark 3:21, 31 and John 7:5). This again would lead us to believe that they did not know about his "miraculous" conception. Mary, too, does not seem to have had much understanding of Jesus (Mark 3:31-35 and John 2:3-5), which is surprising given his divine origin. Since Mary became pregnant long before she came to live with her husband, there certainly must have been public knowledge of Jesus' early birth. But to assume that this factor, together with the conviction that Jesus was the Son of God, engendered the tradition of the virgin birth is at most a hypothesis. We could claim with Rudolf Bultmann that "the virgin birth is inconsistent with the assertion of his [i.e. Jesus'] pre-existence."[31] But this kind of reasoning is flawed, since preexistence implies divine, that is, eternal, sonship, while the virgin birth reflects his coming into the world.

We could assume that though he was born early, Jesus was indeed the son of Joseph and Mary and a virginal conception was just a cover-up. Though this seems to be a plausible hypothesis, it is strange that in antiquity no anti-Christian polemics picked up this argument. Only second-century Jewish Christians claimed that "Jesus was Joseph's natural and

---

29. So Stauffer, *Jesus and His Story*, 16, 208.

30. Brown, *Birth of the Messiah*, 522-23, is very convincing at this point.

31. Rudolf Bultmann, "New Testament and Mythology," in *Kerygma and Myth: A Theological Debate*, ed. Hans Werner Bartsch, trans. Reginald H. Fuller (London: SPCK, 1953), 11.

legitimate son."[32] The anti-Christian polemicists, however, went a different route, suggesting a more tenable alternative to the virginal conception by insinuating that Jesus was an illegitimate son of Mary.[33] It is interesting that Samaritan and Mandaean sources refer to Jesus as the son of Mary with the intention of defaming him, while the Qur'an also refers to him as Jesus, son of Mary (cf. Surah 3:44-45). The Qur'an does so to demonstrate that he was indeed created by God's creative word. Origen in his treatise *Against Celsus* also informs us of Celsus's claim that Mary "bore a child to a certain soldier named Panthera."[34] Of course, Celsus polemicized against the Christians in his *True Word* of A.D. 178. Similarly, from the second century we have a quotation by Tertullian on the charges of Jesus' dubious origin.[35] We may conclude that defaming Jesus on account of his origin was quite widespread. It also seems that some of these accusations can be invalidated by considering that "Pantera could be a family name" which then was used polemically in early Jewish literature.[36] That Jesus, however, is the biological son of Joseph is disputed by the vast majority of sources. This would also weaken the thesis that Jesus was born prematurely. We are immediately confronted with a deep ambiguity: either we remain with the this-worldly aspect or we are open to the transcendent dimension. Jesus' birth is no exception to this rule, provided we accept the textual reliability. We then face the following alternative: in all likelihood Jesus was either born of the virgin Mary, as the Christian and Moslem sources claim and both Christians and Moslems believe, or he was the illegitimate son of Mary, as anti-Christian polemicists assert.

c. Jesus and John the Baptist

In the centerpiece of the famous Isenheim Altar by Matthias Grünewald, John the Baptist (or more correctly the Baptizer) is depicted with an elongated pointing finger, pointing at the crucified Christ. This is the way John is generally perceived, announcing and witnessing to the com-

32. So Brown, *Birth of the Messiah*, 530.
33. For the following see Stauffer, *Jesus and His Story*, 17-18.
34. Origen, *Against Celsus* 1.32 and cf. 1.28, in *ANF* 4:408 and 410.
35. Tertullian, *The Shows* 30, in *ANF* 3:91.
36. So Brown, *Birth of the Messiah*, 536, and Morris Goldstein, *Jesus in the Jewish Tradition* (New York: Macmillan, 1950), 39, who assumes, however, that "Yeshu ben Pantera was given simply as a family name of Jesus in its earliest mention in the Talmud."

ing one. No other person in the Jesus tradition assumed such a prominent role as did John and his message. Yet who was this John?

Josephus (ca. 37–ca. 100) in his *Antiquities of the Jews* tells us in great length about John that "Herod slew him, who was a good man, and commanded the Jews to exercise virtue both as to righteousness towards one another and piety towards God, and so come to baptism; . . . Herod who feared lest the great influence John had over the people might put it into his power and inclination and raise a rebellion. . . . He was sent a prisoner, out of Herod's suspicious temper, to Macherus, the castle I before mentioned and was there put to death."[37] There is no reason to doubt the information given by Josephus, quoted also in full by Eusebius, since it gives no indication of Christian embellishment nor of Josephus's own exaggeration.[38] Josephus does not give us an exact time frame for John the Baptist, except the reign of Herod (Antipas). Here the Gospel of Luke helps a bit further. It introduces the beginning of the mission of John with an interesting sixfold chronological synchronism:

> In the fifteenth year of the reign of Emperor Tiberius, when Pontius Pilate was governor of Judea, and Herod was ruler of Galilee, and his brother Philip ruler of the region of Ituraea and Trachonitis, and Lysanias ruler of Abilene, during the high priesthood of Annas and Caiaphas, the word of God came to John the son of Zechariah in the wilderness. He went into all the region around the Jordan, proclaiming a baptism of repentance for the forgiveness of sins. (Luke 3:1-3)

While some of the intended references are unclear to us and while we do not exactly know from what date onward to calculate the fifteenth year of Tiberius, it is safe to assume that this meant either A.D. 28/29 or 27/28.[39] So John started his ministry around A.D. 28. He preached and baptized within a few miles of Qumran, and it seems likely that he was not unfamiliar with the beliefs and practices there.[40]

37. Josephus, *Antiquities of the Jews* 18.5.2, 540.

38. Cf. the careful deliberations by Charles H. H. Scobie, *John the Baptist* (Philadelphia: Fortress, 1964), 18ff.

39. So Walter Grundmann, *Das Evangelium nach Lukas* (Berlin: Evangelische Verlagsanstalt, n.d.), 100; see also for an extensive discussion of the synchronism Joseph Fitzmyer, *The Gospel according to Luke (I–IX)* (Garden City, N.Y.: Doubleday, 1981), 455-458.

40. So Scobie, *John the Baptist*, 39.

John the Baptist worked in the wilderness area, close to where the river Jordan flows into the north end of the Dead Sea. He baptized in the river Jordan but did not confine himself to one location (Luke 3:3). In the wilderness of Judea he prepared "the way of the LORD" (Isa. 40:3), alluding to the same eschatological expectation which is mentioned by the members of the Qumran community in their "Manual of Discipline."[41] This wilderness situation was indicative of his way of life: "John wore clothing of camel's hair, and a leather belt around his waist, and his food was locusts and wild honey" (Matt. 3:4). Central to John's teaching and preaching was the proclamation of the imminent coming of the end and of judgment. He said to his listeners: "You brood of vipers! Who warned you to flee from the wrath to come? Bear fruit that befits repentance. Do not presume to say to yourselves, 'We have Abraham as our ancestor'; for I tell you, God is able from these stones to raise up children to Abraham. Even now the axe is lying at the root of the trees; every tree therefore that does not bear good fruit is cut up and thrown into the fire" (Matt. 3:7-10). In keeping with the prophetic tradition, these words are simple, clear, and direct. John addressed the entire Jewish nation, even its pious members, and called everyone to repentance. He woke them up from their religious security. Unless they amended their ways and were baptized destruction was inevitable.

Though we do not know much about the baptism John demanded, we may assume with relative certainty that it was not a self-baptism. John administered it himself, most likely by immersion. It had its parallels in the ritual purifications of Judaism, as we know them from Qumran, for instance. As an expression of repentance and conversion from the former ways of sinfulness, John's baptism mediated forgiveness and rescue from the impending judgment. This baptism of repentance had ritual as well as moral implications. It was not a ritual rite to be repeated whenever a person became again unclean: "It marked the once-for-all decision of a person to break with sin and to enter the community of those who sought to prepare for the imminent advent of the Coming One and his twofold baptism of fire and holy spirit."[42]

Both with his message and his baptism John the Baptist becomes important for Jesus. He foretold the advent of a person who would come

41. See the quotation in Scobie, *John the Baptist*, 46.
42. Scobie, *John the Baptist*, 115.

at the quickly approaching end of time to execute judgment and baptize with fire and the Spirit. "The one who is more powerful than I is coming after me; I am not worthy to stoop down and untie the thong of his sandals. I have baptized you with water, but he will baptize you with the Holy Spirit" (Mark 1:7-8). John's prediction of the advent of a mightier one and of the Messianic baptism is recorded both in Q (the hypothetical collection of sayings of Jesus from which the Synoptics are thought to draw) and in Mark, showing not only its reliability but also its significance for the Christian church. Moreover, in the Synoptic Gospels we are also told of Jesus' baptism by John (Mark 1:9-11; Luke 3:21-22; Matt. 3:16-17). According to Matthew and Mark, Jesus goes into the wilderness after this baptism and then his ministry commences. In the Fourth Gospel Jesus' baptism is not directly mentioned. Instead John proclaims Jesus as the "Lamb of God," the one "who baptizes with the Holy Spirit," and who is "the Son of God." John does nothing other than point to Jesus. Yet this portrayal stands in stark contrast to John 3:22-23: "Jesus and his disciples went into the Judean countryside, and he spent some time there with them and baptized. John also was baptizing at Aenon near Salim because water was abundant there." A later redactor must have been uncomfortable in putting Jesus in analogy to John the Baptist and therefore added in John 4:2, "although it was not Jesus himself but his disciples who baptized."[43] It is unlikely that Jesus' baptism was an isolated event at which John and Jesus met and that there was no contact between them before and thereafter. Yet the church had a vested interest in claiming John merely as a precursor or witness to Jesus.

Jesus himself made extensive references to John.[44] He told his audience that John was more than a prophet and that among those born of women there was no one greater than John. He also compared him to Elijah, whom the people expected to return at the end of history. It may very well be that *"through John's mediation Jesus perceived the nearness of the kingdom and his own relation to its coming."*[45] But it is an overstatement when Walter Wink claims: *"The church stood at the center of John's movement*

43. See Raymond E. Brown, *The Gospel according to John (I–XIII)* (Garden City, N.Y.: Doubleday, 1966), 164, in his comments on Jn. 4:2.

44. Cf. Matt. 11:7-19.

45. So Walter Wink, *John the Baptist in the Gospel Tradition* (Cambridge: Cambridge University Press, 1968), 113 (italics author's).

from the very beginning and becomes its one truly great survivor and heir."[46] The church and the Baptist community were not merely on a convergence course. While there was an affinity between Jesus and John the Baptist, there was also a basic difference between the precursor and the coming one. It would simply be impossible to say of John (as one can say of Jesus) that the proclaimer became the proclaimed. Furthermore, we have no trace of a new covenant that John might have initiated. As John must be seen in the larger context of the baptizing movement, comprising among others the Essenes, Nasoreans, and Elkesaites, so Jesus must be seen in the context of the movement of John the Baptist.

It might be more theological desire than historical accuracy to report that Jesus' mission commenced once John the Baptist was imprisoned (Mark 1:14) since this leaves Jesus without a (theological) mentor. The Jesus movement and that of John existed for a (short) while side by side (John 3:26).[47] Yet was it a peaceful coexistence or did they clash, as students and teachers often do once the former exert their own authority? Conjectures about serious clashes are unfounded. The sad comment about John's end is telling: "His [John's] disciples came and took the body and buried it; then they went and told Jesus" (Matt. 14:12). If they felt so close to Jesus to bring him the sad news of John's execution, there could not have been much animosity between them.

There were obvious differences between John and Jesus, as the latter clearly admitted (Matt. 11:18-19). John was an ascetic, while Jesus was not. John remained for the most part in the wilderness, while Jesus traveled freely and even entered the homes of notorious sinners. For John the kingdom was still in the future, while for Jesus it was already present. John preached basically repentance, while Jesus' message also included the good news of God's love. John did not perform miracles, while Jesus did. And finally, for John the right way of living opened the gates of heaven, while according to Jesus we always depend on God's grace even with our best performance. But both agreed on decisive points. They were dissatisfied with current Jewish thought and practice, had fervent eschatological expectations, and were convinced that an immediate decision to surrender one's whole life to God was necessary.

---

46. Wink, *John the Baptist*, 110 (italics author's).

47. So also Jürgen Becker, *Johannes der Täufer und Jesus von Nazareth* (Neukirchen-Vluyn: Neukirchener Verlag, 1972), 15.

While the agreements between John and Jesus are fundamental, Jesus still regarded John as belonging to a different age, the *preparatio evangelii*, the preparation of the gospel (Matt. 11:10 and Luke 16:16). So we need not be surprised that John sent messengers from prison asking whether Jesus was the one who was to come (Matt. 11:3). He was not expecting a supernatural Messiah as in prevalent apocalyptic thought. When he mentioned the untying of the coming one's sandals, he indicated that he looked for an earthly, human figure.[48] Was Jesus then the human figure who would be exalted to become the heavenly judge? Though Jesus' answer was clear, it was as ambiguous as all historical references are by necessity.

d. Duration and Extent of Jesus' Public Ministry

It is very difficult, if not impossible, to ascertain the exact duration of Jesus' public ministry.[49] It must have commenced after John the Baptist made his public appearance, that is, after A.D. 27/28 or 28/29. It came to a close with Jesus' death, which must have occurred before A.D. 33 to 35, the date we can establish for Paul's conversion to the Christian cause. Moreover, the Gospels tell us that Jesus died on a Friday. According to the Synoptics this Friday coincided with the fifteenth day of the Passover month of Nisan, the first day of the feast (Mark 14:12). According to John, however, it was the fourteenth day, the evening on which the Passover lambs were eaten (John 18:28; 19:31). It is possible that the fifteenth of Nisan fell on a Friday in A.D. 30 or 31 (Synoptic chronology) or that the fourteenth of Nisan fell on a Friday in A.D. 30 and 33 (John's chronology). It is therefore likely that Jesus died in A.D. 30, 31, or 33.

There is one more item to consider for the chronology. If we accept the approximate chronological rendering in the Gospels as accurate, then we have in Mark 2:23 an allusion to harvest time (i.e. spring), while at the time of the last Passover it is spring again. If we follow this chronology portrayed in the Synoptics we arrive at no more than two years' public ministry of Jesus. If we follow John, however, we have a mentioning of

---

48. See Scobie, *John the Baptist*, 77-78, for further details on this issue.

49. For details of the chronology see Conzelmann, *Jesus*, 20-25, and Leonhard Goppelt, *Theology of the New Testament*, trans. John E. Alsup, ed. Jürgen Roloff (Grand Rapids: Eerdmans, 1975), 1:20.

Passover in John 2:13 and 23, another feast in John 5:1, which may be identical with the Passover in 6:5, and a final one in 11:55. Thus John's account indicates more than two years for Jesus' ministry. Since Jesus' ministry is easier to arrange in three years than in two, we could even conclude that in terms of the Passover chronology the Synoptics are more correct, while in terms of the length of Jesus' ministry John should be given preference.

Jesus conducted his ministry essentially within that region of Palestine which was settled by Jews. When he went beyond these boundaries it was not to widen his ministry but to elude his opponents or to pass through this "foreign" territory to another destination. He did not intend to establish contact with the Hellenistic world but felt himself sent to Israel (Mark 7:27). In this he distinguished himself from the scribes and Pharisees since they "cross sea and land to make a single convert" (Matt. 23:15). But Jesus himself bore some distinctive marks of a scribe. Like a scribe he was addressed as teacher *(didaskalos)*, and, also in the rabbinic tradition, he had a circle of followers whom he called disciples *(mathētai)*. He also spoke in the style of scribes through dialogues to teach or to refute other teachings, and he coined sayings and parables that could be easily remembered.

His contemporaries realized that he was not just a scribe since "he taught them as one having authority, and not as the scribes" (Mark 1:22). He had a different authority, behaved like a prophet (Mark 8:27), and accompanied his teachings with miracles. The main dialogue partners for him were those who represented the Law, the scribes and Pharisees and, to a lesser extent, the Sadducees. In addition, and also in contrast to his dialogue partners, he concerned himself with those who were neglected in society. This involvement with the untouchables of society may have contributed to his apprehension, conviction, and death.

e. Trial and Death

The actual passion of Jesus begins with his entrance into Jerusalem (Mark 11:1-10), which had undeniable Messianic connotations. The crowd cheered him with "Hosanna!" and spread their garments and palm branches on the road. Yet contrary to political expectations that the Messiah would visibly enter Jerusalem and publicly assume power, Jesus alluded to Zechariah 9:9: "Triumphant and victorious is he, humble and riding on a donkey, on a colt, the foal of a donkey." This humble posture was disappointing for some, since they expected the Messiah to come in glory. Yet they stayed with him during the subsequent days, still expecting something astounding to happen. One event that did occur and engrained itself deeply into the Christian memory was Jesus' farewell supper with his disciples.

We have accounts of the Last Supper in all the Synoptics (Mark 14:22-25; Matt. 26:26-29; and Luke 22:15-20, where the longer version is the original one since the shorter seems to be deliberately abbreviated), a reflection of it is perhaps contained in John 6:53-56, and there is also an account in 1 Corinthians 11:23-25. While the tradition in Mark 14 is the oldest, certain features in 1 Corinthians 11 and Luke 22 are even earlier. According to Mark the Last Supper was a Passover meal (Mark 14:12), a notion which is also supported by Luke (22:15). Yet this contradicts the chronology of John (18:28) according to which Jesus died at the same hour when the Passover lambs were slain in the temple court. While John's chronology may be a theological construct to emphasize that Jesus is *the* Passover lamb, it is not crucial whether John or the Synoptics are correct. Neither the Passover lamb nor the "correct" date was needed for the Passover celebration. Many Jews who did not make the pilgrimage to Jerusalem had to slaughter their lambs themselves without the benefit of the temple ritual. Moreover, there were also different traditions about the exact date of the Passover among various groups within Judaism.[50] We should also note that "the accounts put Jesus' conduct in reference not to peculiarities of the Passover meal, but to the basic elements of every Jewish meal, the breaking of bread and the cup of blessing."[51]

From the traditional celebration of the meal we can infer how the Last Supper proceeded and at which point Jesus introduced something new. To open the meal as the head of the family, Jesus recited the blessing over the meal, to which the table companions responded with an "Amen."[52] While he did this he took the unleavened bread, broke it into pieces, and gave it to his disciples. Though the bread was usually

---

50. For details see Stauffer, *Jesus and His Story*, 114-15.
51. So Goppelt, *Theology of the New Testament*, 1:215.
52. See for the following Joachim Jeremias, *The Eucharistic Words of Jesus*, trans. Arnold Ehrhardt (Oxford: Basil Blackwell, 1955), 106-10.

consumed in silence, Jesus at this meal said, "Take, this is my body." Then came the actual meal at which nothing out of the ordinary happened — so far as we know. The Passover narrative was recited and the Passover psalms were sung (Pss. 113–118). It also seems likely that at the very beginning of the Supper when the bitter herbs were eaten, Jesus dipped some into the bowl and gave them to Judas, singling him out and exhorting him to hasten and complete his mission (Mark 14:18; John 13:26). At the end of the meal Jesus concluded with the rite of thanksgiving: he took the cup of benediction and lifted it up, and at the end of the benediction all responded by saying "Amen." Then he passed around the cup and said: "This is my blood of the covenant which is poured out for many."[53] With these two changes, or rather additions, Jesus "vouchsafed forgiving fellowship by giving himself as the One who died for the benefit of all others. It was not a heavenly body, not a pneumatic substance, that was given, and also not only an atoning power, but Jesus as the One who died for all."[54]

There are still two more phrases which attract attention: "in remembrance of me" (1 Cor. 11:24-25 and Luke 22:19) and the renunciation, "I will never drink of the fruit of the vine until that day when I drink it new in the kingdom of God" (Mark 14:25). While the first phrase might refer to the remembrance of the dead Jesus upon the anniversary of his death and therefore be a later pious addition, it assumes a completely different meaning if it is supposed to mean, "God remembers the Messiah by bringing about his kingdom in the parousia."[55] In this way both references point to eschatological urgency. Jesus will no longer have actual table fellowship with his disciples until he can have it in a redeemed world, in a transfigured creation, at the time of salvation. To this extent his disciples are urged to continue the fellowship meal so that God may hasten the parousia and the coming of the kingdom.

This would mean that with this meal Jesus has taken the ultimate step and has, so to speak, burnt his bridges and is now on the way to another world. In so doing he is vicariously giving — as he expressed in the "words of the institution" — with bread and wine his lifeblood and his very body so that others may participate in the new covenant. The

---

53. Jeremias, *Eucharistic Words of Jesus,* 115.
54. Goppelt, *Theology of the New Testament,* 1:220.
55. Jeremias, *Eucharistic Words of Jesus,* 163.

Last Supper was immediately followed by the betrayal, capture, trial, and execution of Jesus. The Last Supper already had a different tone than one of utter abandonment. It had shown the way to a new stage of reality. This does not belittle Jesus' passion, because it makes clear that only through death can the new reality be achieved.

There have been many thorough investigations into the last days of Jesus, especially insofar as his trial is concerned. The Gospels themselves devote ample space to the events of the last days. Consonant with his mission are his capture and trial. When a fight was about to erupt between his disciples and the helpers of the high priest, Jesus interceded and willingly surrendered himself (Luke 22:47-53). He did not want to be mistaken for a political Messiah to whose aid the heavenly legions would come. When he was questioned by the high priest and the witnesses disagreed, he did not try to escape from the impending doom but, as we will see later, almost forced the verdict upon himself. Thus the saying "the Son of Man is to be betrayed into human hands" (Mark 9:31) becomes true with him.

Even without Jesus' "collaboration" a clash with an influential Jewish segment of society resulting in his demise seemed inevitable.[56] The Jewish leaders perceived Jesus' popularity as a threat to their own standing among the people. Some members of the Sanhedrin, especially the Sadducees, were also afraid that the growing Jesus movement would give the Romans a pretense to intervene and thus the Jews would lose the little independence they still had. The Pharisees of the Sanhedrin also disapproved of his message. Finally, we should not overlook the fact that the people had certain expectations of Jesus which he failed to fulfill. Their obvious enthusiasm for him changed into rejection. But in order to execute Jesus, the Jews needed the Roman authorities, because only they had the right to put someone to death.

The Jewish authorities brought Jesus to Pilate and accused him of political crimes which should compel the Roman representative to act: "We found this man perverting our nation, forbidding us to pay taxes to the emperor and saying that he himself is the Messiah, a king" (Luke 23:2).

---

56. For the following see Josef Blinzler, *Der Prozeß Jesu*, 4th ed. (Regensburg: Friedrich Pustet, 1969), 448, and J. Blinzler, *The Trial of Jesus: The Jewish and Roman Proceedings against Jesus Christ Described and Assessed from the Oldest Accounts*, trans. from the 2nd ed. by Isabel and Florence McHugh (Westminster, Md.: Newman, 1959), 291.

But Pilate was not anxious to act, since Tiberius had reversed his anti-Jewish stance in approximately A.D. 31 and Pilate had been, until then, "the enforcer of this policy," showing his contempt for the Jews whenever he could.[57] Another of his atrocities and he could imperil his position.[58] When he proved to be reluctant to condemn Jesus, the Sanhedrin plainly told him: "If you release this man, you are not a friend of the emperor" (John 19:12). Pilate understood the implied threat.[59] It meant denunciation and the possibility that he would lose his title "friend of Caesar." So he acted in a juridically correct way on behalf of the imperial administration and demonstrated to the Jews a political willingness to oblige. Even as he decided against Jesus he was already thinking how he could strike back at the Jews. John reports that Pilate put an inscription on the cross, "Jesus of Nazareth, the King of the Jews" (John 19:19), meaning that he was executing the petty king of the Jews. When the Jewish authorities protested, he, as protector of the Roman interests, felt secure enough to tell them: "What I have written, I have written" (John 19:22).

Jesus, convicted as an insurgent, died on the cross. His disciples despaired and feared that they would be next in line for persecution. The two disciples on their way to Emmaus expressed eloquently the depth of the disappointment: "But we had hoped that he was the one to redeem Israel" (Luke 24:21). Indeed, God had not vindicated him. Jesus hung helplessly on the cross. When we read Psalm 22, of which, in accordance with Jewish citation practice, only the opening verse is quoted in the passion story, we obtain a different picture of Jesus. Surely, meditating on this psalm, he had realized the depth of the agony he would experience.[60]

However, he did not give up on his God. When we read at the conclusion: "Proclaim his deliverance to a people yet unborn, saying that

57. Goppelt, *Theology of the New Testament*, 1:225-26.

58. Harold W. Hoehner, "Why Did Pilate Hand Jesus over to Antipas?" in *The Trial of Jesus: Cambridge Studies in Honor of C. F. D. Moule*, ed. Ernst Bammel (Naperville, Ill.: Alec R. Allenson, 1970), 90, suggests that for diplomatic reasons Pilate first handed Jesus over to Antipas. While this suggestion sounds convincing, we are not as certain that this episode is as well attested as Hoehner thinks.

59. See Charles H. Dodd, *The Founder of Christianity* (London: Macmillan, 1970), 161-62.

60. This psalm has even been suggested as the original frame for the formation of the passion narrative. See, e.g., John Pobee, "The Cry of the Centurion — A Cry of Defeat," in *The Trial of Jesus*, 92, who claims that "the thought of Ps. 22 runs through the whole chapter" of Mark 15.

he has done it" (Ps. 22:31), we cannot but conclude that beyond and in this agonizing death something else must have dawned.

f. The Empty Tomb and the Epiphanies of the Resurrected One

It is not surprising that the disciples did not expect anything decisive to happen after Jesus' death. Nobody went to the tomb expecting to find it empty, and nobody could imagine that Jesus was not dead. No one had hallucinations or apparitions telling him or her that Jesus must be alive. On the contrary, three women, Mary Magdalene, Mary the mother of James, and Salome, went to the tomb intending to anoint the hastily entombed body of their beloved Lord. When they found the tomb empty and had an unusual encounter at the graveside, "they went out and fled from the tomb; for terror and amazement had seized them; and they said nothing to anyone, for they were afraid" (Mark 16:8).

With one (redactionary) exception (John 20:8), the Easter faith of Jesus' followers was not founded on encountering an empty tomb. As Matthew candidly admits, the empty tomb was subject to different ex- planations.[61] The Jews circulated rumors that "his disciples came by night and stole him away" (Matt. 28:13). Tertullian had an even more incredible story to tell which he found circulating as anti-Christian polemic: "The gardener abstracted [Jesus] that his lettuce might come to no harm from the crowd of visitants."[62] While this polemic surely did not convince many, we must still ask why the stories of finding the empty tomb were included in the Gospels, if they did not prove that Jesus was resurrected. Moreover, three women were presented as the principal witnesses, and women could not serve as official witnesses according to Jewish law. The most convincing reason for the stories concerning the empty tomb is simply that the tomb was indeed empty. The corpse which the followers of Jesus expected to find could not be found there. This corresponds with another incident or a series of incidents, the appear- ances of the resurrected one.

The official record of the Easter appearances is in 1 Corinthians 15:5-8. We read there that Christ "was raised on the third day in accor-

---

61. See the discussion of Woolston (pp. 8-9) and Reimarus (p. 12) above for modern explanations.
62. Tertullian, *The Shows* 30, in *ANF* 3:91.

dance with the scriptures, and that he appeared to Cephas, then to the twelve. Then he appeared to more than five hundred brothers and sisters at one time, most of whom are still alive, though some have died. Then he appeared to James, then to all the apostles. Last of all, as to one untimely born, he appeared also to me." Here the witnesses are all official, all male. Also most witnesses are still alive and can be asked as to what they saw. That "he was raised" is deduced from the "he appeared." In the Petrine sermons we also hear that "God raised [him] from the dead. To this we are witnesses" (Acts 3:15; cf. 2:32; 4:10).

While all four Gospels share the story of the empty tomb, Mark did not contain stories of the appearances of the resurrected one in his shorter version. Yet in Mark 16:7 "an angel" announced Jesus' appearance in Galilee. This is taken up by Matthew (Matt. 28:7-10), who reports one appearance in Galilee (Matt. 28:16-20). In Luke the setting is different (Luke 24:6), and the appearances take place around Jerusalem. John, too, utilizes a tradition which points to Galilee (John 21). Since both Matthew and Luke are influenced by theological considerations in their geography it is difficult to decide in favor of one over the other.[63] It might be that both pointed to something historically valid and neglected other evidence. The most important feature of the appearance stories is the recognition and acknowledgment of Jesus as the resurrected one. This recognition is not based on his visual characteristics but on his deeds, especially in the breaking of bread (Luke 24:30-31). In order to guard against interpretations of the appearances as hallucinations, Luke points out that one could even touch the body of the resurrected one (Luke 24:39) and that the resurrected one could eat (Luke 24:43). While these latter points may be secondary enlargements, they served an apologetic function, rejecting the accusation of delusion or of ghostlike apparitions.

Without exception these appearances of the resurrected one occurred to people who did not believe in his resurrection, but who were led to believe through these encounters. Recognition of Jesus leads to the conviction of his resurrection. The Easter accounts are also commissioning experiences (cf. Matt. 28:18-20; Luke 24:46-49, etc.). Assured that Jesus was indeed vindicated and certain that he did not hold their abandonment of him against them, the disciples were directed to spread the news of who Jesus really was. The proclaimer became the proclaimed.

---

63. Goppelt, *Theology of the New Testament,* 1:240.

Yet before we ask in which sense he became the proclaimed, we must
— at least briefly — focus on his own proclamation.

2. The Proclamation of Jesus

There are many facets of Jesus' proclamation on which one could dwell
— his understanding of God, his ethics, or his compassion for people.
Remembering, however, that on numerous occasions he clashed with the
Pharisees in his interpretation of the Law, we may infer that Jesus'
interpretation of the Law was significant. Since Jesus was close to John
the Baptist, we assume that the announcement of the impending judgment was also important for Jesus. Finally we notice that he does not fit
the prevalent ideas of the Messiah. Thus we must also ask what his
self-understanding was insofar as we can still ascertain it.

a. Jesus and the Law

The first impression Jesus gave to his contemporaries was that he acted
like a scribe. Accordingly he was addressed as "rabbi" (Mark 9:5) or
synonymously as "teacher" (*didaskalos;* Mark 9:17). We hear at the beginning of his ministry that "when the Sabbath came, he entered the synagogue and taught" (Mark 1:21). His more immediate followers are called
"students" *(mathētai),* which is somewhat incorrectly translated as "disciples" (Mark 3:7). He taught his disciples (Mark 8:31), who in turn
instructed others (Matt. 10:7). Jesus may indeed be seen in close connection with the rabbinic tradition, which may also account for the fact that
in the New Testament the term *logos* (word) or *logos theou* (word of God)
denotes the gospel which tells us of Jesus and his sayings. Consequently,
the Swedish New Testament scholar Harald Riesenfeld suggests that
Jesus did not teach indiscriminately or continually. "He imposed certain
limitations on his preaching as he did in the case of his miracles. And
what was essential to his message he taught his disciples, that is, he made
them learn it by heart."[64] He also accompanied his teachings with
miracles (cf. Mark 2:9), something which rabbis usually did not do. The

---

64. Harald Riesenfeld, *The Gospel Tradition and Its Beginnings,* 2d ed. (London: A. R.
Mowbray, 1961), 24.

people therefore remarked that "he taught them as one who had authority and not as the scribes" (Mark 1:22). This estimation was also grounded in the people's perception of him, particularly in his exposition of the Law.

The Pharisaic-rabbinic Judaism, which had gained control of the synagogue in Jesus' day, viewed the Law as a thoroughly performable sum of commandments and prohibitions.[65] Altogether there were 248 commands, corresponding to the 248 members of the human body, and 365 prohibitions, for the 365 days of the year.[66] The commandments were divided into easy and difficult ones depending upon how much (or little) energy or financial investment they required. Each of these commandments was interpreted by the rabbis through numerous stipulations called *halakah* (the way), which were recorded in the *mishna* (the tradition) in the second or third century. The prime concern of the Pharisees was to fulfill the demands of the Torah as interpreted by the Halakah.

Jesus had no intention of revolting against the Law. "Whoever breaks one of the least of these commandments, and teaches others to do the same, will be called least in the kingdom of heaven; but whoever does them and teaches them will be called great in the kingdom of heaven," Jesus said (Matt. 5:19). With such an approach he should have had nothing to fear from the Pharisees, the scribes, and the rabbis who largely followed the rabbinic emphasis on the Law. Yet the coexistence of the Torah and the Halakah caused problems for Jesus. He did not just opt for a more radical interpretation of the Torah, as for instance the Qumran community did, but he drew a sharp distinction between the Torah and the Halakah. When he was challenged on the Halakah (Mark 7:5) he retorted that its adherents "abandon the commandment of God and hold to human tradition" (Mark 7:8). He flatly rejected the Halakah as human precepts and human tradition since it was implicitly designed to restrict the commandment of God in order to circumvent it (Mark 7:9).

While others countered such halakic abuses of the Law with an even stricter interpretation of the Halakah, Jesus did not promulgate such "secondary" radicalism. Rather, he altered the relationship of the people

---

65. Goppelt, *Theology of the New Testament,* 1:88.

66. See Hermann L. Strack and Paul Billerbeck, *Kommentar zum Neuen Testament aus Talmud und Midrasch,* vol. 1: *Das Evangelium nach Matthäus,* 2nd ed. (Munich: C. H. Beck, 1966), 900ff., who provide numerous illustrations.

to the Law itself. We can see this best with Jesus' understanding of the Sabbath. When he intentionally violated the Sabbath law, he knew that he had attacked something constitutive of the Jewish way of life. While the Hellenistic world knew of many holidays, it did not have a special day of rest, the Jewish people did. Yet Jesus pushed aside the Halakah, claiming that "it had been developed only to reduce the area of human responsibility."[67] Jesus did not just question the interpretation of the commandment but the validity of the commandment itself. As he was going to heal someone on the Sabbath day, he asked a rhetorical question: "Is it lawful to do good or to do harm on the Sabbath, to save life or to kill?" (Mark 3:4). This put the whole issue of keeping the Sabbath into a new light. It was no longer just a question of whether a life was at stake. But he introduced the maxim: "At all times and in all places conduct yourself in such a way that life is enhanced and not diminished." In principle Judaism would have agreed to this precept. Yet Judaism held that it was illusory to enact this precept in everyday life. There the commandment (and its Halakah) limited the responsibility of the people to God. Jesus, however, expressed a total and unlimited demand. In healing the sick person he suspended the Sabbath commandment, while showing that through this action God's unrestricted intention of enhancing life had been accomplished. The Jews had only one choice, either to align themselves with Jesus and therewith agree to this suspension of the Law, the very foundation of their faith, or to adhere to the Law and to eliminate its suspender.

Jesus' attitude toward the Law culminates in the so-called antitheses of the Sermon on the Mount (Matt. 5:21-48). He contrasted the halakic "You have heard that it was said to those in ancient times" with his own "but I say to you." He does not establish a new Halakah, but with an emphatic "I" he authoritatively sets his commands, that is, the will of God, in opposition to its traditional understanding. Jesus makes it clear that he does not abolish the Law. "Do not think that I have come to abolish the law or the prophets; I have come not to abolish but to fulfill" (Matt. 5:17). But "the law and the prophets were in effect until John came" (Luke 16:16). Here it becomes clear that with Jesus' proclamation of God's will a new and final disclosure of this will had come. As Ernst Fuchs pointed out, Jesus "dares to affirm the will of God as though he

---

67. Goppelt, *Theology of the New Testament,* 1:93. See 93-94 also for the following.

himself stood in God's place."[68] Jesus did not abolish the commandment concerning the Sabbath or any other commandment (Matt. 5:18). They are here for our life on earth, which is threatened by sinfulness and evil. Decisively, however, Jesus pointed to that which stood behind the Law, God's will for the preservation and enhancement of life. Since in Jesus' life and mission God is present, his proclamation of God's will is of utmost importance for people who want to enter into the kingdom of God. Therefore he told them: "Unless your righteousness exceeds that of the scribes and the Pharisees, you will never enter the kingdom of heaven" (Matt. 5:20). Jesus' authoritative explication of God's will is part of God's eschatological saving activity which had begun in Jesus.

b. Announcing the Kingdom

Jesus and John the Baptist began their ministry in close proximity and, as we have seen, they agreed at many points.[69] But there were also decisive differences between them. Jesus' message was not exclusively one with the somber tone of the impending judgment. For him the time of salvation had already come (Luke 11:20), while for John it was still pending. When John the Baptist sent two of his disciples to ask Jesus whether he was the promised one or whether they should wait for someone else, Jesus referred them to his words and actions. "Go and tell John what you hear and see: the blind receive their sight, the lame walk, lepers are cleansed, the deaf hear, the dead are raised, and the poor have good news brought to them" (Matt. 11:4-5). With this response Jesus claimed that in him the Old Testament images connected with the time of salvation (Isa. 35:5-6) were fulfilled. The claim that he was the bringer of salvation at the end time is frequently attested.[70] For instance, Jesus told his disciples: "Blessed are your eyes, for they see, and your ears, for they hear. Truly I tell you, many prophets and righteous people longed to see what you see, but did not see it, and to hear what you hear, but did not hear it" (Matt. 13:16-17). His disciples experienced what had

---

68. Ernst Fuchs, "The Quest for the Historical Jesus," in *Studies of the Historical Jesus*, trans. Andrew Scobie (Naperville, Ill.: Alec R. Allenson, 1964), 21.

69. See Fuchs, "Quest for the Historical Jesus," 16.

70. For the following see Werner Georg Kümmel, *The Theology of the New Testament according to Its Major Witnesses: Jesus — Paul — John*, trans. John E. Steely (London: SCM, 1974), 1:36-37.

been promised for the end time. Jesus also talked about the new wine that should not be poured into old wineskins (Matt. 9:17). The old time was passed, the time of salvation had been initiated. At one point Jesus stated it even more clearly: "But if it is by the finger of God that I cast out the demons, then the kingdom of God has come to you" (Luke 11:20).

This claim that the kingdom had arrived was a surprise for most Jews, since they expected that with the coming of the kingdom God's power would also become visible. Yet here it is only Jesus' power over the demons which substantiates the assertion that the coming of the kingdom has dawned. But Jesus repeated this claim again, defending himself against the charge that he owed his power over demons to a treaty with the prince of demons: "No one can enter a strong man's house and plunder his property without first tying up the strong man; then indeed the house can be plundered" (Mark 3:27). According to Jewish expectations, only the bringer of salvation at the end time can bind the evil one. Jesus thus indicated through his actions that the eschatological salvation was being accomplished. In Jesus' actions and preaching God was already establishing his rule. One could be included in the saving activity of God if one believed in Jesus and his message.

Albert Schweitzer had convincingly asserted that Jesus' proclamation was a totally eschatological proclamation.[71] But in contrast to those of his contemporaries who preached a message of fire and brimstone, Jesus did not give his listeners a timetable and inform them in detail about the things that were going to happen at some future point. Rather, he addressed his audience in such a way that his address implied an immediate decision.[72] He did not spell out certain eschatological doctrines, but he confronted the people with a radical decision for or against God. This demand for a decision became at the same time a decision for or against Jesus and his actions. His proclamation, his own person, and his actions form a unity that provoked and called for a decision. "Follow me, and let the dead bury their own dead" (Matt. 8:22); "no one who puts a hand to the plow and looks back is fit for the kingdom of God" (Luke 9:62); "and blessed is anyone who

---

71. Albert Schweitzer, *The Quest of the Historical Jesus: A Critical Survey of Its Progress from Reimarus to Wrede,* trans. W. Montgomery, 2nd ed. (London: A. & C. Black, 1922), 328.

72. Rudolf Bultmann, *Theology of the New Testament,* trans. Kendrick Grobel (New York: Charles Scribner's, 1951), 9-10.

takes no offense at me" (Matt. 11:6); these are only a few passages that show the urgency of an immediate decision here and now. The now is the decisive point of history. No longer is the future the decisive point, as in apocalyptic preaching or in the covenant history of the Old Testament. The kingdom of God is in the midst of you, said Jesus. It was not because he was such an important preacher or because he had such an important message that he called for an immediate decision. The kingdom of God has come with his appearance, and thus it is the time of decision. The today of Jesus is the goal of history.

Although Jesus emphasized the decisiveness of his own person and of the present time, he did not point to an impending or immediately coming end of the world, except to reinforce the urgency of an immediate decision for or against God.[73] As far as we know, the oldest tradition of the sayings of Jesus, often called Q, contains no indication that Jesus was a "doomsday prophet" of the immediately approaching end of the world.[74] If there were any authentic words of Jesus about such matters, they would be found in the Q-source. But there is no evidence in Q. This coincides with another finding: neither Jewish contemporaries of Jesus nor Jewish polemicists after Jesus accused him of having falsely announced an immediate end of the world. We cannot imagine that they would not have exploited such false prophecy if it had indeed occurred. Yet if the present assumes such decisive momentum, the future, while not irrelevant, will be of lesser interest. Jesus did not just call for a decision in face of the imminent presence of the kingdom of God. With the coming of the kingdom, salvation had become a present reality.

Jesus used the symbolic language of the Old Testament to proclaim the dawning of the time of salvation.[75] The bright city of God on the top of the hill shines into the dark world (Matt. 5:14). The fields are ripe (John 4:35) and the harvest time has come. New wine as the symbol of the new ages is offered (Mark 2:22). The wedding garment is to be put

73. See Bultmann, *Theology of the New Testament*, 1:29, who even asserts: "The synoptic tradition contains no sayings in which Jesus says he will sometime (or soon) return."

74. Q is an abbreviated form of *"Quelle,"* the German word for "source." Johannes Weiss (1863-1914) appears to have originated the usage. See Stephen Neill with Tom Wright, *The Interpretation of the New Testament (1861-1986)*, 2nd ed. (Oxford: Oxford University Press, 1988), 128 n. 2.

75. For the following see Joachim Jeremias, *New Testament Theology: The Proclamation of Jesus*, trans. John Bowden (New York: Charles Scribner's, 1971), 1:106-7.

on (Matt. 22:11), and the bread of life is given to the children of Israel (Mark 7:27). Jesus announced the now of salvation in word and deed. Through these actions the love of God is shown and the distant threatening God becomes a God who is at hand. In Jesus we encounter the God who seeks out the sinner and who forgives.

Jesus was called "a friend of tax collectors and sinners" (Matt. 11:19). This association, which the Pharisees and many others resented, was an integral part of his self-understanding, since "those who are well have no need of a physician, but those who are sick" (Mark 2:17). In the Gospel according to Luke the parables of the lost sheep, the lost coin, and the lost son (Luke 15:1-32) are narrated to show why Jesus cultivated such friendship with sinners. In each case joy was expressed when the lost was finally found. When Jesus extended fellowship to sinners, through table fellowship, healing the sick, and the summons to become disciples, on each occasion a restoration of fellowship took place. Since Jesus left no doubt that the one who rejoiced over the return of the lost was God himself, it was clear that the searching and forgiving compassion came from God. Therefore God sent the Son into the world not to condemn the world but that the world might be saved through him (John 3:17). Consequently Jesus told of a parable of a king who forgives a slave an incredibly huge debt (Matt. 18:23-35), hoping that this would entice the servant to be similarly merciful to others. To be obedient to the command to love God and neighbor (Mark 12:28), already presented in the Old Testament (Deut. 6:4-5 and Lev. 19:18), is the appropriate response to the loving, caring, and forgiving God whom Jesus portrayed. Yet how could Jesus be so sure that he knew God's will? To address this question we must inquire about his self-understanding.

c. A Different Messiah

Since Jesus' public ministry started without any reported preparations, we may assume that his baptism had a catalytic impact, similar to the call experiences recorded in the Old Testament.[76] Though he may have been conscious of his unique relation to God, it was not until after his baptism that Jesus assumed a public ministry. While he was more than a rabbi or a scribe, even the title of prophet does not do justice to his

---

76. Goppelt, *Theology of the New Testament,* 1:41.

ministry. Although he shared the knowledge of God which had been granted to him, he proclaimed the will of God in such a way that it transcended the category of the prophetic. His preaching and his actions were understood by him to have ultimate significance, and therefore he understood himself as the bringer of salvation.

Most Christians would state without hesitation that Jesus was the Messiah, meaning "the Christ" or the "anointed one." Yet careful study of the New Testament shows that the title Messiah, or *Christos* in Greek, is rarely used in the Synoptic Gospels but quite frequently in the other New Testament writings. It is entirely missing in the oldest source, Q, and so are the titles "son of David," "King of Israel," and "King of the Jews."[77] Mark, the oldest Gospel, does not give us clear evidence that Jesus used the term "Messiah" either. The Gospel of John, which does use the term quite frequently, never uses it in such a way as to indicate that Jesus himself had used it. The term Messiah did not play an important role in the life of Jesus. Jesus probably refused the title Messiah when it was conferred on him.[78] If Jesus had clearly shown Messianic qualities in word and deed, his own self-portrayal should not have caused his ultimate rejection.

In the Jewish creation calendar the year 5000 had awakened Messianic hopes in many people, since the Messiah was supposed to usher in the sixth millennium, the age of the kingdom of God.[79] Thus in the second quarter of the first century A.D. Messianic expectations were especially fervent. For instance, there was the prophet Theudas, who was put to death by the Roman procurator in A.D. 44. A few years later there was an Egyptian prophet who together with his followers attempted to take over Jerusalem. Again the Roman authorities suppressed the rebellion. Josephus also mentions a band of other men who "deceived and deluded the people under the pretense of Divine inspiration, but

77. Vincent Taylor, *The Names of Christ* (London: Macmillan, 1954), 19; and Stauffer, *Jesus and His Story*, 161.

78. Ferdinand Hahn, *The Titles of Jesus in Christology: Their History in Early Christianity*, trans. Harold Knight and George Ogg (London: Lutterworth, 1969), 161. Hahn connects this most probable repudiation of the Messianic title with the observation that "in the life of Jesus any sort of indication of a zealotic tendency in thought or action is entirely lacking."

79. Abba Hillel Silver, *A History of Messianic Speculation in Israel from the First through the Seventeenth Centuries* (Boston: Beacon, 1959 [1927]), 6-7.

were for procuring innovations and changes of the government; and these prevailed with the multitude [in Jerusalem] to act like madmen, and went before them into the wilderness, pretending that God would show them the signals of liberty."[80]

The Messianic expectations usually included the overthrow of the Roman power in Palestine. It was commonly expected that the Messiah would redeem Israel from exile and servitude and even the whole world from oppression, suffering, war, and, above all, from heathenism.[81] Along with redemption from the evil in humanity, the Messiah was expected to save humanity from the evil in nature. The Messianic age would also bring about great material prosperity. The earth would bring forth an abundance of grain and fruit, and humanity would be able to enjoy all of this without excessive toil.

When we review these expectations we must agree with Rudolf Bultmann that Jesus' life and activity were certainly not Messianic when "measured by traditional messianic ideas."[82] Yet to conclude with Bultmann that Jesus did not portray any Messianic aspiration is also overstating the case. Admittedly, Jesus did not conform to the usual political aims connected with Messianic expectations. Some of his followers may have hoped that eventually he would become politically active, especially when he came to Jerusalem to celebrate the Last Supper. But Jesus did not take over the city or assume political leadership (cf. Luke 24:21). Jesus showed no interest in the political and nationalistic expectations connected with the coming of the Messiah, and he did not want to be mistaken for a political liberator. There is no hint whatsoever that he conspired against the Roman occupation army or that he wanted to revolt against it. Though the charges against him were finally of a political nature, he emphatically denied them.

There was another less politically and nationalistically colored title Jesus seemingly used, the title "Son of Man." It occurs eighty-two times in the Gospels, sixty-nine of them in the Synoptics, and only once outside the Gospels (Acts 7:56). The title "Son of Man" has no equivalent in

---

80. Josephus, *Wars of the Jews* 2.13.4, in *The Life and Works of Flavius Josephus*, 683.

81. For this and the following see the helpful summary in Joseph Klausner, *The Messianic Idea in Israel from Its Beginning to the Completion of the Mishnah*, trans. from the 3rd ed. by W. F. Stinespring (New York: Macmillan, 1955), 520ff.

82. Bultmann, *Theology of the New Testament*, 1:27.

secular Greek; it is a translation from the Aramaic. It could simply mean a designation of an individual. It was used in Matthew 8:20 in this way: "Foxes have holes, and birds of the air have nests; but the Son of Man has nowhere to lay his head."[83] Alongside this everyday use developed a more elevated way of speaking. As a result of Daniel 7:13 ("I saw one like a son of man coming with the clouds of heaven") it emerged as a Messianic title. Of course, not all of the Son of Man references in the Synoptics are original, as we can gather from an analysis of the history of tradition. Yet even those which are original need not be traced to Jesus.

It seems strange that this title is virtually confined to the Gospels, and neither the earlier nor the later Christian writings, including those of Paul, used it. It is also significant that it was not used in the Jewish apocalyptic literature after Christ. Only 2 Ezra uses the term, and Rabbi Abbahu (ca. 300) says in the Jerusalem Talmud: "If a man says to you: 'I am God,' then he lies; if, 'I am the Son of Man', he will finally regret it" (j. Ta'an 2:1).[84] It is understandable that Christian literature would avoid using a term which we, too, have trouble understanding in its theological significance. We more likely understand it in its everyday usage denoting the son of a man (and of a woman). But why would the Jewish literature have invectives against it? Because it was once connected with Jesus? The prohibitions might at least indirectly support this thesis. Moreover, why would not the Gospels avoid a potentially misleading title and why would they exclusively use it in sayings of Jesus and never in those about him? In all likelihood "the title was rooted in the tradition of the sayings of Jesus right from the beginning; as a result, it was sacrosanct, and no-one dared to eliminate it."[85] The apocalyptic Son of Man sayings must essentially go back to Jesus himself.[86]

In the sayings of Jesus, as in Jewish apocalyptic, "Son of Man" is a term of glory. When the persecution of the community had reached its climax, he will come suddenly, like a flash of lightning from a clear sky (Matt. 24:27), when no one expects him (Matt. 24:37). "They will see 'the Son of

83. Jeremias, *New Testament Theology,* 1:261-62.

84. Hermann L. Strack and Paul Billerbeck, *Kommentar zum Neuen Testament aus Talmud und Midrasch,* 1:486.

85. So rightly Jeremias, *New Testament Theology,* 1:266.

86. See the careful discussion by Goppelt, *Theology of the New Testament,* 1:178-99, esp. 186 and 193.

Man coming in clouds' with great power and glory" (Mark 13:27). He will be seated at the right hand of God (Luke 22:69), and "then he will send out the angels, and gather his elect from the four winds, from the ends of the earth to the ends of heaven" (Mark 13:27). Then he will hold judgment. The nationalistic hopes for a mighty king from the house of David are superseded here by the transnational hope in the Son of man. When he will come in his glory, he will sit on his glorious throne, and all the nations will be gathered before him (Matt. 25:31-46). He is the bearer of salvation for all the world. As the universal ruler he is the head and representative of the new people of God who will share in his rule.

Jesus always spoke of the Son of man in the third person. To assume that he distinguished between himself and the Son of man is a possible solution. The Son of man would then be another future figure to whom Jesus was pointing. Yet Jesus told John the Baptist that he was the one who was supposed to come. This claim to be the fulfiller excludes the possibility of one coming after him. It could be possible that Jesus referred to the Son of man in the third person because he wanted to distinguish between his own present state and his future state, that he would become the exalted Son of man.[87] This would also agree with another observation. While some Son of Man sayings about his suffering, death, and resurrection may indeed have been formulated after the event, the actual course of Jesus' ministry confronted him with the possibility of a violent death. Jesus clearly foresaw his imminent suffering and announced it several times. He understood it as a necessary and redemptive suffering. In an almost classic way this is expressed in Mark 10:45, where Jesus said, "For the Son of Man came not to be served but to serve, and to give his life as a ransom for many." He applied Isaiah 53 and the image of the suffering servant to himself.[88] He who will judge the world in the name of the Lord must first suffer vicariously for it and reconcile it to God. As the Son of man Jesus lives unknown among the people. In the end time he will appear openly to judge and to redeem, yet already the attitude toward him decides the future of the individual.

---

87. See also Jeremias, *New Testament Theology*, 1:276, who opts for this possibility.

88. Goppelt, *Theology of the New Testament*, 1:198, rightly concludes: "It was in harmony with his ministry that he should apply to himself that singular expression of the Old Testament about the servant of God who died as atonement for all, an expression that was appropriated nowhere in Judaism."

The deepest self-understanding of Jesus, however, cannot be coined into a title. It is a strictly singular phenomenon, namely, that in Jesus there occurred the final self-disclosure of God and thus the end of all history in anticipation.[89] Jesus' confession that he was this direct and final self-disclosure of God led to his conviction as a heretic. But how did he express this self-understanding? In the trial of Jesus, the question was put to Jesus: "Are you the Christ, the Son of the Blessed One?" (Mark 14:61). The high priest concluded from Jesus' answer that Jesus had committed blasphemy. But what is it that is contained in Jesus' answer that would lead to such a devastating reaction? Jesus seemingly recited only Jewish eschatological expectations when he answered: "I am; and 'you will see the Son of Man seated at the right hand of the Power,' and 'coming with the clouds of heaven'" (Mark 14:62).

The issue becomes clear when we consider the Old Testament use of the phrase *egō eimi* (I am). In the Septuagint we find this phrase several times, most prominently in Deutero-Isaiah, rendering the Hebrew *ani hu*, meaning "I [am] He" into Greek. In Deutero-Isaiah the phrase *ani hu* is a solemn statement or assertion that is always attributed to Yahweh (e.g., Isa. 41:4; 43:10; 46:4). Over against claims made by other gods this phrase asserts polemically that only Yahweh is the Lord of history. It also seems to be a concise abbreviation of the longer form of divine self-predication, especially of "I am Yahweh." While the *ani hu* formula as divine self-predication of Yahweh occurs outside Deutero-Isaiah only in Deuteronomy 32:39, the self-predication "I am Yahweh" is rather widespread in the Old Testament. As Ethelbert Stauffer has pointed out, there is also some evidence that the *ani hu* was used liturgically in the worship of the Jerusalem temple, since the Levites presumably sang the Song of Moses, containing Deuteronomy 32:39, on the Sabbath of the Feast of Tabernacles.[90] The use of *ani hu* lived on in the worship service of the temple and of the synagogues and was even known to the Qumran community.

At a few decisive places in the Gospels Jesus uses the term *egō eimi* in a way analogous to the Old Testament theophany formula. For in-

89. Wolfhart Pannenberg, "Dogmatic Theses on the Doctrine of Revelation," in *Revelation as History*, trans. D. Granskou (New York: Macmillan, 1968), 134. The reader is well advised to check the original German over against this often very "free" translation.

90. So Stauffer, *Jesus and His Story*, 179.

stance, according to Mark 13:6, Jesus says: "Many will come in my name and say, 'I am he!' and they will lead many astray." In Matthew this theophanic self-predication is expanded into an explicitly christological statement which reads: "saying, 'I am the Messiah!'" (Matt. 24:5).

Returning to the answer that Jesus gave the high priest in Mark 14:62, we must admit that it could be interpreted without reference to the Old Testament revelational phrase *ani hu* or to any of its variations. It could simply have been a solemn way of saying "yes," as Matthew interprets it in Matthew 26:64. Philip B. Harner, for instance, arrives at the conclusion that "it is not likely that we can understand the *egō eimi* of Mk. 14:62 and Lk. 22:70 in an absolute sense."[91] This is surprising, however, considering that the corollary evidence seems to lead in the opposite direction, namely that the *egō eimi* in Mark 14:62 is indeed used in an absolute sense as a divine self-predication. The matter becomes clearer if we look at the usage of *egō eimi* in other passages in Mark. The phrase appears first in Mark 6:50 at the conclusion of the account of the miracle of the walking on water, where Jesus told his disciples: "Take heart, it is I; do not be afraid." Here the phrase functions almost in a titular sense and as a revelational phrase. In Mark 13:6 Jesus warned his disciples, "Many will come in my name, saying, 'I am he!' and they will lead many astray." Again *egō eimi* is used as a formula of revelation or identification, since its misappropriation leads the believer astray.

We may conclude that Jesus' use of *egō eimi* in Mark 14:62 is more than a simple affirmation. He uses a revelational phrase to disclose himself and identify himself with God. As the words following *egō eimi* show, the Messianic secret is lifted and Jesus unashamedly admits his divine sonship: "In Mk. 14:62 therefore Jesus is making an explicit Messianic claim, the Messianic Secret is being formally disclosed."[92] Since the Messianic secret was carefully hidden in Mark, we may wonder whether Jesus' response does not reflect the theology of the Evangelist more than Jesus' own words. We might be overestimating the historical value of this passage if we would not concede the possibility that this

91. Philip H. Harner, *The 'I Am' of the Fourth Gospel* (Philadelphia: Fortress, Facet Books, 1970), 34.

92. Norman Perrin, "The High Priest's Question and Jesus' Answer (Mark 14:61-62)," in *The Passion in Mark: Studies on Mark 14–16,* ed. Werner H. Kelber (Philadelphia: Fortress, 1976), 82.

passage has been carefully edited to reflect the eschatological hopes of the nascent church.

There is yet another way of determining the historical probability of the *egō eimi* response of Jesus at his trial. As Ernst Fuchs has pointed out, Jesus emphasized in his proclamation the will of God in such a way as only someone could do who stood in God's place.[93] For instance, in his parables Jesus did not simply tell us how God acts, but he told us that God acts the way Jesus acts. Luke wrote that the Pharisees and scribes remarked, "This fellow welcomes sinners and eats with them" (Luke 15:2), then in response Jesus told them parables of God's concern for the lost and sinful, implying that God acts like Jesus. Mark 14:62 would then indicate that at the end of his career Jesus not only acted as if he stood in God's place, but he actually did act in God's place by using the revelational formula *egō eimi*. In all likelihood *egō eimi* was Jesus' own response to the high priest. Since Jesus did not conform to the prevalent Messianic expectations but nevertheless made claims that could only be understood in Messianic terms, the high priests and most other people at that time concluded that Jesus had committed blasphemy.

Another similarly misunderstood theophanic self-predication occurs in Jesus' reply to the Samaritan woman. She said to him in the traditional Messianic expectation, "'I know that Messiah is coming' (who is called Christ). 'When he comes, he will proclaim all things to us.'" Jesus corrected her by saying, "I am he, the one who is speaking to you" (John 4:25-26). He revealed himself as the full self-disclosure of God. But the woman did not understand him. She was too enmeshed in the traditional pattern of Messianic thinking.

The overall impression that Jesus of Nazareth left was of one who had assumed an authority unlike anyone before him. He considered himself empowered to go beyond the Law and point to its real meaning. He claimed to stand in God's place as one who conveys God and God's will to his people. He emphasized that God's will would exalt him as judge and savior of all. Even his disciples could not quite comprehend Jesus' significance. The other people thought so much along nationalistic Messianic lines that they could not understand him. So the people ultimately turned against Jesus and even his disciples deserted him. Then came Easter . . .

93. For the following see Fuchs, "The Quest for the Historical Jesus," 20-21.

3. Jesus the Christ

I have attempted to delineate the history of Jesus. Although some results are more tenuous than others, the internally consistent picture we have received is striking. Once Jesus was no longer among his disciples, his "work" did not collapse as one might have suspected. The survivors of his movement did not simply carry on his legacy, as is the case with most other religious movements on the death of their "founder." Jesus was the "founder" of a new religious movement only in a very limited sense. This cannot be said about Mohammed with regard to the Qur'an or about Buddha with regard to Buddhist teachings. What Mohammed said was constitutive for the Moslem writings and what Buddha taught was essential for Buddhist doctrines. Granted, as the Synoptic tradition shows, the earliest church remembered the message of Jesus and passed it on, albeit usually in a modified form, through its own preaching. The growth of the Jesus tradition also indicates that the church proclaimed in his name in the sense of "what he would have said if. . . ." In this way Jesus was still considered a teacher and prophet. But he was more than that.

In contrast to other religious figures Jesus was not only the bearer of a certain message, but, at least after his death, he was made part of this message and even became its central content. *"The proclaimer became the proclaimed."*[1] There is no doubt that some of this had already started during Jesus' lifetime, for instance, when John inquired about him or when Peter made his famous confession of faith (Matt. 16:14-16). Yet

---

1. Rudolf Bultmann, *New Testament Theology*, trans. Kendrick Grobel (New York: Charles Scribner's, 1951), 1:3.

these statements were still tenuous. John the Baptist clothed his statement in the form of a question, and Jesus called Peter "Satan" soon after he had made his great confession of Jesus' Messiahship (Matt. 16:23) because he misunderstood Jesus' mission. This tenuousness did not change as long as Jesus dwelled among his followers. The turning point came after his death with the event that is commonly called the resurrection. This allowed Jesus to be seen in a new light and opened the way for a continuously expanding and clarifying christological assessment of Jesus.

1. Centrality of the Resurrection

We remember that it can be affirmed with relative certainty that the tomb was empty in which Jesus had presumably been laid. It can also be ascertained that many of his followers were utterly cast down by his death and were frightened that they might share a similar fate. But then they had surprising experiences in which they recognized beyond doubt that their former master was alive. In the case of Paul this one-time persecutor of the Christians was convinced through such an experience that he had been wrong (Gal. 1:13). Similarly, James, the brother of Jesus, together with the entire family of Jesus, had rejected him (Mark 3:21 and John 7:5), but then James had an experience of the resurrected Jesus (1 Cor. 15:7) and became one of the leaders of the Christians. Except for the vision of a "light from heaven" by Paul (Acts 9:3), we have hardly any way of assessing the nature of these experiences. Contrary to detailed descriptions in some apocryphal sources, the act of what was called the resurrection is not described in the New Testament. We read only the firm assertion that "The Lord has risen indeed, and he has appeared to Simon!" (cf. Luke 24:34). Such a statement expresses a strong apologetic tendency, evidently to assure that the body had not been stolen, and that seeing the resurrected one did not result from a hallucination.

The Risen One demonstrated his identity with the earthly Jesus by showing the marks on his hands and feet (Luke 24:39) and the wound on his side (John 20:20). He also demonstrated his corporeality by allowing his disciples to touch him (Luke 24:39) and by eating fish before their eyes (Luke 24:41ff.). These elaborations on the encounter with the resurrected one cannot do away with the overpowering, puzzling, and mysterious nature of the earliest resurrection experiences. "Their eyes were opened" at the breaking of the bread "and they recognized him; and he vanished from their sight" (Luke 24:31). He unexpectedly appeared in a locked room (John 20:19), and "just after daybreak, Jesus stood on the beach" (John 21:4). The disciples did not hesitate to admit that "in their joy they were disbelieving and still wondering" (Luke 24:41).

Why was it so difficult for the first Christians to accept the resurrection of Jesus? First we must remember that among the Jewish contemporaries of Jesus the doctrine of the resurrection of the dead was still a debated subject; the Sadducees rejected the doctrine while the Pharisees subscribed to it (Luke 20:27). Furthermore, "Judaism did not know of any anticipated resurrection as an event in history."[2] Certainly in apocalyptic literature there appears to be a clear concept of a resurrection of the dead at the end of time. 1 Enoch 51:1-5 states:

> In those days, Sheol will return all the deposits which she had received and hell will give back all that which it owes. And he shall choose the righteous and holy ones from among (the risen dead), for the day when they shall be selected and saved has arrived. In those days, (the Elect One) shall sit on my throne, and from the conscience of his mouth shall come out all the secrets of wisdom, for the Lord of the Spirits has given them to him and glorified him. In those days, mountains shall dance like rams; and the hills shall leap like kids satiated with milk. And the faces of all the angels in heaven shall glow with joy, because on that day the Elect One has arisen. And the earth shall rejoice; and the righteous ones shall dwell upon her and the elect ones shall walk upon her.[3]

The Messiah who will rule over the earth will be raised together with the elect. However, when we hear of people being raised from the dead, what takes place is similar to a resuscitation, a return to earthly life: this is not a resurrection to a new life.

Having investigated the resurrection of Jesus as the Messiah in the framework of Jewish expectations, Ulrich Wilckens admits:

2. So Joachim Jeremias, *New Testament Theology: The Proclamation of Jesus*, trans. John Bowden (New York: Charles Scribner's, 1971), 1:308-9.
3. *The Old Testament Pseudepigrapha*, ed. James H. Charlesworth (Garden City, N.Y.: Doubleday, 1983), 1:36-37.

The primitive Christian proclamation of the resurrection of Jesus has no corresponding widespread previous existence in Jewish tradition. It is true that the Christian statements about the installation of Jesus as the mediator in heaven of salvation for the redeemed and as judge of all wicked, are statements which can be shown to be shaped by the character of the various forms of Jewish expectations of the Messiah, but there is no mention in Jewish tradition of the resurrection of the Messiah standing ready and waiting in heaven. There is only a narrow bridge leading to this from Jewish tradition in the observation, in one isolated Jewish text referring to the resurrection, that the prophet Elijah will return to set things aright in preparation for the event at the end of time, and will suffer the same violent death as all the prophets before him, but he will be raised from death. We have to add, however, that Elijah is never expressively given the function of the eschatological mediator of salvation.[4]

With this context in mind it is understandable that the resurrection of Jesus could not simply be inferred from Jewish sources. People were baffled by this event, and some even concluded that it was the beginning of the great resurrection when the Messiah and all the righteous will be raised (cf. Matt. 27:52-53). But Jesus' resurrection could not be comprehended in Jewish apocalyptic terms.

Jesus' resurrection was an act of God *sui generis,* without parallel, not a return to life, but a vindication of his formerly claimed identity with God and a transition to an entirely new form of life. Paul grasped this when he delineated the duality of the resurrected one. Jesus the Christ, according to his human side, was Jesus of Nazareth "who was descended from David according to the flesh." But according to his divine aspect, he was "declared to be Son of God with power according to the spirit of holiness by resurrection from the dead" (Rom. 1:3-4). Therefore he could now be called "Jesus Christ our Lord." The resurrection is not Jesus' own accomplishment but is a mighty deed of that God who is the author of all life and who makes something out of nothingness. Through his resurrection Jesus became the Son of God in a legal sense, the Son of God who stands beside his Father and who participates in the power the Father delegated to him. The resurrection of Jesus was not conceived

---

4. Ulrich Wilckens, *Resurrection: Biblical Testimony to the Resurrection — An Historical Examination and Explanation,* trans. A. M. Stewart (Atlanta: John Knox, 1978), 110.

as a return to earthly life but an elevation to the position of power in heaven as the Son of God. Thus one could even see resurrection and ascension as one.[5] The resurrection then becomes the actual foundation of christology. The earthly Jesus became the risen Lord.

Jesus came into the heavenly position of power as the Christ so that at the Last Judgment he would pronounce the final verdict on all persons and all powers. Just as the risen Lord and God belong together, so the resurrection and the status as Son belong together, and so the title of Lord and the function of savior at the end time. "God has highly exalted him and gave him the name that is above every name, so that at the name of Jesus every knee should bend, in heaven and on earth and under the earth, and every tongue confess that Jesus Christ is the Lord, to the glory of God the Father" (Phil. 2:9-11). Since Jesus was vindicated and his claims were found appropriate, he could be recognized as the fulfillment of the Old Testament promises. A multitude of Old Testament Messianic titles could then be bestowed on him.

Jesus also became the foundation of hope. In 1 Corinthians 15 Paul shows how intimately the generally expected resurrection, Christ's resurrection, and our own resurrection are interrelated: "If there is no resurrection of the dead, then Christ has not been raised; and if Christ has not been raised, then our preaching has been in vain and our faith has been in vain. . . . If Christ has not been raised, your faith is futile and you are still in your sins. Then those also who have died in Christ have perished" (1 Cor. 15:13-14; 17-18). The resurrection of Christ is no isolated event. It is a clear demonstration of the creative power of God. As he overcame the destructive power of death, so he will accomplish the salvation which he has promised to his chosen ones, regardless of the powers of destruction which are at work in the world. Since Jesus was vindicated as the Christ in his resurrection, his overcoming death has universal significance. "For since death came through a human being, the resurrection of the dead has also come through a human being" (1 Cor. 15:21). Jesus Christ opened a new dimension. He guarantees and witnesses to our own future. A new state of being and a new life are possible for us also.

Christ's resurrection is the indication and the proleptic anticipation of the victory over death. Therefore it is different from a resuscitation

5. Wilckens, *Resurrection*, 23.

117

or from a miracle. While resuscitations indicate a return to this life, encountering the same finitude as before, resurrection is the entering into new life, into the fullness of life through which the limitations of this life are overcome. Similarly, the miracles were only pointers to a new future, anticipating it proleptically at one specific point, without having universal impact. But the resurrection, on the other hand, has universal significance because it pertained to the whole being of Jesus and it implied the vindication of this person's equality with God.

It is wrong to surmise that Jesus was resurrected but all those who had died before and after him will not have the same opportunity. On the contrary, in this one resurrection lies the hope for all who have died and will die. The promises contained in this resurrection give a totally new twist to all creation. As Paul cautioned: "Each in his own order: Christ the first fruits, then at his coming those who belong to Christ" (1 Cor. 15:23). The resurrection gives a new direction to creation: "If anyone is in Christ, there is a new creation: everything old has passed away; see, everything has become new" (2 Cor. 5:17). Something new dawned with the resurrection. It was not simply another step further in an ongoing process but fulfillment on a different level. Paul tells us in Romans 8:18-25 that we, together with the whole of creation, are on the way to this new level, not in a process upward but in such a way that something new will break in and the creation will be led to its original intention. God as Creator and Perfecter will endow his creation with its primordially envisioned goodness and glory, and all those who dwell within creation and are touched by the Easter spirit will participate in it. They already have the firstfruit of the Spirit and wait with eager longing for the time of fulfillment.

2. *The Witness of the Synoptics*

Resurrection narratives stand at the conclusion of each Gospel. This conclusion allows for the preceding text and interprets it. Only because the Easter events have occurred is there more than a nostalgic interest in Jesus. This is the consensus of biblical research beginning from Reimarus all the way to the present. There is no interest in a biography of Jesus as would be expected if the eyes of the narrators were turned to the past. The main point which the Synoptic writers wanted to make is that God had disclosed himself and had acted decisively in Jesus of Nazareth.

a. The Markan Witness

Mark, as the oldest Gospel, stands closer than the other Gospel writers to the disturbing situation caused by Jesus' death and resurrection. He begins with the programmatic statement: "The beginning of the good news of Jesus Christ, the Son of God" (Mark 1:1). This clear Messianic statement notwithstanding, he asserted that Jesus did not want an outsider to fully understand the secret of the kingdom of God. Only his disciples, coming from the Easter event, had the privilege of understanding completely the life, destiny, and proclamation of Jesus (Mark 4:11-12).[6] Before Easter the disciples could not truly understand him (6:52; 9:32).

Because of the Easter event the interim period between the resurrection of Jesus Christ and his final coming is not a time of frustrated waiting but of intense activity. It is the time of world mission. However, unlike Matthew and Luke, Mark does not yet reflect on the activities of the exalted Christ during this period, and mentions the emerging church only implicitly in connection with the task of world mission.

From a biographical or historiographical standpoint Mark seems quite imbalanced; the account of the last week of the life of Jesus occupies almost as much room as that of his whole public ministry. But Mark focuses on two main points: God acted decisively through Jesus, and God allowed Jesus to suffer death but also raised him to new life. Both of these points receive equal attention. But the Easter events in the light of which Mark composed his Gospel receive only a brief appendix-like treatment at the end of his account. Perhaps this goes hand in hand with what Martin Dibelius called the "secret epiphanies" in Mark.[7] In the prophetic apocalyptic discourse of Mark 13 the Evangelist records that Jesus designated himself as the "Messiah" (Mark 13:21) and as "the Son" (13:32). These designations were effectively employed by the Evan-

---

6. So rightly Hans Conzelmann, *An Outline of the Theology of the New Testament*, trans. John Bowden (New York: Harper, 1969), 139.

7. Martin Dibelius, *From Tradition to Gospel*, trans. from 2nd rev. ed. by Bertram Lee Woolf (London: James Clark, 1971), 260.

119

gelist, when speaking of the future, to encourage his audience to think of Jesus as the expected Messiah, the Son of God (1:1).

Interesting also is Jesus' Davidic sonship. In relating to us that the blind beggar Bartimaeus designates Jesus "Son of David" and that Jesus heals him (Mark 10:46-52), Mark demonstrates that Jesus used his authority in a merciful way and not as a nationalistic warrior-king. But Mark's primary concern, christologically speaking, is God's understanding of Jesus.[8] God first privately announces to Jesus at his baptism that he is his "Son" (1:11), and then God tells the same to the three uncomprehending disciples at the Transfiguration (9:7). This designation is repudiated by the religious establishment and leads to Jesus' death (14:61). Yet at the end it is uttered by the centurion beneath the cross: "Truly, this man was God's Son!" (15:39). Under God's direction human thought about Jesus can be conformed to God's action.

b. The Matthean Witness

The Gospel of Matthew offers a much more elaborate interpretation of Jesus than the Gospel of Mark. Its leading "theological principle at work here is that of promise and fulfillment."[9] This Gospel aims to show that the Old Testament promises have found their fulfillment in Jesus. He did not come to abolish the Law or the Prophets but to fulfill them (Matt. 5:17-18). He fulfilled the Emmanuel promise (Isa. 7:14; Matt. 1:22-23), the Galilee promise (Isa. 9:1-2; Matt. 4:12-15), the Bethlehem promise (Mic. 5:2; Matt. 2:5-6), the servant of the Lord promise (Isa. 53:4; Matt. 8:17), and many others. Consequently a multitude of Old Testament Messianic titles are bestowed upon him. He is the Messiah, the Son of David, the King of Israel, the Son of God, and the Son of man, to name just a few. He stands in true continuity with the Old Testament. This continuity is crucial, since the historical nation of Israel had neglected and misunderstood its commission to be a light to the nations and lost its election.[10]

Jesus already founded during his life on earth the church as the true Israel which replaces Israel and steps into continuity with the Israel of

---

8. Jack Dean Kingsbury, *The Christology of Mark's Gospel* (Philadelphia: Fortress, 1983), 143, 141.

9. Conzelmann, *Outline of the Theology of the New Testament*, 145.

10. Conzelmann, *Outline of the Theology of the New Testament*, 145.

promise. Though there are specific orders and structures in the church (Matt. 18:15-20), the church is not here to stay. It is only an interim community. It is also far from being a pure community of true believers. Not until the final judgment will the just be separated from the unjust (13:30, 40-43, 47-50). Yet the church is already on its way toward this final judgment when Christ will appear and select the chosen ones.[11] The theme of the coming judgment is consistent throughout the Gospel. The Sermon on the Mount (Matt. 5–7), the sending out of the twelve (Matt. 10), and the apocalypse (Matt. 24) all indicate the judgment as *the* coming event.

In the opening line of the Gospel we read that Jesus Christ is "the son of David, the son of Abraham." By mentioning that Jesus is the "son of Abraham," Matthew wants to show that the entire history of Israel, which had its beginning in Abraham, attains its fulfillment in Jesus (Matt. 1:17). Moreover, in Jesus God makes good his promise to Abraham regarding the Gentiles (Gen. 18:18), so that "many will come from east and west and will eat with Abraham and Isaac and Jacob in the kingdom of heaven" (Matt. 8:11). Jesus is not only the Son of God (2:15), but also from God (1:18) — even in his conception — as Matthew shows in his infancy narratives. As the Son of God Jesus knows God's will and addresses himself in long discourses to such matters as the ethics of the kingdom (chaps. 5–7), instructions on missionary outreach (chap. 10), the secret of the kingdom (chap. 13), community life (chap. 18), and the end time (chaps. 24–25).

Since Jesus is the promised one, the present age is the time of fulfillment. While this age commences with the birth of Jesus and concludes with his parousia as the Son of man, there are two distinct periods denoted respectively by "the kingdom of heaven which is at hand," and "the gospel of the kingdom." Correspondingly we have the ministry to Israel through John the Baptist (Matt. 3:1-2), Jesus (4:16), and the pre-Easter disciples (10:16), and then the ministry to the nations through the post-Easter disciples or the church (26:13). Yet all these ministries are carried out under the commission of Jesus (10:5; 28:18-20; John the Baptist is also clearly designated as forerunner to Jesus). Thus the time

---

11. Günther Bornkamm, "End-Expectation and Church in Matthew," in *Tradition and Interpretation in Matthew*, ed. G. Bornkamm, G. Barth, and H. J. Held, trans. Percy Scott (London: SCM, 1963), 15-51.

of Israel found its fulfillment in the time of Jesus. God has visited his people, gathered them, and made known to them his will.

c. The Lukan Witness

Luke situates Jesus immediately in the context of world history (Luke 2:1-4 and 1:5-6). But the Evangelist does not want to convey the idea that the life and destiny of Jesus are subject to the course of history. Jesus is the focal point of history through whom all history receives its significance and proper validation. Luke distinguishes three main epochs of history: the time of Israel; the time of Jesus as the center of history; and the time of the church. John the Baptist is depicted as the last prophet and not as the forerunner of Jesus (Luke 16:16), since Jesus is without forerunner and without precedent.[12] The whole epoch of the Law and the Prophets leads up to Jesus, and then suddenly Jesus appears as the center of time.

Luke uses the same christological titles as do Mark and Matthew. Yet the term "Messiah" has a much fuller significance than in Matthew's and Mark's usage of the term. At times the titles "Messiah" and "Son of God" come so close that they are virtually synonymous (Luke 4:41). Luke also appropriates the term "Lord" in a very specific way.[13] In the Septuagint "Lord" *(Kyrios)* is the Greek translation for Yahweh. As Lord, God rules over the whole world. Thus the Psalmist says: "Shout to God with loud songs of joy. For the LORD, the Most High, is awesome, a great king over all the earth" (Ps. 47:1-2). Luke applies the term "Lord" to Jesus at his birth when the angel announces to the shepherds: "To you is born this day in the city of David a Savior, who is Christ the Lord!" (Luke 2:11). The idea that Christ was not made Lord until his resurrection is rejected (see also Acts 2:36). Jesus is Lord, and God the Lord exercises his rule over Israel (and over the Gentiles) through him (Luke 1:31-33); that is, Jesus acts with divine authority. This is also clear when we note that Jesus is called the Savior.

In Old Testament and Jewish thought God is the Savior (Isa. 45:21),

---

12. Hans Conzelmann, *The Theology of St. Luke,* trans. Geoffrey Buswell (Philadelphia: Fortress, 1982), 101.

13. For the following see Jack Dean Kingsbury, *Jesus Christ in Matthew, Mark, and Luke,* Proclamation Commentaries (Philadelphia: Fortress, 1981), 99-100.

who delivers his people from bondage, be it from foreign domination or from evil. This sentiment is echoed by Mary when she exclaims in the Magnificat: "My spirit rejoices in God my Savior" (Luke 1:47). Then the angel announces to the shepherds: "To you is born this day in the city of David a Savior" (2:11). This identification shows that God made available through Jesus his salvation, which otherwise only God would accomplish. Yet Jesus is not the triumphant Savior-king whom some nationalists expected. In utilizing material from the Q-sayings source, Luke makes it clear that Jesus carries out his ministry in Israel among the common people, the disenfranchised, and the outcasts of society. He does so in terms of identification, and his revolt is not conducted with means drawn upon from this world. As seen in the Beatitudes, he promises to the "poor" the eschatological kingdom (6:20) and to the "hungry" participation in the Messianic banquet (6:21). Jesus himself is called a "friend of tax collectors and sinners" (7:34), and the parables of the lost sheep, the lost coin, and the prodigal son (chap. 15) again indicate that he was concerned about the people in distress.

When Jesus began his ministry he read from the book of the prophet Isaiah: "The spirit of the Lord is upon me, because he has anointed me to bring good news to the poor. He has sent me to proclaim release to the captives and recovering of sight to the blind, to let the oppressed go free, to proclaim the year of the Lord's favor" (Luke 4:18-19). Jesus' ministry as portrayed by Luke proved to be a "serious challenge to the existing social order."[14] Yet Jesus did not challenge just the social order, but all old ways of thinking, because in him God had announced salvation to the whole world.

Luke knew that someday Jesus would usher in the end of all history and judge the living and the dead. Through Jesus' coming the decisive event has occurred, and the end will bring nothing essentially new concerning salvation. As at his ascension, Christ will return as the exalted Lord.[15] God has now provided the interim as the time of the church. Since

14. So Richard J. Cassidy, in his enlightening study, *Jesus, Politics, and Society: A Study of Luke's Gospel* (Maryknoll, N.Y.: Orbis, 1980), 78.

15. Ulrich Wilkens, "The Understanding of Revelation within the History of Primitive Christianity," in *Revelation as History*, ed. Wolfhart Pannenberg, trans. D. Granskou (New York: Macmillan, 1968), 97. Yet Wilkens seems to see the parousia too much in continuity with the present. Luke was not a proponent of "realized" or "realizing" eschatology.

the gospel is being spread to ever-new shores and since the Christians are empowered by God's Holy Spirit, it is not important how long the church will last and when the end will come. In looking back to the life and destiny of Jesus, we realize that he had announced the end and the coming of God's kingdom. The truth of what he stood for and the truth of his proclamation are guaranteed through his miracles, the resurrection, and his ascension.[16] Christians are no longer alone in the world. The exalted Christ in heaven is active through his word, which is proclaimed in history. His people work in "his name" and in "his spirit." Christians live in this world not with fear nor with utopian expectations but rather with hope. To incorporate the Christian existence into the world, yet to keep it open for the end of all history, is the main concern of Luke both in his Gospel and in the Acts of the Apostles.

When we sum up how Jesus is portrayed by the Synoptic writers, two important items come to the fore: First, Jesus truly is a human being who was born of a human mother and died like any other human being. He ate and drank, he was sleepy, hungry, and exhausted. He was also angry and perplexed at times, and at certain points even in despair. In other words, he experienced the same kind of emotions everyone else experienced. Thus we are not confronted with a docetic or symbolic being but an actual human being. Second, this seemingly simple human being was not just that. He did and said things that caused surprise and are beyond that which is normally expected from a human being. His life is portrayed as a continuous battle against anti-Godly powers. At the beginning stood Satan and temptation to thwart the success of Jesus' ministry (Mark 1:13), and at the end there was Gethsemane, where Jesus struggled to accept his final earthly destiny (Mark 14:32-42). The anti-Godly powers recognized him and exclaimed: "What have you to do with us, Jesus of Nazareth? Have you come to destroy us?" (Mark 1:24). His comprehension of the reality of these powers was affirmed when he stated: "But if it is by the Spirit of God that I cast out demons, then the kingdom of God has come upon you" (Matt. 12:28). The victorious battle against the anti-Godly powers is a sign of the kingdom, because the presence of God and the presence of these powers cannot peacefully (or otherwise) coexist.

16. For the following see Conzelmann, *Outline of the Theology of the New Testament*, 150-51.

Victory over these powers is possible if Jesus sacrifices his life in the pursuit of that victory. His life is therefore described as a life of necessary suffering and dying: "He began to teach them that the Son of Man must undergo great suffering, and be rejected by the elders, the chief priests, and the scribes, and be killed" (Mark 8:31). Such suffering and dying is not an inescapable fate, but it is rather his own plan, "for the Son of Man came not to be served but to serve, and to give his life a ransom for many" (Mark 10:45). This salvific significance of Jesus was illustrated through various titles such as the Christ (Messiah), the Lord, the Son of God, and the Son of man, the latter being a designation used already by Jesus himself.

Such a life and ministry, lived in accordance with God's will and in service to others, could only be carried out through the power of the Holy Spirit. Consequently Jesus' birth was the result of God's life-giving Spirit (Luke 1:35), God's empowering and enlightening Spirit descended upon him at his baptism (Mark 1:10), and the Spirit even drove Jesus out into the desert to be tempted (Mark 1:13), indicating that he had completely surrendered himself to God and the depth of his dedication was to be tested before his ministry started. When his ministry commenced, he made known his identification with the Spirit of God by quoting Isaiah 61:1: "The Spirit of the Lord is upon me" (Luke 4:18). His victories over the destructive forces of darkness are again brought about through the Spirit of God acting in and through him (Matt. 12:28). It is not surprising, then, that his followers will receive the Holy Spirit at Pentecost and baptize in the same Spirit (Matt. 28:19).

3. The Johannine Witness

In many ways John differs from the Synoptics. The differences lie not just in the chronology but also in the language and the theological themes. For instance, the standard Synoptic term "kingdom of God" is only used twice in John; in the first nineteen chapters of the Gospel and in the Epistles the term "Lord" is not used at all. In the Johannine writings the term "Lord" might have clashed with Jesus referring to his disciples as "friends" (John 15:14). The term "Son of God" is only used eight times, and "Son" only sixteen times, but there are thirty references in which Jesus speaks of "my Father."

125

As the opening statement of the Gospel indicates, John had a unique outlook. His opening sentences are a rephrasing of the priestly creation account at the beginning of the Bible ("In the beginning was the Word, and the Word was with God, and the Word was God. He was in the beginning with God. All things came into being through him, and without him not one thing came into being" [John 1:1-3; cf. Gen. 1:1]). John wanted to show that Jesus' coming provides an exact parallel to the creation. Moreover, the *logos* (i.e., word) is the mediator of this new creation, as the *logos* was the mediator of creation at the beginning of time. The personification of the *logos,* to which the Jewish philosopher Philo of Alexandria also attests, reminds us of the personification of wisdom in Jewish thought.[17] Yet John does not expound on who this *logos* is; he assumes that his readers know that. From the beginning of the world, John claims in the prologue to his Gospel (John 1:1-18), the Word was with God. This means that the Word is not identical with God but is in full harmony with him. The *logos* is one with God yet distinguished from God.

In the prologue the whole mission of Jesus is summarized: John the Baptist, being Jesus' precursor, witnessed to Jesus. Jesus came into what was his own: the world which he had created, but which did not accept him. In Jesus, "the Word became flesh and lived among us" (John 1:14). Such a statement is possible neither in Judaism nor in Gnosticism. "It is genuinely Christian."[18] Since the Word became a mortal human being in Jesus, it was possible for Jesus to mediate God and his will. Those who believe in his name, that is, those who believe that he is actually God's self-disclosure, become children of God. They find their proximity to God by accepting Jesus.

Jesus is not only the Word. The identification of Jesus with the Word occurs only in the prologue and is nowhere picked up again. The reason for this "omission" may be that Jesus himself now pronounces the word. But again it is not accepted by the Jews (John 8:37-43). We also read: "Anyone who hears my word and believes him who sent me has eternal life, and does not come under judgment, but has passed from death to life" (5:24), and "whoever keeps my word will never see death" (8:51). Jesus is not only the Word but the one who brings God's word and its

17. Conzelmann, *Outline of the Theology of the New Testament,* 334.
18. Conzelmann, *Outline of the Theology of the New Testament,* 336.

salvific power. This indicates his unity with God. He is the one through whom God presents the choice between death and life to those who encounter him. Jesus' relationship with God seems to be one of complete equality, so that he cannot be distinguished from God. Like the Father, the Son has life in himself (5:26).

John uses the Son of Man sayings analogously to the Synoptics. The Son of man has authority to execute judgment (John 5:27). But it is much more important to show the intimate connection between God and the Son of man. We read that the Son of man has descended from heaven and, from the standpoint of the readers of the Gospel of John, has already ascended into heaven (3:13). From the intimate connection with Jesus it follows that the Son of man will bestow full salvation on his disciples (6:27). The Son of man, that is, Jesus, even permits the *proskynesis* (the worship reserved for a divine being, see 9:38). In this context the Son of man is fused together with the *egō eimi*, which, as we have seen earlier, is a revelational formula.[19] Jesus, the Son of man, is the divine self-disclosure.[20] Small wonder that skeptical Jews took offense at this and accused him of blasphemy, saying, "You, though only a human being, are making yourself God" (10:33). To outsiders it was not evident that Jesus was more than a human being. They did not understand how such a person could be so closely associated with God that God became visible through him. But the Fourth Gospel continues to emphasize that Jesus was indeed exceedingly close to God. He was in the Father and the Father was in him (10:38), and whoever saw the Son saw the Father (14:9).

It is also significant that John, as the only Gospel which provides a clear statement on incarnation (John 1:14), contains several statements that assert his preexistence prior to his coming to this earth. We read that Jesus was loved by the Father "before the foundation of the world" (17:24), that he was "before Abraham" (8:58), and that the Father will glorify him with his own glory, which he had "before the world existed" (17:5). John leaves the impression that Jesus' life here on earth was only an episode that "interrupted" his preexistent and eternal glory. To indicate the difference between any other figure and Jesus we are also told

19. See above, chap. 2.
20. Werner Georg Kümmel, *The Theology of the New Testament according to Its Major Witnesses Jesus — Paul — John*, 276-77.

that Jesus is the Father's "only Son" (1:14 and 3:16). Jesus is without precedent, parallel, and successor. He is unique.

In the characteristically long discourses we also hear that Jesus is a vital gift to his listeners. He is "the bread of life" (John 6:35), "the light of the world" (8:12), "the gate" (10:9), "the good shepherd" (10:11), "the true vine" (15:1), "the resurrection and the life" (11:25), and "the way, and the truth, and the life" (14:6). In these "I am" statements Jesus was not speaking metaphorically about himself but rather presenting himself as the true shepherd, light, vine, and so on.[21] He set himself apart from other figures who claimed to be bearers of salvation. With the "I am" statements he made the exclusive claim that final salvation is mediated only through him. And these are not just ontological statements about Jesus' being but functional statements which describe God's saving activity through Jesus. God's salvation is being actualized in the person and word of the human being Jesus. His life, work, and destiny, of course, are carried out in unity with the Holy Spirit (cf. 1:32-34).

The so-called farewell discourses (John 14–16) contain five sayings in which the "Paraclete" is mentioned (14:16-17, 26; 15:26; 16:7-11, 13-15). The term "Paraclete" occurs in the New Testament only once outside these passages—in 1 John 2:1. The figure of the Paraclete is equated in John 14:17 and 15:26 with the "Spirit of truth" and in 14:26 with the "Holy Spirit." As Werner Georg Kümmel (1905-) suggested, "There can be no doubt that John intends with 'Paraclete' to denote the same reality as with 'Spirit.'"[22] But in John 14:16 Jesus said: "I will ask the Father, and he will give you another Advocate [Paraclete], to be with you forever," indicating that this term is used for Jesus himself as the one sent to this earth by God.[23] Who is this Paraclete? In the Greek and Hellenistic world it is a legal advisor, helper, or advocate in court. The New Testament use only fits this description in part. More fitting is the notion of a heavenly advocate as found in Jewish and Old Testament ideas (cf. Job 16:19-22 and Zech. 1:12). Jesus himself is regarded as such a Paraclete during his earthly ministry.

After Jesus' departure another Paraclete would come to continue his

---

21. Kümmel, *Theology of the New Testament,* 283ff.

22. Kümmel, *Theology of the New Testament,* 315.

23. So rightly Johannes Behm, *"Paraklētos,"* in *TDNT* 5:800; see also n. 1 there for the discussion.

work and remain forever with and in the disciples. This is the Spirit, who is sent to the disciples by God or by Jesus to teach them with comprehensive authority and yet with strict adherence to Jesus and his message. He would maintain, expand, and complete the work of Jesus and lead his followers in all truth. The world would not receive the Paraclete since it does not perceive and understand him. The witness of the Paraclete to Jesus (John 15:26) turns into an accusation of the world before God. The world is convicted with regard to sin, righteousness, and judgment. The Paraclete makes known the sins on the side of the world, and righteousness and triumph on that of Jesus (16:8-11).

The Paraclete represents the continuing impact of Jesus after his death and exaltation. Where the Paraclete is at work, there the words of Jesus are recalled and interpreted. The mission of Jesus continues through and beyond his death and resurrection. John himself stands in this tradition and wrote his account so that "you may come to believe that Jesus is the Messiah, the Son of God, and that through believing you may have life in his name" (John 20:31). Knowing who Jesus is already imparts salvation, because such knowledge is not noetic or intellectual but shapes one's life in the light of the God to whom Jesus witnesses.

4. The Pauline Witness

It is not for chronological reasons that we present Paul as the last important representative of New Testament christology. Indeed, Paul's writings are the earliest we have in the New Testament, and in that sense he should be listed first. But of the writers mentioned so far, he is the only one who definitely was not a disciple or a follower of Jesus during Jesus' life on earth. Once a persecutor of the early Christian community, he became one of its most fervent advocates. As he himself admits, he was a latecomer (1 Cor. 15:9).

The Epistles which bear Paul's name comprise nearly three-fifths of the nonnarrative part of the New Testament. This great scope of the Pauline corpus of letters and the uniqueness of what we know about Paul set them apart from the rest of the New Testament and convince us that Paul's theological thought not only forms the center of the New Testament, but also decisively dominated the development of early

Christian thought. Paul's significance in the development of this thought lies in the fact that he had been a Jewish rabbinic scholar and now, as a converted Christian, became "the first Christian theologian."[24] This means he also decisively advanced and clarified christological thinking. It is beyond question that Paul was and understood himself as a recipient and bearer of the Christian tradition. Concerning the Eucharist and the resurrection Paul handed on the tradition which he himself received (1 Cor. 11:23; 15:3-8). The words used in these two passages, "delivered" and "received," are technical terms denoting the mediation of tradition.[25]

It can also be established that Paul's traditions included sayings of Jesus. With regard to divorce, for instance, he emphasized to his readers that he was not espousing his opinion but a dictum of the Lord (1 Cor. 7:10-11). Similarly, he writes: "The Lord commanded that those who proclaim the gospel should get their living by the gospel" (9:14). Next to the specific citations of the words of the Lord which have their parallels in the Synoptics there are allusions to teachings of Jesus (cf. Rom. 12:14), though they are more difficult to detect. We may conclude that Paul was familiar with the traditions concerning Jesus' teachings and used certain elements of that teaching. But direct references or quotations from Jesus' teachings are relatively sparse in Paul. Also he says nothing about Jesus' life. "Paul does not appeal to Jesus as an earthly teacher or to his sayings as the instruction of a distinguished rabbi. His appeals are to the risen, reigning *Christ*, the church's *Lord*."[26] Jesus is not an authority of the past, but, as the risen Christ, he is a present reality who guides his people. This goes hand in hand with Paul's interchangeable use of the name "Jesus" and the title "Christ" for the earthly Jesus and for the resurrected one. It is the Spirit of God "who raised Jesus from the dead" and in the same sentence God "who raised Christ from the dead" (Rom. 8:11), and then "Christ being raised from the dead" (6:9). Paul also asserts that "we proclaim Christ crucified" (1 Cor. 1:23), and he is certain that he did not proclaim "another Jesus" (2 Cor. 11:4). For Paul the earthly Jesus was identical with the risen Lord, and he was

24. Kümmel, *Theology of the New Testament*, 139.
25. Friedrich Büchsel, *"Paradosis,"* in *TDNT* 2:172.
26. So rightly Victor Paul Furnish, *Theology and Ethics in Paul* (Nashville: Abingdon, 1968), 56.

convinced that his own proclamation referred to Jesus of Nazareth and included Jesus' work and message.

Paul also considered Christ's appearance to him to be equal to his appearance to Peter (cf. 1 Cor. 15:8). He was also convinced that he was "called to be an apostle" and "set apart for the gospel" (Rom. 1:1). Throughout his ministry Paul uncompromisingly asserted the validity of his apostolate and his understanding of Christ. "For I want you to know, brothers and sisters, that the gospel which was proclaimed by me is not of human origin; for I did not receive it from a human source, nor was I taught it, but I received it through a revelation of Jesus Christ" (Gal. 1:11-12). Clearly Paul was commissioned by the resurrected one to preach "the cross of our Lord Jesus Christ" (6:14).

When Paul introduced himself to the Christian community in Rome, he concisely delineated the significance of Christ:

> Paul, a servant of Jesus Christ, called to be an apostle, set apart for the gospel of God, which he promised beforehand through his prophets and the holy scriptures, the gospel concerning his Son, who was descended from David according to the flesh and declared Son of God with power according to the spirit of holiness by resurrection from the dead, Jesus Christ our Lord, through whom we have received grace and apostleship to bring about the obedience of faith among all Gentiles for the sake of his name, including yourselves who are called to belong to Jesus Christ. (Rom. 1:1-6)

The gospel which Paul proclaimed had as its central figure the Messiah, Christ Jesus, crucified, risen, and returning to the completion of salvation. Important also for Paul was that Jesus Christ was the fulfillment of the Old Testament prophecies and that he lived here on earth as a descendant of David. This established the continuity between Paul's proclamation and the Old Testament faith. It was equally important that through his resurrection Jesus of Nazareth was exalted as the Lord Jesus Christ and designated Son of God. This establishes and emphasizes the continuity between the Old Testament promises and the resurrection of Jesus Christ. According to the Old Testament expectations and promises, the series of final events had started with Jesus' coming, and with his death and resurrection.

Through his death and resurrection, Jesus as the Christ had taken his position at the right hand of the Father in heaven. What remained was his parousia and the coming of the kingdom of heaven in power and glory. The ethnic particularity of salvation had become obsolete since Jesus, formerly the Messiah of the Jews, had been enthroned as Lord and Savior of the whole world. Our Savior is at the same time the Lord of the universe (Phil. 2:9-11): all of humanity, all cosmic powers, and the whole universe belong to him. Through Christ's enthronement all people have access through faith to his kingdom and to salvation. "This fact constitutes the gospel for the non-Jewish people. Paul was chosen to proclaim this gospel in the interval between the resurrection of Jesus Christ and his coming in power."[27]

When Paul presented Christ to his listeners he concentrated on Christ's death and resurrection. "The cross of Christ" (Gal. 6:12) can even become an abbreviated form of the sum of the gospel. The death of Jesus is not an isolated event in world history, but an act of God that shows his power, an eschatological event. The crucified one is none other than the "Lord of glory" (1 Cor. 2:8). The death of Jesus was no accident but integral to God's plan and purpose for humanity. Having been educated in rabbinic thought, Paul applied to Christ's death juridical thinking and formulations. He died "at the right time" (Rom. 5:6), since God "gave him up" (8:32), and Jesus was then "obedient to the point of death" (Phil. 2:8). Jesus' death was God's own action, and Jesus "was handed over to death for our trespasses" (Rom. 4:25). God "did not withhold his own Son, but gave him up for all of us" (8:32). So he "has died for all" (2 Cor. 5:14). The reason for this sacrifice was that we were all sinners and stood in bondage to the powers of this age. The crucifixion was a sacrificial, atoning act in which Christ "gave himself for our sins to set us free from the present evil age, according to the will of our God and Father" (Gal. 1:4).

We "were bought with a price" (1 Cor. 6:20). Christ was born "under the law" (Gal. 4:4), assumed "the likeness of sinful flesh" (Rom. 8:3), and was made "to be sin" (2 Cor. 5:21) though he was not a sinner. Jesus thereby met sin on its own turf and effectively broke its power (Rom. 8:3). In the eyes of the world this sacrificial death was sheer "foolishness" (1 Cor. 1:21). But God deliberately chose the weak, low, and despised act of the cross to achieve his salvational act. Consequently, Paul can

27. Hans Schwarz, *On the Way to the Future,* rev. ed. (Minneapolis: Augsburg, 1979), 67.

boast in the cross of Christ (Gal. 6:14), since it expresses God's love for us. Christ gave himself up to death through which we are freed from the law (i.e., from sin and death) and are granted life. The Son of God loved us and gave himself up for us (Gal. 2:20).

"The 'power of the cross,' however, is not intelligible apart from Christ's resurrection."[28] Paul emphasized this point when he picked up an early confessional formula and wrote: "If you confess with your lips that Jesus is Lord and believe in your heart that God raised him from the dead, you will be saved" (Rom. 10:9). Christ's Lordship and his resurrection go together. Jesus Christ is Lord because he was resurrected. "God raised the Lord and will also raise us by his power" (1 Cor. 6:14). It is important to know "the power of his resurrection" (Phil. 3:10), since Christ's resurrection was a mighty demonstration of God's sovereignty and constitutes the decisive commencement of the "coming age." One could even say that the resurrection was an event of "world history," since it was God's victory over the powers of this age, over sin and death (1 Cor. 15:54-57).

Paul can look back to the cross and perceive its power, since "the Lord" was crucified there. Here we encounter God's redeeming power breaking into the world. Through his death and resurrection Christ has already been enthroned in power to exercise his dominion in the present age (Phil. 2:9). But the ultimate goal is the full sovereignty of God, when the anti-Godly powers of this present age will have been completely destroyed (1 Cor. 15:24). There is a tension in Paul's thought between the "already" and the "not yet" and an eschatological proviso which presses on toward its resolution.

Since the dying and rising of Christ have been accomplished on our behalf, Christians are made participants of this event. This means that believers hope that they are united with Christ in his death and resurrection (Phil. 3:10-11). Since Christ "has died for all; therefore all have died" (2 Cor. 5:14) so that they may live as he lives. "Christ's death and resurrection are not merely events which produce benefits for the believer, but also are events in which the believer himself partakes."[29] This participation of the believer in Christ's death and resurrection is best illustrated with Paul's interpretation of baptism.

28. So rightly Furnish, *Theology and Ethics*, 168.
29. So rightly Robert Tannehill, *Dying and Rising with Christ: A Study in Pauline Theology* (Berlin: Alfred Töpelmann, 1967), 1, in his introduction.

Christians have "died so sin," since they "were baptized into his death, . . . so that, just as Christ was raised from the dead by the glory of the Father, so we too might walk in newness of life" (Rom. 6:2-4). Paul speaks here of our death in Christ as an event in the past. We have been baptized with and in him. As sinners we have died and have been freed from the dominion of sin in the same way as we have died from the dominion of death. This does not mean that sin and death cease to exist. The power of sin and death is broken though the final triumph over them still has to come. Christians have Christ as their new sovereign as symbolized through baptism in Christ's death and resurrection. Yet baptism is not the saving event. It initiates us into the actual saving event, namely Christ's death and resurrection. Priority is given here to what Christ has accomplished for us. It is a one-time event for us, something to which we look back so that we can step forward and walk in newness of life. Through baptism we obtain the hope in the resurrection that "we will certainly be united with him [i.e., Jesus Christ] in a resurrection like his" (Rom. 6:5). The future tense describing the salvation process is important. Christians can look forward because they look back.

Christians then "walk not according to the flesh but according to the Spirit" (Rom. 8:4). There is a new quality of life engendered through the dying and rising with Christ. This new quality must be made manifest by Christians. "The 'newness' of the Christian's life consists in the fact that it is no longer in bondage to the law, sin, and death, but is yielded to God (righteousness) for obedience."[30] Robert Tannehill (1934-) reminds us rightly that "dying with Christ is without meaning unless God is now exercising his power for life in the midst of this dying and unless God manifests this power for life fully through the resurrection of the dead."[31] This means there are two points to be observed: Already a new power is present in the Christian life. We might call this new state of existence a proleptic anticipation of the hoped-for goal. Second, a final resolution of the hope is envisioned, a resolution through which the prolepsis may find its actual fulfillment. The Christian existence therefore is an eschatological existence which is oriented toward the end from which it receives its power to life. We should be careful not to construe

30. Furnish, *Theology and Ethics,* 175-76.
31. Tannehill, *Dying and Rising,* 131.

Paul's thoughts as entailing some kind of Christian mysticism. Our being is not fused together with Christ's, although we do belong to Christ. While Paul may indeed have employed the symbolism of mystery religions, he is clear that the dying and rising is a one-time occurrence. Our association with Christ is of an intensely relational but not mystical nature. So he can even "in human terms" speak of us becoming "slaves of righteousness" (Rom. 6:18-19) so that we are "slaves" *(douloi)* "in the new life of the Spirit" (Rom. 7:6).

Paul also uses the eschatological title "Christ" to express who Jesus is. Thereby "Christ" is almost always used as a proper name, mainly in the theologically undifferentiated connection of Jesus Christ or Christ Jesus.[32] Seldom is the term "Jesus" used alone, and even for the pre-existent One Paul uses the name "Christ": "they drank from the spiritual rock that followed them, and the rock was Christ" (1 Cor. 10:4). Paul talks about the "Lord" *(Kyrios)* and the Son of God, but does not use the term "Son of Man." Christ is also seen as the mediator of creation (1 Cor. 8:6), but he is not equated with God. Although in him "the whole fullness of deity dwells bodily" (Col. 2:9), he still remains "the image of the invisible God, the firstborn of all creation" (1:15). There is an (ontological) difference between God and Christ. Since Christ stands so close to God, his life and destiny have cosmic relevance. Even though he was instrumental in reconciling all things to God (1:20), "the creation waits with eager longing" (Rom. 8:19) until it will be set free from its bondage to decay. With the coming of Jesus Christ to this earth, with his life, death, and resurrection, a new age has dawned that presses forward to its full disclosure. This was Paul's understanding of Christ. It was from this point that the emerging church had to begin in its christological reflections.

---

32. Kümmel, *Theology of the New Testament*, 154.

4. Stations of
Christological Reflection

It is not my intent to be exhaustive in portraying the turning points in christological reflection, but I would like to point out those stations along the way at which crucial decisions were made. At each instance I will ask whether they led to clarifications of the person and accomplishment of Jesus Christ or strayed away from the New Testament vision. If tradition means the passing on of that which has been received, tradition is not necessarily bad. Quite the contrary, it is necessary in order for continuity to be preserved. Without tradition we would be in danger of veering away from the originally envisioned direction. The first major decisions concerning the interpretation and meaning of the christological reflections contained in the New Testament occurred within the first centuries. While the New Testament had emphasized that Jesus was indeed the Messiah, postbiblical generations reflected upon the consequence of that assertion, especially upon how the sender of salvation is related to the bringer of salvation. This question led directly into the trinitarian reflections of the early church.

1. The Early Church

Two questions especially troubled the early church: Is Jesus Christ, our Savior, identical with God, or is he some kind of semi-god? And, if Jesus Christ is divine, how is this divinity related to his humanity? For us in the twentieth century these questions may seem irrelevant, but if we

137

consider them in the context of the time in which they were posed we discover their truly existential nature. In the Hellenistic context semi-gods abounded. Quite often these semi-divine emissaries came to the help of humans. But they were subject to the laws of this world and its finitude, and their help could at most be of a temporary nature. If Jesus Christ can provide lasting salvation, he must be truly divine. This option, however, posed the danger of polytheism. Would not the true divinity of Christ impair the Jewish monotheism out of which most Christians initially came? If there was more than one God, these "gods" would have to fight for supremacy among one another or each of them would have only a limited sphere of influence. Considerations like these influenced the so-called trinitarian controversy, actually a misnomer for these discussions, since the Holy Spirit was given only ancillary attention.

The subsequent christological controversy again confronted truly existential questions. If Jesus had not really assumed human nature, so common thought went, he could not actually redeem humanity, since he seemed to be aloof from it. Yet if he had taken on human nature, did this not threaten his divinity from which salvation would necessarily come forth? But even if both "natures" were maintained, how could they ever be joined to form one being? Would not a savior composed of two "natures" almost resemble a monster, totally unlike a truly divine or truly human being? One can easily imagine that questions like these defied easy answers or simple solutions.

a. The Trinitarian Controversy

The New Testament does not contain an explicit doctrine of the Trinity, nor even trinitarian formulas. Though God the Father, Jesus Christ, and the Spirit are mentioned often and in close proximity to each other, we only encounter triadic formulations such as "The grace of the Lord Jesus Christ, and the love of God, and the communion of the Holy Spirit be with all of you" (2 Cor. 13:13), or, in the Great Commission, "Make disciples of all nations, baptizing them in the name of the Father and of the Son and of the Holy Spirit" (Matt. 28:19). Though one may assume that Father, Son, and Holy Spirit belong together and are actually one, this is nowhere explicitly stated. The only exception is the Johannine Comma in 1 John 5:7-8. While the widely attested text states: "There are three that testify: the Spirit and the water and the blood, and these three agree," a later editor, apparently feeling the need to give a more explicit statement of the Trinity, changed the text to: "There are three that testify in heaven, the Father, the Word, and the Holy Spirit, and these three are one. And there are three that testify on earth: the Spirit and the water and the blood, and these three agree." This insertion seems to have emerged from a trinitarian interpretation of this triad in Spain and Africa during the late fourth or fifth century.[1] This comment stands at the conclusion rather than at the beginning of trinitarian reflection.

At the beginning are rather simple statements that nevertheless show the necessity of regarding Jesus as fully divine. We read in 2 Clement 1:1-2: "We ought to think of Jesus Christ just as we do of God, as the Judge of the living and the dead; nor ought we to belittle our salvation. For when we think little of him, we also hope to receive but little."[2] Jesus Christ is our Savior only if he is truly divine. But how is he related to God the Father in his divinity? To this Ignatius responds: "There is one Physician: both flesh and spirit, begotten and unbegotten, in man, God, in death, true life, both from Mary and from God, first passible and then impassible, Jesus Christ our Lord" (*Ign. Eph.* 7:2).[3] Here we are again confronted with the assertion of the true divinity of Christ but now with more intensive reflection indicating two ways of looking at Christ, the human and the divine ways. How the two are related is not yet enunciated. Here the first eminent theologian of the early church, Origen of Alexandria (ca. 185–ca. 253) put forth a decisive elaboration. That a clarification was needed is evident from Justin Martyr's (ca. 100–ca. 165) designation of Christ simply as "another God and Lord."[4] No wonder his Jewish opponent objected to such unreflected polytheism.

To avert the danger of a pluralism within the divinity, monarchianism, meaning "one primordial power," was advanced. But whether in the dynamistic form which saw an impersonal divine power active in the human being Jesus, or in the modalistic variety which argued that the Son and the Spirit are simply modes of the appearance of the one God, monarchianists claimed, to which Eusebius of Caesarea (ca. 260–ca. 340)

1. See C. Draina, "Johannine Comma," in *New Catholic Encyclopedia* (1967), 7:1004.

2. Robert M. Grant and Holt H. Graham, eds., *The Apostolic Fathers: A New Translation and Commentary*, vol. 2: *First and Second Clement* (New York: Thomas Nelson, 1965), 112.

3. Grant and Graham, *The Apostolic Fathers*, vol. 4: *Ignatius of Antioch* (New York: Thomas Nelson, 1966), 38.

4. Justin Martyr, *Dialogue with Trypho* 56, in *ANF* 1:223.

rightly objected, "that the Savior was merely human."[5] While the proponents of monarchianism "saved" monotheism, they sacrificed the divinity of Christ to do so. More clarity was introduced by Irenaeus (ca. 130-202), who wrote:

> Therefore the Father is Lord, and the Son is Lord, and the Father is God and the Son is God; for He who is born of God is God. And thus God is shown to be one according to the essence of His being in power; but at the same time, as the administrator of the economy of our redemption, He is both Father and Son: since the Father of all is invisible and inaccessible to creatures, it is through the Son that those who are to approach God must have access to the Father.[6]

Irenaeus avoids a divine pluralism and emphasizes the unity of God. In talking about the economy of redemption he introduces a salvation-historical approach that nearly leads him to a modalistic concept of the relation between Father and Son as if they were merely appearances of the one God. It is also noteworthy that the Spirit is not mentioned here, though Irenaeus does mention him at other points.

Tertullian (ca. 155–ca. 245), the first prominent theologian to use Latin, introduced another aspect into the discussion. He proposed a distinction between the three persons of the Trinity and their common substance; there are three persons in the Godhead but one common substance.[7] Tertullian also talks about Christ "coming out from God like the ray's procession from the sun, and the river's from the fountain," indicating a strict subordinationism.[8] This dialectic of equality and distinction between Father and Son was then further advanced by Origen.

Although the doctrine of the Trinity was not a major concern of

---

5. Eusebius, *The History of the Church from Christ to Constantine* 5.28, trans. G. A. Williamson (Minneapolis: Augsburg, 1965), 235.

6. Irenaeus, *Proof of Apostolic Preaching* 47, in *ACW* 16:78.

7. He wrote in his tract against Praxeas, "I must everywhere hold one only substance in three coherent and inseparable (Persons)." Tertullian expresses his conception of the relation of the three persons even more forcefully earlier in the same tract: "One cannot believe in One Only God in any way than by saying that the Father, the Son, and the Holy Ghost are the very selfsame person.... [They are] three, however, not in condition, but in degree; not in substance, but in form; not in power, but in aspect." Tertullian, *Against Praxeas* 12 and 2, in *ANF* 3:607 and 3:598. This distinction proved most useful, as shall be seen later.

8. Tertullian, *Against Praxeas* 22, in *ANF* 3:617.

Origen, it is wrong to say that "he made little contribution to the church's understanding of it."[9] Though Origen did not offer a solution, he went decidedly beyond Irenaeus and Tertullian. Origen was influenced by Platonic thought, and consequently he put great emphasis on the unity of God. Origen addressed some of the fears of polytheism. The consequence of these fears was that people either denied that the Son had a distinct nature of his own besides that of the Father and made him out to be God the Father in all but name, or they denied the Son's divinity and attributed to him an existence that fell outside the sphere of the Father. Against such overreactions Origen asserted that there is only one God in his own right *(autotheos)*.[10] But there are other gods, godly only through participation in God. Then there is the firstborn, who is associated with the gods as their archetypal image. He gives them their godliness and transcends them, because he continually dwells with the Father. God is the "unbegotten God and Father" and the Son is thus only the begotten Son.[11]

If Christ is the intermediary between God and the created, it is decisive for christological reflection to know whether he is situated in the middle or whether he belongs to one side or the other. Origen decides that the fact that Christ "is the image of God's goodness sets the Savior higher above lesser beings than the fact of being good sets God above the Savior."[12] Christ is closer to God than to creation. Origen is emphatic that "we worship one God, the Father and the Son . . . the Father of truth, and the Son, who is the truth; and these, while they are two, considered as persons or subsistences, are one in unity of thought, in harmony and in identity of will."[13] Origen also asserts that Christ is "the perfect essence of God the Father" and that he eternally proceeded from the Father, indicating a closeness and even sameness of the two.[14]

There are two problems immediately apparent in Origen's christological proposal. If, on the one hand, the oneness of Father and Son is emphasized too much, it is difficult to distinguish between the two; but

9. So in contrast to Joseph Wilson Trigg, *Origen: The Bible and Philosophy in the Third-Century Church* (Atlanta: John Knox, 1983), 103.

10. Origen, *Commentary on John* 2.2, in *ANF* 10:323.

11. Origen, *Against Celsus* 8:14, in *ANF* 4:644.

12. Origen, *Commentary on St. Matthew* 15:10, according to Jean Daniélou, *Origen*, trans. Walter Mitchell (New York: Sheed and Ward, 1955), 255.

13. Origen, *Against Celsus* 8:12, in *ANF* 4:643-44.

14. Origen, *De principiis* 4.1.28, in *ANF* 4:377.

if, on the other, the subordination of the Son to the Father is emphasized too much, the Savior becomes a semi-God. While Origen held oneness and subordination in dialectic tension, his successors did not exhibit the same skill. The resulting problems were either of the right-wing Origenist type which shortchanged the independence of the Son, or of the left-wing Origenist type which minimized the godhead of Christ. Both approaches advanced beyond the older economic type of relation between Father and Son which suggested a successive (i.e., economic) disclosure of persons in the Trinity and which understood the Trinity as a reference to God's eternal being.

Arius (256-336), a presbyter in Alexandria, was the most prominent exponent of the left-wing Origenists. He advocated a strict subordination of the Son. He did not pose the threat of a new polytheism[15] nor deny God's revelation in Jesus Christ as he understood it. On the contrary, he was afraid that elevating Christ to the level of God the Father would indeed threaten monotheism. In order to preserve faith in one God he relentlessly subordinated Christ to God the Father. In 320 he wrote a letter to his bishop Alexander in which he outlined his faith. He claimed that he had learned this faith from his bishop, namely that

> we know one God — alone unbegotten, alone everlasting, alone without beginning, alone true, alone possessing immortality, alone wise, alone good, ... who begot an only-begotten Son before eternal times, through whom he made the ages and everything.... There are three *hypostases.* God being the cause of all is without beginning, most alone; but the Son, begotten by the Father, created and founded before the ages, was not before he was begotten.[16]

Arius held on to the concept of three hypostases. But this term was almost entirely unrelated to the rest of his trinitarian thought, since he portrayed God the Father as immovable and unchangeable, while Jesus Christ, though still being the mediator of creation, was created before the ages and therefore did not exist before he was created. He also has

---

15. Contrary to the otherwise excellent description of Arius's position by Bernhard Lohse, *A Short History of Christian Doctrine,* trans. F. Ernest Stoeffler (Philadelphia: Fortress, 1966), 50.

16. Arius, "Letter to Alexander of Alexandria," in *The Trinitarian Controversy,* trans. and ed. William G. Rusch (Philadelphia: Fortress, 1980), 31-32.

no "being with the Father," nor is he "part of the same substance," with which words Arius denied the *homoousia* of the Son.[17] The letter was signed by several presbyters, deacons, and bishops, but Alexander could not see much similarity in it to his own thought. He took special exception to the idea that "only-begotten" should allow for the assumption that there was a time when he was not and that he differed in his divinity from God the Father.[18] Alexander of Alexandria excommunicated Arius and those who associated themselves with him.

When Constantine became emperor, he sent his advisor Hosios of Cordoba to Alexandria to mediate in the dispute. But the conflict had already spread far beyond Alexandria. When Hosios was on his way back to Constantine's residence in Nicomedia, he stopped in Antioch and called together a synod to decide who should fill the vacant bishop's seat there. The synod did not confine itself to the election process but also pursued the issue of the Arian heresy.[19] This synod in the winter of 324/325 was rather modest in tone and put forth a creed which affirmed faith in one God and in one Lord Jesus who was "not begotten from nothing but from the Father" and "who always is and not at a prior time was not."[20] This creed decisively rejected the Arian proposal, yet the full unity with God was not touched upon. At that time Constantine was already planning to convene a council of the whole empire at Nicea. After addressing a variety of issues, this council took up the Arian controversy. Constantine felt it was his duty to remove error and to propagate the true religion. He also feared that a divided church would offend the Christian God and bring vengeance upon the Roman Empire and its emperor. Constantine was present at the Council of Nicea and even participated in the debates.[21] He instructed the bishops to reach unanimous agreements motivated not by hate or partiality, but by a desire

17. Arius, "Letter to Alexander of Alexandria."

18. Alexander of Alexandria, "Letter to Alexander of Thessalonica" (A.D. 324), in *Trinitarian Controversy,* 38.

19. See for details Adolf Martin Ritter, "Dogma und Lehre in der Alten Kirche," in *Handbuch der Dogmen- und Theologiegeschichte,* ed. Carl Andresen (Göttingen: Vandenhoeck & Ruprecht 1982), 1:164.

20. "The Synodal Letter of the Council of Antioch" (A.D. 325), in *Trinitarian Controversy,* 47.

21. So Aloys Grillmeier, *Christ in Christian Tradition,* vol. 1: *From the Apostolic Age to Chalcedon (451),* trans. John Bowden, rev. 2nd ed. (Atlanta: John Knox, 1975), 258.

to seek out the principles of the church and of the apostles. In comparing his own theology with the decisions of the council, we notice that his interest was to bring unity to the church and not to impose his theological preferences upon the council's statements of faith.[22]

The Creed of Nicea was the first creedal formula issued by an ecumenical synod, and therefore it was the first that could in a legal sense claim universal authority.[23] Expanding considerably on earlier creeds, the council professed faith in

> one Lord Jesus Christ, the Son of God, begotten from the Father, only begotten, that is, from the being of the Father, God from God, Light from Light, true God from true God, begotten not made, of the same being with the Father, through whom all things were made, those in heaven and those on earth, who because of us humans and because of our salvation came down and became flesh, becoming human, suffered and rose again.

Three hundred and eighteen bishops had assembled at Nicea and signed the creed. Only a few of those present refused to sign, among them Arius and his friends, preferring instead to go into exile.

The Nicene Creed was mainly a reply to the Arian position. In the Apostles' Creed biblical terminology had been used to explain how Jesus was related to the Father; now it was no longer sufficient for clarifying the issue without compromising the Christian faith with heretical positions. Thus the phrases "from the being of the Father," "true God from true God," "begotten not made," and "of the same being with the Father" were formulated to ensure that Jesus Christ was not subordinate to God. The council insisted that God had to dwell fully in Jesus Christ in order to offer salvation to humankind.

Yet did not the identity of Christ with God that the Nicene Creed professed jeopardize Christ's full humanity? Was he still considered a human being who once lived among us and with us? Even Athanasius was reluctant to admit that Christ was *homoousios* (of the same being with the Father).[24] Moreover, it seems that the Nicene Creed, its ecumenical status notwithstanding, was far less known than we might assume. It took

22. Grillmeier, *Christ in Christian Tradition*, 1:261-62.
23. So J. N. D. Kelly, *Early Christian Creeds*, 3rd ed. (London: Longman, 1972), 207.
24. For the following see Kelly, *Early Christian Creeds*, 257ff.

a good thirty years until Latin translations were published and Bishop Hilary of Poitiers (ca. 315-367) introduced the West to the crucial text of the Arian controversy. The question that was not addressed at Nicea was how the *homoousios* should be understood, that is, the Son being "of one being with the Father." Was it, in the Western sense, a notion of one substance and three persons? Or was it more the emphasis on the "begotten, not made" that Eastern theologians were wont to make? Most likely it was intended to be understood in the latter sense.

As might have been expected, the council decision did not settle the theological controversy. At Nicea the actual battle only started. The main champion of the anti-Arian cause was Athanasius, bishop of Alexandria from 328 until his death in 373. Initially his main emphasis was on the divinity of the *logos*. He compared Father and Son, for instance, to the water of a river. "For like as the well is not a river, nor the river a well, but both are one and the same water which is conveyed in a channel from the well to the river, so the Father's deity passes into the Son without flow and without division."[25]

Through his banishments in Treves (335-337), Rome, and Aquileia (339-346), Athanasius became more acquainted with the Western notion of interpreting the *homoousios*. He realized that this was an excellent term to assert the unity of God and the distinction in the Godhead between Father and Son. The *homoousios* refers much more to the unity of the Godhead, while the differentiation of the persons of the godhead, though much more feasible now without threatening their equal divinity, is not yet clearly enunciated.[26] Here the work of the great Cappadocian theologians began. Only later in his career did Athanasius mention the divinity of the Spirit: "The Holy Spirit is not a creature, nor external, but proper to and inseparable from the Essence of the Father and the Son."[27]

---

25. Athanasius, "Statement of Faith," in *NPNF 2*, 4:84.

26. Athanasius elaborates on his interpretation of the Western notion of Godhead: "For they [i.e., Father and Son] are one, not as one thing divided into two parts, and these nothing but one, nor as one thing twice named, so that the Same becomes at one time Father, at another His own Son, for this Sabellius holding was judged an heretic. But They are two, because the Father is Father and is not also Son, and the Son is Son and not also Father; but the nature is one." Athanasius, "Four Discourses against the Arians" 3:4, in *NPNF 2*, 4:395.

27. Athanasius, "Tome or Synodical Letter to the People of Antioch" 5, in *NPNF 2*, 4:484.

The three Cappadocians, Basil the Great (ca. 330–ca. 379), Gregory of Nyssa (ca. 335–ca. 394), the younger brother of Basil, and Gregory of Nazianzen (ca. 329–ca. 390) pursued much further the issue of the Trinity, including the differentiation between the three persons. In his "Fifth Theological Oration" Gregory of Nazianzen elaborated on the doctrine of the Trinity and posed the question of whether one should even ask about the Holy Spirit, "this strange God of Whom the Bible is silent."[28] His answer was in the affirmative and was well argued with ample scriptural references. He admits that "the Old Testament proclaimed the Father openly and the Son more obscurely. The New manifested the Son, and suggested the Deity of the Spirit. Now the Spirit Himself dwells among us, and supplies us with a clear demonstration of Himself."[29] Then he proceeds to show how the Spirit was involved in the ministry of Jesus. This moved him to argue that we should "worship God the Father, God the Son, and God the Holy Spirit, Three Persons, One Godhead, undivided in honor and glory and substance and kingdom."[30]

Once the full deity of the Spirit is asserted, the question of tritheism emerges: are there now actually three gods? Gregory responded in this way:

> When then we look at the Godhead, or the First Cause, or the Monarchia, that which we conceive is One; but when we look at the Persons in Whom the Godhead dwells, and at Those Who timelessly and with equal glory have their Being from the First Cause — there are Three Whom we worship.[31]

There is a unity of the godhead which is differentiated in three persons. There is not simply a numerical distinction or one of name among the persons of the Trinity, but one which highlights the respective peculiarities of the persons.[32] Gregory is candid enough to admit that though

---

28. Gregory of Nazianzen, "The Fifth Theological Oratory" 1, in *NPNF* 7:326.

29. Gregory, "The Fifth Theological Oratory" 26, in *NPNF* 7:318.

30. Gregory, "The Fifth Theological Oratory" 28, in *NPNF* 7:327.

31. Gregory, "The Fifth Theological Oratory" 14, in *NPNF* 7:322.

32. Gregory explains concerning the relationship between and the properties of the persons: "The very fact of being Unbegotten or Begotten, or Proceeding has given the name of Father to the First, of the Son to the Second, and of the Third, Him of Whom we are speaking, of the Holy Ghost that the distinction of the Three Persons may be preserved in the one nature and dignity of the Godhead." "The Fifth Theological Oratory" 9, in *NPNF* 7:320.

146

he has looked everywhere for analogies, he has been unable "to discover anything on earth with which to compare the nature of the Godhead."[33] The triune God is so unique that he has no equal.

Once the differentiation within the Trinity had been elucidated, it also became necessary to consider christology officially in the context of the Trinity. At the Ecumenical Council of Constantinople in 381, the original Nicene Creed was updated and clarified. Now the brief comment that Christ "became incarnate" was expanded to "was incarnate from the Holy Spirit in the Virgin Mary." The Holy Spirit was elevated to the same level as Father and Son in the article concerning the Holy Spirit.[34] Yet these important formulations, known to us as the Niceno-Constantinopolitan Creed, did not at first gain wide circulation. Until recently scholars were not even sure that this creed had indeed been issued at the Council of Constantinople.[35] When it was officially read at the Council of Chalcedon in 451 and received into its minutes together with the Nicene Creed, many of the council participants probably heard it for the first time. But it soon became the baptismal creed of the Eastern churches, and for a while also enjoyed popularity in the West.

The decision of the Ecumenical Council of 381 was not one of simply reiterating New Testament formulations. The *homoousios* expressed there and previously at Nicea was not a surrender to the Hellenistic spirit. Yet with the conceptual tools available at that time the church asserted that in Jesus Christ God encounters us completely and fully. Salvation is truly present in Jesus Christ. Analogously, in the Holy Spirit God is totally present in and with his church. Thus the church could continue to feel assured that it was not an association dedicated to the memory of Jesus or a free agent determined to mold the world according to its own ideas. On the contrary, God's presence in this world constituted the people of God who attempted to live in his Spirit and carry out his mission.

In the West Augustine (354-430) gave a definite understanding to

---

33. Gregory, "The Fifth Theological Oratory" 31, in *NPNF* 7:328.

34. The text was expanded to read that the Holy Spirit is "the Lord and life-giver who proceeds from the Father, who with the Father and the Son is together worshipped and together glorified." The council refrained from saying that the Spirit is "one in being with the Father and the Son."

35. For the discussion of its origin see Kelly, *Early Christian Creeds*, 305-31.

the Trinity in his fifteen-volume treatise *The Trinity,* written between 399 and 419. Central for him was the emphasis on the unity of the godhead so as to avoid all suspicion of advocating tritheism. Thus he stated: "Whatever is spoken of God in respect to Himself and of each single person, that is, of the Father, the Son, and the Holy Spirit, and together of the Trinity itself, is to be predicated in the singular of each divine person and not in the plural."[36] While he admits that he does not venture "to use the formula one essence and three substances, but rather one essence or substance and three persons," he does not want to use the generic designation *person* to show their independent individuality but rather their common essence.[37] The term "person" is used of God the Father "in respect to Himself, not in relation to the Son or to the Holy Spirit."[38] The Father is then a person only in himself, but not in relation to the person of the Son or that of the Holy Spirit. Beyond that necessary differentiation we cannot represent the Trinity inseparably, though Father, Son, and Holy Spirit work together inseparably.[39] Yet actually "the works of the Trinity are not separable . . . when any One of the Three is named in connection with some divine action, the whole Trinity is to be understood as involved in that action."[40] While in themselves the persons in the Trinity are to be distinguished, toward us they form a unity. Thus adoration and praise are always addressed to the whole Trinity even if just one person is mentioned.

As we have seen, the doctrine of the Trinity evolved only as an offspring of christological reflection. From the beginning almost to the very end, the discussion in the first centuries was dominated by the quest for christology: Who is the one whom we call Christ? Once it was clarified that he is indeed God, then the question had to be addressed as to how the divine and the human "aspects" are related in him. Again we could assume that this was basically a speculative question. Yet salvation was at stake here too, because the conviction soon emerged that if God had not really come down to us in Jesus Christ we could never come up to

36. Augustine, *The Trinity* 5.8.9, in *FaCH,* 45:186-87.

37. Augustine, *The Trinity* 7:4:8-9, in *FaCH* 45:235-36; quotation, 5.9, in *FaCH* 45:187.

38. Augustine, *The Trinity* 7.6.11; in *FaCH* 45:236.

39. Augustine, *The Trinity* 4.21.30, in *FaCH* 45:170.

40. Augustine, *Enchiridion* 12.38, in *Library of Christian Classics,* vol. 7: *Augustine: Confessions and Enchiridion,* trans. and ed. Albert C. Outler (Philadelphia: Westminster, 1955), 363.

him. Others, however, were more afraid that the divine might be too much dragged down into our sphere and thereby lose its salvific power.

The unresolved christological problems similar to those regarding the Trinity go right back to the New Testament, since the New Testament had neither a conceptually and intellectually developed christology nor an actual doctrine of the Trinity. It was clear for the New Testament sources that Jesus Christ had been an actual human figure in whom God had been truly present. For reasons of adhering to a strict monotheism, seldom is Jesus referred to as God. Yet the early church had always considered Jesus as God. His preexistence was an indisputable fact for Paul. Paul had also set the tone for the dominant strain of christological reflection when he asserted that Jesus Christ "was descended from David according to the flesh and was declared to be Son of God in power according to the spirit of holiness" (Rom. 1:3-4). Contained therein is an understanding of Christ's twofold status, human and divine.

At the beginning of christological reflection we encounter other influential strands. Certain Jewish Christians advocated the so-called Ebionite christology, which initially did not differ much from mainline Christianity.[41] After their exodus to Pella, in present-day Jordan, in anticipation of the destruction of Jerusalem in A.D. 70, their perception of Christ (whom they also considered to be the Messiah) changed. They came to believe that, as the only person who had completely fulfilled the law, Christ had been appointed Messiah, and with reference to Psalm 2:7 was adopted by God at the time of his baptism. His death had no salvific significance and the Last Supper was a mere remembrance of the table fellowship with Jesus. As the Son of man Christ will come someday on the clouds of heaven to usher in his reign and the final judgment. This kind of christology was strongly rejected by the early church, though adoptionistic tendencies survived even in the main church through the centuries.

Another christological development was docetism, which was especially strong in Gnostic circles under the influence of Marcion (ca. 85–ca. 160). The strict dualism in Gnosticism does not allow for a coming together of the creator and the created.[42] The Savior, it was said, only became

41. For the following see Hans Joachim Schoeps, *Jewish Christianity: Factional Disputes in the Early Church*, trans. Douglas R. A. Hare (Philadelphia: Fortress, 1969), 61ff.

42. See Robert Haardt, *Gnosis: Character and Testimony*, trans. J. F. Hendry (Leiden: E. J. Brill, 1971), 4-5.

human in a limited way and only until the day of crucifixion, since he could not die on the cross. Docetism flourished in the first two centuries, though docetic tendencies have continued to surface until the present time.

Logos christology was another early christological development. It contained more promise for ecclesial acceptance than did docetism. The Apologists carried on the Johannine tradition, calling Christ the Word, "the first-born of God," "Lord, and God the Son of God," but also identified the Logos as God's incarnate word with the Logos of Greek philosophy.[43] The incarnate Christ was identified with the reason that is inherent in the order of the world. Christ was not only the Word which appeared in history but the universal mind (of God) and the cosmic principle. On this basis it was then easy to assert that all truth of Greek philosophy came ultimately from the Logos, Jesus Christ. What in its universal presence had seemed fragmentary and imperfect had now been revealed fully and finally in Jesus Christ.

Mainly because of Origen's influence, Logos christology became virtually the dominant christological stream in the third century. Origen claimed that the Word, being divine itself, can be known only to God. The Word is the only mediator, and it must then be the true self-disclosure of God.[44] The Word is thus considered synonymous with Reason, Wisdom, and Truth. All of these are eminent philosophical concepts that show the universal character of the logos which became incarnate and therefore individuated in Christ. By asserting the universal significance of Christ it was even more important to ascertain how the divine was disclosed to the human in the one person of Christ.

Again it was Tertullian who came up with a lasting solution. After thinking through all possible options, which were later fiercely discussed (primarily in the East) he concluded:

> We see plainly the twofold state, which is not confounded, but conjoined in One Person — Jesus, God and Man. . . . The property of each nature is so wholly preserved, that the Spirit on the one hand did all things in Jesus suitable to Itself, such as miracles, and mighty deeds, and wonders; and the Flesh, on the other hand, exhibited the affections which belong to it.[45]

---

43. Justin Martyr, *First Apology* 21, in *ANF* 1:170; Justin Martyr, *Dialogue with Trypho* 128, in *ANF* 1:264, and Justin Martyr, *First Apology* 5, 1:164.

44. For the following see Origen, *De principiis* 2.6.1ff., in *ANF* 4:281-82.

45. Tertullian, *Against Praxeas* 27, in *ANF* 3:624.

There is one Jesus Christ who is the Son of God and at the same time fully human. While Tertullian touched on Nestorius's idea (d. 451) that the human movements of Christ are accomplished by his human nature and the divine by his divine nature, he nevertheless emphasizes the unity of the person of Christ, which consists of two natures that are present in his person unchanged and unmixed.

Unfortunately the East did not take notice of Tertullian and pursued its own deliberations, which resulted in painful controversies. The first noteworthy position in the East is that of Athanasius and then later that of Apollinaris of Laodicea (ca. 315–ca. 392). Athanasius was then engaged in his bitter struggle with Arius. The Arians denied the presence of the human soul in the incarnate Logos. According to their way of reasoning, the incarnate Logos took the place of the human soul in the body of Jesus. Athanasius was not that far removed from Arius in his own reflections; he did not reject the idea that by coming into Jesus the Logos took on the form of a creature. He only objected when they claimed that this proved the creaturely aspect of the Logos. For Athanasius it was of prime importance that Jesus was divine throughout the incarnational process. There must be a direct and real union of God with humanity in Christ. In his treatise on the *Incarnation of the Word* he argued that the one who "has filled all things everywhere . . . takes a body of our kind."[46] The incorruptible Son of God clothes all of humanity with incorruption.[47] God came to us so that we could become God-like. While this interpretation would suffice to explain the atoning quality of Jesus, the question concerning his real human nature is not even addressed. The Arians justifiably asked, "If He were very God from very God, how could He become man?"[48] Athanasius replied that the Scriptures contain a double witness to Christ as the Savior: he is eternally God and he became incarnate.[49] The dominant force in Jesus is still the Godhead. The human aspect served the Godhead because it belonged to God.[50] The human person of Jesus is

---

46. Athanasius, *Incarnation of the Word* 8, in *NPNF 2*, 4:40.

47. Athanasius, *Incarnation of the Word* 9, in *NPNF 2*, 4:41.

48. As cited by Athanasius, *Five Discourses against the Arians* 3:27, in *NPNF 2*, 4:408.

49. Specifically Athanasius writes that Jesus "was ever God" and "that afterwards for us He took flesh . . . and was made man." *Five Discourses against the Arians* 3:29, in *NPNF 2*, 4:409.

50. No clearer statement of this view can be found than the following: "The flesh

151

therefore rather lifeless. While Athanasius does not mention a human soul, he also does not say that Jesus Christ was without a human soul. Yet "for practical purposes, he regards Jesus, as the Arians did, as Logos plus body or flesh."[51]

Apollinaris of Laodicea, a friend of Athanasius and also a fierce enemy of Arianism, openly taught what his friend only implied: Jesus was indeed less than a complete human being. He focused so much on the divine aspect of Christ that he exclaimed: "O new creation and divine mixture! God and flesh completed one and the same nature!"[52] Through the incarnation something new was formed, a new creation of human/divine origin. Indeed, only the body and soul of Christ could be said to be human; Christ's spirit was the Spirit of God. Christ was rightly called "the human being from heaven."[53] The intellect which was divine moved the flesh so that it would act in the proper manner. God did not come down to us, but rather our human body was lifted up to the divine and therewith removed from its misery of imperfection and sinfulness. The Logos replaced the human intellect, and the human flesh was sanctified and redeemed. Incarnation therefore consisted of the divine Logos assuming a body so that the divine nature could remain dominant.[54] It was evident to Apollinaris that in order to achieve redemption the divine had to be the active agent and the human form had to be relegated to total passivity. But in doing so, Apollinaris sacrificed the integrity of the human nature of Christ and actually presented a docetic picture. The divine did not become human but assumed the decisive function within a human being.

Gregory of Nazianzen rightly argued against this position. God has to become really human in order for humans to become divine.[55] In

---

ministered to the works of the Godhead, because the Godhead was in it, for the body was God's." Athanasius, *Five Discourses against the Arians* 3:31, in *NPNF 2*, 4:410.

51. So rightly Richard A. Norris, trans. and ed., *The Christological Controversy* (Philadelphia: Fortress, 1980), 20, in his introduction.

52. Apollinaris of Laodicea, "Fragments" 10, in *Christological Controversy*, 108.

53. Apollinaris, "Fragments" 25, in *Christological Controversy*, 108.

54. Apollinaris writes, "The human race is saved not by the assumption of an intellect and of the whole human being but by the assumption of flesh, whose nature it is to be ruled. What was needed was unchangeable Intellect which did not fall under the domination of the flesh on account of its weakness of understanding." "Fragments" 76, in *Christological Controversy*, 109.

55. Gregory flatly states that salvation is impossible when the divine and the human

contrast to Apollinaris, Gregory emphasized the presence of two aspects in Jesus, the human and the divine, without any mixture or diminution:

> Passible in his flesh, impassible in his Godhead; circumscript in the body, uncircumscript in the Spirit; at once earthly and heavenly, tangible and intangible, comprehensible and incomprehensible; that by one and the same [Person], who was perfect man and also God, the entire humanity fallen through sin might be created anew.[56]

Apollinaris and his teachings on christology were rejected at the Council of Constantinople in 381. Yet, as Athanasius had shown, if one operates with a Logos christology and wants to assert that Christ is truly divine one can hardly escape the position espoused by Apollinaris.

But there was still another line of thought, which was initially put forth by Eustatius of Antioch (ca. 285–ca. 337) in the so-called School of Antioch, then further developed by Diodorus of Tarsus (ca. 315–ca. 394) and Theodore of Mopsuestia (ca. 350-428/429). Significant for the Antiochene School was the concept of the indwelling of the divine in Jesus Christ. How does God's indwelling in a Son take place?

> It means that having indwelt him, he united the one assumed as a whole to himself and equipped him to share with himself in all the honor in which he, being Son by nature, participates, so as to be counted one person in virtue of the union with him and to share with him all his dominion, and in this way to accomplish everything in him, so that even the examination and judgment of the world shall be fulfilled through him and his advent.[57]

In this view there is more a moral harmony or union than an ontological one.[58] The human and the divine came together in a unity of intention and action, yet not in a unity of the person. Theodore borders

---

are wholly separate with no chance of personal encounter; "That which he has not assumed he has not healed; but that which is united to his Godhead is also saved." Gregory of Nazianzen, "Letter to Cledonius against Apollinaris" Ep. 101, in *The Library of Christian Classics,* vol. 3: *Christology of the Later Fathers,* ed. Edward R. Hardy (Philadelphia: Westminster, 1954), 218.

56. Gregory, "Letter to Cledonius," 216.

57. Theodore of Mopsuestia, *On the Incarnation* 7.2, in *Christological Controversy,* 117.

58. So also Rowan A. Greer, *Theodore of Mopsuestia: Exegete and Theologian* (London: Faith, 1961), 58.

on a dangerous dualism when he attempts to explain the union of the divine and human in Jesus Christ. In distinguishing the natures, "we say that the person of the man is complete and that that of the Godhead is complete. But when we consider the union, then we proclaim that both natures are one person."[59] The same problem opens up when he claims that Mary is both the mother of man and the mother of God.[60]

In contrast to the position developed by Athanasius, it is clear that for Theodore the human was not simply swallowed up by the divine. One must also remember that the indwelling motive is biblical and that Theodore's theology is more informed by biblical exegesis than by Greek (ontological) conceptuality. Yet the Greek-minded Christians longed for a more physical salvation, a redemption from this present world, which did not seem to be forthcoming from a primarily moral guidance of the human through the divine. Diodorus and Theodore were not opposed in their teaching during their lifetime. Only much later (499 and 553 respectively) were they labeled heretics. But then they were long dead and unable to defend their case. Nestorius was not so fortunate.

Soon after Nestorius became bishop of Constantinople (428), he was asked whether he taught that Mary gave birth to God *(theotokos)* and to a human being *(anthropotokos)*. He clearly declined the first.[61] Yet he did not plainly come out in favor of the latter. He argued that out of the virgin the Holy Spirit formed a temple for God the Logos in which he dwelled. Christ is "at once God and man"; therefore, the designation "mother of God" is at the least one-sided.[62] He held on to the unity of the person of Christ when he stated by way of illustration:

> If you want to lift up someone who is lying down, do you not touch body with body and, by joining yourself to the other person, lift up the hurt one while you, joined to him in this fashion, remain what you were? This is the way to think of the mystery of the incarnation.[63]

While this position may indeed be more biblically informed than the one represented by Cyril of Alexandria (376-444), who attacked him

---

59. Theodore, *On the Incarnation* 8.8, 120.
60. Theodore, *On the Incarnation* 12.11, 121.
61. Nestorius, "First Sermon against Theotokos," in *Christological Controversy,* 124.
62. Nestorius, "First Sermon," 129.
63. Nestorius, "First Sermon," 125.

fiercely, the unity of the person was still not well maintained.[64] Does this not sound somewhat like a docetic Christ? Cyril thought so and was not satisfied with the answer given by Nestorius that Nicea did not teach the *theotokos* and that at most one could say that Mary gave birth to Christ *(christotokos)*.

Cyril of Alexandria asserted the strict unity of the Logos with the flesh so that there is not only a unity of will, but "the Word substantially united to himself flesh, endowed with life and reason, in a manner mysterious and inconceivable."[65] Because of this unity in the flesh he calls the Virgin Mary "mother of God" *(theotokos)*.[66] He rejected the notion that the Logos would indwell in a human being but stated that "he was actually united with flesh, without being changed into it."[67] Yet when he addressed the issue of Christ's death, he hardly moved beyond the position assumed by Nestorius when he said that "we proclaim the fleshly death of God's only-begotten Son, Jesus Christ."[68] Does this mean that God in Christ died too? Or, as Nestorius argued, that Christ died only in his humanity? Cyril was silent at this point.

Cyril of Alexandria was quite insistent that Nestorius's formulations were wrong, and in 430, after consultation with Pope Celestine, put forth twelve statements which Nestorius had to renounce.[69] But were his own positive elaborations as orthodox as he had assumed? For instance, he claimed that the one nature of the divine Logos had become flesh.[70] The potential heresy of this position was averted by Cyril's elaboration that Jesus Christ definitely had a human soul, since the Logos united itself with the full human nature. This shows how tricky the conceptual distinctions had become and how unintentionally one lapsed into heresy. The positive contribution of Cyril was the insight that one could not distinguish or separate the two natures of the incarnate Logos. Since Jesus Christ was considered to be consubstantial with God, it was clear

64. This is evident in Nestorius's statement: "God has been joined to the crucified flesh, even though he has not shared its suffering." Nestorius, "First Sermon," 130.

65. Cyril of Alexandria, "Second Letter to Nestorius" 3, in *Cyril of Alexandria: Selected Letters,* ed. and trans. Lionel A. Wickham (Oxford: Clarendon, 1983), 5ff.

66. Cyril, "Second Letter to Nestorius" 7, 9ff.

67. Cyril, "Third Letter to Nestorius" 4, in *Cyril of Alexandria,* 19.

68. Cyril, "Third Letter to Nestorius" 7, 23.

69. Cyril, "Third Letter to Nestorius" 12, 29-33, for the text.

70. Cyril, "Third Letter to Nestorius" 8, 25; cf. Lohse, *Short History,* 89.

that the main interest was in his divinity and this interest carried the discussion.

A council was convened in Ephesus at 431. Cyril and his followers arrived early and had Nestorius condemned. The formally convened synod led by Nestorius in turn condemned Cyril. Yet Cyril succeeded in having his synod recognized as the Third Ecumenical Council, and Nestorius remained deposed. Later a reconciliation was effected between Cyril and some of the followers of Nestorius. But the controversy flared up again and was finally decided at the Council of Chalcedon (451).

Influential at Chalcedon was a doctrinal letter of Pope Leo the Great (ca. 400-461), called Leo's *Tome* (June 13, 449), which he had sent to Constantinople on reports of controversy preceding Chalcedon. Leo picked up the christological position of the West as advocated by Tertullian and later writers such as Hilary of Poitiers, Ambrose (ca. 333-397), and Augustine.[71] He used Tertullian's language in asserting that "the characteristic properties of both natures and substances are kept intact and come together in one person."[72] He maintained that Christ existed "in a novel order of existence, yet without departing from the glory of his Father."[73] There is a unity of the person which does not lead to a dissolution of the respective characteristics, since "each 'form' carries on its proper activities in communion with the other."[74] The two entities are so intensely present in the unity of the person that it comes to a *communicatio idiomatum,* an exchange of the respective properties or attributes of each nature.[75] But he does not follow through on the implication of the *communicatio idiomatum* and says that he endured his suffering and crucifixion not in his "divine nature in virtue of which, as Only Begotten, he is coeternal and consubstantial with the Father, but in the weakness of his human nature." This is very reminiscent of the position which Nestorius had taken when he claimed that the divine was unable to suffer and die in Jesus Christ.

---

71. See Lohse, *Short History,* 91-92, for details.
72. Pope Leo I, "Letter to Flavian of Constantinople" 3, in *Christological Controversy,* 148.
73. Leo I, "Letter to Flavian" 4, 149.
74. Leo I, "Letter to Flavian" 4, 150.
75. This *communicatio idiomatum* is clearly evident in Leo's statement that "the Son of man came down from heaven (since the Son of God took on flesh from the Virgin of whom he was born), and conversely . . . that the Son of God was crucified and buried." Leo I, "Letter to Flavian" 5, 151, for this and the following quotation.

Since Leo's *Tome* insisted on the unity of the human with the divine in Jesus Christ and at the same time distinguished between the two natures of Christ, his letter was well received and became the decisive document in the controversy. Together with Cyril's "Second Letter to Nestorius" and "Letter to John of Antioch," which accepted the formula of reunion between followers of Nestorius and Cyril's own party, the *Tome* became part of the authoritative documents of Chalcedon. But the Emperor Marcian, who had just succeeded Theodosius II and had called the council together at Chalcedon, also wanted a fresh pronouncement to which the bishops could be held accountable. Against their original intentions the council delegates did not simply reiterate the Creed of Nicea and Constantinople but promulgated their own confession. In that statement they agreed that Jesus Christ

> is complete in his deity and complete — the very same — in his human-ity, truly God and truly a human being. . . . The very same one was born in the last days from the Virgin Mary, the Mother of God, for our sake and the sake of our salvation: one and the same Christ, Son, Lord, Only Begotten, acknowledged to be unconfusedly, unalterably, un-dividedly, inseparably in two natures, since the difference of the natures is not destroyed because of the union, but on the contrary, the character of each nature is preserved and comes together in one person and one hypothesis, not divided or torn into two persons but one and the same Son.[76]

The unity of Christ is emphasized by stating that Christ is in two natures, which might imply a composite being. That Mary is Mother of God *(theotokos)* is reiterated. The two natures were clearly affirmed, thus rejecting any notion of one nature.

Now comes the most important insight of the council. After stating that Jesus is truly God and truly a human being, the council did not actually state what this new being was like, but decided to establish parameters or boundaries outside of which the unity could no longer be affirmed. Four negatives were set forth: "unconfused" *(asynchytos)* and "unaltered" *(atreptos)*, which were safeguards against Apollinarian thought, and "undivided" *(adihairetos)* and "unseparated" *(achoristos)*,

---

76. The Council of Chalcedon, "Definition of the Faith," in *Christological Controversy*, 159.

which were safeguards against Antiochian tendencies. These four negatives plus the Western affirmation of truly God and truly a human being
may have looked like a compromise.[77] It was indeed a compromise. The
church finally admitted that while it must affirm that Jesus Christ was
truly divine and truly human, it cannot positively assert how he could
be such. It could only state, and so it did, how one should not talk about
that unity.

One could also say that "in the Chalcedonian Creed the West gave
its answer to the East."[78] It provided the positive basis on which undue
speculation could be rejected. Chalcedon "rightly elected to take a position midway between neutrality, on the one hand, and, on the other, a
speculative attempt to plumb the depth of the mystery which meets us
in the person of Jesus Christ." Speculation was not eliminated but shown
its boundaries. The definitions also told Eastern representatives that their
initial attempts to define the person of Jesus Christ were futile, since
these would require a definition of God. If one wants to determine how
the divine and the human factors in Jesus Christ are related to each other,
one first has to define each of these factors. Yet such a definition of the
divine, of God, is humanly impossible lest it result in a caricature. We
can only retell the story about God's coming to us which he first told us
(cf. Matt. 1:20).

The Chalcedonian decision did not put an end to the controversy.
On the contrary, it poured new oil onto the flames. For some Alexandrian
extremists the statement was not strong enough, and for the Nestorians
it was too strong. Of course, national rivalries also played an important
role. The emperor whose heavy hand was felt at Chalcedon also tried
to win back the monophysite party, so-called after Cyril's claim that "the
one nature *(mia physis)* of the Logos became flesh." In the sixth century
Justinian I (527-565) convened an ecumenical council which integrated
Chalcedon along the line of a hypostatic union of the two natures, since,
as some claimed, without this phrase one could still think of the two
persons of Christ. Yet this Fifth Ecumenical Council at Constantinople

---

77. See the reservations by Wolfhart Pannenberg, *Jesus — God and Man*, trans.
Lewis L. Wilkins and Duane A. Priebe, 2nd ed. (Philadelphia: Westminster, 1988), 285,
where he called the formulation "problematic," since it does not take the concrete unity
of the historical human being Jesus as its point of departure, but rather the difference
between the human and divine creaturely being.

78. Lohse, *Short History*, 93-94, for this and the following quotation.

in 553 did not lead to unity either. The movement toward national monophysite churches in Syria and Egypt continued unabated, while the large Nestorian constituency in present-day Iran and reaching far into India felt even more alienated.

Then there occurred a shift in the other direction. Since it had been decided that there were two natures in Christ and that in Aristotelian thought a nature implied a substance and that again a will, one had to assert that there were two natural wills and two natural energies unconfoundedly, unalterably, undividedly, and inseparably present in the person of Jesus Christ. This dyotheletism (i.e., doctrine of the two wills) was sanctioned at the Sixth Ecumenical Council in Constantinople in 681 over against the rival opinion of monotheletism. Of course, the decision was correct within the framework of Chalcedon. Yet one wonders whether it did not imply dangerous implications in terms of the life and ministry of Jesus. When did he use the divine will and when the human? Such questions show that one cannot set off one nature of Christ against the other.

Again it was the emperor who saw to it that the decision fostered "unity." But in the end the church was fragmented and weakened. In Egypt and Syria monophysite national churches were established and large segments of the Christian population in Iran and far into India, China, and Central Asia constituted themselves as Nestorian churches independent of Constantinople. That a large part of the East succumbed so quickly to Islam may not be unrelated to the fact that, at least initially, these national groups felt more protection under Islamic rulers than under an emperor who wanted to dictate their religious affairs.

In the East christological concerns dominated many aspects of religious life. Even the iconoclastic controversies (disputes over the status of the images of saints and of Christ) had christological overtones. If there is such an intimate unity of the human and the divine in the person of Jesus Christ, it would be blasphemous, some argued, to depict Christ. This would imply a depiction of the deity. Such a move was forbidden in the Bible. The issue was rescued by the insight that the divine Logos had in fact become human. Images are simply a remembrance and an illustration of the Logos being human.[79] Since "the honor given to the

---

79. For the following see John of Damascus, *Exposition of the Orthodox Faith* 16, in *NPNF* 2, 9:88.

image passes over to the prototype," the image represents that which it typifies.[80] So the honor given to the images returns to Christ, for whom also the saints stand, and eventually even to God. The West was less inclined to pursue such christologically interpreted folk piety and understood the images more as didactic materials. With the iconoclastic controversies, which severely destabilized the Eastern church, we leave the formative christological age.

2. Medieval Trends

As we enter the medieval era, we immediately notice that the focus of debate had changed. In the center no longer stood Jesus Christ as that human and divine person and in his relation to God the Father, but rather the works of Christ. How could the One, who was truly God in human form, execute our redemption? The deliberations went, for the first time, in a more ecclesial direction, emphasizing the Lord's Supper, the sacrament of the real presence of Christ, but they also were directed more theologically to the issue of satisfaction. How could Jesus Christ achieve satisfaction before God, undoing our willful and sinful alienation from God? Before we briefly delineate the theory of satisfaction, culminating in the proposal of Anselm of Canterbury (ca. 1033-1109), we must first deal with an issue of a more trinitarian nature that contributed to the schism between East and West, the so-called *filioque* clause, meaning that the Holy Spirit proceeded from the Father *and* from the Son.

The *filioque* clause had come to the attention of the Patriarch of Constantinople about 883, when he wrote: "That some of those from the West are introducing the idea that the divine and Holy Spirit proceeds not only from God and the Father, but also from the Son."[81] Yet this *filioque* clause was known much earlier to Eastern theologians. Already during the pontificate of Leo III, who died in 816, some Latin monks on the Mount of Olives in Jerusalem reported that a Greek monk named John from the monastery of St. Sabas had accused the Franks of heresy

80. John of Damascus, *Exposition* 16, quoting Basil.
81. For this and the following quotation see Jaroslav Pelikan, *The Christian Tradition: A History of the Development of Doctrine*, vol. 2: *The Spirit of Eastern Christendom (600-1700)* (Chicago: University of Chicago, 1974), 183.

for teaching the *filioque*. They appealed to the pope, "prostrate on the ground and in tears to deign to investigate in the holy fathers, both Greek and Latin, who composed the creed, where it is said [that the Holy Spirit] 'proceeds from the Father and the Son.'" Yet the *filioque* dates back even further. It is already mentioned in the Athanasian Creed, which most likely dates back to the fifth or sixth century and states that "the Holy Spirit proceeds from the Father and the Son." This formulation, like many other assertions of the Athanasian Creed, shows dependence on Augustine.[82]

In his book *On the Trinity* Augustine had used the *filioque* formula when he wrote:

> God the Father alone is He from whom the Word is born, and from whom the Holy Spirit principally proceeds. And therefore I have added the word principally, because we find that the Holy Spirit proceeds from the Son also. But the Father gave Him this too, not as to one already existing, and not yet having it; but whatever He gave to the only-begotten Word, He gave by begetting Him. Therefore He so begat Him as that the common Gift should proceed from Him also, and the Holy Spirit should be the Spirit of both.[83]

Since Augustine emphasized the interrelatedness and interpenetration of Father, Son and Holy Spirit, for him the *filioque* was natural, since it showed the interrelating link between Father and Son and also emphasized with implicit reference to the Gospel of John that Jesus was the one who was sending the Spirit. For Augustine this did not mean a diminution of the status of the Spirit, as he showed in "Tractate 6" of *On the Gospel of St. John*, where he wrote: "For the Holy Spirit is God, even as the Son of God is God, and the Father God. I have said 'God' thrice, but not three Gods; for indeed it is God *thrice* rather than three Gods; because the Father, and the Son, and the Holy Ghost are one God."[84]

The *filioque* was only slowly accepted even in the Western church. Only when in Spain adoptionistic tendencies arose and it was said that the Son of God assumed the Son of man, who was then adopted and called "God," did the *filioque* gain increasing interest in combating this

---

82. Roger John Howard Collins, "Athanasianisches Symbol," in *TRE* 4:331.
83. Augustine, *On the Trinity* 15.19.29, in *NPNF 1*, 3:216.
84. Augustine, *On the Gospel of St. John* (Tract. 6.2), in *NPNF 1*, 7:39.

heresy.[85] The unity of the person was at stake here; in adoptionist thought the person was thought to be composed of two entities, since at Christ's conception the Son of man was thought to have been taken up into the unity of the person of the Son of God. The Synod of Frankfurt (794) rejected this kind of Sabellian heresy, and in 796-97, under strong influence from Charlemagne (ca. 742-814), the *filioque* was received in the creed of 381. But Pope Leo III (ca. 750-816) was reluctant to approve that change. The *filioque* safeguarded the essential equality of Father and Son, though Eastern theologians noted that the Son was moved closer to the Father than the Spirit was. They did not object so much to the theological as to the ecclesial implications. Pope Leo III seems to have known what was at stake, since he did not promulgate the *filioque* as a papal dogma. Yet he permitted the *filioque* to be taught and even confessed his own faith in "the Holy Spirit, who proceeds equally from the Father and the Son."[86] The East, however, questioned whether Rome had the authority to impose on the entire church such an addition to the Nicene Creed. The Eastern church considered the move by the Western church an act of apostasy since the Nicene Creed had been set forth by an ecumenical council of the whole church and therefore its wording could only be changed by another council. If the Western church taught differently it had abandoned its catholicity and left the union of the church. The *filioque* therefore was one of the major points of contention in the schism between East and West which occurred in 1054.

In his work *Cur Deus homo* ("Why God Became Man"), Anselm of Canterbury (ca. 1033-1109) made the first attempt to present the doctrine of redemption in a harmonious and logically consistent interpretation. A major part of his achievement was the discrediting of an older view of redemption called the "ransom theory" which maintained that humans were redeemed from the rights of the devil. The ransom theory dates back at least to Jerome, who spoke of "the devil's rights" over the human race.[87] Origen gave this view its widely popular and lasting shape. "Christ, who gave his own blood as the price for us, is rightly said to

85. See Reinhold Seeberg, *Text-Book of the History of Doctrine,* trans. Charles E. Hay (Grand Rapids: Baker, 1954), 2:30, for details.

86. As quoted by Pelikan, *The Christian Tradition,* 2:187. See Pelikan also for details.

87. So Joseph M. Colleran, in the introduction to his translation of Anselm of Canterbury, *Why God Became Man* and *The Virginal Conception and Original Sin* (Albany, N.Y.: Magi Books, 1969), 43.

have bought us back."[88] According to Origen, the devil purchased us by giving us the "money" of theft, false testimony, greediness, violence, and other wrongdoing, which are "the devil's property" that we receive when we act according to them. So we are all "his slaves who have received however insignificant a coin from this property." Christ "is said 'to buy . . . back with his precious blood' those whom the devil bought with the cheap wages of sin." Christ's redemption was accomplished by purchasing us with his own blood from the devil, who had initially bought us through the sins which we have committed.

Some theologians in the early church, like Gregory of Nyssa, adopted the statement that the ransom of Christ was paid to the devil.[89] Others, however, rejected it. John of Damascus (ca. 676-ca. 754), for instance, exclaimed: "God forbid that the blood of the Lord should have been offered to the tyrant [i.e., the devil]."[90] Since we have sinned against God, John found it more plausible that God would receive the ransom for us and that we should thus be delivered from condemnation. John spoke of a bait by which death is lured into releasing all those who would have forfeited their lives through sin. He writes: "Wherefore death approaches, and swallowing up the body as a bait is transfixed on the hook of divinity, and after tasting of a sinless and life-giving body, perishes, and brings up again all whom of old he swallowed up."

Augustine wrote in similar terms: "The Devil exalted when Christ died, and by that very death of Christ the Devil was overcome: He took food, as it were, from a trap. He gloated over the death as if he were appointed a deputy of death; that in which he rejoiced became a prison for him. The cross of the Lord became a trap for the Devil; the death of the Lord was the food by which he was ensnared."[91] Yet Augustine's mentor, Ambrose of Milan, still advanced the ransom theory. According to Ambrose, the devil had reduced the human race to perpetual captivity by the heavy debt of inherited liability, "which our debt-laden ancestor had transmitted to his posterity by inheritance. The Lord Jesus came, He offered His death for the death of all, He poured out His Blood for

---

88. See for this and the following quotations Origen, "Exodus Homily 6.9," in *FaCH* 71:296.

89. Gregory of Nyssa, *The Great Catechism* 22-24, in *NPNF* 2 5:492-4.

90. For this and the following quotation see John of Damascus, *Exposition of the Orthodox Faith* 3.27, in *NPNF* 2 9:72.

91. Augustine, "Sermon" 263.1, in *FaCH* 38:392.

the blood of all."[92] We were already in debt through the transgression of Adam and we contracted heavy debts by our own sins. Christ then paid this debt with his innocent suffering. Other theologians were more reluctant to introduce the idea that we were bought by the devil and instead were content to say that we were "abandoned by God" and "given over to the Devil."[93]

The ransom theory did not present a dualistic picture of God and the devil, but simply alerted us to the fact that we had left the domain of God and therefore were abandoned by him. Nevertheless it seemed to give too much weight to the devil. It also smacked more of a folk tale than of the biblical drama of redemption. But the ideas that humanity was in the grip of the devil and that because of humanity's sinful ways the devil had a right to keep us in his domain were just too graphic and convincing to die out easily. Even Boso, Anselm's dialogue partner in *Cur Deus homo* narrates: "We usually say, moreover, that to set man free, God must have acted against the devil more through justice than through fortitude."[94] He implicitly acknowledged that the ransom theory was still popular in his time. The main objection now brought forth by Boso against this theory was a theological one. Since both humanity and the devil are under God's dominion, it would be inconsistent and demeaning for God to plead a cause with his own creature or to make payment to it. Since justice is involved, a payment must be made, but to God and not to the devil. It was not yet recognized that the whole terminology of ransom, money, and indebtedness simply did not fit the relationship between God and humanity. In this situation Anselm introduced a novel approach that was both intellectually satisfying and no longer needed to be clothed in financial terms.

In his investigation *Why God Became Man,* Anselm of Canterbury wrestled with the following question: "For what reason or by what necessity did God become man, and by His death, as we believe and acknowledge, restore life to the world, although He would have accomplished this by means of another person, whether angelic or human, or simply by an act of His will?"[95] Having posed this question on the very

---

92. Ambrose, "Letters" 41.7, in *NPNF 2,* 10:446.
93. So John Chrysostom, "Homily 68 on the Gospel of John," in *FaCH* 41:241.
94. Anselm, *Why God Became Man* 1.7, in Colleran, 71-72.
95. Anselm, *Why God Became Man* 1.1, 64.

first page of his book, he sets out to give a reasonable explanation for the incarnation and the death of Jesus Christ. While Anselm does not cite any scriptural texts to construct his theory of atonement, his treatise and his thoughts are scripturally informed. Moreover, it was the historic achievement of Anselm to realize that the sacrifice of Christ, the redemption of humanity through Jesus Christ, was an act "addressed to God, not to man or to the devil" and that it was also compatible with the immutability of God.[96] While the notion of satisfaction finds its analogy in Germanic law, according to which someone whose honor had been violated must be compensated accordingly, the most obvious source may lie in the penitential system of the church as it was developing at that time. But already Tertullian had talked about making "satisfaction to the Lord" through repentance for sins.[97] The term "satisfaction" had a long history in theology which now came to a new high point in Anselm's satisfaction theory.

For Anselm sin is withholding from God the honor which is due him:

> A person who does not render God this honor due Him, takes from God what is His and dishonors God, and this is to commit sin. Now, as long as he does not repay what he has plundered, he remains at fault. Neither is it enough merely to return what was taken away, but on account of the insult committed, he must give back more than he took away.[98]

This puts humanity immediately in an impossible situation. We can return to God only what we have taken away, since at the most we can do what we are expected to do. We can do no more. Of course, Anselm argues, in his divine mercy God could remit our sins. Such action, however, is most unlikely, since "it is not fitting for God to do anything unjustly or inordinately."[99] If honor is withheld, punishment must follow, or some other kind of satisfaction must be obtained to reestablish the violated order. If God were to pursue the way of punishment, humanity

---

96. Jaroslav Pelikan, *The Christian Tradition*, vol. 3: *The Growth of Medieval Theology (600-1300)* (Chicago: University of Chicago Press, 1978), 139.

97. Tertullian, *On Repentance* 5, in *ANF* 3:660.

98. Anselm, *Why God Became Man* 1.11, 84.

99. Anselm, *Why God Became Man* 1.12, 87.

would be permanently ruined and God would not have accomplished his purpose of reestablishing order. The problem now arises that no one but God can make satisfaction to God, since no one can do more than what God would require from us. Any aberration from that norm could never be compensated by a human being. While God could accomplish this, he is not in need of satisfaction, since he has not fallen away. No one ought to make satisfaction except a human being.

Anselm finally arrives at the conclusion: "If no one but God can make that satisfaction and no one but man is obliged to make it, then it is necessary that a God-Man make it."[100] Such a "God-Man" must be truly divine, otherwise he would not have the means to accomplish satisfaction. And such a God-Man must be truly human, otherwise such satisfaction would never be applicable to humanity. For the honor of God this divine human being must do something for which he is not already under obligation to do so. This action cannot consist in the obedient fulfilling of God's will, since every rational creature is under the obligation to do that. The free surrender of his infinitely precious life to death would suffice, since in Anselm's opinion "mortality is a property not of pure human nature, but of corrupted human nature."[101] This means that a truly human and divine being would not have had to die. Jesus Christ, the divine human being, was truly divine and therefore his life was of infinite value and more than sufficient as payment for all the sins of the whole world. His incarnation and suffering as God-Man would satisfy the divine honor. If God were to leave them unrewarded, he would either be unjust or incapable of providing redemption. Since God cannot give anything to the Son, who needs nothing, the reward is then to the advantage of those for whom the Son died. "What greater mercy could be imagined, for example, than for God the Father to say to the sinner condemned to eternal torments and having no way to redeem himself: 'Receive my only begotten Son and present Him instead of yourself'; and for the Son Himself to say: 'Take me and redeem yourself!'"[102] Thus the sins of humanity are remitted. In this way both divine justice and mercy are preserved.

While the early church only implicitly assumed the inner necessity for the divinity of Christ, Anselm explicitly laid it out as the presupposi-

---

100. Anselm, *Why God Became Man* 2.6, 124.
101. Anselm, *Why God Became Man* 2.11, 134.
102. Anselm, *Why God Became Man* 2.20, 161-62.

tion for our salvation. In this way the divinity of Christ and his salvific work were intimately connected. Anselm also made the cross of Christ intelligible. Significant for Anselm were primarily Christ's death and to a lesser extent his incarnation. His active life on earth was of much lesser significance. Also the exclusively legal relationship between God and humanity including Jesus Christ's own activity bore the mark of Western Christianity. In contrast to this way of thinking, the New Testament is more multifaceted. The idea of a God who was so anxious to protect his honor and who could not forfeit satisfaction led centuries later to the Reformation question of how to obtain a gracious God.

Peter Abelard (ca. 1079-1142), a contemporary of Anselm, while he did not quote *Cur Deus homo*, reacted very strongly to Anselm's satisfaction theory. He in turn advanced a counterposition. Since through the works of the law no one can become righteous, God made his love manifest in Christ by assuming our nature. As our teacher and example he remained faithful unto death. The love of God manifested in Christ awakens in our heart the same kind of love toward God and humanity. Abelard wrote: "It seems to us that we are justified in the blood of Christ and reconciled to God in this, that through the singular grace manifested to us in that his Son took our nature and that teaching us by both word and example he persevered even unto death, Jesus bound us closer to himself by love, so that, fired by so great a benefit of divine grace, true charity would no longer be afraid to endure anything for his sake."[103] The work of Christ therefore inspires us to Christ-like actions. Teaching us through his example, Christ leads us to responsive love and piety.

While Abelard rejects the work of Christ as either a ransom paid to the devil or a satisfaction to God the Father, Christ does not simply become the example whom we should follow, as some of his critics have claimed.[104] Abelard leaves no doubt that Christ indeed suffered for humanity and bought and redeemed us with his blood.[105] One must also see that for Abelard the emphasis was on Jesus Christ not as the man of sorrows but as the divine Logos who would disclose to humanity the

103. Peter Abelard, *Epist. ad Romans* II.3 col. 836AB, as quoted in Jeffrey G. Sikes, *Peter Abailard* (New York: Russell & Russell, 1965), 208.

104. So correctly George P. Fedotow, *Peter Abelard*, vol. 5 of *Collected Works of George Fedotow*, ed. Richard S. Haugh, trans. Alexander I. Lisenko (Vaduz, Liechtenstein: Büchervertriebsanstalt, 1988), 186.

105. See the quotations provided by Fedotow, *Peter Abelard*, 194-95.

path of righteousness. Therefore it is understandable, though unfortunate, that he was accused of Pelagianism. It is certainly not coincidental that the reform-minded monk Bernard of Clairvaux (1090-1153) was adamantly opposed to Abelard and attempted to have him silenced by the official church. Medieval piety was more interested in satisfaction and atonement than in a Christ who taught us love and compassion. This became yet more noticeable in the Reformation quest for a gracious God, where again the works of Christ and not his teachings reigned supreme.

3. The Reformation Emphasis

Since the Reformers considered themselves as reformers within the church catholic, they had no interest in espousing new christological doctrines. This becomes at once evident when we read Article 2 of the Augsburg Confession (1530). There the Chalcedonian decision of the true divinity and true humanity of Jesus Christ is wholeheartedly accepted. Nevertheless some significant emphases in Reformation christology were made, especially by Martin Luther (1483-1546).

In 1518 at the famous Heidelberg Disputation Luther outlined his theology of the cross by saying: "That person does not deserve to be called a theologian who looks upon the invisible things of God as though they were clearly perceptible in those things which have actually happened (Rom 2:20). . . . He deserves to be called a theologian, however, who comprehends the visible and manifest things of God seen through suffering and the cross. . . . A theology of glory calls evil good and good evil. A theology of the cross calls the thing what it actually is."[106] These theses were specifically directed against scholastic theologians and their elaborate speculative theology. According to Luther, the Trinity and the person of Christ were not matters of logical inquiry or metaphysical speculation but of intense existential concern. Luther was primarily aided in his theological reasoning not by the logic of philosophy, but by the principle of *sola Scriptura* (Scripture alone). The cross, Luther discovered, was the hermeneutical key to God's salvation history and more specifically to the Christ event. Nobody, he claimed, could have invented the cross as a means of salvation. It must reflect true history and God's

---

106. Martin Luther, *Heidelberg Disputation* (1518; theses 19ff.), in *LW* 31:52-53.

working in that history toward our salvation. Therefore "the cross alone is our theology."[107] Or, as he wrote: "True theology is practical, and its foundation is Christ, whose death is appropriated to us through faith."[108] By practical theology Luther meant existential theology. This becomes at once clear in his explanation of the second article of the Apostles' Creed in *The Small Catechism.*

> I believe that Jesus Christ, true God, begotten of the Father from eternity, and also true man, born of the virgin Mary, is my Lord, who has redeemed me, a lost and condemned creature, delivered me and freed me from all sins, from death, and from the power of the devil, not with silver and gold but with his holy and precious blood and with his innocent sufferings and death, in order that I may be his, live under him in his kingdom, and serve him in everlasting righteousness, innocence, and blessedness, even as he is risen from the dead and lives and reigns to all eternity.[109]

Once the true divinity and true humanity of Jesus Christ were asserted, this "twofold nature" had immediate consequences for salvation. Salvation was accomplished by the innocent suffering and death of Christ.

While Luther was opposed to scholastic speculation, one cannot but be struck by the closeness of his thought to Anselm's theory of satisfaction.[110] Yet Luther's faith was not seeking understanding, as Anselm's faith was; rather, Luther started with the fact of the christological dogma and then deduced its existential implications. The proper relation between the divine and the human person of Christ was not to be explored but simply presupposed as the necessary basis for discerning Christ's work. Luther uses the image of "bridegroom" for Christ and the "believ-

---

107. Martin Luther, *Explanation of Ps. 5:12,* in *Operationes in Psalmos* (1519-21), in *WA* 5, 176.32-33.

108. Martin Luther, "Table Talk No. 153" (1531-32), in *LW* 54:22.

109. Martin Luther, *Small Catechism* (1529), in *The Book of Concord,* trans. and ed. Theodore G. Tappert (Philadelphia: Fortress, 1959), 345.

110. Jaroslav Pelikan, *The Christian Tradition,* vol. 4: *Reformation of Church and Dogma (1300-1700)* (Chicago: University of Chicago Press, 1984), 161, however, asserts that it does not contain any specific echo from Anselm's version of the doctrine of atonement. While Luther's argument certainly runs differently from that of Anselm, at the center of both reflections is the doctrine of satisfaction, each time focused on Christ's death, and with Chalcedon as its presupposition.

ing soul" as his bride. Since Christ is the bridegroom, Luther argues, "he must take upon himself the things which are his bride's and bestow upon her the things that are his." Since Christ is God and man in one person,

> he has neither sinned nor died, and is not condemned, and he cannot sin, die, or be condemned; his righteousness, life, and salvation are unconquerable, eternal, omnipotent. By the wedding ring of faith he shares in the sins, death, and pains of hell which are his bride's. As a matter of fact, he makes them his own and acts as if they were his own and as if he himself had sinned; he suffered, died, and descended into hell that he might overcome them all. . . . Thus the believing soul by means of the pledge of its faith is free in Christ.[111]

By this miraculous and joyful exchange Christ takes over our sins and we are endowed with his righteousness and his life.

There is not only the exchange between Christ and us and the participation in each other's destiny, but also the exchange between Christ's human and divine nature and the participation in each other's properties. This *communicatio idiomatum*, through which Christ's human nature participates in the properties of the divine nature, especially in the ubiquity, is applied by Luther to his understanding of Christ's real presence in the Lord's Supper. "If God and man are one person and the two natures are so united that they belong together more intimately than body and soul, then Christ must also be man wherever he is God. If he is both God and man at one place, why should he not also be both man and God at a second place? If he is both man and God at a second place, why not at a third, fourth, or fifth, and so forth, at all places?"[112] From the intimate relation between the human and the divine natures follows the exchangeability of the properties respective to each nature. This allows the human nature to participate in the properties of the divine nature and thereby makes possible the bodily presence of Christ in every Eucharist meal. Though Luther tries to explain how such can happen, he finally admits that he does not know the answer; he is relying on God's word as related to us in the Gospels. With this admission of divine sovereignty Luther distinguished himself notably from Zwingli.

111. Martin Luther, *The Freedom of a Christian* (1520), in *LW* 31:351-52, for this and the preceding quotation.
112. Martin Luther, *Confession concerning Christ's Supper* (1528), in *LW* 37:229.

Since Christ had ascended into heaven and was sitting at the right hand of the Father, it was clear for Huldreich Zwingli (1484-1531) that Christ could not at the same time be present in the Lord's Supper. At the most he could be spiritually present. For Luther, the right hand of God was not a specific geographic location; rather, it was a metaphor for God's almighty power in which Christ participates. Luther thus writes: "The Scriptures teach us, however, that the right hand of God is not a specific place in which a body must or may be, such as on a golden throne, but is the almighty power of God, which at one and the same time can be nowhere and yet must be everywhere."[113] God's almighty power cannot be circumscribed and measured and therefore Christ can be bodily present in and at any place including the Lord's Supper.

Luther's insistence on Christ's bodily presence in the elements of the Lord's Supper was also the result of his emphasis on Scripture alone. Since Christ has said that he would be present, Luther concluded that there was no reason to doubt his word, even if reason cannot fully comprehend how such a presence might be possible. Similar to Christ's coming to us, his presence in the elements was also a gift for the faithful that God had graciously extended to us. Christ is therefore God's gracious word to us. He did not simply render satisfaction for our sins on the cross but also fulfilled that which we could not fulfill ourselves. For instance, Luther claims: "The Law was not put in our hands for us to fulfill, but it was put in the hands of Christ who was to come for Him to fulfill."[114] He accomplished that which we were unable to do, and therefore we were placed again on God's side and stand no longer in opposition to God and his will.

With respect to the Trinity, Martin Luther emphasized its unity. He stated: "In the Godhead there is highest unity."[115] Though he did not coin the term "triune," this term seems to have come into common use due to Luther's influence.[116] In each of the persons of the Trinity the whole Godhead is present as if there were no other persons. Yet no person is for itself, as if there were no other persons who are also the

113. Martin Luther, *This Is My Body* (1527), in *LW* 37:57.
114. Martin Luther, *Lectures on Galatians* (1519) 3:20, in *LW* 27:270.
115. Martin Luther, "Sermon of June 16, 1538," in *WA* 46:436.7-8.
116. So Emmanuel Hirsch, *Hilfsbuch zum Studium der Dogmatik* (Berlin: Walter de Gruyter, 1937), 17.

Godhead.[117] Each person of the Trinity represents the whole Godhead. But none of the persons is taken on his own; they act and indeed are always together. Luther picks up here the insight of Augustine that the works of the Trinity toward the world are undivided, while within the Trinity there is a differentiation between the works of the respective persons:

> Father, Son, and Holy Spirit are a single creator, not three, against the created. This is how far the Turks and the Jews and the heathens come. But we should not see God only from the outside in his works, but God also wants to be recognized by us from the inside. But what is he inside? There he is Father, Son, Holy Spirit. This means that we do not adore three gods. Internally it is one single being in three persons.[118]

Luther admits that the Trinity is not rationally explicable. Only when we die will we be confronted with this mystery and see it. In the above quotation Luther pointed out that the activities of Christ and of the Holy Spirit are not just confined to the Christian sphere. Since they are one with God the Father, they are also present outside the Christian domain, working in the created order and preserving it. In this capacity they are recognized by Christians and non-Christians alike.

In the *Loci communes* of 1521, written by Philipp Melanchthon (1497-1560), Luther's co-worker, a decidedly existential emphasis is noticeable. Melanchthon claims that Christ "has been given as a remedy for us, or to use the language of scripture, 'for our salvation,' in some other way than that exhibited by the Scholastics."[119] Therefore to know Christ is "to know his benefits and not as they teach, to perceive his natures and the mode of his incarnation." Then he tries to describe the work of Christ in the language of Paul, so that some scholars have suggested that his *Loci communes* comes close to being a commentary on Paul's Letter to the Romans. In his later years Melanchthon elaborated more extensively on the doctrine of the Trinity.

In regard to the ubiquity of Christ, Melanchthon claimed that Christ

---

117. Cf. Martin Luther, "Thesen zur Promotion von Georg Major" (1544), *WA* 39/2:28.21-22 (theses 9-10).

118. Martin Luther, "Sermon of December 25, 1541," in *WA* 49:239.4-9.

119. Philipp Melanchthon, *The Loci Communes,* trans. Charles L. Hill (Boston: Meador, 1944), 68-69, for this and the following quotation.

is everywhere present according to his person. But he did not extend the ubiquity to the body of Christ.[120] According to Melanchthon there is no ubiquity of the human nature of Christ as such but only of his person. The person of Christ is then still understood to be actually present in the Lord's Supper.

We noted that Huldreich Zwingli rejected Luther's claim of the ubiquity of the human nature of Christ and its real presence in the Lord's Supper. According to Zwingli's more literalistic view, Christ's body is spatially limited and, since his ascension, is present at a certain locale in heaven.[121] Zwingli does admit the communication between the respective properties of both natures of Christ. He speaks, for instance, of Christ as eternal God and of Christ as having died for us, but at the same time he strictly distinguishes between the two natures of Christ.[122] The limited cannot become unlimited, since it is created.[123] Zwingli maintained the tradition that Mary can rightfully be called "mother of God"; "she has borne the one who is God and man according to his humanity, since nobody can give birth to the Godhead."[124] Zwingli was correct in emphasizing the unity of the person of Christ, but he could not see the need for the togetherness of the two natures, fearing that the human would be swallowed up by the divine. Therefore he restricted Christ's actual presence to his presence at the right hand of God the Father, while in the Lord's Supper he conceded at the most Christ's spiritual presence. It is not surprising that Luther accused Zwingli of advocating Nestorian teachings, since in his divinity Christ seemed to be removed from the earth.[125]

John Calvin (1509-64), on the other hand, cautioned that "if to fill all things in an invisible manner is numbered among the gifts of the glorified body, it is plain that the substance of the body is wiped out, and that no difference between deity and human nature is left."[126] Calvin

---

120. Philipp Melanchthon, *CR* 7:780, in a letter to Osiander of May 1, 1551.

121. Huldreich Zwingli, *Amica exegesis . . . ad Martinum Lutherum* (1527), in *CR* 92:695.3–696.9.

122. Zwingli, *Amica exegesis,* in *CR* 92:679-82.

123. Huldreich Zwingli, "An den Rat von Nürnberg" (July 2, 1526), in *CR* 95:640.2-3.

124. Huldreich Zwingli, *Eine Antwort, Valentin Compar gegeben* (1525), in *CR* 91:117.29ff.

125. Martin Luther, *Von den Konzilien und Kirchen* (1539), *WA* 50:591.9-21.

126. John Calvin, *Institutes of the Christian Religion* 4.17.29, ed. John T. McNeill, trans. Ford Lewis Battles (Philadelphia: Westminster, 1960), 2:1398-99.

continually tried to emphasize the difference between the two natures in Jesus Christ. In a way similar to that of the unity of body and soul in the human person, both entities of the whole can retain their peculiar properties. He wrote: "For we affirm his divinity so joined and united with his humanity that each retains its distinctive nature unimpaired, and yet these two natures constitute one Christ." Yet then he continued a little later to write that the Scriptures attribute to Christ sometimes those things that "must be referred solely to his humanity, sometimes what belongs uniquely to his divinity; and sometimes what embraces both natures but fits neither alone. And they so earnestly express this union of the two natures that is in Christ as sometimes to interchange them. This figure of speech is called by the ancient writers 'the communication of properties.'"[127] The strict distinction between the two natures in Jesus Christ is mitigated by scriptural influence and even leads Calvin to assert an actual communication of the respective properties of each nature. He differs here from Zwingli, who is more influenced by philosophical consideration and who admits a communication of the properties only in a metaphorical way.[128]

Calvin does not go as far as Luther in asserting that Christ is present in the Lord's Supper in his true humanity. Christ "declares his flesh the food of my soul, his blood its drink."[129] Yet Christ does not descend to us, since "the secret working of the Spirit, which unites Christ himself to us," makes such descent unnecessary. According to Calvin our souls are united with Christ, who remains in the celestial kingdom at the right hand of the Father. As in the case of Luther, however, an existential interest comes to the fore here when Calvin declares: "For that is to possess of Christ entire, crucified, that we may enjoy all his benefits."[130] A bodily and real presence in the Lord's Supper is not needed, since the benefits of the Lord's Supper are union with Christ. Calvin does not regard this as a union with Christ in and with the elements but rather with the celestial Christ through the elements. The intentions of Calvin and Luther are quite similar if not identical. Yet the means of achieving

---

127. For this and the preceding quotation see Calvin, *Institutes* 2.14.1; 1:482-83.

128. So also Karl-Heinz zur Mühlen, "Jesus Christus IV: Reformationszeit," in *TRE* 16:764.

129. For this and the following quotation see Calvin, *Institutes* 4.17.31-32; 2:1403.

130. Calvin, *Institutes* 4.17.33; 2:1405.

them is quite different, the one looking to the heavenly Christ at the right hand of the Father, and the other to the Christ present in the elements of the Lord's Supper.

The christological controversies between Calvinist and Lutheran theologians and also among Lutheran theologians themselves concerning the mode of the actual presence of Christ went on for at least another century after the deaths of both Luther and Calvin. Like the christological controversies following Chalcedon, these post-Reformation controversies pursued dead ends. They led away from the central emphasis of the Reformation, that Christ being truly divine and truly human is not just a logical theory to be explored in all its ramifications, but foremost the way in which God worked out salvation for humanity. The Reformers did not talk only about the works of Christ but also of his office. By this they primarily meant his task of bringing salvation to humanity and not so much his threefold office as king, priest and prophet, which was emphasized initially by Calvin and later by Lutheran and Reformed Orthodoxy.[131]

4. The Modern Era

When we come to the modern era, we want to pay attention to the Enlightenment and Pietism, which in many areas go hand in hand, then to the nineteenth century, and then to the classical voices of the twentieth century, before surveying the present scene. Already at the time of the Reformation there was one stream which in some ways bore decidedly modern marks, that of the antitrinitarian movement.

Antitrinitarians were found among representatives of the Anabaptists, the Spiritualists, and the Enthusiasts. Usually they were persecuted wherever found, as we see in the cases of Michael Servetus (1511-53), who was burned in Geneva, and Valentino Gentile (1520-66), who was decapitated in Berne. In Transsylvania Saxony they were temporarily given refuge, and also in Poland, where they founded their own settle-

---

131. For Luther's doctrine of the office of Christ see the quotations in Hirsch, *Hilfsbuch zum Studium der Dogmatik* , 50-66, who emphasizes this aspect as one of the new developments in christology. It is interesting that Karl-Heinz zur Mühlen does not mention this aspect. Also Jaroslav Pelikan is remarkably silent regarding this teaching.

ment in Rakow in the district of Sandomierz. There they came mainly from among the Anabaptists and were influenced after 1580 by Faustus Socinus (1539-1604). The Italian names of many leading anti-trinitarians betrays a close affinity to Italy, especially to Italian humanists. It is interesting that though Faustus Socinus put himself totally at the service of his Polish brethren, he never actually became a member of the Anabaptists, since he did not allow himself to be rebaptized. In the *Tractate concerning God, Christ, and the Holy Spirit,* written after 1580, he claimed that nowhere in Scripture is the Holy Spirit designated as God. Often things are attributed to him that are proper to God. God is essentially one; he is neither triune nor twofold. Even when Christ is named God in the Bible, this does not refer to his being but only to the peculiarity of his being.[132] This means Jesus is divine only insofar as the human person Jesus is designated by God in a special way. Since the true divinity and the true humanity of Christ were discredited, Socinus saw no reason for an exchange of the divine and human properties in Jesus. Whatever Jesus did or said refers to the actual human being Jesus of Nazareth. Though conceived by the Holy Spirit, Jesus was not son of God according to his body and a human being according to the spirit. The two "natures" of Jesus existed only on account of his divine origin and his sinless life.

While Socinus continuously cited biblical passages to support his claims, it was only a question of time until the same kind of statements would be made without explicit reference to the Bible. Moreover, Socinus depicted Christ primarily as a teacher and not so much as a savior providing satisfaction for our sinfulness or undergoing the punishment that we would have deserved. Rather, Christ aids us in our ethical striving for perfection and in our general development. Thus ethics seems to replace dogmatics.[133] When we encounter actual representatives of the Enlightenment, both references to Scripture and interest in trinitarian issues have subsided. It is now clearly understood that there is only one God, if any, whose involvement with the world and with humans can be fathomed by human reason.

---

132. Fausto Sozzini, *Traktat über Gott, Christus und den Heiligen Geist,* in *Der linke Flügel der Reformation,* ed. Heinold Fast (Bremen: Carl Schünemann, 1962), 413.

133. Walter Sparn, "Jesus Christus V: Vom Tridentinum bis zur Aufklärung," in *TRE* 17:7-8.

Indicative of the reductionistic mood that we encounter in the commencing phase of the Enlightenment is Gottfried Wilhelm von Leibniz (1646-1716) and his *Discourse on Metaphysics* (1710). Leibniz deals extensively with God, his activity in the world, and the universal happiness and perfection he will bring about. Only in the last chapter does he even mention Jesus Christ, under the heading: "Jesus Christ has revealed to men the mystery and the admirable laws of the kingdom of heaven and the greatness of the supreme happiness which God has prepared for those who love him."[134] Leibniz concedes that the ancient philosophers knew very little of these important truths, and therefore Jesus Christ expressed them "divinely well. . . . His gospel has entirely changed the face of human affairs. It has brought us to know the kingdom of heaven, or that perfect republic of spirits which deserves to be called the city of God. He it is who discovered to us its wonderful laws. He alone has made us to see how much God loves us and with what care everything that concerns us has been provided for." Jesus Christ is the teacher who instructs us concerning the loving will of God, who wants our best, and who will bring us to everlasting happiness. God is in ultimate control and cares more for our souls than for the whole world. We could concede that Leibniz still maintains an existential interest in christology, since Christ shows us what God has wrought for us. Yet the content of his christology is almost exclusively one of ethical instructions on how to lead a good life. Though eternal life is presupposed and stands at the end and culmination of all human and divine endeavors, Jesus as a figure of history has become rather pale. As Adolf von Harnack (1851-1930) said a few centuries later, he is only the one who points us to the Father.

The position of Leibniz represents the leading intellectual sentiment in Europe of his time. Yet there was also a different current — Pietism. Like the Enlightenment movement, it was ecumenically oriented, appealing both to the educated and to the general population. Its emphasis was on rebirth, on loving the neighbor in word and deed as Jesus has taught us, and on redemption from death and the devil, forgiveness of sins, and eternal happiness, wrought through Jesus' sacrifice. Jesus again occupied

---

134. For this and the following quotation see Gottfried Wilhelm von Leibniz, *Discourse on Metaphysics* 37, in *The Rationalists: René Descartes, Benedict de Spinoza, Gottfried Wilhelm Freiherr von Leibniz*, trans. George Montgomery, rev. Albert R. Chandler (New York: Doubleday, 1960), 453.

the central stage of theological reflection, not just as the teacher of righteousness, but also as the one who provides our redemption.[135] The theological leader of Pietism was Philipp Jacob Spener (1635-1705), who portrayed a mystical spiritualism that soon became part of the official church's teachings and especially its hymnody. His main writing, *Pia Desideria,* or *A Cordial Desire for a God-Pleasing Improvement of the Truly Protestant Churches Including Some Simple Christian Proposals in That Regard* (1675), was immediately translated into Latin to gain wider circulation. In 1666 Spener was elected senior pastor in Frankfurt/Main, in 1686 he was appointed court preacher in Dresden, the most prestigious position that a pastor could obtain at that time in Germany, and in 1691 he became senior pastor at St. Nicolai in Berlin, where he stayed until his death. The latter was actually the most important position, because there he exerted immense influence on the Prussian Court, making Berlin the spiritual center of Germany. Spener picked up the central Lutheran concerns, such as the miraculous and happy exchange between Christ and us through which we come to stand in Christ's place and are accorded righteousness and that we are exempted from God's judgment.[136] The work of Christ becomes important as he redeems us from sin, secures justification for us, and allows us to be reborn through the gospel and the Holy Spirit.

Count Nicholas Ludwig von Zinzendorf (1700-1760) was a Pietist of a very special kind. Zinzendorf was born of a noble family and educated in Halle, where he became acquainted with Pietism. Against his own intentions he became the supervisor and counselor of a newly organized congregation of Moravian immigrants in Herrnhut, Silesia. Though initially working at the court in Dresden, he became a pastor, adopted Lutheranism, and was also consecrated bishop of the Brethren Community (1737). He traveled extensively to the United States, Great Britain, Switzerland, and the Netherlands. Interesting for us is his special devotion to Jesus, which in metaphors and action became almost excessive, especially his devotion to the wounds of Christ or his explicit references to the Song of Solomon. At the end of his life he returned to a more sober appreciation of the Christian faith.

135. Philipp Jacob Spener, *Pia Desideria* (excerpts), in *Das Zeitalter des Pietismus,* ed. Martin Schmidt and Wilhelm Jannasch (Bremen: Carl Schünemann, 1965), 19-20.
136. See Philipp Jacob Spener, "Sermon 52" on Jeremiah 23:6, in *Das Zeitalter des Pietismus,* 49.

In his explanation of the second article of the Apostles' Creed, Zinzendorf emphasized that not only for oneself, but also for proclamation's sake, it is important to know who Christ was according to his person and his office.[137] Similarly, one will not be freed from sin and become pious unless one has recognized Jesus as one's savior. This emphasis on the primacy of Jesus as savior is a clear rejection of the Enlightenment tendency to reduce Jesus to an educator of an upright and God-pleasing life. Zinzendorf states: "We must believe: 1. that he [Jesus] is a savior of the sinful who has died for the sins of all the world. . . . [and] that he has bought, reconciled and saved us and has loved us so much that he has given his life for us, that he also, since he has deemed our souls as so important and has bought them so dearly, has the first right to us and that he alone should be accorded all our devotion."[138] Though Zinzendorf leaves no doubt that Jesus Christ is our savior and tries to show this with many biblical references, he does not once mention that Jesus is truly human and truly divine, though there is no reason to doubt his adherence to this tenet.

Central to Zinzendorf's christology is Christ the Savior. He is the chosen head in whose nail wounds we discover our divine election.[139] Through his cleft side he leads our souls to him; he is the lamb who was slain and the bridegroom of our souls, who loves us above everyone else. When we know about his death, we know about God's essence: he is a loving God. Jesus died for us on the cross and is the friend of our soul who gives us absolution. These are some of the metaphors which Zinzendorf used and for which he was severely criticized. Essentially Zinzendorf presents a Lutheran theology of the cross, albeit often clothed in mystical terminology. This mysticism, centered in Christ's passion and in him as the bridegroom of our soul, even advocates the image that Jesus becomes our friend and brother.[140] This implies, however, the

137. See for the following Nikolaus von Zinzendorf, "Erste Rede über die Erklärung des zweiten Artikels des christlichen Glaubens" (1738), in *Das Zeitalter des Pietismus,* 320.

138. Zinzendorf, "Erste Rede über die Erklärung des zweiten Artikels des christlichen Glaubens," 324.

139. For the following see his poem "Aufrichtige Erklärung, wies ihm ums Herz ist" (1734), in *Das Zeitalter des Pietismus,* 309ff.

140. See Leiv Aalen, *Die Theologie des jungen Zinzendorf* (Berlin: Lutherisches Verlagshaus, 1966), 313, who, however, does not draw on these consequences, which also become evident in Schleiermacher, who, in turn, was influenced by Zinzendorf.

danger that Christ be so drawn into our sphere that he becomes one of us and is basically our guide and our teacher in terms of right living. Zinzendorf unintentionally furthered the emphasis on the humanness of Jesus, which is the nearly exclusive topic of Enlightenment christology.

Gotthold Ephraim Lessing (1729-81) may suffice to illustrate the general trend of the Enlightenment. We have encountered him already as the editor of the *Wolfenbüttel Fragments,* in which capacity he showed how problematic it was to secure reliable information on the Jesus of history in order to provide a foundation for Christian dogma. But Lessing was a multifaceted person. As shown in his editing of the *Wolfenbüttel Fragments,* he was quite hesitant to volunteer his own theological position. The influence of Leibniz can be seen, for instance, in the posthumously published fragment *The Christianity of Reason* (ca. 1752/53). In a deductive way he arrived at the notion that "God created from eternity a being lacking no perfection which he himself possessed. This being is called in Scripture the Son of God, or, which would be still better, the Son-God. A God because he lacks none of the attributes which belong to God."[141] Since the greatest harmony must exist between two things which have everything in common with each other, "the harmony which exists between them is called by Scripture *the Spirit which proceeds from the Father and Son.*" Since the harmony is contingent upon God the Father and God the Son, and both could not be God unless this harmony existed, Lessing further concluded that *"all three are one."* Though Lessing called Christ created and conceived of the Spirit only as the provider of harmony between Father and Son, he nevertheless maintained with tradition that the Spirit proceeds from the Father and the Son and that all three are one. Whether that was his actual standpoint is difficult to judge. It could just have been a logical exercise, since this fragment is stringently deductive in tone.

Quite different and much more typical of Lessing's own convictions is a one-page manuscript of 1780 called *The Religion of Christ.* Because of the conciseness of this document and the significance of its statements, and also because of its analogy with many items mentioned in the *Wolfenbüttel Fragments,* I quote this manuscript in its entirety:

141. See Gotthold Ephraim Lessing, *The Christianity of Reason,* in *Lessing's Theological Writings,* trans. Henry Chadwick (London: Adam & Charles Black, 1956), 99-100, for this and the following quotations.

1. It is a question whether Christ was more than a mere man. That he was a real man if he was a man at all, and that he never ceased to be a man, is not in dispute.
2. It follows that the religion of Christ and the Christian religion are two quite different things.
3. The former, the religion of Christ, is that religion which as a man he himself recognized and practiced; which every man has in common with him; which every man must so much the more desire to have in common with him, the more exalted and admirable the character which he attributes to Christ as a mere man.
4. The latter, the Christian religion, is that religion which accepts it as true that he was more than a man, and makes Christ himself, as such, the object of its worship.
5. How these two religions, the religion of Christ and the Christian religion, can exist in Christ in one and the same person, is inconceivable.
6. The doctrines and tenets of both could hardly be found in one and the same book. At least it is obvious that the former, that is, the religion of Christ, is contained in the evangelists quite differently from the Christian religion.
7. The religion of Christ is therein contained in the clearest and most lucid language.
8. On the other hand, the Christian religion is so uncertain and ambiguous, that there is scarcely a single passage which, in all the history of the world, has been interpreted in the same way by two men.[142]

Lessing marked here the starting point of a contemporary christology from below. He claimed that Jesus was certainly a historical human being and questioned whether he was more than that. Then he distinguished between the religion of Christ and the Christian religion. The former was reduced to that which general revelation makes accessible to humanity; Jesus was an exponent of general religion. The Christian religion claims on the basis of a special revelation that Jesus is more than a human being and then makes him the object of its worship. Since the Christian religion is based on revelation and since revelation is

142. Lessing, *The Religion of Christ*, in *Lessing's Theological Writings*, 106.

susceptible to many different interpretations, there is no agreement among Christians what the Christian religion ought to be. This stands in contrast to the religion of reason, since the latter relies on a general revelation which is uniform in all humanity. There is little doubt as to what Lessing opted for — not the Christian religion but the "religion of Christ." But even this kind of religion had become questionable since at least Kant. According to Kant, it is at the most a practical necessity, arising from our perception of the inadequacy of this world and the need for a final resolution of its contradictions. Yet such a religion, as Ludwig Feuerbach (1804-72) has reminded us, may simply result from wishful thinking as a projection of our desires on the screen of transcendence. This means that the so-called religion of Christ is not any more universal and warranted than the Christian religion. At the end of the Enlightenment it was realized that if one wanted to continue to talk about religion, one was no better off with the religion of Christ than with the Christian religion. So why not stay with the Christian religion? This was the avenue that was pursued by Friedrich Schleiermacher (1768-1834).

During the Enlightenment Jesus was often considered to be just an epiphenomenon of God.[143] Friedrich Schleiermacher provided the first effort to establish Jesus Christ again in his own right. Schleiermacher was not just the first one who lectured regularly on Jesus of Nazareth, but in his dogmatics, *The Christian Faith,* he also attempted to found his christology on the historical Jesus, though he consistently called him Christ and not Jesus.[144] Schleiermacher considered Jesus to be the perfect human being.[145] He constructed his christology exclusively from Jesus' peculiar activity and not from his being. Christ's dignity was seen to be identical with his activity and was to be evaluated with the whole of his life in view.[146] Nevertheless God was in Christ Jesus. "What comes into existence through the being of God in Christ is all perfectly human, and in its totality constitutes a unity, the unity of a natural life-history, in

143. See John Macquarrie, "Jesus Christ: VI Neuzeit (1789 bis zur Gegenwart)," in *TRE* 17:16-42, who deals extensively with the God issue (deism, natural religion, etc.) in the first part of his article, since this was the emphasis of that earlier period.

144. Macquarrie, "Jesus Christ: VI Neuzeit," *TRE* 17:19, calls Schleiermacher's christology "a classical example" of "a Christology from below."

145. Friedrich Schleiermacher, *The Christian Faith* §92, ed. H. R. Macintosh and J. S. Stewart (Edinburgh: T. & T. Clark, 1948), 374.

146. Schleiermacher, *The Christian Faith* §93.1, 377.

which everything that emerges is purely human."[147] With this presupposition it is no surprise that Schleiermacher understands Jesus to be a
child of his time, "since mind and understanding drew their nourishment
solely from this surrounding world."[148] Since he considered the union
between the human and the divine in Jesus to be one of the person, a
communication of the properties of each nature would cancel their union
and was therefore rejected by Schleiermacher.[149] Even the propriety of
the term "nature" was questioned. According to Schleiermacher nature
is the summary of all finite existence, which makes it problematic to
attribute a nature to God and to talk about the divine nature of Christ.[150]
Schleiermacher preferred to talk about the unity of the essence. This
unity shows itself such that "the human God-consciousness becomes an
existence of God in human nature."[151] Jesus mediates all existence of
God in the world and all revelation of God through the world, since he
develops in himself the potency of a unique God-consciousness.

Schleiermacher does not need then the resurrection and ascension
of Christ or "the prediction of his return to judgment" as properly
constituent parts of the doctrine of the person of Christ. "The redeeming
efficacy of Christ depends upon the being of God in Him, and faith in
Him is grounded upon the impression that such a being of God indwells
Him."[152] Since the disciples recognized Jesus as Son of God without
knowing of the resurrection and ascension, we do not need these items
either in acknowledging Jesus Christ as Son of God. Schleiermacher did
not take into consideration how ambivalent any pre-Easter confessions
of Christ were; there is a continuity of the impression that Jesus made
throughout history. The salvational activity of Christ consists in his
exerting his influence upon his followers, in the "person-forming divine
influence upon human nature." The activity of the redeemer is "world-
forming, and its object is the human nature, in the totality of which the
powerful God-consciousness is to be implanted as a new vital principle."[153] Jesus is no longer the ethical example, as in classical Enlight-

---

147. Schleiermacher, *The Christian Faith* §97.3, 409.
148. Schleiermacher, *The Christian Faith* §93.3, 382.
149. Schleiermacher, *The Christian Faith* §97.5, 413.
150. Schleiermacher, *The Christian Faith* §96.1, 392.
151. Schleiermacher, *The Christian Faith* §94.2, 388.
152. Schleiermacher, *The Christian Faith* §99.1, 417-18.
153. Schleiermacher, *The Christian Faith* §100.2, 427, for this and the preceding quotation.

enment christology, but he is, so to speak, the opening in the human sphere through which God exerts his influence on us and shapes us into new beings. Jesus is no divine-human being as in Chalcedonian christology, but a truly human being in whom the divine is present under the guise of the human. Any superhuman phenomenon, such as the virgin birth or the resurrection, is seen as dogmatically irrelevant. An ontological difference between us and Jesus Christ would be difficult to maintain.

While Schleiermacher shied away from stating that Jesus was more than a unique human being, Georg Wilhelm Friedrich Hegel (1770-1831) had no such hesitations and considered it to be most logical that in the human person Jesus the divine was indeed present to bring out the uniqueness of Jesus Christ. Hegel wrote in his youth an essay on the life of Jesus. This concern for the Jesus of history is still prevalent in *The Positivity of the Christian Religion* (1795-1800), of which the first two parts were written when Hegel was twenty-five years old and the third part a few years later. The treatise, which was only posthumously published, states in a tone similar to that of Kant that Jesus "was the teacher of a purely moral religion, not a positive one."[154] Jesus was a teacher of the religion of reason and not of a specially revealed religion. The content of his teachings was basically morals. His miracles were not intended to form the foundation of doctrines, for they cannot rest on observed facts. They were simply meant to awaken the attention of a people deaf to morality. Since the Jews expected a Messiah who was to rebuild the Jewish state from its foundations, Jesus could not exactly contradict their Messianic ideas if he wanted to gain a hearing. Nevertheless he "tried to lead their messianic hopes into the moral realm and dated his appearance in his glory at a time after his death."[155]

We hear that "much of the confidence and attention which Jesus won" from the Jews must be ascribed to his miracles.[156] But Hegel also pointed out that "we must also notice the command which Jesus gives to his disciples after his resurrection to spread his doctrine and his name.

---

154. For this quotation and the following see Georg Wilhelm Friedrich Hegel, *The Positivity of the Christian Religion* §4, in G. W. F. Hegel, *Early Theological Writings*, trans. T. M. Knox (Chicago: University of Chicago, 1948), 71.

155. Hegel, *Positivity* §8, 77.

156. Hegel, *Positivity* §9, 78.

This command (especially as worded in Mk. 16:15-18) characterizes the teacher of a positive religion just as markedly as the touching form of his parting words before his death characterizes the teacher of virtue. . . . The religion of Jesus became a *positive* doctrine about *virtue*."[157] Like Kant, Hegel maintained that both the religion of Jesus and the Christian religion focus on morality or virtue. But there are two distinct differences from the Kantian position. First, Hegel is much more interested in the Jesus of history than is Kant; and second, he gives the historical accounts of the Gospels much more credence (including miracles and the resurrection) than either Kant or Schleiermacher had done. Hegel also indicates that the transition from a natural religion to a positive religion is based on (divine) authority. This positive religion is rooted in the life of Jesus.[158]

In his 1821 *Lectures on the Philosophy of Religion* Hegel moved a decisive step further. "Christianity, as distinct from all other religions, . . . is the perfect religion," since it is "the outcome and expression of the eternal dialectic immanent in God's own being as it works itself out under the conditions of time and space."[159] Hegel arrives at a synthesis of biblical insight and the logic of dialectic. Though quite often he sounds otherwise, he knows that it makes sense to argue theologically not from the standpoint of philosophical speculation or speculative thinking but from history. When he presses therefore for the unity of the divine and human nature, he sees that in Christianity it has obtained "for humanity the form of immediate, sensible perception and external existence; it appears as something seen and experienced in the world. . . . *In order for this divine-human unity to become certain for man, God had to appear in the world in the flesh.*"[160] This union of the divine and the human had to occur in a single human being, because if it had happened in humanity in general, the singularity and particularity of the union could not have been maintained.

157. Hegel, *Positivity* §§14-15, 83 and 86.

158. Therefore it is correct to say with James Yerkes, *The Christology of Hegel* (Missoula, Mont.: Scholars, 1978), 309, that Hegel wanted to refute the epistemological skepticism and the vague and vacuous religious subjectivism that he encountered in Kant.

159. So rightly Bernard M. G. Reardon, *Hegel's Philosophy of Religion* (New York: Barnes & Noble, 1977), 59.

160. Georg Wilhelm Friedrich Hegel, *The Christian Religion: Lectures on the Philosophy of Religion*, part 3: *The Revelatory, Consummate, Absolute Religion*, ed. and trans. Peter C. Hodgson (Missoula, Mont.: Scholars, 1979), 181.

185

The appearance of God in humanity has two aspects for Hegel: "The first concerns the content of the appearance, which is the unity of the finite and the infinite, the fact that God is not an abstraction but a concrete God." The second aspect is more philosophical: "God, considered in terms of his eternal Idea, has to generate the Son, has to distinguish himself from himself; he is this process of differentiating, namely, love and Spirit."[161] This would mean that Jesus as the Son of God is posited by God over against himself as his other. Hegel, of course, has no problem in seeing not only a relational unity but also an ontological one between Jesus and God the Father. Jesus is both divine and human. When Hegel mentions the teaching of Jesus and emphasizes thereby the centrality of love, one could again be reminded of a moral gospel. Yet such a notion is immediately pushed aside when he states that such a love is directed against the established order of Judaism, against everything established, and therefore is a breaking away from the usual.[162]

Quite interesting is Hegel's interpretation of Jesus' death. His death represents, first, "the highest pinnacle of finitude."[163] It is, second, "the highest love," because "Christ [has been] given up *for us,* [and that his death] may be represented as a sacrificial death, as the act of absolute satisfaction."[164] Death is, in general, the extreme limit of finitude and at the same time the dissolution of limitation. Jesus' death, "this suffering, the anguish of death, is the moment of the reconciliation of Spirit with itself, with what it contains implicitly."[165] Hegel even goes one step further, stating: "God has died: This is the negation, and this is a moment of the divine nature, of God himself. In this death, accordingly, God is satisfied. God cannot be satisfied by something else, only by himself. The satisfaction consists in the fact that the first moment, that of immediacy, is negated; only then does God attain peace with himself, only then is spirituality posited."[166] Yet Hegel does not stop with the death of God, as later death-of-God theologians would do. He proceeds so to speak from Good Friday to Easter Sunday, claiming: "The process does not

161. Hegel, *The Christian Religion,* 3:190-200.
162. Hegel, *The Christian Religion,* 3:188.
163. Hegel, *The Christian Religion,* 3:201.
164. Hegel, *The Christian Religion,* 3:202.
165. Hegel, *The Christian Religion,* 3:203.
166. Hegel, *The Christian Religion,* 3:209-10.

come to a halt at this point; rather, a reversal takes place: God, that is to say, maintains himself in this process, and the latter is only the death of death. God rises again to life, and thus things are reversed."[167] Hegel rightly refers here to the resurrection but cautions that in essence it belongs to faith, since it is not an external history suitable for unbelief.

In an amazing and daring way, Hegel combined his logic of dialectic with biblical insights. In Jesus the divine-human encounter validated itself, and the universal principle of history became concrete in a single human being. While Hegel did not remain captive to the Enlightenment spirit that eliminated everything in Jesus which went beyond that which could be expected to occur to a strictly human being, he turned Jesus into such a paradigmatic and universalized human being that the temptation arose again to detach Jesus from history, as David Friedrich Strauss would do later.[168] Positively, Hegel showed that logic need not mitigate against that which is central to the Christian understanding of Jesus, that he is truly human and divine. To the contrary, only from that point of departure does it make sense to talk about the Christian religion.

Albrecht Ritschl (1822-1889) was one of the leading Protestant theologians of the latter half of the nineteenth century. In his christology he was influenced by Schleiermacher, but in its philosophical undergirding also by Kant. Like Schleiermacher, Ritschl emphasized that the vocation of Jesus was central to his person and mission. He tried to construct a christology from below, stating: "The estimate of Christ . . . is intentionally directed with the greatest possible exactness to the historically certified characteristics of His active life, but at the same time it is undertaken from the standpoint of the community of the kingdom of God founded by Him. These two criteria, historical and religious, for the understanding of His person, should be coincident, inasmuch as the purpose of Christ was directed to the founding of a community in which He was to be recognized in religious faith as the Son of God."[169] With this emphasis on the historically verifiable, there were many items, such as Jesus' preexistence, his ascended state, or the relationship of the divine

---

167. Hegel, *The Christian Religion*, 212.

168. For the contribution of D. F. Strauss, see chap. 1 above.

169. Albrecht Ritschl, *Introduction in the Christian Religion* §25, trans. Alice Mead Swing, in Albert Temple Swing, *The Theology of Albrecht Ritschl,* together with *Instruction in the Christian Religion* (London: Longmans, Green, and Co., 1901), 200.

and human natures, that were of no interest to Ritschl. They are not "historically certified characteristics of Jesus' active life."

Ritschl wanted to restrict himself to the purely human aspect of Jesus and evaluate this theologically. According to Ritschl, Jesus was conscious of the new and hitherto unknown relation to God, and said so to his disciples; and his aim was to bring his disciples into the same attitude toward the world as his own, and to the same estimate of themselves, that under these conditions he might enlist them in the worldwide mission of the Kingdom of God, which he knew to be not only his own business, but theirs.[170]

Jesus is the model and the leader who will bring his followers to the same understanding of God and the world that he displayed. This holds true not only for his disciples but also for us, since "only through the impulse and direction we receive from Him, is it possible for us to enter into His relation to God and to the world."[171] It is interesting that Ritschl continually compares Jesus to founders of other religions, such as Zoroaster, Buddha, Moses, or Mohammed. Thus he does not stay within the narrow confines of the Christian faith and give us a simple historical portrait. As a result of his comparison, he is convinced that Jesus "brings the perfect revelation of God, so that beyond what He brings no further revelation is conceivable or is to be looked for." We can do nothing other "than regard Christ as the Bearer of the final revelation of God."[172]

The closeness of Jesus to God is not seen in ontological terms, since they cannot be historically ascertained, but in strictly relational categories. Again the ethical aspect is dominant, which is demonstrated by Ritschl's picking up Irenaeus's notion that God became human so that humanity might become God-like. Through this deification process the members of the community of Christ should gain mastery of the world. Important for Ritschl is Christ's priesthood, not in terms of his self-sacrifice, but in that Christ as priest stood in the highest possible relation with God and exercised this fellowship at each moment of his life. "Every

170. Albrecht Ritschl, *The Christian Doctrine of Justification and Reconciliation*, trans. H. R. Mackintosh and A. B. Macaulay (New York: Charles Scribner's, 1900), §44, 386.
171. Ritschl, *Christian Doctrine of Justification and Reconciliation*, §44, 387.
172. For this and the preceding quotation see Ritschl, *Christian Doctrine of Justification and Reconciliation*, §44, 388.

act and word of His vocation arose out of His religious relation to God."[173] Jesus brought humanity together through the motif of universal love by including all in the Kingdom of God. In bringing about this union Jesus was conscious of exercising in his own person the lordship of God, since he enjoyed such a certainty in his own particular vocation. According to Ritschl, such action presupposes that he apprehended himself as the Son of God, a relationship which he continuously exercised. Even Jesus' death cannot be seen as a satisfaction of divine justice but rather as the fulfillment of his vocation.[174] Since Jesus was faithful to God, he is the highest example for overcoming the world, and in doing so, Jesus served God's intention for him. It is important that Jesus was ready to suffer everything, even death, for the sake of his calling. This showed both his dominion over the world and his faithfulness to God.

Can we conclude from Ritschl's remarks that he considered Jesus to have been just an exceptional human being who was unwaveringly true to what he was supposed to be? Certainly Ritschl avoids any ontological signification of Jesus. For this he earned the wrath of his orthodox colleagues. But then, we read about Jesus: "Accordingly, His resurrection through the power of God is the consistent completion, corresponding to the worth of His personality, of the revelation through Him, which is final both in respect to the actual will of God and to the destiny of man."[175] Ritschl does not give us any clues as to how the resurrection ought to be interpreted. It almost looks as if the resurrection is a reward for Jesus for being faithful to his call. Should this mean that Ritschl works with an implicit christological ontology that he did not dare to bring out in the open because he wanted to stay within what was acceptable for nineteenth-century materialism? Perhaps one should give Ritschl's christology more credence than some of his orthodox contemporaries were willing to do.

Another nineteenth-century figure, Søren Kierkegaard (1813-55), was unwilling to succumb to the dominant materialistic stream of his time. His christology as well as most of his philosophy can be understood as a vehement protest against the prevailing trends of his time. Jesus as

---

173. Ritschl, *Christian Doctrine of Justification and Reconciliation*, §50, 482.

174. For the following see David L. Mueller, *Introduction to the Theology of Albrecht Ritschl* (Philadelphia: Westminster, 1969), 61.

175. Ritschl, *Introduction in the Christian Religion* §23, 198-99.

depicted by Kierkegaard is a human being, not an idealized God or some kind of docetic being.[176] Yet this human being Jesus is also the Son of God who can only be encountered in this strictly human being through a personal relation. In full conformity with the decision of Chalcedon, the starting point for Kierkegaard's christology is the person of Jesus Christ as truly human and truly divine. "This doctrine of the God-man is for him the Absolute Paradox."[177] Important for Kierkegaard is what follows from this presupposition: the existential significance which the God-man has for the life of the believer. How does this paradox of the divine-human person determine our existence as Christians? For Kierkegaard the Christian faith is not a doctrine but rather focuses on a person to whom I entrust myself without any reservations. In contrast to Socrates, the master does not render himself superfluous once he has instructed his disciples, but the faith stands or falls with the master.[178] This is different from a doctrine, which can be appropriated independently of its instructor. Christianity can never be understood apart from the person of Christ. Since the Christian faith is based on an existential decision, one cannot prove Christ's divinity, as it has been attempted, for instance, on account of his miracles. For Kierkegaard the miracles do not become unnecessary, since they focus our attention on Christ so that we can no longer overlook the paradox of his person and have to take a stand for or against him.[179] But not until we recognize God in Christ is the immediate proof of Christ's divinity apparent.

Kierkegaard's emphasis on christology is derived from the paradox of the incarnation, because there occurs the personal identity of God with the particular human being Jesus of Nazareth. "In Christ, God meets man *personally*."[180] From thereon, every human being, wherever he or she may live, can have a personal relationship with God. Yet the reality of the incarnation is often left unappreciated, since we do not realize that God came into the world for each of us. In the incarnation God shows the

176. Cf. the emphasis on this point by Bradley R. Dewey, *The New Obedience: Kierkegaard on Imitating Christ* (Washington: Corpus Books, 1968), 58.

177. Eduard Geismar, *Lectures on the Religious Thought of Søren Kierkegaard* (Minneapolis: Augsburg, 1937), 63.

178. So rightly Louis Dupré, *Kierkegaard as Theologian: The Dialectic of Christian Existence* (New York: Sheed and Ward, 1963), 137.

179. Dupré, *Kierkegaard as Theologian*, 141. Italics added.

180. Dupré, *Kierkegaard as Theologian*, 148.

greatness of his own love. Since "the theme of the coming together of God and man in the Christ is central to Kierkegaard's christology, and to his religious thought as a whole,"[181] Kierkegaard does not present a christology from below but from above. According to Kierkegaard, Christ "is the paradox, the object of faith, exists only for faith. But all historical communication is the communication of *knowledge*; consequently, one can come to know nothing about Christ from history."[182] The fact that an individual human being is God is an immense offense against our intellect. Therefore history can have no redeeming or enlightening value. Kierkegaard then continues: "The demonstrations for the divinity of Christ that Scripture sets forth — his miracles, his resurrection from the dead, his ascension — are indeed only for faith, that is, they are not 'demonstrations.'"[183] At the most, Kierkegaard concludes, it can be demonstrated that Jesus Christ was a great man, perhaps the greatest of all, but not that he was God. If we begin with the assumption of faith that Jesus Christ was God, then the time elapsed between the life of Jesus of Nazareth and our own life is canceled out and he becomes contemporaneous with us. If, on the other hand, we want to ascertain from that which we know about Jesus from history that he was God, then this whole attempt, Kierkegaard declares, is blasphemy.[184] We have no other access to Christ than through faith, and acceding to the fact "that God has lived here on earth as an individual human being is infinitely extraordinary."[185]

Since God is present in a truly human being who has all the marks of a human being, Jesus Christ begins his life in lowliness and leads it in abasement to the very end. This means that "temporality in its entirety was suffering and abasement; not until eternity is there victory, loftiness."[186] Jesus did not transcend lowliness while he was on earth. He began his life in poverty and ended it with an ignominious death, crucified like a criminal. Only then did he ascend on high. Yet his death has infinite importance as a death of atonement. Since he had finished

---

181. So Paul Sponheim, *Kierkegaard on Christ and Christian Coherence* (London: SCM, 1968), 173.

182. Søren Kierkegaard, *Practice in Christianity* 12.24, ed. and trans. Howard V. Hong and Edna H. Hong (Princeton: Princeton University Press, 1991), 25.

183. Kierkegaard, *Practice in Christianity*, 12.25, 26.

184. Kierkegaard, *Practice in Christianity*, 12.25, 26.

185. Kierkegaard, *Practice in Christianity*, 12.29, 31.

186. Kierkegaard, *Practice in Christianity*, 12.169, 182.

his test as a human being, and passed it, "he is now the perfect one and has been taken up on high."[187] Jesus is not simply a model for Christians to follow. Beyond all imitation he brought to us salvation through his suffering and humiliation. God's judgment on humanity and his love for humanity coincided in the death of Christ. "His death is the ultimate manifestation of man's sin, but it also marks the beginning of man's redemption."[188] While Kierkegaard never worked out a full systematic statement on an objective theory of atonement, it is clear for him that no cooperation is possible between God and humanity. "The fellow-worker with Christ in relation to the atonement thou canst not be, not in the remotest way. Thou art wholly in debt, He wholly makes satis-faction."[189] Salvation is totally Christ's business, accomplished through the God who meets us in the human person of Jesus.

In many ways Kierkegaard set the tone for christological reflection in the twentieth century, especially for those theologians representing neo-Reformation or dialectical theology. While Kierkegaard shared with Luther an existential interest in christology, unlike Luther he differ-entiated between the Jesus of history and the Christ of faith. Yet Kierke-gaard did not reflect on how the Christ of faith is related to the Jesus of history but only reiterated continuously that Jesus Christ was a truly human being. Kierkegaard and those who followed him presupposed a solid knowledge of the historical Jesus as portrayed by Scripture without ever reflecting on it. It is also noteworthy that for Kierkegaard Jesus Christ was a totally uneschatological figure. Resurrection and ascension are only consequences of Christ's obedience, not the turning point of history toward a new creation. Regardless of all claims to the contrary in neo-Reformation theology, this kind of approach to christology con-tinued far into the latter years of the twentieth century.

The doctrine of incarnation is also primary for Karl Barth (1886-1968).[190] And again like Kierkegaard, Barth shows a disinterest in the

---

187. Kierkegaard, *Practice in Christianity,* 12.170, 183.

188. So Dupré, *Kierkegaard as Theologian,* 151.

189. So Søren Kierkegaard, *Christian Discourses,* in *Christian Discourses,* and *The Lilies of the Field and the Birds of the Air,* and *Three Discourses at the Communion on Fridays,* trans. Walter Lowrie (London: Oxford University Press, 1952), 308. Cf. also the comments by Sponheim, *Kierkegaard on Christ and Christian Coherence* 190-91.

190. Stephen W. Sykes, "Barth on the Centre of Theology," in *Karl Barth: Studies of His Theological Method,* ed. Stephen W. Sykes (Oxford: Clarendon, 1979), 29.

historical Jesus. The reason for this disinterest lies first of all in Barth's conviction that "Jesus as the Christ, as the Messiah, is the End of History. . . . As Christ, Jesus is the plane which lies beyond our comprehension. The plane which is known to us, He intersects vertically, from above. Within history, Jesus as the Christ can be understood only as Problem or Myth."[191] Barth does not only claim that Jesus as the Christ transcends empirical verification, but also that once the divine enters the human, it is present there as a problem, an enigma, or a paradox. Any christology from below would have to contradict the historical meaning of the empirically verifiable dimension. In 1959 Karl Barth still claimed that the subject of theology is the word of God. "Theology is a science and a teaching which *feels itself responsible* to the living command of this specific subject and to nothing else in heaven or on earth."[192] This does not mean that theology has its own method and its own science, but that the starting point is God's self-revelation through the Word, through Jesus Christ.[193] "Since Barth identifies Jesus Christ with revelation, his insistence that Christian theology must begin with revelation means that it must begin with Jesus Christ."[194] More specifically, revelation begins with the divinity of Jesus Christ, because Jesus Christ is of the same divine essence as God the Father and the Holy Spirit. Revelation begins with the triune God. In contrast to Schleiermacher, Barth views the Trinity not as a theological conclusion of Christian theology but its very presupposition. Barth claims: "It is the doctrine of the Trinity which fundamentally distinguishes the Christian doctrine of God as Christian — it is it, therefore, also, which marks off the Christian concept of revelation as Christian, in face of all other possible doctrines of God and concepts of revelation."[195]

As in his reticence about a christology from below, starting with

191. Karl Barth, *The Epistle to the Romans,* trans. by Edwyn C. Hoskyns from the 6th ed. (London: Oxford University Press, 1963 [1933]), 29-30, in his comments on Romans 1:3-4.

192. Karl Barth, foreword to the Torchbook edition of *Dogmatics in Outline,* trans. G. T. Thomson (New York: Harper, 1959), 5. Italics in original.

193. Jeffrey C. Pugh, *The Anselmic Shift: Christology and Method in Karl Barth's Theology* (New York: Peter Lang, 1990), 127.

194. Charles T. Waldrop, *Karl Barth's Christology: Its Basic Alexandrian Character* (New York: Mouton, 1984), 89-90.

195. *CD* I/1:346.

the Jesus of history, Karl Barth does not want to begin with a general notion of God and then gradually work his way up to the Christian understanding of God. In contrast to any general notion of God he immediately begins with the Christian understanding of God, being derived from the triune God as disclosed in Jesus Christ. In Hegelian fashion, Barth postulates that God has the freedom to differentiate himself from himself, to become unlike himself and yet remain the same. So he is not only God the Father but also God the Son.[196] Barth arrives at a trinitarian form of revelation, since God in his divinity is not just revealer, but the revelation and the revealedness.[197] This kind of trinitarian method does not lend itself to historical investigation. Nevertheless, Barth claims: "It belongs to the concept of Biblically attested revelation, to be an historical event," since it occurred to concrete historical people.[198] The "objective reality" of God's revelation for us is Jesus Christ, God's incarnate Word. Barth asserts: "The Word or Son of God became a Man and was called Jesus of Nazareth; therefore this Man Jesus of Nazareth was God's Word or God's Son."[199] Jesus Christ is not a demi-God or an ideal human being, but someone like you and me. In that truly human person he presents God to us and he presents us to God. "In this way He is God's revelation to us and our reconciliation with God."[200] In his twofold existence Jesus can mediate God to us and be our mediator with God. Though in Christ God took up our nature (which is the same as our fallen nature), Jesus does not succumb to fallenness.

Important for Karl Barth's understanding of incarnation is the dogma of the virgin birth. It contains the insight that God really comes down to us as one of us and becomes one of us. It emphasizes that

> God does it all Himself. The dogma of the Virgin birth is thus the confession of the boundless hiddenness of the *vere Deus vere homo* and of the boundless amazement of awe and thankfulness called forth in us

---

196. *CD* I/1:367.

197. See Otto Weber, *Karl Barth's Church Dogmatics: An Introductory Report on Volumes I:1 to III:4*, trans. Arthur C. Cochrane (Philadelphia: Westminster, 1953), 34-35; and John Macquarrie, *TRE* 17:34, who rightly points out the problematic nature of this construct.

198. *CD* I/1:373.

199. *CD* I/2:13.

200. *CD* I/2:151.

by this *vere Deus vere homo*. It eliminates the last surviving possibility of understanding the *vere Deus vere homo* intellectually, as an idea or an arbitrary interpretation in the sense of a docetic or ebionite Christology.[201]

God himself accomplishes his incarnation. It is not a human act or a human and divine cooperative act, but completely and totally God's own doing. He comes down to our plane, becoming one of us.

Another important facet in Barth's christology is the significance which divine election plays in understanding Jesus Christ. One can even go so far as to say that for Barth's dogmatics the doctrine of election constitutes the structural as well as the hermeneutical key.[202] Again election has to do with incarnation, because Jesus Christ is "on the one hand the electing God and on the other the elected man."[203] In Jesus Christ the electing God and the elected man coincide. Barth emphasizes that we must look to this same Jesus Christ, since word *(logos)* and work are identical. God's word is Jesus Christ, and God's activity is God's redemptive event in Jesus Christ.[204] The election of Jesus Christ has two sides, the one in which election is being executed by and through Jesus Christ and the other as the election which occurred to him. "That the elected man Jesus had to suffer and die means no more and no less than that in becoming man God makes Himself responsible for man who became His enemy and that He takes upon Himself all the consequences of man's action — his rejection and his death."[205]

Clothing it in the Calvinistic doctrine of election and predestination, Barth introduces Luther's paradigm of the miraculous and joyful exchange between Christ and the believer. This becomes evident when he cautions that in speaking of predestination one must always speak of election and reprobation, predestination to salvation and to perdition. Barth then continues: "We may say already that in the election of Jesus Christ which is the eternal will of God, God has ascribed to man the former, election, salvation and life; and to Himself He has ascribed the

201. *CD* I/2:177.
202. So rightly Douglas R. Sharp, *The Hermeneutics of Election: The Significance of the Doctrine in Barth's Church Dogmatics* (Lanham, Md.: University Press of America, 1990), 1.
203. *CD* II/2:59.
204. Karl Barth, *Dogmatics in Outline,* 67.
205. *CD* II/2:124.

latter, reprobation, perdition and death."[206] In Christ's death God assumed our own lot so we would be freed from that which should have truly been ours. Of course, Jesus' death is not the final word of God:

> The Word of divine steadfastness is the resurrection of Jesus from the dead, His exaltation, His session at the right hand of the Father. By these events God confirms the fact that the Elect is the only-begotten Son of God who can suffer death but cannot be holden of death, who by His death must destroy death. By these events, God makes manifest the vindication of His positive will as Creator against the assault of Satan, a vindication which He made by the offering up of His Elect.[207]

The resurrection is again seen as an exclusive act of God, in which God is revealed in the one humiliated on the cross.[208]

In conclusion it must said that Karl Barth's christology is truly a christology from above, one that is reminiscent of the early church, like, for instance, that of Athanasius. Central to this type of christology is neither the proclamation of Jesus nor his work as a person. Rather, it is the salvific significance of the incarnation, the cross, and the resurrection which occupies center stage. Ontological concerns are of primary importance, while relational considerations fade in the background. Barth initially started with existential concerns — how Jesus Christ can be contemporaneous with us today — but as his *Church Dogmatics* progressed, ontological considerations gained the upper hand. Barth mapped out a territory which, though attractive and lavish, is nonetheless foreign to citizens of this world. And it is this foreign territory that Barth beckoned the citizens of this world to enter.

A christology from above, though from a very different perspective, is presented by Paul Tillich (1886-1965). The second volume of his three-volume *Systematic Theology* is devoted to christology. Since sin and evil are also treated in this rather slim volume, christology proper is allotted less than ninety pages. In the introduction Paul Tillich asserts, "There is no logically necessary or deductive step from . . . God to the

---

206. *CD* II/2:163.

207. *CD* II/2:125.

208. For a more detailed treatment of the significance of the resurrection in this context, see David L. Mueller, *Foundation of Karl Barth's Doctrine of Reconciliation: Jesus Christ Crucified and Risen* (Lewiston, N.Y.: Edwin Mellen, 1990), 408ff.

Christ."[209] That there is a Christ, meaning that God assumed humanity, or, to stay within Tillichian terminology, that essence lived under the condition of existence, is totally nonrational and paradoxical.

One would assume that Paul Tillich is constructing a christology from below when he claims: "Jesus as the Christ is both a historical fact and a subject of believing reception."[210] That is, a Christian theology is completely undercut if the historical fact or the believing reception is completely ignored. But then Tillich talked about the research into the historical Jesus and its failure, and assured us that not the historical argument but participation, meaning the immediacy of the self-consciousness of the believer, warrants the reality of the event upon which Christianity is based.[211] Analogous to Kähler's claim, the "Biblical historical Christ is normative for Tillich" and not the historical Jesus.[212] This does not mean that Tillich constructed a biblical christology, but that the biblical imagery became informative for his christology.

Humanity, according to Tillich, has left its essential nature and lapsed into existence. Thereby it forfeited its theonomy and asserted its autonomy. The estrangement from its essential nature is overcome for human existence through an ecstatic experience which gives birth to theonomy. This is accomplished in the experience of the New Being "as symbolized in Jesus who is the Christ."[213] Jesus is this New Being insofar as in him there is the undistorted manifestation of his essential being within and under the conditions of existence.[214] Christ is the end of existence lived out in estrangement, conflict, and self-destruction.

> The Christ is essential man. He represents man to man, that is, he shows what man essentially is. But he also represents God to man, because essential man has embedded within him the image of God. Therefore, essential manhood and essential God-manhood are identical.[215]

209. *Systematic Theology (ST)* 2:3.

210. *ST* 2:98.

211. *ST* 2:114.

212. So rightly A. T. Mollegen, "Christology and Biblical Criticism in Tillich," in *The Theology of Paul Tillich*, ed. Charles W. Kegley (New York: Pilgrim, 1982), 269.

213. Carl J. Armbruster, *The Vision of Paul Tillich* (New York: Sheed and Ward, 1967), 168.

214. *ST* 2:119.

215. So the fitting summary of Tillich's position in Armbruster, *Vision of Paul Tillich*, 179.

For Tillich, similar to Barth, Christ is the perfected human being. Yet Tillich is very hesitant to accept the paradigm of the incarnation, because he is convinced that its intention (to say that God changed into something that is not God) cannot be maintained theologically. Rather, he opts for the Johannine metaphor that the *logos* became flesh. "Flesh" signifies historical existence, and "becoming" indicates that God participates in that which is estranged from him.

In Jesus the New Being was and is actualized, and estrangement of existence has been overcome. Jesus Christ as the New Being rescues us from our estranged human situation. The expression of the New Being in Jesus as the Christ can be seen in Christ's words, in his deeds, and in his suffering.[216] With regard to the last item we are surprised to hear that Tillich declared: "The suffering on the Cross is not something additional which can be separated from the appearance of the eternal God-Manhood under the conditions of existence; it is an inescapable implication of this appearance."[217] Christ's suffering on the cross is a mere consequence of his becoming human. The salvific function of Christ is no longer centered in cross and resurrection but in Jesus as the Christ, because in him "the conflict between the essential unity of God and man and man's existential estrangement is overcome."[218] This was the biblical picture of Jesus as the Christ that Tillich gleaned from the New Testament.

Tillich saw in the cross of Christ and in his resurrection central symbols of the universal significance of Jesus. The resurrection becomes "the decisive test of the Christ-character of Jesus of Nazareth. A real experience made it possible for the disciples to apply the known symbol of resurrection to Jesus, thus acknowledging him definitely as the Christ."[219] Tillich interpreted the resurrection of Jesus as the Christ with the help of the restitution theory. This restitution "is rooted in the personal unity between Jesus and God and in the impact of the unity on the minds of the apostles. . . . In an ecstatic experience the concrete picture of Jesus of Nazareth became indissolubly united with the reality

216. *ST* 2:121ff.

217. *ST* 2:123-14, and Armbruster, *Vision of Paul Tillich,* 198, who rightly cautions that this close connection of the cross with the significance of Jesus the Christ allows for "no room whatsoever for the sacrificial aspect of the crucifixion."

218. *ST* 2:125.

219. *ST* 2:154.

of the New Being. He is present wherever the New Being is present."[220] While Tillich rejected the interpretation of the resurrection as a spiritualistic or psychological event, one wonders whether his own restitution theory does not ultimately issue from his positing a psychological event that occurred in the mind of the disciples and continues to occur in each Christian who recognizes the significance of Jesus as the Christ.

The problem seems to stem from Tillich's own christology. While he agrees with the decisions of Nicea and Chalcedon, that Christ is truly divine and that in him the human and the divine are equally present, the human being Jesus only serves as the paradigm of the manifestation of the New Being.[221] When Tillich claims: "Christology is a function of soteriology," we can agree only in part, since the emphasis must be first on Christ and then on salvation.[222] Salvation is dependent on Jesus as the Christ and not vice versa. If it were the other way around, salvation could also be found in other ways and at other places than in Jesus Christ.[223] We should remember that the Reformation concern for christology was of an existential nature, whereby christology came first and the existential question second. The problem with Tillich does not simply lie in a reversal of christology and soteriology. His dogmatic system first postulates the emergence of the New Being under the guise of existence. Then essential elements of the historical-biblical Christ are used to illustrate the philosophic postulate of the manifestation of the New Being. Tillich therewith presents a christology from above in which the New Testament witnesses are used as illustrations. Such an approach is dogmatically convenient, since one need not deal with the problematic nature of historical research and its results. Moreover, as we have seen with Rudolf Bultmann (1884-1976), or with narrative theology, this approach is advocated by some New Testament scholars, who can then attempt to stay above the changing tides of biblical research.

Once christology has lost its historical moorings, the danger emerges that the Christian faith be considered more a timeless myth than a religion anchored in history. Moreover, one loses sight of the essential

---

220. *ST* 2:157.

221. *ST* 2:145.

222. *ST* 2:150.

223. Cf. also the caution expressed here by Alexander J. McKelway, *The Systematic Theology of Paul Tillich: A Review and Analysis* (New York: Dell, 1964), 177.

claim of biblical christology that God entered the human sphere bounded by space and time. In this situation it was only fitting that Wolfhart Pannenberg (1928-) in his "Dogmatic Theses on the Doctrine of Revelation" (1961) claimed: "The proclamation of Christ presents, for those who hear it, a fact (to be reasonably and reliably true) that in the fate of Jesus of Nazareth, God has been revealed to all men. The proclamation of the gospel cannot assert that the facts are in doubt and that the leap of faith must be made in order to achieve certainty."[224] We cannot resort to faith and dogma to establish our Christian faith but must ground it in history. Pannenberg subsequently showed that a credible christology which can reasonably be defended in our age of critical reason can only be constructed from below, a christology which begins with that which is historically ascertainable about Jesus of Nazareth.

---

224. Wolfhart Pannenberg, "Dogmatic Theses on the Doctrine of Revelation," in *Revelation as History*, ed. Wolfhart Pannenberg, trans. David Granskou (New York: Macmillan, 1968), 138.

Part III
The Relevance of
Jesus Christ for Today

We have looked at the quest for the historical Jesus, taken account of the biblical testimony, and considered its assessment throughout history. Now it is time to take stock: What is the significance of Jesus Christ for today? After all, Jesus of Nazareth lived nearly two thousand years ago in a corner of what was then the Roman Empire. By the most generous estimates his public ministry lasted four years, and at the end of a relatively short life he was executed by the Roman occupation army. Nevertheless, this Jesus has impacted human history like no other person. While his adherents comprise the largest religious group on earth, the official influence of the religion named after him seems to be waning. There is no agreement among his adherents as to who he actually was and what he intended to accomplish. And then there is Islam, the old rival of Christianity, that has a very peculiar estimate of Jesus, quite different from that of the Christian religion. So, who is this Jesus of Nazareth for us today, and what is his potential for our present understanding of world history?

5. The Human Face of God

There is insufficient material in the biblical and extrabiblical sources for us to write a biography of Jesus. Yet contrary to what some critics still claimed at the turn of the century, it is important that this Jesus was a person who lived on this earth and was not a mythical figure. This Jesus, with whom the whole Christian movement is intimately connected, was an actual person who said and did certain things. The Christian faith is based on the history connected with a certain human being. Yet Jesus is not considered just the founder of the Christian movement; he is its very focus of devotion, since he is believed to be the human face of God. With this kind of assertion, an ugly broad ditch opens between the accidental truth of history and the timeless truth of human self-awareness.

1. Bridging the Ugly, Broad Ditch

In 1806 the German idealistic philosopher Johann Gottlieb Fichte (1762-1814) wrote: "Only the metaphysical but not the historical contributes to our salvation; the latter only makes it intelligible."[1] Before Fichte, Gotthold Ephraim Lessing had pointed out that it is difficult to bridge "the ugly, broad ditch" between the accidental facts of history and the necessary facts of reason.[2] These examples, which could easily be multiplied, show

---

1. Johann Gottlieb Fichte, *Die Anweisung zum seligen Leben,* ed. Fritz Medicus (Hamburg: Felix Meiner, 1954), 97, in his sixth lecture.
2. Gotthold Ephraim Lessing, *On the Proof of the Spirit and of Power* (1777), in *Lessing's Theological Writings,* trans. Henry Chadwick (Stanford, Calif.: Stanford University Press, 1957), 55.

us that history does not provide a trustworthy enough foundation for faith and salvation. Rudolf Bultmann poignantly expressed this apparent dilemma when he admitted that all knowledge of the historical Jesus is very uncertain. "Here research ends with a large question mark," was his conclusion. Contrary to others, however, he did not give up in despair but concluded his observation with the assertion: "And here it ought to end."[3] For Bultmann the history of Jesus of Nazareth is only an accidental historical event. Nevertheless, he insisted that this historical event encounters us with the claim that it is God's revelation. Therefore we are called to accept that God has acted decisively in this human being. Bultmann wanted to bridge the ugly, broad ditch by an appeal to faith. One must have faith contrary to all evidence.

In evangelical quarters especially, one is often called to faith and summoned to believe something. Evangelicals often understand "faith" as a move to trust something or someone trustworthy. But how can an accidental event in history ever become normative for more than its own eventfulness? Acknowledging that Jesus once lived, acted, and preached does not necessarily change our own self-understanding. The situation only changes once we recognize that Jesus is not an isolated event. In his proclamation he drew on the promissory history of Israel, used the apocalyptic imagery of Judaism, and stood in the context of the Messianic expectations of his time. This contextualization allows us to perceive with more understanding the historical figure of Jesus. It shows that Jesus stands in continuity with the salvational expectations of Israel and even anticipates them proleptically in his own person; that which was thought to occur on a universal scale at the end of history had already occurred with him on an individual scale.[4] This is most clearly pronounced in the opening sentence of the Letter to the Hebrews, where the author states: "Long ago God spoke to our ancestors in many and various ways by the prophets, but in the last days he has spoken to us by the Son, whom he appointed heir of all things, through whom he also created the worlds" (Heb. 1:1-2). The God who once spoke through the prophets is identical

3. Rudolf Bultmann, "Liberal Theology and the Latest Theological Movement" (1924), in *Faith and Understanding*, ed. Robert Funk, trans. Louise P. Smith (London: SCM, 1969), 1:30.

4. This has also been claimed by Wolfhart Pannenberg in thesis 4 of his "Dogmatic Theses on the Doctrine of Revelation," 139.

with the God who spoke in the Son.[5] In other words, the God of the Old Testament is identical with the God of the New Testament.

Beyond the continuity of the sameness of God, there is a strict discontinuity: In these final days the time of old has come to an end. With God's speaking in the Son something new has commenced. Jesus stands in continuity with the promissory history of Israel. This history has now come to an end, since God no longer communicates indirectly through prophets and has communicated himself through his Son. The Son-of-God christology which is presupposed in Hebrews corresponds to the Johannine statement: "Whoever has seen me has seen the Father" (John 14:9). With this assertion we are either confronted with a faith statement of the Evangelist, telling us that there is an identity of God with Jesus, or Jesus himself claims this intimate affinity with God. But how do we know which side of the alternative is correct? Even if one concedes that Jesus made this statement, how does one know that he was correct?

Before we simply rely on historical facts, we should recall Philipp Melanchthon's caution: "Unless one knows why Christ took upon himself human flesh and was crucified, what advantage would accrue from having learned his life's history?"[6] To acknowledge something as historically true is different from realizing its existential import. Even an overwhelming amount of data, which science, for instance, continuously compiles, is rather useless unless it is brought into a coherent whole and comes to stand in a respective frame of reference. Similarly, when historians want to know what really happened, they must interpret the historical facts available to them by placing them into the web of history that seems most plausible to them and their readers. In the same manner, when we are confronted with the facts concerning the life, mission, and destiny of Jesus, we should not simply resort to faith or to the help of the Holy Spirit in order to understand what we read. Such a procedure would introduce a "God of the gaps" and borders on incredulity.

Wolfhart Pannenberg in his discussion with kerygmatic theology on the one hand and confessional Lutheran theology on the other asserted

5. See for the following Hans-Friedrich Weiss, *Der Brief an die Hebräer* (Göttingen: Vandenhoeck & Ruprecht, 1991), 137ff., in his explanation of Heb. 1:1-2.

6. Philipp Melanchthon, *The Loci Communes,* trans. Charles L. Hill (Boston: Meador, 1944), 68.

vehemently that there is no special knowledge of faith or special decision of faith which is not based on natural knowledge. He wrote: "I admit that I cannot understand any knowledge as other than 'natural.' . . . Reference to the message does not help here at all, since it only raises the question whether the message is true."[7] Pannenberg shows that a simple recognition of historical facts does not suffice, since one has to understand history in its own sense as something which involves oneself. Moreover, according to Pannenberg, history does not only include that which historical positivism would acknowledge as historical, but also Jesus' resurrection from the dead and his incarnation. Pannenberg is convinced that God has left the incognito character of his self-revelation at Easter and made himself known to the nations (Rom. 16:25-26).[8] Pannenberg then claims:

> Men must first be brought to reason in order that they may really perceive the event that reveals the truth of God's deity. For this truth, as evident as it is in itself, and no matter how much it may also be presented as evident — otherwise faith would be without foundation — is opposed by prejudgments which commonly prejudice men. It is true that the sweeping away of such prejudgments can never be a matter of rational argument alone because these prejudgments are themselves irrationally rooted, provided that we *are* dealing with prejudgments. To this extent, a kind of illumination is needed in order for the truth, which is clear in itself and demonstrable as true, to dawn upon the individual man, too.[9]

While Pannenberg is correct that faith cannot be added to history as some external supplement to make us aware of its existential significance, he seems to have overstated his case. The resurrection of Jesus Christ was not a historical event in the strict sense of the word, as Pannenberg would have us believe. The resurrection of Jesus Christ, in contrast to a resuscitation, transcended the space- and time-bound limits of history. Even the concept of a resurrection was not universally accepted in the religious milieu of Jesus. We should remember that a significant segment of Jewish society, the Sadducees among them, re-

7. Wolfhart Pannenberg, "Insight and Faith," in *Basic Questions in Theology: Collected Essays*, trans. George H. Kehm (Philadelphia: Fortress, 1971), 2:33-34.

8. Pannenberg, "Insight and Faith," 2:41 n. 22.

9. Pannenberg, "Insight and Faith," 2:40-41.

jected the notion of a resurrection. While it is true that in later Judaism the resurrection was perceived in an apocalyptic context as that to which all history was moving, another large segment of society held to a much more worldly expectation, the nationalistic reestablishment of the Davidic kingdom. The resurrection of Jesus Christ was also subjected to different interpretations. Some claimed it was a fraud and that the disciples had removed the corpse from the tomb, while others claimed they had seen Jesus after he had been resurrected to new life.

It is strange then that Pannenberg admits that some people, by normal count a rather sizable contingent, would need some kind of illumination to perceive history in its true existential significance. One wonders whether "illumination" is not another term for the traditional reference to the aid of the Holy Spirit through which one understands the true significance of Jesus.

It would be preferable not to focus on Jesus' ultimate destiny, his resurrection, but to include in an evaluation of his significance all the verifiable historical facts concerning his life and proclamation. In so doing, one soon realizes that Jesus lived and acted like a normal human being. His portrayal as an itinerant preacher in a small geographic region of Palestine is certainly accurate. On the other hand, there were certain incidents in his life, whether the result of later embellishments or an actual reflection of history, which transcended the usual life of a human being. His actual father seemed to be unknown, his family wanted to declare him insane, he performed unusual acts which were interpreted as miracles, and the tomb in which he was laid after his death was found empty. Of course, all these items can and have been explained as referring to ordinary incidents within space and time. Yet the picture gets more complicated once we consider his message. The final verdict was blasphemy, since at numerous times Jesus interpreted anew God's word which was known through tradition and behaved as if he stood in God's place.

The historical dilemma which confronts us is perhaps best expressed in the so-called graffito of Alexamenos dating from A.D. 85 discovered at the Palatine in Rome. This caricature shows a youth standing before a cross on which hangs a figure with the head of an ass. The subscription in Greek reads: "Alexamenos worships his God." There is indeed an alternative which we must face. Either this Jesus of Nazareth was out of his mind, he actually was an ass, or indeed he was the one he claimed to be, the human face of God. Any attempt to bridge the ugly broad ditch, to tip the scales more in favor of one or the other, is empirically unwarranted. An actual verification and vindication can only come at the end of history. But would this not imply that Jesus as an accidental phenomenon of history is less trustworthy than the necessary truth of reason? This is not necessarily true, since reason itself is pluriform. It can be employed as aprioristic reason, as understanding reason, and as historical reason.[10] First, in its a priori form, reason uses certain principles and applies it to experience. Reason then is not just a principle which helps us order reality, but it filters the possibilities of that which we perceive as reality. Whatever does not fit this filter is eliminated. This would explain the tension between natural reason and revelation. Revelation does not occur in natural reason and is excluded by the latter. Second, there is perceiving reason, which tries to relate reality to that which looms behind whatever we encounter. Reason searches for that timeless truth that is expressive of the fundamental laws of nature. Finally, there is historical reason, which opts for an ultimate verification of reality at the end of all history, when variety and diversity, unity and wholeness become discernible, since no future developments will disturb the then-extant configurations.

It has become clear that there is a historical dimension to reason unless it is reduced to a nonhistorical ideology. As long as there is advancement in knowledge, whether in the sciences or in the humanities, the present assessment and insight of reality is valid only unless refuted by future insight or correspondingly modified. Reason therefore stands under an eschatological proviso. Its insights still lack ultimate verification. The necessary truth of reason does not have an advantage over the accidental truth of history. This does not mean that all historical accidents have equal truth value. As we can see with Jesus, it is important that they be in agreement with a certain historical tradition out of which they emerge. It is equally important that they do not remain fragmented in the manner of the often-heard idiosyncratic statement: "The way it looks to me." They must be related to reality as a whole and have integrative power.

It is important that the life, message, and destiny of Jesus remained significant not only for the followers of Jesus during his lifetime and a

---

10. This distinction is made by Wolfhart Pannenberg, "Faith and Reason," in *Basic Questions in Theology*, 2:55-59.

few converts who joined the movement later, but that this figure became the rallying point for an ever-expanding faith. It even became influential for other religious persuasions, as demonstrated by the high esteem that Jesus carries in Islam and the central Christian tenets which found their way into Marxist theory and Gandhi's teachings. While one may ask whether these adaptations properly understood Jesus and his teachings, it is noteworthy that the life and ministry of Jesus have an impact beyond the confines of the Christian faith. The accidental truth of history embodied in Jesus transcends any historical accident. The ultimate empirical verification which Christians hope for and which non-Christians disclaim is not simply the final vindication of two equally probable and credible possibilities. It is that which seems most probable and most sensible in its context then and its context now. Since we are unable to bridge the ugly, broad ditch by empirical demonstrability, we are still called to trust that our faith will not be in vain.

2. The Jewishness of Jesus

Jesus was not just a historical person claiming universal validity but also a member of the Jewish community which claimed a special historical relationship with God. How can we evaluate Jesus and his message, given the fact that the Jewish tradition has historical priority?

When we talk about Jesus as a Jew we must keep in mind that this statement is understood differently by different people. Christian and non-Christian Arabs are likely to interpret this as meaning that Jesus was an Israeli.[11] While Christians may understand Judaism quite often as their predecessor religion, for Muslims there is a unilateral development from Judaism via Christianity to Islam. Though there is certainly a historical progression from Judaism to Christianity and finally to Islam, it would be difficult if not impossible to assert empirically that one is more advanced than the other. At this point it is much more beneficial to talk about different ways of believing. That the Christian church had no problems with Jesus' Jewishness is illustrated by the fact that his mother Mary was received into the Apostles' Creed.

11. This has been rightly pointed out by Markus Barth, *Jesus the Jew: Israel and the Palestinians*, trans. Frederick Prussner (Atlanta: John Knox, 1978), 11.

According to orthodox rabbinic law, a Jew is any person who has a Jewish mother or converted to Judaism. Therefore, Martin Buber (1878-1965) could talk about his brother Jesus:

> From my youth onwards I have found in Jesus my great brother. That Christianity regarded and does regard him God and Saviour has always appeared to me a fact of the higher importance which, for his sake and my own sake, I must endeavor to understand. My own fraternally open relationship to him has grown ever stronger and clearer, and today I see him more strongly and clearly than ever before.
>
> I am more than ever certain that a great place belongs to him in Israel's history and that this place cannot be described by any of the usual categories.[12]

For a Jewish person Jesus is not just any brother but a Jewish brother. Jesus' hand which is extended to a Jew so that he or she would follow him is not perceived by a Jew to be the hand of the Messiah. It is also not thought of as a divine hand but the hand of a human person in which the furrows of deepest sorrow have been engraved. It is the same hand that touches both Christians and Jews, since it is the hand of a great witness to faith. Jesus' faith is one of unconditional trust in God and demonstrates a readiness to put oneself totally under the will of God. This kind of attitude embodied in Jesus can bind together Jews and Christians. This means the faith *of Jesus* unites while faith *in Jesus* separates.[13] The faith of Jesus comes to expression in the Sermon on the Mount, in the parables of the fatherhood of God and of his kingdom, and in the Lord's Prayer which Jesus taught his disciples. Yet faith in Jesus as the Messiah, as the second person of the Trinity, and as the singularly righteous one who substitutingly suffers for us, separates Christians and Jews. Jews restrict their estimate of Jesus to the strictly human level. While a Jew (or a secular historian) may admit that there was some inkling of a Messianic calling in Jesus' own consciousness, he or she will argue that the Messiahship of Jesus is as little a matter for Jewish faith as for historical research. Jesus' divinity does not enter the horizon of either the historian or the Jew.

---

12. Martin Buber, *Two Types of Faith*, trans. Norman P. Goldhawk (New York: Macmillan, 1951), 12-13.

13. So very tellingly Schalom Ben-Chorin, *Jesus im Judentum* (Wuppertal: Rolf Brockhaus, 1970), 51.

In trying to remove potential misunderstandings between Jews and Christians, the Jewish scholar Pinchas Lapide (1922-) makes three claims:[14]

1. Jesus did not reveal himself to his people as their Messiah. Consequently, Israel could not recognize him as their savior.
2. The majority of the Jewish people whom Jesus addressed gave him an enthusiastic reception. It follows, therefore, that one cannot blame them for Jesus' death on the cross.
3. Jesus never rejected Israel, since his undivided love beyond his death belongs to his people. Therefore they cannot be considered rejected by Jesus.

The first thesis, that Jesus did not understand himself as Messiah, seems to be the easiest to substantiate. There is no indication in the Gospels that Jesus called himself the Messiah. Lapide also refers to Rudolf Bultmann, who wondered whether Jesus reinterpreted the traditional concept of Messiah.[15] Even the healings, exorcisms, and other miraculous deeds which Jesus performed need not be associated with Messianism. Lapide points out that Bar Kochba had been considered for nearly three years as Messiah without having accomplished a single miracle.[16] Even the notions that the Messiah must suffer as described in the suffering servant song of Isaiah 53 or that he will be resurrected were not part of Jewish Messianic thinking. At the time of Jesus it was generally believed that various figures would be resurrected, but none of them was thought to be the Messiah. The claim of Messiahship was not unusual at that time. Messianic pretenders were quite frequent during the century in which Jesus lived. While none of them accomplished salvation, they led thousands of credulous Jews to death and slavery. When Jesus asked his disciples who people thought he was, they answered that he was John the Baptist, Elijah, or even Jeremiah. Only Peter called Jesus the Messiah, the Son of the living God (Matt. 16:16). Jesus and the other disciples neither rejected Peter's confession nor rejoiced over it (cf. Mark 8:29-30). Jesus even forbade them to spread it around.

14. Pinchas Lapide and Ulrich Luz, *Jesus in Two Perspectives: A Jewish-Christian Dialog*, trans. Lawrence W. Denef (Minneapolis: Augsburg, 1985), 25.
15. Lapide and Luz, *Jesus in Two Perspectives*, 30.
16. Lapide and Luz, *Jesus in Two Perspectives*, 30.

Lapide sums up why the Jewish people at the time of Jesus supposedly could not recognize him as their Messiah:[17]

1. Jesus did not publicly disclose himself as the Messiah.
2. Jesus admonished his disciples and his friends not to reveal the secret of his suffering.
3. Jesus repeatedly stole away from the ovations of the people and usually performed healings secretly.
4. Jesus' parables of the Messianic redemption do not disclose details about the coming of the kingdom, but shrouded it in mystery.
5. If it is true, as Paul said: "How are they to believe in one of whom they have never heard?" (Rom. 10:14), then it is certainly true that the vast majority of the Jewish people at that time could not believe in Jesus and become Christians, since they had never heard of him.

According to Lapide, when a Jew reads the Gospels he or she is surprised to see more than fifty references from the Hebrew Bible which are used in such a way as to prove Jesus' Messiahship.[18] But these passages were never intended to be read in that way, and therefore their fulfillment is still expected today. Lapide also suggests that the Greek word *parousia* should be interpreted not as return (of the Messiah) but as advent, which would mean that both Jews and Christians live in hope and are on the way to salvation, as Paul says, "until he comes" (1 Cor. 11:26). Pinchas Lapide concludes that Jesus did not disclose himself as Messiah, and he was not the Messiah.

But what about the second charge made by many Christians that Israel rejected Jesus? Lapide starts with the Johannine assertion "He came to what was his own, and his own people did not accept him" (John 1:11) as the key passage that from the beginning Christendom has understood as the expression par excellence of the unbelief of the Jews. He asks: "Why this wave of hatred, this scarlet thread that reaches from Golgotha to Auschwitz? Why this condemnation of God's biblical people, whose 'perfidy' consists in remaining true to their faith through three millennia — the faith of Abraham, Moses, David, and last not least, Jesus of Nazareth, who, though not the Messiah of Israel, like us, longingly

---

17. Lapide and Luz, *Jesus in Two Perspectives*, 45-46.
18. For the following see Lapide and Luz, *Jesus in Two Perspectives*, 51.

hoped for the Messiah's coming."[19] Lapide sees no trace that *the* Jews rejected Jesus, since even that key passage in the first chapter of John continues: "But to all who received him, who believed in his name, he gave power to become children of God" (John 1:12). Jews invited Jesus into their homes, Jews became his disciples and remained faithful beyond his death, and they believed in him as the coming Messiah. Without these Jews there would not have been any Christendom. All the original apostles were pious Jews who found no contradiction between their Jewishness and their faith in Jesus. Moreover, many other people in Israel applauded Jesus.

Why would then the Gospel of John paint such a dark picture of the Jews whereby the "Johannine dogma concerning Israel's unbelief"[20] is carried to absurdity in the same Gospel as we can see in John 7:11-13:

> The Jews were looking for him at the festival in saying, "Where is he?" And there was considerable complaining about him among the crowds. While some were saying, "He is a good man," others were saying, "No, he is deceiving the crowd." Yet no one would speak openly about him for fear of the Jews.

The Evangelist seems to distinguish between the Jews who were of mixed opinion about Jesus and the Jews of whom the "Jews" were afraid. Lapide explains this anti-Judaism in terms of the late date of the Gospel. At that time Jerusalem had been destroyed, the Jewish people were dispersed, and they were shunned throughout the entire Roman Empire as indefatigable rebels. Therefore, Jesus being a Jew and being killed like a zealot by the Romans was a double handicap for the nascent Christian mission to the Gentiles. Consequently the Evangelist reduced the complicity of the Romans in the death of Jesus to a minimum, while blaming the "Jews" for the death of their compatriot. In this way it was hoped that the persecutions against the emerging church would be lessened and the Roman authorities would be moved to tolerate this new religion.[21] This anti-Judaism was a matter of self-defense, not actually directed against the Jews but much more a ploy by which the Christians sought to appear in a good light before the Romans.

19. Lapide and Luz, *Jesus in Two Perspectives*, 59.
20. Lapide and Luz, *Jesus in Two Perspectives*, 71.
21. For the preceding see Lapide and Luz, *Jesus in Two Perspectives*, 77.

The reality was that the death of Jesus was the result of a military and political execution in which the Jews had no part. The people of Israel, insofar as they were in touch with Jesus, were generally open to him and his message and were often even enthusiastic about him. Yet their admiration was focused on the teacher, the preacher, the miracle-worker, the mighty person of God, and the prophet from Galilee, but not, as in later Hellenism, the God-man who by dying on the cross substitutingly atoned for the sins of humanity, since such a death was "a stumbling block to Jews" (1 Cor. 1:23). Since the Jews did not reject Jesus, it follows that he did not reject them either. Lapide states:

> Jesus' teaching as a whole and his preaching which he "always taught in synagogues and in the temple, where all Jews come together" (Jn. 18:20), are permeated with this all-embracing love for his people — a love which knows as little about the rejection of Israel as it knows about the replacement of Israel by the Gentiles.[22]

How does a Christian react to such an assessment of Jesus? Ulrich Luz (1938-), professor of New Testament at Bern, responded to Lapide in the above-cited publication. Luz agrees that most likely Jesus did not understand himself as Messiah in the theo-political sense of Israel's hope and he never pretended to be such a Messiah. Yet the Jewish expectations of a savior figure who was to appear at the end time were pluriform. There was the high priest of the end time, the prophet, and above all the heavenly Son of man as hinted at in Daniel 7:13-14. Luz is open to the notion that Jesus took himself to be that Son of man whom God would exalt and enthrone as the coming Son of man.[23] When the New Testament confessed Jesus as the Messiah, it did not mean the Jewish political Messiah, who was supposed to liberate Israel from the yoke of the Gentiles. Through his proclamation, action, death, and resurrection Jesus fulfilled the traditional Messianic expectations in a new way, trans-forming and superseding them to some extent. It was no longer necessary for a Jew who believed in Jesus to expect another Messiah. Since Jesus did not consider himself to be the theo-political Messiah which Israel expected, Israel did not betray its own faith by rejecting Jesus. When a Jew says that Jesus was not the expected Messiah, he or she does not

22. Lapide and Luz, *Jesus in Two Perspectives*, 99.
23. Lapide and Luz, *Jesus in Two Perspectives*, 130.

mean by the term "Messiah" the same as a Christian denotes with the term "Christ" when confessing Jesus to be the Christ.[24] Both Christians and Jews talk past each other.

Concerning the second thesis of Lapide that the Jews did not reject Jesus, Luz agrees that especially the Galilean and also the Judaic masses applauded Jesus. But he was rejected by the Sadducees in Jerusalem, the highest stratum of the priestly caste, since they felt he endangered their cultic privileges, the political peace, and the status quo. That the Jews delivered to the Roman authorities a fellow Jew who had announced the destruction of the temple and of Jerusalem was nothing new in that century.[25] Many Pharisees also rejected Jesus, since they disliked his liberal understanding of the Sabbath law and the fact that he took exception to the prescriptions of cultic purity. On the other hand, there were many points of contact between Jesus and the Pharisees. We also do not hear that any of them was involved in Jesus' trial. But how did the schism between those who believed in Christ and the other Jews occur after Easter? Non-Christian Jews and Christian Jews appealed to the same God and the same Scripture, but in a very different way. The result was a quarrel, a fight among brethren. Then came estrangement, distancing, and finally severed relations. This allowed one faction to perceive the other in the abstract, no longer as real and living human beings.

Luz agrees with Lapide that Jesus did not reject Israel. He knew that he was sent to his own people. Jesus was not primarily interested in the Israel of history that was constituted through the covenant at Mount Sinai and through God's election. The selection of his twelve disciples indicates that he was much more concerned with the eschatological Israel which God in boundless love would gather from all of Israel and also from its despised members. Jesus removed the boundaries for God's love, extended this love, and deepened it. With his mission Jesus did not simply confirm the election of Israel but rather established it anew, because, as Paul said, "If God so loves us Gentiles, how much more will He remain faithful to his own people, for whom election and the promises were intended and still remain in effect!"[26]

24. Lapide and Luz, *Jesus in Two Perspectives*, 134-35.
25. Lapide and Luz, *Jesus in Two Perspectives*, 141.
26. Lapide and Luz, *Jesus in Two Perspectives*, 156.

Paradigmatically we have seen in Lapide a genuinely Jewish and sympathetic interpretation of Jesus. Jesus is a brother in the Jewish faith and, to some extent, even an example of that faith. According to this view Jesus is not the Messiah and never intended to be. In Jewish eyes, the usual claim is that it was not theology but the political situation which led to the demise of Jesus. Even Jesus' pronouncement of the forgiveness of sins need not have led to the charge of blasphemy, since this action could be understood as synonymous for healing or for expelling demons.[27] Jesus was not a prophet in the Old Testament sense, but rather a teacher of the law.[28] He taught in the customary way of his time, explaining canonical texts and narrating parables. Since there were many prophets who served the rebel leaders, offering them miraculous help in dire political situations, the term "prophet" carried with it distinctly pejorative overtones.[29] In claiming spiritual authority to underpin his charismatic activities, Jesus could be considered to be a saint from Galilee.[30]

Yet there is good reason to think of Jesus as being akin to the Pharisees.[31] This would explain his admonishment to his followers: "Therefore, do whatever they [the Pharisees] teach you and follow it; but do not do as they do, for they do not practice what they teach" (Matt. 23:3). There were two great Pharisaic schools at this time. From the school of Hillel Jesus appropriated the golden rule as documented in Matthew 7:12 and for which the love of neighbor was central. From the school of Shimei he took the stricter interpretation of the Old Testament law. Yet his own contribution was the interiorization of the law in which love was the decisive and energizing element. Jesus taught like a Pharisee or a rabbi but with more authority and therefore in opposition to many of their representatives. Some of the Pharisees warned him of Herod's plan to kill him (Luke 13:31), and others invited him to dinner (Luke 11:37). The Pharisee Nicodemus visited Jesus by night, confessing: "Rabbi, we know that you are a teacher who has come

27. So Geza Vermes, *Jesus and the World of Judaism* (Philadelphia: Fortress, 1983), 10.

28. So Ben-Chorin, *Jesus im Judentum,* 54.

29. Geza Vermes, *Jesus the Jew: A Historian's Reading of the Gospels* (Philadelphia: Fortress, 1973), 98-99.

30. So Vermes, *Jesus and the World of Judaism,* 11.

31. So Ben-Chorin, *Jesus im Judentum,* 55, and Pinchas Lapide, *Ist das nicht Josephs Sohn? Jesus im heutigen Judentum* (Stuttgart: Calwer Verlag, 1976), 82-83.

216

from God" (John 3:1-2); finally, Joseph of Arimathea, another Pharisee, asked for Jesus' corpse so that he could bury it according to Jewish rites. We have no reason to doubt that the Pharisees were very close to Jesus, though he did not always agree with all of them. His demise did not come from the Pharisees, the largest religious group at the time, but from the representatives of the establishment.

Herod Antipas in Galilee and the chief priests and their council in Jerusalem had the unenviable task of maintaining law and order and averting major catastrophes. In their eyes Jesus was jeopardizing the status quo. His revolutionary propaganda was contrary to the law of the Roman provincial administration, and it was also murderously foolish, since it could arouse the spirits of his fellow Jews and jeopardize the survival of Judaism in Palestine. Therefore it was better for one man to die for the people "than to have the whole nation destroyed" (John 11:50).[32] The fact that Jesus could have been taken for a zealot shows that he identified with the aspirations and hopes of his people. His use of kingdom language and his preaching and ministry pointed in the direction of redemption for his people, something which could easily be misunderstood as political liberation. Jesus therefore ended on the cross as a political instigator. In despair he cried out: "My God, my God, why have you forsaken me?" (Mark 15:34). Jesus died feeling he had been abandoned by God.

In the Jewish view, Jesus ended as somebody who had tragically failed. But as Schalom Ben-Chorin tells us, this does not diminish his greatness, at least not for the Jewish understanding. "Jesus of Nazareth is a tragic failure whose eyes were blinded out of love for Israel."[33] He can be seen in the same way as Rabbi Akiba, who thought Bar Kochba was the Messiah and paid for this error with his own life. Jesus belongs to Judaism. He died as one for many. Yet he did not die like Bar Kochba in trying to arouse the people to resist Roman domination. His own ministry was one of healing and forgiveness, and of association with sinners. In this way he sought to obtain redemption for his people. "For his contemporaries the way to redemption lay via the destruction of Israel's enemies, not via the forgiveness and invitation to the feast of those who wittingly or unwittingly were the instruments, that is, those

---

32. See the comments by Vermes, *Jesus and the World of Judaism*, 12.
33. Ben-Chorin, *Jesus im Judentum*, 63.

who collaborated with the foreign powers or neglected the carefully established boundaries between Jews and Hellenists."[34]

Perhaps it is tragic that Israel even to the present day has never picked up the transformed Messianic vision of Jesus and still clings to the theo-political vision of traditional Messianism. Their vision remains as precarious as ever, while the other vision, even if it did not lead the Jews to an acceptance of Jesus as their Messiah, would at least offer the perspective of peace. Underlying this is the fundamental difference between the Jewish perception of Jesus and the Christian view of Jesus. In the Jewish perception Jesus is at the most a brother, whereas in the Christian view he is the savior. A brother can only add another voice to the chorus. He cannot fundamentally change or transform tradition. Thus Jesus, for a Jew, can offer another view, but not *the* view. But for those who see him as savior, Jesus does not just add another voice but is *the* voice, the saving one. A transformation is possible, even in that which is entailed by the Messiah. The Jewish Jesus stays on the human level and does not mediate God. He only gives a different interpretation of the law. But Jesus' word and deed cannot be separated. As the human face of God he is both word and deed.

3. Jesus As Word and Deed

The affirmation of Nicea (A.D. 325) that Jesus was of one being with God the Father decisively and inalterably influenced the development of christology. The problem arose when one attempted to express how this Jesus of Nazareth, who was of one being with the Father, could also be a truly human being. The attempt to show intelligibly that a once self-consistent divine nature and a self-consistent human nature came together in one individual human being in such a way that both natures still remained distinct led to blind alleys of doctrinal development and almost unceasing theological controversies.[35] As would be expected, the

34. John Riches, *Jesus and the Transformation of Judaism* (London: Darton, Longman & Todd, 1980), 188, who rightly juxtaposes the political and the nonpolitical options in first-century Judaism.

35. Wolfhart Pannenberg, *Jesus — God and Man*, trans. Lewis L. Wilkins and Duane A. Priebe, 2nd ed. (Philadelphia: Westminster, 1977), 287.

divine side of Jesus always won at the expense of the human side. This was true of monophysite tendencies, which advocated that in Christ two hypostases were joined into one physis, but also of tendencies which advocated a communication between the respective properties of the two natures, and in the idea that there exists a mutual penetration or perichoresis of the divine and human nature. The result is a theanthropic reality, divine actions are conducted in a human way, and human suffering is borne in a divine way and therefore glorified. Since the divine nature of Christ was considered dominating, it was clear to the average believer that he or she should not dare to communicate immediately with Jesus Christ. One had to substitute more human intermediaries. Therefore either icons were substituted for the human face of God, or Mary and the saints filled the gap between us and the divine pantocrator.

With the emergence of critical reason a glorified Christ became more and more suspect. The result was a concentration on the human Jesus. Friedrich Schleiermacher, for instance, presented in his christology the classical example of a christology from below in which he attempted to explain the significance of Jesus Christ from his human side.[36] He called Christ the redeemer, or the one "in Whom the creation of human nature, which up to this point had existed only in the provisional state, was perfected."[37] In this way Jesus shows a solidarity with all of humanity, while at the same time there is a uniqueness in him. He is free from sin and enjoys an unimpaired God-consciousness. Schleiermacher identified this exceptional God-consciousness with God's existence in Christ, saying: "To ascribe to Christ an absolutely powerful God-consciousness, and to attribute to Him an existence of God in Him, are exactly the same thing."[38]

In spite of Schleiermacher's attempt to rid himself of a christology that focused on being, he lapsed back into a terminology that sounds suspiciously ontological. This suspicion is confirmed when Schleiermacher explained how the God-consciousness became so powerful in Jesus. Schleiermacher wrote: "The beginning of His life was also a new

36. So John Macquarrie, "Jesus Christus VI," in *TRE* 17:19.

37. Friedrich Schleiermacher, *The Christian Faith* §92.1, Engl. trans. of the 2nd German ed., ed. H. R. Mackintosh and J. S. Stewart (New York: Harper & Row, 1963), 2:374.

38. Schleiermacher, *The Christian Faith* §94.2, 2:387.

implanting of the God-consciousness which creates receptivity in human nature. . . . That new implanting came to be through the beginning of his life, and therefore that beginning must have transcended every detrimental influence of His immediate circle."[39] What does such implanting mean? Though certainly used metaphorically, it conjures up images of the God-consciousness as some distinct "thing" which is inserted into the person of Jesus Christ.[40]

Schleiermacher ran into problems similar to those of the church fathers in their christological reflection. There is a human Jesus, and in this Jesus something transcendental or divine is inserted. Jesus is neither fully human nor fully divine, since the insertion is surrounded by humanity. But the affirmation of the *vere deus et vere homo*, the truly God and truly human, is essential for Christian theology. Yet this cannot be maintained when two substances come together, since then we have neither the truly human nor the truly divine but either a conglomerate or an individual being in which one or the other dominates. As Wolfhart Pannenberg reminds us: "The formula of the true divinity and true humanity of Jesus begins with the fact that one describes one and the same person, the man Jesus of Nazareth, from different points of view."[41]

The underlying problem is a wrong approach to the phenomenon of Jesus. We cannot do justice to him by trying to fathom his ontological placement in relation to God, but, as the New Testament would tell us, we encounter Jesus both in word and in deed. It neither suffices to concentrate just on his message, as it continues to be fashionable, especially if one preselects those passages that are amenable to one's cause. Nor is it faithful to Jesus to focus on his actions, for instance, his solidarity with sinners and outcasts of society, with women and other underprivileged. Such a Jesus becomes a supporter of one's own agenda instead of being allowed to speak for himself. Word and deed interpret each other and support each other.

Through historical critical research the credibility of the New Testament sources, especially as they relate to the life and activity of

39. Schleiermacher, *The Christian Faith* §95.3, 389.

40. Cf. the reservations of John Macquarrie, *Jesus Christ in Modern Thought* (London: SCM, 1990), 208, who even speaks here of "a logical defect in Schleiermacher's christology."

41. Pannenberg, *Jesus — God and Man*, 284.

Jesus, has been severely shattered. But a retreat to a dogmatic Christ or an ideologically construed Christ who supports one's own agenda is the wrong way out of the dilemma. It has always been a claim peculiar to the Christian faith that it is rooted in history.[42] In contrast to Platonists or any other kind of philosophical idealists, Christians put their trust in an ideal that is not removed from history but has taken shape under the historical conditions of this world. The Logos did not just mediate itself but took on human form and lived among us (John 1:14). This concrete historical assertion provides not only an anchor in history (including its geographic and ethnic rootedness) for Christianity, but it imparts to our present world hope and trust that the self-manifestation of the Logos in history will not remain an isolated incident. Of course, this rootedness in history also makes the Christian faith vulnerable because one is continually prone to check whether any assertion is actually connected to that history.

From the very beginning Christianity displayed a strong tendency to impose on its historic particularity certain dogmatic and philosophical concepts. This began with the innocuous glorification of the historical Jesus, it continued with the Hellenistic two-nature terminology of the divine-human relation, and it concluded with theories of the atonement. Though these concepts usually did not result from abstract considerations but were developed through existential interests, the existential questions of humanity dare not become the starting point of christological reflection. If this were the case, the danger of a human projection would be all too real. Rather, we must pursue the opposite route, take as our starting point the words and deeds of the historic person of Jesus of Nazareth, and ask whether any existential relevance issues from them. This means that the Reformation question, "How do I obtain a gracious God?" must first be transformed into the primary question, "Does the human person of Jesus of Nazareth show us the graciousness of God, and if so, how is that done?" Unlike Martin Kähler we should not be afraid to delve into the "quagmire" of historical-critical research or fear that in so doing we become dependent on the ever-shifting results of New Testament exegesis.

On the surface, hardly any position concerning Jesus of Nazareth has not been taken up by one New Testament exegete or another in the

---

42. This has been convincingly pointed out by Macquarrie, "Jesus Christus VI," in *TRE* 17:45.

last two hundred years. We must also be mindful of the depth of historical skepsis as it has left its imprint on many theologians through Rudolf Bultmann's verdict that it matters only that God acted decisively in Jesus, not who Jesus actually was. When we look at present-day historical research we notice on the one hand a proliferation of specialization. But, on the other hand, there is also a decided effort to bridge fragmentation and prevent atomization in favor of a more holistic approach. Even biblical theology is no longer a bad word in face of the theologies of Q, Mark, the various Pauline epistles, and so on. This renewal of a holistic approach has also influenced the assessment of that which is credible about the Jesus of history. There is a body of information concerning the life and proclamation of Jesus on which most New Testament scholars virtually agree. Of course, the tide may turn again to more pronounced skepticism. If that happens, then we can take comfort that just as the tide has once before turned, so it will return again to the opposite direction.

If we start our christological reflections with the historical Jesus and not with the dogmatic Christ, are we then not simply conceding that Jesus was only a human being? By its very presuppositions historical research can never show us that Jesus was the Christ or that Jesus of Nazareth was the historic manifestation of the divine Logos. Historical research can only show us the human person of Jesus insofar as this person is still traceable. While the results of historical research must be acknowledged, we must also keep in mind that with this Jesus of Nazareth there originated a new religious and spiritual movement. He was identified with the historical manifestation of the divine Logos. Historical research will and can never tell us whether this identification was correct. If it were to do this, it would clearly overstep its boundaries. The decisive question is whether such identification is even permissible. Any help in allowing us to answer this question in the affirmative cannot come from supposedly unique events such as the virgin birth, miracles, or Christ's resurrection. Historians are always able to destroy historical singularity by adducing parallel evidence from other figures and events in history. When we consider Jesus' words and deeds we get the overall impression, as Ernst Fuchs has pointed out, that on occasions Jesus acted as if he stood in God's place. Something transpires here that poses either that Jesus was insane, a religious fanatic, and an impostor, or that he was indeed right in his self-understanding.

While people followed Jesus out of various motivations, some of them may have had an inkling, however faint, that this Jesus was someone to watch and to follow.[43] As the hopes and expectations were not fulfilled in the direction in which they were traditionally looking and in the time frame in which they thought at that time, Jesus was rejected by the vast majority. Only after his death and resurrection could Peter remind his fellow Jews: "Therefore let the entire house of Israel know with certainty that God has made him both Lord and Messiah, this Jesus whom you crucified" (Acts 2:36). Jesus was vindicated both in his words and in his deeds. The same vindication pertained to his self-awareness.

4. Jesus' Self-Awareness

After Rudolf Bultmann had declared that he did not know and did not want to know what Jesus felt in his heart, most serious theologians were hesitant to continue investigating Jesus' self-understanding. The time of romantic books about a gentle Jesus who was kind to women and children and who had a soft heart for people in misery was irrevocably gone. Yet the days of extreme skepticism were over too. Hans Conzelmann (1915-89), a close student of Rudolf Bultmann, denied that we can extrapolate Jesus' self-understanding from the christological titles used by the Gospel writers. At the same time he conceded that Jesus understood himself as the one who issued the final call. "His position is unique, because after him nothing else will 'come' but God himself. . . . In action and teaching he confronts the respective person through himself *immediately* with God."[44] Since Jesus did not leave a confused impression, we may conclude that he knew his own identity, which included a unique relationship to God. When christological reflection later called him truly God and truly human, this could be understood neither as being strictly descriptive nor exhaustive of his own self-identity.[45]

43. It is therefore unwarranted to claim with John Macquarrie: "From the synoptic Gospels it clearly follows that the first disciples who followed Jesus saw in him a human being and nothing else" (Macquarrie, "Jesus Christus VI," in *TRE* 17:50).

44. Hans Conzelmann, "Jesus Christus," in *Religion in Geschichte und Gegenwart*, 3rd ed. (Tübingen: J. C. B. Mohr [Paul Siebeck], 1965), 3:633.

45. For the following see Raymond E. Brown, "Did Jesus Know He Was God?" *Biblical Theological Bulletin* 15 (April 1985), 77-78.

Today there is no longer a problem in perceiving Jesus as a fully human being, as was the case in antiquity. The question posed today is what it means to call Jesus truly God. There is first the picture of Jesus as a rabbi or a teacher. He was called teacher by the people (Mark 9:17), by his disciples (4:38), and even by those who were opposed to him (12:14). But Jesus was not like other rabbis. While a disciple chose his teacher, Jesus himself called those who were to follow him. Therefore we hear in John 15:16: "You did not choose me, but I chose you."[46] There is also no indication that his disciples would sooner or later become rabbis in their own right. As apostles the former disciples became at the most witnesses to Jesus' life and teaching. Since Jesus did not just teach but also proclaimed in an authoritative way and even worked miracles, many considered him a prophet. Here there is an affinity with the Islamic assessment of Jesus as a prophet. But to call him just a prophet would be a misunderstanding, since no Old Testament prophet acted in such independence of the Mosaic law as did Jesus. It is also significant that in reference to Jesus we never find in the New Testament a prophetic formula such as "the Word of God came to Jesus of Nazareth."

The Word did not come to Jesus, since he already had it, or, as John formulated it in the prologue to his Gospel, Jesus *was* the Word. It is no surprise that we read in the New Testament: "Something greater than Jonah is here" (Matt. 12:41). The claim is even made that "something greater than Solomon is here" (12:42).[47] Since the end time was supposed to bring the complete renewal of God's past salvific activity, Jesus related this expectation to his own presence. But he did not announce that he was the expected prophet of the end time. Rather, he made a call for a final renewal. But who was he that he could stand before the people without analogy, being more than a rabbi and a prophet? It is not without significance that in all the layers of the Synoptic tradition a distinction was always made when Jesus talked about God as his Father. He never included his disciples in talking about the Father, but distinguished between "his Father" and "their Father."[48] The only exception is in the Lord's Prayer, where Matthew exchanged the original "Father" (Luke

46. See Leonhard Goppelt, *Theology of the New Testament*, trans. John E. Alsup, ed. Jürgen Roloff (Grand Rapids: Eerdmans, 1981), 1:164, on this passage.
47. See for more details Goppelt, *Theology of the New Testament*, 1:166.
48. See for the following Goppelt, *Theology of the New Testament*, 1:203.

11:2) for the traditional Jewish "Our Father" (Matt. 6:9). All solidarity with his people notwithstanding, Jesus carefully distinguished between him and them with regard to God. Jesus had a unique relationship to God.

There is also the odd-sounding saying in Matthew 11:27: "All things have been handed over to me by my Father; and no one knows the Son except the Father, and no one knows the Father except the Son and anyone to whom the Son chooses to reveal him." A mutual knowing between God and Jesus in the New Testament is usually mentioned only in the Johannine writings (cf. John 10:14). We encounter such mutual knowing also in Hellenistic mysticism and in Gnostic literature, where it points to an ontological relationship. According to this saying Jesus demanded unrestricted authority, since he knew God in an exclusive way. He knows the Father because he is related to him as the Son. Archibald Hunter (1906-) rightly calls this "unshared sonship" the deepest form of Jesus' self-understanding: "a filial relationship, expressed in the phrases 'My Father' and 'the Son,' to which there is no parallel, this is the last secret of the words and works of Jesus."[49] This I-Thou relationship, initiated and sustained by God and fulfilled by Jesus' own response of obedience and love, also shines through in Jesus' prayers, where he addressed God as Father (Mark 14:36).

Addressing God as "abba" ("father") was unique at that time and must have left such a lasting impression on the disciples that even in the Hellenistic church the Aramaic term was still used (cf. Rom. 8:15). "Abba" was the confiding, affectionate address of a child to its father. In Jesus' usage it illustrates his unique and trusting relationship and dedication to his father. Jesus surrendered himself to God's will as a child completely trusts its father. If there existed this kind of relationship between God and Jesus, we may conclude that Jesus' self-understanding was not fixed and settled in every respect once he started his earthly mission. We may properly assume a development in his existential knowledge of what this relationship implied for his life. That he struggled with it until the very end of his earthly sojourn is documented in the moving episode of Jesus' prayer in Gethsemane (Mark 14:32-42) prior to his arrest and capture. This kind of development does not diminish

---

49. Archibald M. Hunter, *The Work and Words of Jesus*, rev. ed. (Philadelphia: Westminster, 1973), 106, including the following quotation.

the fact that there was a unique relationship between God and Jesus, and Jesus knew about it.

When Jesus talked about himself as son or as the Son, he did not just refer to the Old Testament tradition in which Yahweh was considered the Father of Israel and the Israelites sons and daughters of Yahweh (Deut. 32:6; 14:1).[50] He did not talk about God the Father because he was a Jew, but because it allowed him to express his unique relationship with his God. How much was implied already and how much was later developed in christological reflection is difficult to say. For him the Son and Father image provided a picturesque expression of the intimate knowledge he had of God's ultimate will for humanity. This was also illustrated through his use of the Hebrew term "Amen," which was without analogy in Judaism.[51] "Amen" was used by the Jews as a response at the end of prayer, doxology, and Scripture-reading to endorse the words they just heard. Yet Jesus prefaced his own words with "Amen, I say to you" and did not simply respond with "Amen" to something others had said.[52] There are sixty examples of this usage in the Gospel sources (Mark 13; Q 9; Matt. 9; John 25), and all are found on the lips of Jesus. While this may remind us of the Old Testament prophets, who began their pronouncements with "Thus says the LORD," there is a decisive difference. A prophet never dared to say "Amen, I tell you," since he was only a spokesperson of God. The "Amen, I tell you" sayings of Jesus deal with the kingdom of God (Mark 9:1), with those who sacrificed everything for the sake of Jesus (Mark 10:29), with the coming judgment (Matt. 10:15), and with many other central facets of his message. We encounter here a unique feature of Jesus' speech, and it expresses the certainty of the one who knew and promulgated what he had learned from his Father. While a prophet introduced his message with "Thus says the LORD" to indicate that it was not his own wisdom but a divine message, Jesus uttered this message on his own authority.

It was the conviction of the nascent Christian church that there existed a personal union between God and Jesus. This union was also

---

50. Georg Fohrer, "huios, B. Old Testament," in *TDNT* 8:351-52.

51. See for the following Joachim Jeremias, *New Testament Theology: The Proclamation of Jesus*, trans. John Bowden (New York: Charles Scribner's, 1971), 35-36.

52. See for the following the insightful comments of Hunter, *Work and Words of Jesus*, 111.

expressed through the many titles that were conferred upon Jesus. That any of these titles belonged to Jesus' self-awareness is often denied. Günther Bornkamm (1905-90), for example, declares: "It is the special character and work that Jesus is to be found *in* his word and *in* his actions, and that he does not make his own rank a special theme of his message prior to everything else."[53] This is to say that he did not use any of the Messianic titles that tradition had made available. According to Bornkamm, Jesus was superior to any of these concepts which were conferred upon him. Indeed, it does not change our estimate of Jesus whether he used any Messianic titles that were bestowed upon him either in his own time or at a later date. Through him God's rule was inaugurated. But Jesus was not simply a pawn in the inauguration of that rule of God. He was a person in his own right.[54] He had a certain self-understanding, and, for historical accuracy, we must again ask whether this was also expressed in appropriate terminology associated with the expectation of salvation.

A more differentiated analysis of the New Testament sources allowed for some advancements in deciphering Jesus' self-understanding. Since William Wrede (1859-1906) scholars declared that the Messianic secret was just a theory introduced by Mark the Evangelist. This was still the opinion of Rudolf Bultmann and his followers.[55] Since then the concept of a Messianic secret has been found in four discrete layers. The oldest can be traced back to Jesus himself. He talked about the coming of the kingdom, its completion, and the Son of man in terms which are difficult to understand. Then there are sayings about the secret of the kingdom (Mark 4:11) and the partial hiddenness of revelation (Matt. 11:25-26). Again, these sayings could go back to Jesus or at least to the early Christian community. It was only upon this foundation that Mark erected his own scheme of the Messianic secret, which was again transformed by Matthew and Luke until we finally read in John 10:24-25: "How long will you keep us in suspense? If you are the Messiah, tell us plainly." Jesus answered: "I have told you, and you do not believe," an incident that could just as easily be narrated in Matthew

---

53. Günther Bornkamm, *Jesus of Nazareth,* trans. Irene and Fraser McLuskey (London: Hodder and Stoughton, 1969), 169.

54. See the deliberations by Goppelt, *Theology of the New Testament,* 1:160.

55. Goppelt, *Theology of the New Testament,* 1:177.

or Luke. Jesus did not enter the marketplace and declare "Come and see, I am the Messiah." His activity could be easily understood neither in strict analogy to Old Testament expectations nor to hopes currently in vogue among his contemporaries. The same is true for the much debated concept of the Son of man.

Apart from the Gospels the title "Christ" is used over four hundred and fifty times in the New Testament. But within the Gospels it was used only seven times as a self-designation by Jesus himself.[56] The conclusion seems unavoidable that "Christ" was the favorite title of the later Christian church to describe the person and work of Jesus. Most likely it was not used by Jesus with reference to himself. Yet when we come to the title "Son of man," the evidence is very different. It is used only once in the rest of the New Testament, but sixty-nine times in the Synoptics as a self-designation of Jesus. This would make it difficult to substantiate that the early church created this title and conferred it upon Jesus. The New Testament authors would have had to use great care to see that this title appeared virtually exclusively in the Gospels and then only in sayings of Jesus. The church would also have had to be careful not to use this "favorite title" of Jesus in their own designation of him. It would have put a title into the mouth of Jesus that later came into disuse. This conclusion also seems very unlikely.

We may conclude that it is very probable "that Jesus himself made use of the Son of man concept as a model and filled it in such a way that it became a central expression of his mission."[57] In this way he talked about the Son of man who, as the eschatological mediator of salvation, conducts the final judgment and establishes God's rule. Similarly, Jesus talked about the Son of man in his present authority. He was the Lord over the Sabbath (Mark 2:28) and had authority to forgive sins on earth (2:10). Furthermore, he came in humility and had "nowhere to lay his head" (Matt. 8:20). He also came to eat and drink with tax collectors and sinners (11:19), the outcasts of society. Even the sayings of the Son of man who was to suffer and be rejected should not simply be explained

---

56. See for the following the remarks by Robert H. Stein, *The Method and Message of Jesus' Teachings* (Philadelphia: Westminster, 1978), 144.

57. This is also the conclusion of Goppelt, *Theology of the New Testament*, 1:186, after careful analysis of the present state of the discussion.

as later interpretations that were projected back onto Jesus.[58] At least for Mark 9:31 ("The Son of man is to be betrayed into human hands") there is broad agreement that this announcement of the passion dates back to Jesus.[59] The passive mode of the saying focuses everything on God's activity. God allowed the cataclysmic events that Jesus perceived as rushing toward him. He entered them because he understood this to be an eschatological necessity and was convinced that God would not abandon the one who represented him. The statement in Mark 9:31 seems to reflect an Aramaic origin. Since it fits together well with the imagery associated with Mark 10:38, a saying which most likely dates back to Jesus, the former one also seems to be original.[60]

Jesus saw his way as the avenue on which the final salvational activity of God reaches humanity. Since he considered himself not just one of many righteous people, but the one who is more than a prophet and more than a righteous person, he appropriated the suffering servant imagery of Isaiah 53 and applied it to himself. He connected the coming of salvation with himself as the suffering servant of God and announced in the pronouncements of the suffering Son of man that which was applicable to himself.[61] One must concede that in Jewish apocalyptic the Son of man was not supposed to suffer. Yet in Daniel 7 the visionary image of the Son of man is related to the people of God who had to suffer under the powers of this earth. In applying this image to himself, Jesus wanted to help his disciples understand his way of suffering as the avenue by which God's salvational activity comes to fulfillment.[62]

But why would Jesus have used this term to refer to himself? We must first notice that this title was by no means unambiguously defined.

58. This was still the position of Rudolf Bultmann, *Theology of the New Testament*, trans. Kendrick Grobel (New York: Charles Scribner's, 1951), 1:31.

59. So Jürgen Roloff, *Neues Testament* (Neukirchen-Vluyn: Neukirchener Verlag, 1977), 133. The reason why "Son of man" sayings which include the announcement of suffering are not found in Q can be easily be explained by the fact that they are closely associated with the passion story. The passion story is also missing in Q (Roloff, *Neues Testament*, 12).

60. Goppelt, *Theology of the New Testament*, 1:189.

61. It is interesting that Pannenberg, *Jesus — God and Man*, 327, cautions that one should not assume that Jesus knew himself to be the suffering servant of Isaiah 53. Pannenberg also assumes that when Jesus spoke of the Son of man he meant another person. Pannenberg seems to represent here a somewhat dated exegetical position.

62. This is also the conclusion of Goppelt, *Theology of the New Testament*, 1:193.

It was open enough that Jesus could fill it with the content appropriate to his mission. Second, it was not related to the this-worldly Messianic aspirations prevalent in the Israel of that time. It enabled him to declare his unique unity with humanity, especially with the humble and despised. It also illustrated his special function as the representative of the new Israel he was creating and as the bearer of God's sovereignty and judgment. "It was thus at once a title of majesty and of humility."[63] While in Judaism the two figures of the Son of man and the servant of the Lord had existed more or less separately, Jesus knew he was called by God to fuse in his own person the two roles of the Son of man and the servant of the Lord. "He was born to suffer, born a king." A person thinking of himself so highly can only be understood in one of three ways: "Christ either deceived mankind by conscious fraud, or he was himself deluded, or he was divine. There is no getting out of this trilemma."[64] In the New Testament the answer was clearly given with the third option. This was phrased in the terms of Jesus' incarnation, his preexistence, and his virgin birth.

Excursus: Incarnation, Preexistence, and Virgin Birth

Incarnation, preexistence, and virgin birth are different ways in which the biblical writers point out the unique relation between Jesus' divine origin and his human existence. All three of them have their analogue in the history of religions and have been highly debated since the inception of rationalism, a movement which disclaimed the facticity of anything in Jesus that went beyond that which could be expected of a mere human being.

The concept of incarnation is related to concepts such as manifestation or epiphany, meaning that the godhead manifests itself or appears in this world. In Tibetan Buddhism, the Dalai Lama is understood as an incarnation of a certain bodhisattva. In Hinduism, the concept of *avatar* is similar to incarnation, meaning that the godhead appears in different human or animal forms and is partially or totally present in

---

63. See Hunter, *Work and Words of Jesus,* 108, for this and the following quotation.
64. John Duncan, *Colloquia Peripatetica* (Edinburgh, 1870), 109, as cited in Hunter, *Work and Words of Jesus,* 112.

these forms. In the intertestamental period and in late Judaism, there was the expectation of a heavenly, angel-like being who would appear on earth in the last days.

It is not surprising that the Christian concept of incarnation has come under heavy attack. In 1977 historian of religion John Hick (1922-) edited a book entitled *The Myth of God Incarnate,* "and it immediately set off the biggest theological controversy in Britain since *Honest to God* fifteen years earlier."[65] In the first eight months it sold 30,000 copies, 24,000 of them in Great Britain alone. Apart from Michael Goulder's claim that "Paul appropriated the idea of Jesus' incarnation in the course of dialectic with the Samaritan [Christian] missionaries in Corinth and Ephesus between A.D. 50 and 55," nothing in this collection of essays was actually new.[66] For instance, we are told:

> Jesus cannot be a *real* man and also unique in a sense different from that in which each one of us is a unique individual. A literal incarnation doctrine, expressed in however sophisticated form, cannot avoid some element of docetism, and involves the believer in claims for uniqueness which seem straightforwardly incredible to the majority of our contemporaries.[67]

Or: "To reduce *all of God* to a human incarnation is virtually inconceivable." Instead, we are offered the following alternative: "I find salvation in Christ, because in him God is disclosed to me as a 'suffering God.'"

One argues here on two different planes, first on the theological, claiming that incarnational thinking leads to docetism. As God incarnate, Jesus is not an actual human being. Second, on the plane of contemporary secular thinking, the concept of incarnation is disclaimed on the ground that it could not point to an actual historical occurrence. The alternative introduced here of a suffering God who is disclosed in Jesus is supposed

65. So Michael Goulder, foreword to *Incarnation and Myth: The Debate Continued,* ed. Michael Goulder (Grand Rapids: Eerdmans, 1979), vii.

66. Michael Goulder, "The Two Roots of the Christian Myth," in *The Myth of God Incarnate,* ed. John Hick (London: SCM, 1977), 64-86 (quoted from p. 79). See also Graham Stanton, "Samaritan Incarnational Christology?" in *Incarnation and Myth,* 243, who comes to the conclusion that it is extremely unlikely "that Paul's 'incarnational' christology has been influenced by Samaritan views."

67. For this and the following quotations see Frances Young, "A Cloud of Witnesses," in *The Myth of God Incarnate,* 32, 35, 38.

to circumvent the problem that contemporary secular sentiment might have with the notion of the majesty of God. Instead of the grandeur of God, solidarity with human suffering is called for. Yet unless such a God has the power to change present conditions, it remains dubious how he could ever provide any salvation in a true sense. At the most he could be a sympathetic fellow-sufferer.

Incarnation, of course, does not imply that God Almighty has abdicated in favor of his Son. "It means that the Son shares the Father's nature, and that the God to whom universal worship will be given is the one who has disclosed himself as Jesus."[68] Jesus is, so to speak, the window through which God allows us to perceive God's will. Jesus of Nazareth discloses God for us and thereby becomes the criterion for our understanding of the nature and will of God. Jesus' humanity mediates God to us and therefore God's love is communicated to us "by God's own incarnate presence here in our midst."[69] The concept of the incarnation is the peculiarly Christian way of speaking of God's dealings with humanity and humanity's experience and knowledge of God. Three points are noteworthy in the notion of incarnation: First, the initiative is from God and not from humanity; second, God is deeply involved in his creation; and third, the center of this initiative and involvement is Jesus Christ.[70] Incarnation signifies an act of God at a definite point in space and time at which God became human in his Son as Jesus of Nazareth, born of Mary, "a virgin espoused to a man called Joseph, a Jew of the tribe and lineage of David, and towards the end of the reign of Herod the Great in Judea."[71] This divine involvement with the created order by no means implies that in some Hegelian fashion God merged with or into his own creation. The difference between God the Father and the Son and the created order is safeguarded by the concept of preexistence.

---

68. Michael Green, "Jesus in the New Testament," in *The Truth of God Incarnate*, ed. Michael Green (Grand Rapids: Eerdmans, 1977), 23.

69. Brian Hebblethwaite, *The Incarnation: Collected Essays in Christology* (Cambridge: Cambridge University Press, 1987), 35.

70. See John Macquarrie, "Christianity without Incarnation? Some Critical Comments," in *The Truth of God Incarnate*, 143, who lists these three points.

71. Thomas F. Torrance, *Space, Time and Incarnation* (London: Oxford University Press, 1969), 52. When Torrance says here that "the Son of God became man" he skirts the issue that God became human; hence ancient christology talked about Mary as *"theotokos,"* mother of God.

The New Testament scholar Martin Hengel (1926-) rightly claims: *"There was an inner necessity about the introduction of the idea of pre-existence into christology."*[72] The Old Testament bears witness that God sent angels, special people, and prophets who represented God and announced his will. Because of their ontological difference from God, they were his true and full representatives only in a limited sense. Jesus was completely different, for in him there occurred a complete self-disclosure of God as God's Messiah. "In Jesus the pre-existent Word became embodied in a single human individual who was so faithful a reproduction of it as to be its complete reflection and incarnation. But there is no suggestion that this individual was not a man in every sense of the word."[73] To safeguard the notion that Jesus was fully human he was depicted as having descended from the heavenly sphere and having become humiliated, as described in Philippians 2:6-11. On the divine side, the notion of preexistence subsumed the attributes initially accorded to wisdom in Judaism, such as the mediation of creation and of salvation.[74] It was emphasized that in Jesus Christ "are hidden all the treasures of wisdom and knowledge" (Col. 2:3). This assertion implied that in Jesus of Nazareth God's self-disclosure had occurred in an unsurpassable and final way.

The association of Jesus with wisdom was not simply a later elaboration, a retrospective reflection on his life and destiny from the perspective of the resurrection. As the source Q (which exclusively contains sayings attributed to Jesus) shows, from the very beginning Jesus' followers collected sayings of the one whom they understood to be the Messiah. This occurred in analogy to the collection of sayings attributed to King Solomon in *The Wisdom of Solomon*. It was clear for them that "someone greater than Solomon is here!" (Luke 11:31). Jesus was considered the representative of divine wisdom.

In the *logos* christology of the prologue to the Gospel of John, there occurred the consequent finalization of merging the notion of the preexistent Son of God with that of traditional wisdom. He was in the beginning, and all things came into being through him. Yet now the concept

---

72. Martin Hengel, *The Son of God: The Origin of Christology and the History of Jewish-Hellenistic Religion,* trans. John Bowden (Philadelphia: Fortress, 1976), 71. Italics author's.
73. John A. T. Robinson, *The Human Face of God* (London: SCM, 1972), 152-53.
74. See for the following Hengel, *The Son of God,* 72.

of *sophia,* that is, wisdom, was replaced by the term *logos,* Word of God, since the former concept was tainted too much by mythological speculation. In the Western tradition the notion of wisdom has been largely forgotten. In the Orthodox liturgy of Eastern Christendom, however, wisdom *(sophia)* is closely connected with the reading of Scripture, reminding us that in the Bible the wisdom of God is contained, since it is the reflection of God's self-disclosure. It is only natural that Paul would call Christ "the power of God and the wisdom of God" (1 Cor. 1:24), since he is prior to all created things and has power over nature and history.

Is a preexistent Jesus not an anemic human figure with a strong tinge of docetism, as the writers of *The Myth of God Incarnate* surmised? The Epistle to the Hebrews disperses such doubts. On the one hand, it describes Jesus Christ as "the reflection of God's glory and the exact imprint of God's very being . . . [who] sustains all things by his powerful word" (Heb. 1:3). On the other hand, Jesus is introduced as "a Son" whom God "appointed heir of all things" (Heb. 1:2). Moreover, "he learned obedience through what he suffered; and having been made perfect, he became the source of eternal salvation for all who obey him" (Heb. 5:8-9). The high christology in Hebrews is balanced by a low christology which might even imply adoptionistic trends, leading us to believe that Jesus came to his unparalleled status once he had been found faithful to his calling. Such a conclusion might tempt us to talk about a retroactive christology, saying that the full godhead was bestowed upon Jesus only after his mission was accomplished. Yet such thinking runs counter to this letter: "Therefore he had to become like his brothers and sisters in every respect, so that he might be a merciful and faithful high priest in the service of God, to make a sacrifice of atonement for the sins of the people" (Heb. 2:17). In conclusion it must be stated that Jesus was both completely human in that he did not take recourse to some elevated status while living on earth, and completely divine in that he had always been and always will be with God.[75]

Earlier Paul had pursued the same tendency as the Epistle to the Hebrews. In Romans 1:3 Paul writes about the gospel "concerning his Son, who was descended from David according to the flesh and was

75. For very insightful comments on this issue see Robinson, *The Human Face of God,* 158ff.

declared to be Son of God with power according to the spirit of holiness by the resurrection from the dead." While this statement might lend itself to a retroactive christology, meaning that from the perspective of the resurrection Jesus was then declared Son of God, Galatians 4:4 would mitigate such thinking: "But when the fullness of time had come, God sent his Son, born of a woman, born under the law, in order to redeem those who were under the law." Until the time is ready God's Son waits to be sent to his people. While in every respect he is a human being born like the rest of us, he nevertheless completely embodied the divine initiative and saving presence.

When we come to Philippians 2:5-11, we are not confronted with a Gnostic redeemer myth which says that the divine being Jesus was sent into this world and upon accomplishment of his mission was restored to his former glory. The Gnostic myth which talks about the sending and return of a heavenly redeemer figure postdates Philippians 2. Moreover, unlike Jesus, the redeemer in this myth did not become an actual human being and his return to his former glory was not the result of his obedience but of his heavenly constitution.[76] Philippians 2, a hymn which Paul picked up from the early Christian community, employs various concepts to show that Christ went from preexistence to humility and on to final exaltation. Yet for Paul the emphasis is not on the transition from one phase to another, but on the humility, obedience, and selflessness of Christ. Paul wanted to show the Philippians the way of Jesus as an example for their own lives.[77]

When we now turn to the Gospel of John, we are confronted with a two-source theory. Jesus has a heavenly Father and an earthly mother. There is no contradiction for John in Jesus' being sent from God and

---

76. While Robinson, *The Human Face of God*, 163, writes of "a Gnosticizing version of the distinctively Christian message," Gerhard Friedrich, "Der Brief an die Philipper," in *Die Briefe an die Galater, Epheser, Philipper, Kolosser, Thessalonicher und Philemon,* by J. Becker, H. Conzelmann, and G. Friedrich, Das Neue Testament Deutsch, vol. 8 (Göttingen: Vandenhoeck & Ruprecht, 1985), 151, clearly denies this. It is also strange that Robinson always rejects the notion that Christ would have come from high and instead emphasizes his human status. The two do not seem to exclude each other. To the contrary, only because this human being was once on high could he return to that former state and provide salvation for us there. Exaltation is not a reward for Jesus' faithfulness but the consequence of his former state and his accomplished mission.

77. Friedrich, "Der Brief an die Philipper," 152.

being utterly and genuinely human. He is "the man called Jesus" (John 9:11). John the Baptist declares about Jesus: "After me comes a man who ranks ahead of me" (1:30). We also read that "God did not send his Son into the world to condemn the world, but in order that the world might be saved through him" (3:17). Jesus asks: "Can you say that the one whom the Father has sanctified and sent into the world is blaspheming because he said, 'I am God's Son'?" (10:36). Jesus is a full human being and at the same time God's Son who was sent into the world. Preexistence and the full humanity of Jesus do not exclude each other.

Preexistence should not be construed to mean that Jesus waited in some heavenly realm until the time "was fully come," and then he could be incarnated. As the analogy and even interchangeability of logos, sophia, and Jesus indicates, preexistence does not imply a preexistent person but the certainty and insistence that that which appeared in the human form of Jesus of Nazareth was indeed of divine origin and had occurred with divine sanction. In Jesus the fullness of the Godhead is present in human form. Just as any talk about the preexistent person of Jesus leads to undue speculation, it is unnecessary to talk about the triune God prior to the Christ event. Only from there do we know that God is triune as Father, Son, and Holy Spirit. Relocating the triune God into the Old Testament leads to speculation. Similar to incarnation, preexistence is a necessary concept to express that God was indeed fully present in Jesus.

It is interesting that in those New Testament writings where the notion of preexistence occurs we do not find the concept of virgin birth, and vice versa. At least since Rudolf Bultmann it has been claimed, even by Wolfhart Pannenberg, that "the legend of Jesus' virgin birth stands in an irreconcilable contradiction to the Christology of the incarnation of the pre-existent Son of God found in Paul and John. According to this legend, Jesus first *became* God's Son through Mary's conception."[78] Yet Pannenberg wants to maintain the theological content of the legend of the virgin birth (that Jesus from the very beginning has been Son of God and therefore is God's Son in person). But do the notions of the virginal conception and of the preexistence of Jesus need to exclude

---

78. Pannenberg, *Jesus — God and Man*, 143; see also Rudolf Bultmann, "New Testament and Mythology," in *Kerygma and Myth*, ed. Hans-Werner Bartsch, trans. Reginald Fuller (New York: Harper & Row, 1961), 34-35.

each other? Are they not complementary assertions that Jesus is the Son of God? While the one emphasizes the miraculous conception, the other points to his preexistence.[79] If both have the same goal, it is not surprising that one notion is missing where the other one is used, and vice versa. Yet it would be wrong to assume that with the concept of the virginal conception Jesus' existence as the Son of God started at his birth, whereas with the notion of preexistence it started before the beginning of the world. The emphasis is not on temporality, but on ontology. While Jesus' earthly origin is an act of God, through his ontological union with God Jesus always has been and always will be.

"Commonly the virgin birth is regarded as a 'theological statement' without historical content."[80] Indeed, when we claim that Mary has always been a virgin we could leave historical ground and simply talk about the theological significance of Mary's virginity, that Mary completely surrendered herself to the salvation-historical service of God.[81] But when we look at the biblical narratives, the virginal conception has little to do with Mariology and much to do with christology. In the Gospel according to Matthew, the Gospel writer tells the reader that Mary's pregnancy is caused by the Holy Spirit. Any human sexual agent in begetting the child is ruled out, as well as any sexual relations between Mary and Joseph after the child had been conceived until Jesus was born (Matt. 1:18-22). Armed with this knowledge, the reader cannot misunderstand Mary's situation the way Joseph did. Yet even Joseph had to act the way God wanted him to. He did not divorce Mary, and, by accepting Jesus as his son, he became his legal parent and transferred to him the Davidic ancestry. All of this, according to the Gospel writer, was done through God's will.

In a way similar to that in which preexistence rules out adoptionism, the divine sonship through the work of the Holy Spirit excludes the

79. See Karl-Josef Kuschel, *Born before All Time? The Dispute over Christ's Origin*, trans. John Bowden (New York: Crossroad, 1992), 318, who follows here the suggestion of Gerhard Lohfink.

80. So Heikki Räisänen, "Maria/Marienfrömmigkeit. I. Neues Testament," in *TRE* 22:118.

81. Karl Rahner, "Dogmatische Bemerkungen zur Jungfrauengeburt," in *Zum Thema Jungfrauengeburt*, ed. K. Suso Frank et al. (Stuttgart: KBW, 1970), 157, who draws out the theological significance of the eternal virginity of Mary as being part of the faith of the church.

adoption of Jesus as the Son of God at some point during his life. But "there is no suggestion of an incarnation whereby a figure who was previously with God takes on flesh," as with the notion of preexistence.[82] Yet preexistence christology and virginal-conception christology were soon brought together so that the preexistent word of God was described as taking flesh (John) in the womb of the virgin Mary (Matthew and Luke). While in the New Testament both concepts are still used by different writers, the story is different when we come to the church fathers. Justin Martyr, for instance, writes: "And when we say also that the Word who is the first-birth of God was produced without sexual union, and that He, Jesus Christ, our Teacher, was crucified and died, and rose again," citing virtually in one breath both Christ as the eternal *logos* and Christ as the one born by a virgin.[83] The virginal conception is no longer directed against the adoptionistic heresy, but signifies the point at which the human face of God entered this world.

For Matthew and Luke the virginal conception was not just a symbol regardless of what had taken place historically. In all likelihood both of them regarded the virginal conception as historical. But when the ancient creeds confessed that Jesus was "born of the virgin Mary," this confession echoed Paul's assertion that Jesus was "born of a woman" (Gal. 4:4), meaning that Jesus was an actual human being who had a certain mother and who found his death under Pontius Pilate. The virginal conception as such was of lesser interest, since it was used to underscore the full humanity of Jesus. Today our interests have shifted. We also want to know whether it makes sense to believe in the virginal conception of Jesus. We should note here that the interest of the Evangelists is not scientific. There is no indication that they ever bothered to contemplate whether a virginal conception was biologically possible. They simply asserted the virginal conception of Jesus Christ. This makes all discussions about the possibility of a pathenogenesis of a human being irrelevant.[84] For the Evangelists it was clear that God could bring it about if he wanted.

---

82. Raymond E. Brown, *The Birth of the Messiah: A Commentary on the Infancy Narratives in Matthew and Luke,* new ed. (Garden City, N.Y.: Doubleday, 1993), 141.

83. Justin Martyr, *The First Apology* 21, in *ANF* 1:170.

84. So rightly Archibald M. Hunter, *The Work and Words of Jesus,* 33. See also the elaborations on pathenogenesis by Robinson, *The Human Face of God,* 50-51.

But do the biblical accounts of the virginal conception not simply reflect similar stories of the pagan world or of other world religions which were then transferred onto Jesus? In these so-called parallels, of which there are many, we consistently find that a divine male impregnates a woman either through normal sexual intercourse or through some other substitute. According to the New Testament, however, Jesus is begotten through the creative power of the Holy Spirit. "There is no clear example of *virginal* conception in world or pagan religions that plausibly could have given first-century Jewish Christians the idea of the virginal conception of Jesus."[85]

When we look into Judaism for parallels, we do not find any. The only parallel would be Isaiah 7:14, where the prophet announces: "Look, the young woman is with child and shall bear a son, and shall name him Immanuel." This was then altered in Matthew 1:23 to read: "Look, the virgin shall conceive and bear a son, and shall name him Immanuel." This would indicate that in Christian exegesis Isaiah 7:14 was reinterpreted in the light of an existing Christian tradition of the virginal conception of Jesus. Yet neither in Judaism nor in present-day exegesis has Isaiah 7:14 been interpreted to refer to a virginal conception. The impetus for such an interpretation could not have come from Judaism, but from Christian sources.[86]

The question still needs to be resolved whether Christians could ever have found out about such a virginal conception. The only item that could have been public knowledge was that Mary became pregnant before she came to live with her husband. We can deduce, for instance, from the anti-Christian work of Celsus who claimed that Mary was convicted of adultery with a Roman soldier named Panthera, that for the opponents of Jesus such an early birth supplied evidence of illegitimacy. For Christians, however, Jesus' birth was explained in terms of a miraculous conception while his mother was still a virgin, that is, before she came to live at Joseph's house.[87] So the historically warranted alternative to the virginal conception is not a conception in wedlock but an illegitimacy through Mary's adultery.

On the issue of historicity we should not forget the initial slant of

---

85. Brown, *Birth of the Messiah*, 523.
86. Brown, *Birth of the Messiah*, 524.
87. For examples of anti-Christian polemics see Brown, *Birth of the Messiah*, 534-35.

the assertion of the virgin birth, namely, that Jesus was indeed born by a human mother as every human being is born. Yet the stories of the virginal conception affirmed that already at birth Jesus was God's special Son born through a special act of God. Here lies the difference between Jesus and other human beings, who could also be called sons and daughters of God. The church fathers used the notion of the virgin birth to emphasize the divinity of Jesus and therefore the full efficacy of his salvational activity.[88] In the formation of the Christian dogma, the virginal conception of Jesus soon became an item that proved the sinlessness of Jesus. Since he was conceived without the sexual nature of human propagation and the sensual appetites aroused by that, he was free from original sin. In the long run Jesus' virginal conception was not considered sufficient to ensure his sinlessness, and the church stated that Mary, too, had been immaculately conceived. In order to free Jesus from the entanglement of sin, it was thought that in no way could he have been marred by a sexually produced conception. Small wonder that such kind of reasoning bordered on docetism. Contrary to the original notion of virginal conception, Jesus could not have been a fully human being. But "in its origins, the virginal conception shows no traces whatsoever of an anti-sexual bias and should not be made to support one. For the evangelists it was a visible sign of God's gracious intervention in connection with the becoming of His Son."[89]

We should keep in mind that the virginal conception is not primarily an explanation but "an affirmation of mystery."[90] It affirms that God is at work in bringing Jesus into this world as his own Son. This affirmation is then clothed in the narrative of a physical miracle. Whether one accepts this primarily as poetry and as a symbol or as a historic occurrence, one should not overlook the important message it conveys: God's self-disclosure in history is not a human possibility. It is a divine gift of grace since it discloses to us the one who was before all creation and through whom all creation has been made. In bringing to us his divine fullness God bridges the ugly, broad ditch that separates us God-alienated beings from our source of origin, our inspiration for living, and our ultimate destiny.

---

88. So K. Suso Frank, "'Geboren aus der Jungfrau Maria: Das Zeugnis der Alten Kirche'," in *Zum Thema Jungfrauengeburt*, ed. Frank, 95.

89. So rightly Brown, *The Birth of the Messiah*, 530.

90. Hunter, *The Work and Words of Jesus*, 34.

6. Cross and Resurrection

Once a human life has come to its earthly conclusion one can assess it in its entirety. The cross of Jesus as the means by which he suffered death signifies the conclusion of his human life. Any assessment of his person, life, and ministry must take this cross as its starting point. At the same time it would be historically inaccurate to dwell exclusively on the cross, since it is the deep conviction of the Christian community that Jesus did not remain in death but was resurrected as the Christ. This claim and its historical roots mark the other side of an appropriate interpretation of Jesus. It is important not to collapse the two into one or to emphasize one at the expense of the other. The cross and the resurrection are neither identical nor are they, so to speak, two sides of the same coin. It is sufficient to say that the cross signifies the historically verifiable end point of Jesus' life. Just as any human being dies, Jesus also faced death. But there is no analogy to the resurrection of Jesus in our human sphere. If any reality pertains to it, it must be a divine reality which goes beyond that which can be expected for the destiny of a human life.

When we turn to accounts of Jesus' death, we are confronted with suggestions that he did not enter death without being fully aware of its significance. Unlike most human beings he did not confront death without knowing why. Jesus clearly addressed the question of the meaning of his death, especially in connection with the so-called Last Supper. While it is often claimed that other announcements and predictions of his death were introduced by the believing community after the fact, no such claims are made about the interpretation of Jesus' death in the context of the Last Supper. Here it is commonly argued that we encounter genuine Jesus material. Yet even predictions such as "The Son of man has to be betrayed into human hands" (Mark 9:31) should not be too quickly relegated to the status of later additions.[1] They are not just announcements of what will happen, but they indicate that what will happen is anything but accidental. It is part of God's plan, which Jesus must accept. A simple prediction would have been too self-evident, since, knowing about the Jewish law and about the destiny of most prophets, Jesus knew very well what destiny he would eventually face. The important point is not that Jesus foretold his death (that would have been a very simple matter!), but that he gave his death a very significant interpretation.

1. Jesus' Self-Interpretation of His Death (Eucharist)

In the New Testament we have three independent traditions concerning the Last Supper: Mark 14:22-25 with its parallel in Matthew 26:26-29; 1 Corinthians 11:23-25; and Luke 22:15-20. The oldest version is represented by Paul, who probably wrote his first letter to the congregation in Corinth in A.D. 54. Yet the account which Mark offers to us dates back to an even earlier stage of the tradition, though it was written later than Paul's version. It is characterized by numerous Semitic-sounding words and terms, altogether at least twenty-three, while all the other traditions (including that of Paul) present a rather Greek-sounding text.[2] The Lukan account is preserved in two versions, the shorter one comprising Luke 22:15-19a and the longer one extending to Luke 22:20. While usually a shorter version is regarded as the older one, here it is the virtually unanimous opinion that the longer one is the original. This is also supported by the fact that most ancient manuscripts contain the longer version.[3] Altogether then we have a very well-documented tradition, so that there can be no doubt of the historic fact that Jesus held a last supper with his disciples.

---

1. See Leonhard Goppelt, *Theology of the New Testament*, trans. John E. Alsup, ed. Jürgen Roloff (Grand Rapids: Eerdmans, 1981), 1:188ff., where he shows that the often accepted opinion that the announcements of Jesus' suffering are *vaticina ex eventu* is historically and theologically untenable.

2. So Joachim Jeremias, *"Das ist mein Leib..."* (Stuttgart: Calwer Verlag, 1972), 17-18.

3. Jeremias, *"Das ist mein Leib,"* 20.

Some scholars, however, have claimed that the so-called Last Supper has analogies in Hellenistic mystery cults, which can hardly be reconciled with the claim that its origin was in Palestine, that is, in Jerusalem.[4] Indeed, Justin Martyr (ca. 100–ca. 165) complained that "the wicked devils have imitated [the Lord's Supper] in the mysteries of Mithras, commanding the same thing to be done. For, that bread and a cup of water are placed with certain incantations in the mystic rites of one who is being initiated, you either know or can learn."[5] While Justin Martyr noticed a similarity between the Lord's Supper and the sacred meals in the Mithras cult, he also implicitly admitted that sacred meals are not unique to Christianity. In antiquity there were a variety of meals that in some way or other were connected with cultic rites, sacrifices, or meals in memory of the dead.[6] Justin Martyr correctly observed the similarity in the cultic execution of the rite. But it is not what is done that is decisive, but what is meant by the rite. In the mystery cults, one wanted to get in touch with the godhead. But the intention of the Last Supper was quite different. Moreover, the frequent Semitic expressions in the text of the Last Supper mitigate against a Hellenistic origin. The connections point much more to Judaism and the Old Testament.

The Last Supper must also be considered in the context of Jesus' table fellowship. The Last Supper was not the only meal (though it was the most important one) which Jesus had with his disciples and which they continued to have after Easter.[7] In oriental understanding, having table fellowship was not a casual affair but the sign that one was granted peace, confidence, community, and forgiveness. Table fellowship signified a mutual sharing of lives. Since it was customary in Judaism at the time of Jesus to pray before and after the meal, there was also present a religious dimension, since one was joined together under God's auspices. It is not surprising that other Jews took offense at Jesus being the guest of sinners (cf. Luke 19:7). By having table fellowship with them, he demonstrated that he was forgiving them their sins. In representing

4. For the validity of these charges see Goppelt, *Theology of the New Testament*, 1:214-15.

5. Justin Martyr, *The First Apology* 66, in *ANF* 1:185.

6. So rightly Gerhard Delling, "Abendmahl II," in *TRE* 1:48.

7. So Jeremias, *"Das ist mein Leib,"* 7.

God, he showed the sinners that he did not exclude them. He wanted to have table fellowship with them.

Since Peter had recognized Jesus as the Messiah (Mark 8:29), table fellowship with Jesus had taken on an even more significant meaning. If Jesus was the Messiah, then each meal with him that his disciples enjoyed was a proleptic anticipation of the meal at the time of salvation.[8] These kinds of meals were then continued when the early Christians day by day "broke bread at home and ate their food with glad and generous hearts, praising God and having the goodwill of all people" (Acts 2:46-47). In so doing they followed his command: "Do this in remembrance of me" (Luke 22:19). The followers of Jesus should always come together for a common meal so that the Messianic community becomes visible, and they should plead to God that he bring about the Messianic fulfillment. In their celebration of the Lord's Supper Christians proclaim the commencement of salvation and at the same time ask God to complete it.

What was now the special significance of this Last Supper? According to Mark, the Last Supper was a Passover meal (Mark 14:12): "On the first day of the unleavened bread, when the Passover lamb is sacrificed, his disciples said to him, 'Where do you want us to go and make the preparations for you to eat the Passover?'" While this reference to a specific date, the first day of the feast of the unleavened bread, occurs only within the narrative of the Last Supper, in Luke we find the same reference within the actual meal when Jesus says: "I have eagerly decided to eat this Passover with you before I suffer" (Luke 22:15). The Gospel of John presents a different chronology: "They led Jesus from Caiaphas to Pilate's headquarters. It was early in the morning. They themselves did not enter the headquarters, so as to avoid ritual defilement to be able to eat the Passover" (John 18:28). According to this version Jesus was arrested the evening before the Passover day and was crucified on the day of the Passover, meaning that he died at the same time when the Passover lambs were slaughtered in the temple. With two different dates and therefore two different contexts of the Last Supper we are confronted with the following options: we can side either with the Synoptic writers or with John. Or we can pass by the historical anchoring altogether and say that the Synoptics try to locate the Last Supper histori-

---

8. See for the following Jeremias, *"Das ist mein Leib,"* 12-13.

cally as a Passover meal in order to emphasize that Jesus was the true Passover lamb. John's emphasis then was on the crucifixion, by which he showed that Jesus was indeed the Passover lamb.[9]

While it is likely that the Last Supper presupposes a Passover meal, we can no longer ascertain its original historical setting. This concession does not render us helpless concerning the exact meaning of the Last Supper, since the narratives show that Jesus' actions at that Supper are connected not specifically with a Passover meal but with the basic elements of any Jewish meal, the breaking of the bread and the cup of blessing. But when we relate it to a Passover meal many details become understandable and their significance is clearer.[10] Four elements in the Last Supper are significant:[11] the eschatological reference (Mark 14:25: "Truly I tell you, I will never again drink of the fruit of the vine until the day when I drink it new in the kingdom of God"); the reference concerning the bread; the reference concerning the cup; and the command to continue these meals (1 Cor. 11:24: "Do this in remembrance of me").

The eschatological reference is phrased by Paul in the following words: "For as often as you eat the bread and drink of the cup, you proclaim the Lord's death until he comes" (1 Cor. 11:26). While Paul closes with this eschatological outlook on the coming of the Lord, as is fitting for liturgical use, both Mark and Luke have it in the beginning, together with Jesus' announcement that he will never again drink of the fruit of the vine until that day when he drinks it anew in the kingdom of God (Mark 14:25; Luke 22:18). With this statement Jesus prefaces the whole meal.[12] Jesus announces that his communion with his disciples is now ending. It will only be renewed with the visible inbreaking of the kingdom of God.

---

9. Eduard Lohse, *History of the Suffering and Death of Jesus Christ*, trans. Martin O. Dietrich (Philadelphia: Fortress, 1967), 53-54, seems to eliminate the historical issue altogether by simply applying a theological interpretation. Yet it is important to anchor the crucifixion of Jesus historically even if we cannot pinpoint the exact date. Otherwise we are sailing on the nonhistorical plane of mythology and risk becoming just another mystery cult tossed about by the changing winds of the times.

10. See Goppelt, *Theology of the New Testament*, 1:215, who offers here very good insights in the problematic of the exact date and its relevance.

11. These four items have been pointed out by Goppelt, *Theology of the New Testament*, 1:215-16, whom we will follow in our considerations.

12. Goppelt, *Theology of the New Testament*, 1:216.

What is the reason for this unusual arrangement? Why does Jesus invite his disciples for the meal and then refrain from eating with them?[13] An answer can be found in the words by which he interpreted the bread and wine. If they refer to his body and blood, then it would be quite unusual that he would eat them, consuming himself, so to speak. Another reason might be that his last hours on earth are approaching. Unlike somebody who was to be executed and who was allowed to have one more good meal on earth, Jesus already eliminates the feast from his life. He has decided to go that final way to which his Father leads him and dedicates his life totally to God (cf. John 17:19). It is not without significance that the Christian congregations in Asia Minor who celebrated the Christian Passover at the same time that the Jews held their Passover, maintained the original staging with one significant difference. They fasted the evening of the Passover feast and consumed the meal in the morning when the cock crowed. Epiphanius (ca. 315-403) gives the following reason for this: "And when the Jews are feasting, do you fast and wail over them, because on the day of their feast they crucified Christ; and while they are lamenting and eating unleavened bread in bitterness, do you feast."[14] The fasting should be counted as an expiation for the unbelief and sinfulness of the Jews. Most likely this custom reflects Jesus' own doing. He fasted and prayed that his people might recognize what was good for them and for their salvation. Jesus opened this Last Supper by interceding for those who were supposed to fall under God's judgment, offering himself as a sacrifice.

What should the disciples do after his death? Were they now eliminated from communion with Jesus? The subsequent words of Jesus pointed in a different direction. There was to be a new kind of communion with him. At the same time, they felt they should continue to fast for Israel, hoping for the union between church and synagogue.

After this unusual introduction Jesus proceeded with the meal, just as a Jewish householder would. At the beginning of each meal the man of the house took the bread into his hand and after saying the usual blessing, "Blessed are you who bring forth bread from the earth," he broke the bread into pieces and gave it to the other participants in the meal. At this point

---

13. See on this question Joachim Jeremias, *The Eucharistic Words of Jesus*, 3rd ed., trans. Norman Perrin (New York: Charles Scribner's, 1966), 128.

14. *Constitution of the Holy Apostles* 5.17, in *ANF* 7:446-47.

Jesus spoke the unusual words: "Take; this is my body" (Mark 14:22). "Body," or "flesh," a term more likely used, signifies the human being or the person. With these words Jesus announced that he was going to die, and now he gave himself again to his followers, since the gift mentioned in these words is the person of Jesus as it confronts us after his death. At the end of the meal he took the cup with wine, as in Jewish custom, lifted it slightly above the table, said grace over it for the meal, and handed it to his disciples. As they drank from it, he told them: "This is my blood of the covenant, which is poured out for many" (Mark 14:24). As Leviticus 17:11 indicated: "The life of the flesh is in the blood"; the blood that is poured out is the life that Jesus gave through his dying.

The blood of Jesus does not necessarily mean that he is sacrificed like an animal and could be compared to a Passover lamb. While an animal is always sacrificed as a victim, Jesus intentionally gave his life for many. The term "many" does not mean to imply that some might be excluded from this gift of life. In English and Greek "many" stands in contrast to "all." But in the original Hebrew or Aramaic there is no term to indicate "all," and therefore the term "many" also stands for "all."[15] Paul illustrates this usage when he changes in the same sentence from "many" to "all," indicating the transition from an original Hebrew or Aramaic term to the Greek language: "Because there is one bread, we who are *many* are one body, for we *all* partake of the one bread." Jesus pointed beyond the group of his disciples, indicating that his death has universal significance. He is dying for all, for the whole of humanity. Isaiah 53:12 may loom here in the background with its saying concerning the servant of God: "He poured out himself to death, and was numbered with the transgressors; yet he bore the sin of many, and made intercession for the transgressors." Jesus did not understand his death as the end of a mission which had failed, but as the end of his earthly salvific activity. He died for us so that we might have new life.

The mentioning of a covenant reminds us of the new covenant which God promised to make with the house of Israel and the house of Judah (Jer. 31:31). This is not the renewal of the covenant with Israel, since the new covenant, erected through Jesus' death, goes beyond Israel and comprises all of humanity. In Jesus' death the enigmatic figure of the servant of God

---

15. Eduard Lohse, *History of the Suffering and Death of Jesus Christ*, 51. The Hebrew word *kol* does not correspond to our word "all" since it does not form a plural. It denotes a totality (all of Israel) but not a sum total (everyone in Israel).

and the expectation of a new covenant come to fulfillment. It may even be likely that the death of Jesus was interpreted by his followers along the lines of the death of the martyrs who were regarded as dying for the people in order that the wrath of God against the nation might come to an end.[16] This might also explain why the Christians did not simply ignore Israel but still interceded before God for this nation and hoped, as Paul had done, that they too might embrace Jesus as their Messiah. Whether or not Jesus' Last Supper was a Passover meal, the Christian saw it in that light and rightly detected that Jesus' blood had redeeming value in a manner similar to the blood of the first Passover (Exod. 12:13). God will spare his people from death and through the blood of the Passover lamb new life and new hope will ensue. Through the Last Supper the Christian community understood itself as the new covenant community, while Jesus in this Supper anticipated his death and its saving consequences.

Those who continue to celebrate the Lord's Supper look back to his death and are reminded of the salvific significance of this death. Yet the Christian Eucharist is not simply a memorial meal. *"After Easter the disciples did not think up a presence of the resurrected One in their regular table fellowship, but expected his coming in keeping with the promise which had been given to them on the night of his betrayal."*[17] The Last Supper was an eschatological meal. It anticipated the coming of the kingdom of God in its fullness.[18] The eating of bread and the sharing of the cup then and now are more than symbolic actions. By eating the bread and drinking the cup the participants in the Eucharist express the acceptance of all that is signified by the body and blood of Jesus. The Eucharistic celebrations focus on Jesus' death as the possibility for a new covenant between God and his people. Yet the Eucharist also anticipates the heavenly meal to which Jesus looked forward in sharing the Last Supper with the Twelve.

Today the Lord's Supper is seen as the meal between the ages at which in an anticipatory way the Lord himself presides as our host. Because of this eschatological aspect the Eucharist is not an occasion for mourning over Jesus' death but rather for rejoicing in his presence and

16. So I. Howard Marshall, *Last Supper and Lord's Supper* (Grand Rapids: Eerdmans, 1981), 147-48.

17. Goppelt, *Theology of the New Testament*, 1:221. Italics are the author's in the German version (*Theologie des Neuen Testaments,* 1:269).

18. Vincent Taylor, *The Life and Ministry of Jesus* (London: Macmillan, 1961), 191.

for giving thanks for the benefits procured by his death.[19] The recent liturgical emphasis in the Eucharistic celebration, away from a somber tone and rediscovering a more joyful approach, is very much in order. Yet the Lord's Supper should not be misunderstood as a fun experience. Paul rightly cautioned the Corinthians: "For all who eat and drink without discerning the body, eat and drink judgment against themselves" (1 Cor. 11:29).

Those who do not discern the Eucharist as something unique will incur judgment upon themselves. Through eating bread and drinking wine we receive new life as the benefit of Jesus' sacrifice of his body and blood and are included in the new covenant. If we do not discern these elements as something unique, we profane them and exclude ourselves from the salvific benefit. The salvific presence of Christ in the elements stands against our indifference.[20] Paul and the church rightly understood that Jesus' self-interpretation of his death was not some escape route by which Jesus made a last-ditch attempt to make the impending disaster shine in a better light. The church concurred with Jesus that he was right in attributing salvific significance to his death. They celebrated the Eucharist as a saving event and turned the cross into a symbol of victory.

2. The Salvational Significance of Jesus' Death

Given its Jewish and Hellenistic context, it is not surprising that the Christian community pointed to the salvational significance of Jesus' death. Paul mentioned that "our paschal lamb, Christ, has been sacrificed" (1 Cor. 5:7), alluding to the rabbinic idea that the death of the Passover lambs had expiatory significance for the Israelites.[21] Similarly his rendering of the words of the institution of the Lord's Supper, "this cup is the new covenant in my blood" (1 Cor. 11:25), is reminiscent of Exodus 24:8: "Moses took the blood and dashed it on the people and said, 'See the blood of the covenant that the LORD has made with you

---

19. So rightly Marshall, *Last Supper and Lord's Supper,* 153.

20. For the preceding see Gerhard Delling, "II. Urchristliches Mahl-Verständnis," in *TRE* 1:55.

21. See Goppelt, *Theology of the New Testament,* 2:94-95, who points to this and the following analogies.

in accordance with all these words.'" Paul also writes of "the redemption that is in Christ Jesus, whom God put forward as a sacrifice of atonement by his blood, effective through faith. He did this to show his righteousness, because in his divine forbearance he had passed over the sins previously committed" (Rom. 3:24-25). Christ's death is seen here in analogy to the atoning death of the animals sacrificed by Aaron, who was making "atonement for himself and for the people" (Lev. 16:24).

We should also consider the similarities between the death of Jesus and that of the martyrs.[22] Like the martyrs Jesus was innocent of any crime against his people or against the state. Like them he was put to death by hostile authorities. Like them he was killed for reasons which the political authorities considered pragmatic but which he understood to be the unavoidable outcome of his unmitigated faithfulness to God. As in the case of the martyrs, it was believed that Jesus had been vindicated by God, that his death was not the final point but rather the prelude to exaltation and glory. The idea that the undeserved death of an exceptionally worthy person could effect expiation for others was then applied to the death of Jesus. We could also look here at Greek mythology in which Heracles and Achilles voluntarily accepted death and were consequently venerated as gods and led immortal lives.[23] Or we could consider the fate of Socrates, who drank the cup of hemlock without hesitation and became the prototype of the martyr who fearlessly confronts death for the sake of truth.

We should not overextend the significance of these analogies. It must be conceded, because of these numerous analogies, that the message of the death of Jesus of Nazareth, the Son of God, who died on the cross for all people, was not incomprehensible for either educated Jews or Christians. But in contrast to these analogies, it was the death "of a Jewish craftsman of the most recent past, executed as a criminal, with whom the whole present and future salvation of all men was linked," and not

22. See Sam K. Williams, *Jesus' Death as Saving Event: The Background and Origin of a Concept*, Harvard Dissertations in Religion, vol. 2 (Missoula, Mont.: Scholars, 1975), 253-54, who wants to show that the notion of the salvational significance of Jesus' death originated among Christians "who were also thoroughly at home in the Greek-Hellenistic thought world" (230). He points here also to the influence of 4 Maccabees. As will be seen, such conclusions are unwarranted.

23. See the analogies provided by Martin Hengel, *The Atonement: The Origins of the Doctrine in the New Testament*, trans. John Bowden (Philadelphia: Fortress, 1981), 4-5.

with the death of a religious or political hero.[24] Because of this "embarrassing fact" the earliest Christian missionaries always also included the teaching, the actions, and the passion of their Messiah in their message. They did not only preach the cross of Christ but clothed it in the narrative of him as a Messianic person.

It is important to remember that there is an undeniable continuity between Jesus' own interpretation of his death and the salvific significance which the nascent Christian community attributed to it. "It was not primarily their own theological reflections, but above all the interpretative sayings of Jesus at the Last Supper which showed them how to understand his death properly."[25] Surprisingly, New Testament exegetes invariably point to the Last Supper as the place from which to gather an understanding of Jesus' view of his death and its enduring significance, while systematic reflection has almost unanimously ignored this. When Paul mentioned that "Christ died for us" (Rom. 5:8), then the underlying notion that Jesus' death has expiatory efficacy for others is, of course, prefigured in Jesus' words at the Last Supper that his blood "is poured out for many" (Mark 14:24).[26] The Son of Man saying, "For the Son of man came not to be served but to serve, and to give his life as ransom for many" (10:45), points in the same direction. Remember that "for many" is to be understood as meaning "for all," since both expressions were identical in Hebrew. Jesus' Last Supper, which he celebrated with his disciples, occupied a central place in the memory and worship of the Christian community, because in it he had dedicated to his disciples, indeed all his followers, the fruits of his violent death.

Similarly, Paul's statement that Christ "was handed over to death for our trespasses and was raised for our justification" (Rom. 4:25) has its antecedent reference in Jesus' own words: "The Son of man is to be betrayed into human hands" (Mark 9:31). Jesus referred here to the realization of God's eschatological plan of salvation, which Paul connected with Isaiah 53 — the servant of God "bore the sin of many" (Isa. 53:12). The continuity between Jesus' self-interpretation of his death and the subsequent interpretation by the Christian community indicates that Jesus'

24. So Hengel, *Atonement*, 31.
25. So very rightly Hengel, *Atonement*, 73.
26. For the following see Hengel, *Atonement*, 73, and Goppelt, *Theology of the New Testament*, 2:93-94.

last days were not characterized by a spirit of mere resignation, nor was he caught by surprise.[27] Jesus knew that he was going to die, but at the same time he was in "control of the situation." Not for a moment did Jesus treat his passion and death as something merely to be endured. The significant point of Jesus' self-evaluation of his death was that he was going to fulfill a ministry for all people before God. When we today see the love of God and even the suffering love of God in the cross of Jesus, then this is different from what Jesus himself viewed.[28] It is a view in the light of one's own history and experience, but not an unfolding of the purpose and meaning of Jesus' passion and death. As far as we can discern, Jesus' last days on this earth demonstrated his perfect obedience to God's will, by which he submitted himself to God's judgment upon sin and by which, as Jesus perceived it, he atoned for the sins of humanity.[29]

While the doctrine of atonement proved to be one of the most important teachings for the self-understanding of the Christians, the initial explication of the Christian teaching beyond the New Testament took relatively little cognizance of this fact. In confrontation with heretical teachings and Greek philosophy the Christian faith was initially presented as the true teaching and the true philosophy.[30] Ignatius (d. ca. 110) called Jesus "our only teacher" (*Magn.* 9:12), and Barnabas mentions in his letter that the Lord Jesus "by His personal manifestation" redeemed "our hearts from darkness" (*Barn.* 14:9). The Christians have the "new law" of their Lord Jesus Christ (*Barn.* 2), and since "the days are evil, and Satan possesses the power over this world," they ought to give

---

27. See for the following C. F. D. Moule, *The Origin of Christology* (Cambridge: Cambridge University Press, 1977), 110.

28. This caution is rightly expressed by Vincent Taylor, *Jesus and His Sacrifice: A Study of the Passion-Sayings in the Gospels* (London: Macmillan, 1965), 302-3, against the Abelardian moral theory of atonement. This Abelardian sentiment also seems to lie behind Jürgen Moltmann's claim that the Christian faith stands and falls "with the knowledge of the crucified Christ, i.e., with the knowledge of God *in* the crucified Christ or, to use Luther's even bolder phrases: with the knowledge of the 'crucified God.'" *The Crucified God: The Cross of Christ as the Foundation and Criticism of Christian Theology*, trans. R. A. Wilson and John Bowden (Minneapolis: Fortress, 1993), 64. Not by accident does Moltmann's treatise on the theology of the cross ensue in an appeal for socio-political action.

29. Taylor, *Jesus and His Sacrifice*, 307ff.

30. See for the following Hans Kessler, *Die theologische Bedeutung des Todes Jesu: Eine traditionsgeschichtliche Untersuchung* (Düsseldorf: Patmos, 1970), 22-23.

heed to themselves, and "diligently inquire into the ordinances of the Lord" (*Barn.* 2). Jesus is the new teacher and law-giver, and Christians ought to be patient and obedient to their Lord. Then they can rejoice in wisdom and understanding. Of course, the biblical testimony that Jesus "died for us, and for our sakes was raised again by God from the dead" (Polycarp, *Phil.* 9) is not suppressed, but the emphasis is on exercising patience and following Jesus even in martyrdom.

Ignatius was an exception in emphasizing the true suffering of Christ as the criterion of right teachings. Against docetic ideas, he countered that Jesus "suffered truly, even as also He truly raised up Himself, not, as certain unbelievers maintain, that He only seemed to suffer" (*Smyrn.* 2). Jesus was truly nailed to the cross under Pontius Pilate and Herod the tetrarch "for us in His flesh" (*Smyrn.* 1). Through Jesus' death "our life has sprung up again" (*Magn.* 9). Since for Ignatius the cross of Christ is central for Christian teaching, he admonishes the Trallians "for, since you are subject to the bishop as to Jesus Christ, you appear to me to live not after the manner of men, but according to Jesus Christ, who died for us, in order that, by believing in his death, you may escape from death" (*Trall.* 2). While Jesus' death has saving power, the emphasis is on the example of Christ which empowers Christians to live Christ-like lives. In confrontation with Hellenistic literature and thought patterns it was important to show Christ as teacher and example. Once the Christian message had gained widespread acceptance, then one could put more emphasis on the saving significance of Christ's death.

The need to rethink one's own approach was also prompted by rampant Christian Gnosticism. This diminished the significance of Jesus' saving activity by emphasizing more and more the believer's own possibilities of achieving salvation.[31] In this situation Irenaeus cautioned that all our knowledge is only fragmentary and we should not indulge in "endless conjectures concerning God, but we should leave such knowledge in the hands of God Himself."[32] In contrast to Gnostic speculations, Irenaeus emphasized that "God cannot be known without God . . . for the Lord taught us that no man is capable of knowing God, unless he be taught of God."[33] This self-disclosure of God occurred through his

31. Carl Andresen, "Erlösung," in *RAC* 6:130.
32. Irenaeus, *Against Heresies* 2.28.7, in *ANF* 1:401.
33. Irenaeus, *Against Heresies* 4.6.4, in *ANF* 1:468.

Son, Jesus Christ. Jesus is not just the teacher who enlightens and guides us the right way but is also the one who "wrought salvation."[34] He did, "through His transcendent love, become what we are, that He might bring us to be even what He is Himself."[35] Salvation does not consist in our being lifted up to a higher plane, somehow escaping the created order, but in a "regeneration."

According to Irenaeus, there is both a restitution of the beginning, that is, a regeneration, and also a completion of the progressive historical process. Irenaeus advanced his theory of recapitulation (Greek: *anakephalaiosis*), a term gleaned from Ephesians 1:10, where it says that in Christ the plan has been set forth for the fullness of time "to gather up" all things in him. He considered Jesus as the anti-type of Adam, who, through his death, frees humanity from bondage to sin into which Adam brought humanity through his disobedience. Irenaeus wrote:

> For by summing up in Himself the whole human race from the beginning to the end, He also summed up its death. From this it is clear that the Lord suffered death, in obedience to His Father, upon that day on which Adam died while he disobeyed God. Now he died on the same day in which he did eat. For God said, "In that day on which ye shall eat of it, ye shall die by death." The Lord, therefore, recapitulating in Himself this day, underwent his sufferings upon the day preceding the Sabbath, that is, the sixth day of the creation, on which man was created; thus granting him a second creation by means of His passion, which is that [creation] out of death.[36]

At the end Christ will complete and transform the whole creation; Jesus' death has saving significance for the whole of humanity and beyond that even for the whole of creation. Jesus did this by waging war against the enemy of humanity, the devil, most notably by obediently hanging on the tree, since the first disobedience occurred in connection with a tree by which the virgin Eve "was unhappily misled."[37] Jesus overcame the devil by being obedient throughout his life and even into death. With this kind of obedience, which stands in stark contrast to the disobedience of the first human being, Jesus achieved salvation for us.

34. Irenaeus, *Against Heresies* 4.33.4, in *ANF* 1:507.
35. Irenaeus, *Against Heresies* 5 preface, in *ANF* 1:526.
36. Irenaeus, *Against Heresies* 5.23.2, in *ANF* 1:551.
37. Irenaeus, *Against Heresies* 5.19.1, in *ANF* 1:547, and 5.21.1 in *ANF* 1:548.

We encounter in Irenaeus what Gustav Aulén (1879-1977) termed "the classic type" of the doctrine of atonement.[38]

In the classic type, atonement is accomplished by God in Christ. For this action the passive form can also be used, namely that God is reconciled with the world. Both modes, the active and the passive, belong together, since God is reconciled only because he himself reconciles the world with himself and himself with the world. This understanding is often coupled with the motive of divine warfare against the devil, who holds humanity in bondage, and the subsequent triumph of Christ. The emphasis is not on the satisfaction of God's justice but on God's grace through which God brought humanity back to him. In contrast to that theory, Aulén perceived a Latin (Western) type in which "the images and analogies are taken continually from the law-courts in the manner dear to the Latin mind." God's justice is violated through human sinfulness and a subsequent payment is required for his satisfaction. The satisfaction is achieved by Christ, who offers himself as the sinless human being on behalf of sinners. Atonement can still be regarded as God's work, as God has planned this procedure all along. The third type which Aulén portrayed emphasizes the action not so much of God but of humanity. Conversion and amendment are prominent, and Christ is considered the perfect example, the ideal human being, and the head of the human race whom humanity is supposed to follow. This type we saw to some extent in the Apostolic Fathers, and we will see it again in modernity as a result of the Enlightenment.

The Latin type has its roots in Tertullian, the initiator of Latin theology. Tertullian was trained in law and rhetoric like many of the leading Western theologians, and for some time he was a lawyer in Rome.[39] Yet legal categories are not used to talk about the salvational significance of Jesus' death. Rather, they are applied to our relationship with God: "God as Judge presides over the exacting and maintaining of justice, which to Him is most dear."[40] Since we know "the divine precepts," we know these things from which God bids us to abstain, the

---

38. See for the following Gustav Aulén, *Christus Victor: An Historical Study of the Three Main Types of the Idea of Atonement*, trans. A. G. Hebert (London: SPCK, 1970), 145-46.

39. According to Kessler, *Die theologische Bedeutung des Todes Jesu*, 59.

40. Tertullian, *On Repentance* 2, in *ANF* 3:658.

things which are accounted sin and "offend the Lord."[41] God has then "destined penalty by means of judgment" for all sins committed by deed or will, and he will "grant pardon by means of repentance."[42] Beyond that Tertullian also emphasized some kind of recapitulation when he says that Christ came down from heaven, preached and humbled himself even to death — the death on the cross (cf. Phil. 2:8). "He loved, of course, the being whom He redeemed at so great a cost. . . . Our birth He reforms from death by a second birth from heaven; our flesh He restores from every harassing malady."[43] Christ as the perfect one overcame our imperfection, and as the imperishable one he overcame our finitude. Christ brought restitution and not something new.[44]

Two more points ought to be mentioned which proved to be important for the West though they have their origin in the East: the interpretation of Jesus' death as a ransom paid to the devil and Jesus' death as expiation through a sacrifice offered to God. Both facets are present in Origen's understanding of Christ's death. Origen emphatically stated that "it was for the benefit of mankind that He should die on their account."[45] In this process God first delivered the Son "to the prince of this age, and to the rest of its princes, and then by them delivered [Him] into the hands of men who would slay Him."[46] But then they were laughed at "by Him who dwells in the heavens, and might be derided by the Lord, inasmuch as, contrary to their expectation, it was to the destruction of their own kingdom and power, that they received from the Father the Son."[47] The devil could not hold on to the pure soul of Jesus and therefore had to release him, whereby the human souls were freed from the power of the devil and his demons, since Jesus had been given to him as a ransom.

The other line of thought started with the notion that all sins need expiation in order to be forgiven. This expiation can only be met through a sacrifice that is spotless and sanctified. Since Jesus is this purest of all

41. Tertullian, *On Repentance* 3, in *ANF* 3:658.
42. Tertullian, *On Repentance* 4, in *ANF* 3:659.
43. Tertullian, *On the Flesh of Christ* 4, in *ANF* 3:524.
44. See Tertullian, *On Monogamy* 4, in *ANF* 4:61, where he emphasizes that the "Paraclete is rather *re*stitutor than *in*stitutor."
45. Origen, *Against Celsus* 1.54, in *ANF* 4:420.
46. Origen, *Commentary on Matthew* 13.8, in *ANF* 10:480.
47. Origen, *Commentary on Matthew* 13.9, in *ANF* 10:481.

living beings, he can be the sacrifice for sins, "a very holy offering."[48] "And this man indeed took our sins and has borne infirmity because of our iniquities, and the chastisement due us has come upon him, that we might be disciplined and regain peace."[49] The understanding that Christ through his death offered a sacrifice that reconciled us to God remained dominant in the West. Usually it was also connected with the idea of a ransom from the power of the devil.[50]

Anselm of Canterbury (1033-1109) then brought to its culmination the idea of Jesus giving satisfaction to God for our sins. At the same time he rejected the notion that the devil has anything to do with the process of salvation; it is God's sovereign act. According to biblical testimony, sin separates us from God and hands us over to death. Through his death Christ suffered in a substituting and expiatory way to end our separation from God and our subjection to death. Anselm's emphasis was not on Christ representing us and expiating our sins but on Christ satisfying God's justice.[51] Anselm laid out his theory of satisfaction in his book *Cur Deus homo,* completed in summer of 1098. Since it is not fitting for God to allow anything to be in disorder in his kingdom, "it is not fitting that God should forgive sin that goes thus unpunished."[52] A sinful person cannot attain salvation if that person "does not repay what he seized by sinning."[53] Yet humans have nothing which they could give to God to achieve restitution. Even the smallest sin is of immense magnitude, since it is against God's order, and salvation is irrevocably forfeited. Yet humans were created to enjoy eternal bliss. This goal can only be attained by Jesus Christ and not by sinful human beings, but he can help them obtain this goal. He is completely human and completely divine. Our debt to God "was so great that only God was able to pay it, although only a man ought to pay it; and, thus, the same [individual] who was divine was also human."[54] Jesus voluntarily sacrificed to God that which

---

48. Origen, *Homilies on Leviticus 1–16,* 5.3, in *FaCH* 83:93.

49. Origen, *Commentary on John* 28.165, in *FaCH* 89:326.

50. See Kessler, *Die theologische Bedeutung des Todes Jesu,* 89-90, who emphasizes this point.

51. Goppelt, *Theology of the New Testament,* 2:97.

52. Anselm of Canterbury, *Cur Deus homo,* in *Anselm of Canterbury,* ed. and trans. Jasper Hopkins and Herbert Richardson (Toronto: Edwin Mellen, 1976), 3:69.

53. Anselm, *Cur Deus homo* 1.19, 86.

54. Anselm, *Cur Deus homo* 2.18, 130.

he was never obligated to sacrifice, namely his life. Since God is a just God, he could not but repay the Son for that. Christ in turn gave this reward as a ransom for sinners though he was not indebted to them. Satisfaction was achieved and humanity was redeemed. In a logically conclusive way Anselm had attempted to solve the question why God had to become human and what was achieved by that. Though Anselm's theory is still fascinating today, it is a strictly logical treatise isolating the issue of satisfaction from the larger context of Jesus' ministry and from its biblical roots.[55]

How can we still express today the salvational significance of Jesus' death? Is it still possible for us to talk about a substituting punishment that Jesus took upon himself in his passion and death?[56] Dorothee Sölle, for instance, talks about "the absent God whom Christ represents and who is 'helpless' in the world."[57] Long before that Dietrich Bonhoeffer claimed: "God lets himself be pushed out of the world on to the cross. He is weak and powerless in the world, and that is precisely the way in which he is with us and helps us. . . . The Bible directs man to God's powerlessness and suffering; only the suffering God can help."[58] Jürgen Moltmann has even written a book entitled *The Crucified God*, in which he asked the question: "Why did Jesus die? He died not only because of the understanding of the law by his contemporaries or because of Roman power politics, but ultimately because of his God and Father."[59] Of course, Jesus died because God allowed him to die, just as he has allowed millions of people to die, from the victims in Auschwitz to victims of traffic accidents, wars, heart attacks, and old age.

In all likelihood Jesus knew that he would encounter a violent death, and as he entered into it he realized more and more that God would not

---

55. Cf. also Pannenberg's reservations to Anselm's proposal in Wolfhart Pannenberg, *Jesus — God and Man*, trans. Lewis L. Wilkins and Duane A. Priebe, 2nd ed. (Philadelphia: Westminster, 1988), 277.

56. Pannenberg, *Jesus — God and Man*, 280, opts for this while having reservations on the typological identifications of Jesus' way, as drawn out by early Christendom, with the cultic and prophetic tradition of the Bible (274-75).

57. Dorothee Sölle, *Christ the Representative: An Essay in Theology after the "Death of God,"* trans. David Lewis (Philadelphia: Fortress, 1967), 150.

58. Dietrich Bonhoeffer, *Letters and Papers from Prison*, enlarged ed., ed. Eberhard Bethge, trans. Reginald Fuller et al. (New York: Macmillan, 1971), 360-61.

59. Moltmann, *The Crucified God*, 149.

spare him from that final, bitter end. But in Psalm 22 (which Jesus may have prayed on the cross) we find not only the frequently quoted opening line: "My God, my God, why have you forsaken me?" (Ps. 22:1). There is also the confident assertion: "For he did not despise or abhor the affliction of the afflicted; he did not hide his face from me, but heard when I cried to him" (Ps. 22:24). If Jesus' death had been his ultimate end, his words of institution at the Last Supper would simply have been wrong. If there were no salvational significance to be associated with his body and blood, Jesus would have been a failure. Even Martin Luther, who claimed that the cross of Christ is the true theology and recognition of God, did not claim that he could make sense of the cross in isolation.[60]

For Martin Luther the cross as an abbreviation stands for two things: First, the cross is the end point of God's historical involvement in Jesus with this earth. It is diametrically opposed to any speculative theology that constructs its tenets without reference to God's activity in history. Second, the cross shows us that God always works under the appearance of the opposite, since nobody would expect that anything good could come out of the cross. This would mean that only the resurrection lends distinctiveness to the Christian phrase: "Christ died for us."[61]

Christ's death does not show the powerlessness of God. It also does not demonstrate the agony of God, since the only person we see is a human being who suffers and dies. If anything, Jesus' death shows the depth of perversity of which humanity is capable. Jesus suffered through this perversity knowingly and voluntarily. He did not take an escape route. He did not have it easier because he was the human face of God. If anything, it was more difficult for him, because he knew that he did not deserve this death or any other death. In this sense he was the only one who died unnecessarily. The amazing thing is that God did not cut short the history of humanity when humanity killed God's only Son and rejected God's human face. On the contrary, God brought his Son back to new life. With this action God defied all life-negating human perversity and showed us that life is possible in and beyond death. Jesus, who knew of no sin, bore

---

60. Martin Luther, *Operationes in Psalmos* (1519-21), in *WA* 1:362.18-19 (explanation of Ps. 5:12).

61. See Moule, *Origin of Christology*, 122, who rightly mentions here incarnation and resurrection, since only from the resurrection can one legitimately talk about incarnation. If Christ is with God as the resurrected one, it also makes sense to assume that at one point he became human.

the sins of humanity, and God in Christ Jesus overcame the anti-Godly powers of death and destruction. In this way both ideas finally came true — the Old Testament substitution theory and the more folksy notion of cheating death and the anti-Godly destructive powers of their final claim on life. Yet is it possible to rest the truthfulness of the salvific significance of Jesus' death on the fact of his resurrection?

3. The Enigmatic Character of Christ's Resurrection

When we turn to Christ's resurrection, we are confronted with a different nomenclature. In talking about Jesus we referred to a person who had lived in space and time on our earth. With Christ the situation is different. We are told that the resurrected one is no longer confined to space and time. Moreover, the resurrection of Jesus Christ is a singular event which defies any correlation with preceding events.[62] To underscore that through his resurrection Jesus is removed from the strictures of space and time, the title "Christ" is usually accorded to him. Reflecting on Jesus and his significance, Paul, for instance, omits the historical name "Jesus" altogether and just talks about "Christ."

The idea of the resurrection emerged relatively late in the context of Israel and of later Judaism. The only text in the Hebrew Bible referring to a resurrection which remains unquestioned by Old Testament exegetes is Daniel 12:2-3, where it says: "Many of those who sleep in the dust of the earth shall awake, some to everlasting life, and some to shame and everlasting contempt. Those who are wise shall shine like the brightness of the sky, and those who lead many to righteousness, like the stars forever and ever." The second verse emphasizes the assertion of the first one, that not all but some, meaning the chosen ones, will be resurrected. This conviction emerged under the trials of the Maccabean Wars and found its expression in the text, which was presumably put in its final shape between 168 and 164 B.C.[63] How much the idea of a resurrection

---

62. See Heinzpeter Hempelmann, *Die Auferstehung Jesu Christi — eine historische Tatsache? Eine engagierte Analyse* (Wuppertal: R. Brockhaus, 1982), 48, who emphasizes the singular event of "Jesus' resurrection."

63. For the following see Günter Stemberger, "Auferstehung I/2 Judentum," in *TRE* 4:444-45.

was debated in the late second century B.C. is shown in 2 Maccabees 12:43ff., in which one gloss states that it is "superfluous and foolish to pray for the dead," while another one emphasizes that a sin offering for the dead is beneficial. The final redactor then harmonizes the two positions by saying: "For if he were not expecting that those who had fallen would rise again, it would have been superfluous and foolish to pray for the dead."

If the disciples of Jesus had been Sadducees, Good Friday would have meant for them the end of their hopes and the final demise of Jesus' mission.[64] Had they been Gnostics, they would have been happy over Good Friday because Jesus would have been redeemed from his body and his soul would have left its earthly prison. Most likely they would even have cursed the thought of a bodily resurrection (cf. 1 Cor. 12:3). Since they were schooled, however, in Pharisaic thought, they could understand the resurrection as something positive.

Outside Judaism, there were various belief systems of dying and rising gods. Some of them had little relevance for the concept of individual destiny beyond death, while others, such as the myth of the Egyptian god Osiris, were thought to show personal existence beyond death.[65] There was also the report of Apollonius of Tyana, a contemporary of Jesus, who had appeared after his death (Philostratus, *Life of Apollonius* 8.31). Yet this was seen by his followers to have been just another miracle and not a unique act of God which revealed his intention for them and beyond them for all of the created order.[66] It was this latter interpretation that was applied to Christ's resurrection by the Christians.

Regardless of his numerous controversies with the Pharisees, Jesus seems to have been close to them in many ways. We may conclude that his disciples shared this affinity too, and were prepared, like the Pharisees, for something beyond death. Yet what inspired and empowered the disciples to found such an enduring movement? Significantly enough, the decisive event is nowhere described in the New Testament. "No individual of the primitive community ever claimed to

---

64. Pinchas Lapide, *The Resurrection of Jesus: A Jewish Perspective*, trans. Wilhelm C. Linss (Minneapolis: Augsburg, 1983), 65.

65. Hans Wissmann, "Auferstehung I/1: Religionsgeschichtlich," in *TRE* 4:443.

66. See E. P. Sanders, *Jesus and Judaism*, 2nd ed. (London: SCM, 1987), 320, who draws out the parallels between Jesus and Apollonius of Tyana but also points to the differences.

have seen or experienced Jesus' resurrection as an event, a fact, a happening."[67] It is not until the middle of the second century that we find in the *Gospel according to Peter* a description of the resurrection.[68] On the one hand this reluctance of the evangelists to paint in daring colors a resurrection which they had not seen may give added credence to their conviction that Jesus Christ was resurrected.[69] Yet we could also conclude more skeptically that the resurrection expresses "*merely* a belief, without specifying witnesses, and what is more, without being in the least able to specify witnesses."[70] The resurrection of Jesus Christ is based on circumstantial evidence, on the appearances of the resurrected one and on the empty tomb.

Concerning the appearances of the resurrected one, we can say quite confidently that witnesses saw Jesus who had been crucified.[71] They claimed that after his death they had seen him and expressed this "vision" in different ways, already including a partial interpretation of what they saw. By a process of reflective interpretation they arrived at the statement that "Jesus has been raised by God, he is risen." While the Easter narratives in the Gospels present a later stage of the written tradition, the earliest text in the New Testament is 1 Corinthians 15:4-5, which speaks of the resurrection of Jesus Christ from the point of view of the witnesses. This text can be dated to A.D. 50, and the information contained therein to somewhere in the fourth decade of the first century, probably in the first half of that decade.[72] This would take us back to a dozen years after the death of Jesus. Paul writes here concerning Jesus "that he was buried, and that he was raised on the third day in accordance with the scriptures, and that he appeared to Cephas, then to the twelve." This text contains two important assertions. The first is that Jesus Christ "was raised" and

67. Willi Marxsen, "The Resurrection of Jesus as a Historical and Theological Problem," in *The Significance of the Message of the Resurrection for Faith in Jesus Christ*, ed. C. F. D. Moule (London: SCM, 1968), 24.

68. Edgar Hennecke, *New Testament Apocrypha*, ed. Wilhelm Schneemelcher, Engl. trans. and ed. R. Mcl. Wilson, vol. 1: *Gospels and Related Writings* (Philadelphia: Westminster, 1963), 1:185-86.

69. So rightly Lapide, *Resurrection of Jesus*, 54.

70. Marxsen, "Resurrection of Jesus as a Historical and Theological Problem," 24.

71. For the following see Marxsen, "Resurrection of Jesus as a Historical and Theological Problem," 30.

72. Gerhard Delling, "The Significance of the Resurrection of Jesus for the Faith in Jesus Christ," in *Significance of the Message of the Resurrection*, 78.

was not observed by anybody, while the second, which refers to a historical occurrence, is that "he appeared to Cephas, then to the twelve." Evidently the first assertion is a conclusion drawn from the second.[73]

With the term "he appeared" Paul also cites his own experience of the resurrected one at Damascus (1 Cor. 15:8). He is the only Easter witness who personally wrote down his experience. In using the passive mode Paul shows that this was an occurrence in which the one who appeared was the active agent. Jesus appeared and made himself known just as God appeared from hiddenness and addressed individuals. This kind of language was already used when God disclosed himself in Old Testament times. For instance, in Genesis 12:7 we read: "Then the LORD appeared to Abram." To conclude from the appearances that the resurrection had indeed taken place is not just possible but even necessary. Jesus disclosed himself as being present and therefore he must have been resurrected. The frequently used formulation that Christ was "raised from the dead" (cf. 1 Cor. 15:12) underscores the theophanic significance of Jesus' resurrection. Presupposed here is the Israelite faith in God who has power over life and death (cf. Deut. 32:39). After Jesus had been "with the dead" in Sheol, God raised him to new life. Through this action the apocalyptic expectation of the end-time resurrection of the dead (held by the Pharisees among others) found expression in an exemplary way.[74] What had been expected at the end of time had occurred in a singular way in Jesus as the Christ.

The appearances of the resurrected one did not happen because people believed in them. On the contrary, "the resurrection was the cause of a faith which did not previously exist."[75] Doubt and unbelief concerning the message of the resurrection are as old as this message itself. The Evangelists unashamedly tell us that some of the disciples initially did not believe; unbelief was not reserved for the proverbial doubting

---

73. So also Goppelt, *Theology of the New Testament*, 1:235.

74. Paul Hoffmann, "Auferstehung II/1: Neues Testament," in *TRE* 4:486. When he mentions that the resurrection of the dead is a revivification of the whole person, who in a shadowy existence resided in the realm of the dead, he remains unconvincing. As Paul emphasizes and as the Easter narratives in the Gospels also try to demonstrate, this was no return of Jesus to his former way of life but an advance to a new form of life (cf. 1 Cor. 15:42ff.).

75. Moule, "Introduction to the English Edition," in *Significance of the Message of the Resurrection*, 2.

Thomas (John 20:24-29).[76] In Matthew 28:17 we read: "But some doubted." Similarly Mark 16:14 relates: "Later he appeared to the eleven themselves as they were sitting at the table; and he upbraided them for their lack of faith and stubbornness, because they had not believed those who saw him after he had risen." In the Gospel according to Luke we read: "But these words seemed to them an idle tale, and they did not believe them" (Luke 24:11).

The unbelief may have resulted partly from the fact that it was women who first spread the news that Jesus had been resurrected. In all four Gospels we find that women found the tomb of Jesus empty and then returned to the other disciples to tell them this news. If the story of the resurrection had been a literary invention, the authors would not have made women the key witnesses to this fact, since in rabbinic Judaism women did not have any credibility in court.[77] It is not surprising that Paul, who wanted to present an official and legally tenable testimony of the resurrection, does not mention any women. Yet the women, too, had their problems in initially recognizing the resurrected one. Mary Magdalene first mistook him for the gardener (John 20:14-15).

With Mary Magdalene as well as with other followers of Jesus we notice that the initiative of recognizing the resurrected one always started with Jesus.[78] Jesus did not primarily make himself known as the resurrected Christ by the way he looked but by the way he acted and talked.[79] His way of speech and action dispersed the doubt present in his disciples. His followers recognized him as the Christ, as the one who lived beyond his death to new life and who is their present Lord. Their response is adoration (Matt. 28:16 and implicitly John 20:17). Although the disciples had deserted Jesus while he was hanging on the cross, he now returned to them and reestablished communion with them. Yet this was not a

76. Lapide, *Resurrection of Jesus,* 39.

77. Lapide, *Resurrection of Jesus,* 95.

78. Edward Schillebeeckx, *Jesus: An Experiment in Christology,* trans. Hubert Hoskins (New York: Random House, 1981), 331, 347.

79. See for the following Goppelt, *Theology of the New Testament,* 1:243. It is doubtful whether one can ascertain that for the Judeo-Christian community the resurrection did not constitute a central theme and that this occurred only with the Judeo-Hellenistic Christians, who made the cross and resurrection of Jesus Christ their central mission motif (see also Ulrich Wilckens, "The Tradition-History of the Resurrection of Jesus," in *Significance of the Message of the Resurrection,* 74).

return to the communion which they enjoyed with him before his death. Similar to the Old Testament call experiences when God appeared and sent prophets, the disciples also experienced a new call and a mission to spread the news of salvation in Jesus Christ.[80] Interestingly, these appearances, with the exception of that to Paul, were confined to people who had been close to Jesus during his earthly career.

When we attempt to localize the appearances of the resurrected one, we encounter some difficulties. Since Jesus was crucified on a Friday afternoon and was resurrected early Sunday morning, he had been in the tomb for only one and a half days, not for three days as the biblical writers tell us. Most likely the reference to the "third day" is not to be construed as an indication of an exact time span, but expresses God's compassion and grace.[81] The divine grace occurring on the "third day" is often mentioned in the Old Testament. On the "third day" there was thunder and lightning on Mount Sinai (Exod. 19:16). On the "third day" Abraham lifted up his eyes (Gen. 22:4). Jonah was three days in the belly of the fish before he was rescued (Jon. 2:1). And in Hosea 6:2 we read: "After two days he will revive us; on the third day he will raise us up." The rabbis wrote in Midrash Rabba: "The Holy One, blessed be his name, never allows the righteous one to remain longer than three days in anguish." The extension of the appearances to forty days (Acts 1:3) is a similar construct.[82]

Another point of controversy has often been caused by attempts to locate geographically the site of the first appearances. In Matthew 28:16-17 we read: "Now the eleven disciples went to Galilee, to the mountain to which Jesus had directed them. When they saw him, they worshipped

---

80. See also Jürgen Moltmann, *Theology of Hope: On the Ground and the Implication of a Christian Eschatology,* trans. James W. Leitch (Minneapolis: Fortress, 1993), 195, who calls the Easter appearances "phenomena of vocation."

81. See for the following Lapide, *Resurrection of Jesus,* 92.

82. It is strange that Joachim Jeremias, *New Testament Theology: The Proclamation of Jesus,* trans. John Bowden (New York: Charles Scribner's, 1971), 1:304, argues very strongly for the three days, while at the same time claiming that the appearances of the resurrected one occurred over a long time span and that only relatively late were they finally restricted to forty days (301). Bruce M. Metzger, "A Suggestion concerning the Meaning of I Cor. XV.4b," in *Journal of Theological Studies* 8 (1957): 123, offers another persuasive explanation for the "third day." In the Orient "three days" are counted as a transitional habitation, while "four days" are recognized as permanent. When Jesus was raised after "three days," this underscored that Sheol was not yet his permanent habitation.

him; but some doubted." In Mark we read that the women were told: "But go, tell his disciples and Peter that he is going ahead of you to Galilee; there you will see him, just as he told you" (Mark 16:7). In the Lukan text we read: "While staying with them, he ordered them not to leave Jerusalem, but to wait there for the promise of the Father" (Acts 1:4). Consequently we do not find any appearances of the resurrected one to his followers in Galilee. Some exegetes try to reconcile the differing localities by claiming:

> It was the appearances of the risen Jesus in Galilee which inspired belief in the resurrection and led to the founding of the primitive community. On this basis, the resurrection of Jesus came to be the fundamental assumption in everything the community thought and did. Moving to Jerusalem, the community found in existence the women's story of the discovery of the empty tomb. They regarded it as a confirmation of the belief in the resurrection which they had already brought with them from Galilee.[83]

Pinchas Lapide proposes another theory which has even more plausibility.[84] He reminds us that *galil* and the feminine form *galilah* means in Hebrew "region" or "environs." Isaiah 9:1 mentions the "area of the Gentiles" (Heb.: *galil hagoyim*), from which the Northern mountainous province Galilee received its name, which in Greek transcription comes close to *galilah*. But Ezekiel 47:8 also knows of a *galilah kadmonah*, an "eastern region," which corresponds to the area east of the temple in or near Jerusalem. Most likely this could be the neighborhood of Bethany, which was well known to the disciples. That this area of Jerusalem *(galilah Yerushalayim)* was meant was difficult to understand for later Greek-speaking people who were not familiar with Palestine topography and its exact naming. Consequently some of the Gospel writers understood the appearances to have occurred in Jerusalem, and other writers in Galilee. Most likely the disciples went into hiding but did not go as far as Galilee. They simply stayed with friends outside the city.

Most likely the journey of the women on Easter morning to the tomb was the starting point of the chain of events. Whether Mary Magdalene, Mary the mother of James, and Salome (Mark 16:1) or just Mary Mag-

---

83. Wilckens, "Tradition-History of the Resurrection," 73-74.
84. Lapide, *Resurrection of Jesus,* 113-14.

dalene alone (John 21) witnessed the tomb was empty and then returned to the disciples to tell them of the startling news may well remain undecided.[85] It is important to note that the empty tomb is not incidental to the Easter experiences, but is their initial geographical and historical starting point. It is simply wrong to claim that attempts to prove the historical truth of the empty tomb have been unsuccessful.[86] If the Christian community really had invented the story of the empty tomb, it would not have mentioned as its main witnesses one or three women. It is also hard to maintain that the empty tomb resulted from the dogmatic assertion of the third day, because in 1 Corinthians 15:4 we have already the mentioning of the third day without any reference to an empty tomb.[87] It is not without significance that Jewish polemic does not deny the fact of an empty tomb but offers a different explanation, namely, that the disciples had stolen the corpse (Matt. 28:15) or that the gardener had removed it (John 20:15). It is most likely that indeed the women found a tomb that was empty. They held it to be the tomb in which Jesus had been laid.

We should also remember that the historical fact of an empty tomb did not found the belief in the resurrected one. It was Jesus who showed himself as the Christ and initiated the resurrection faith. Since nobody could come up with the corpse of the dead Jesus, there remains the alternative of either the confession in the resurrected one or the theft of the corpse (by the disciples).[88] We are confronted again with the ambiguity of history. Perhaps the Jewish author Pinchas Lapide is right when he reasons: there was this anxious group of disciples who were just about to discard everything. All of them had betrayed their master and fled the city in despair. But suddenly, or overnight one might say, they changed into a self-assured and dedicated missionary troop. Such a change could not have been caused by a vision or some self-deception. Often a singular vision suffices to found a sect, a school, or even religious

---

85. Jeremias, *New Testament Theology,* 304-5, claims, not without justification, that the story in Mark 16:1-8 has its older historical antecedent in John 20:1-2.

86. This is the skeptical position adopted by Marxsen, "Resurrection of Jesus as a Historical and Theological Problem," 24-25.

87. For the following see Goppelt, *Theology of the New Testament,* 1:246.

88. See the careful analysis and the conclusions reached by Hans Freiherr von Campenhausen, *Der Ablauf der Osterereignisse und das leere Grab,* 2nd ed. (Heidelberg: Carl Winter, 1958), 51-52.

order. Yet this cannot account for the origin of a world religion which soon was to conquer the vast Roman Empire.[89] The enigma is not so much the resurrection — this was a singular act of God — but what it engendered, the inception of a worldwide mission the end of which we have not yet seen. The resurrection can indeed be called a turning point.

4. The Turning Point of the Resurrection

For a whole day (October 12, 1964), in the small town of Sittensen near Hamburg, Germany, more than two thousand people followed a discussion on the resurrection of Jesus Christ between two theologians, Ernst Fuchs of the University of Marburg and Walter Künneth (1901-1997) from Erlangen University.[90] This shows paradigmatically that this event which is said to have occurred nearly two thousand years ago is still of immense significance for us today. Yet the resurrection of Jesus Christ cannot be fathomed by purely historical research. Such research can only state, as it has abundantly done, that the followers of Jesus had experiences which they interpreted to mean that Jesus had appeared to them. A smaller group of New Testament scholars may also include that which is historically verifiable: that followers of Jesus claimed that a tomb which they thought was the one in which Jesus was laid was empty after a certain interval. We can also ascertain historically that these appearances (and the empty tomb) led the followers of Jesus to the belief that Jesus was resurrected as the Christ. Given these historically verifiable facts, we must now ask whether this kind of interpretation by the first Christian community that Jesus was indeed resurrected was correct.

Liberal historicism attempted to demonstrate that a psychological development within the disciples made them believe in something which they termed a resurrection. This resulted in visions of the resurrected one.[91] More recent theology has abandoned this kind of psychologizing approach. Hans Conzelmann posed the fundamental issue of New Testa-

89. Lapide, *Resurrection of Jesus,* 125-26.
90. Christian Möller, foreword to *Die Auferstehung Jesu Christi von den Toten: Dokumentation eines Streitgesprächs,* by Ernst Fuchs and Walter Künneth (Neukirchen-Vluyn: Neukirchener Verlag, 1973), 5.
91. For a brief summary of the positions up to the 1960s see Goppelt, *Theology of the New Testament,* 1:230-31.

ment theology very correctly when he asked: "Why did faith maintain the identity of the Exalted One with Jesus of Nazareth after the resurrection appearances?"[92] What kind of event was it that led them to hold on to the faith that the exalted Christ was identical with Jesus of Nazareth? Since nobody within the Christian community had seen or experienced Jesus' resurrection, Willi Marxsen (1919-92) rightly concludes that "witnesses, after the death of Jesus, claimed that something had happened to them which they described as seeing Jesus, and reflection on this experience led them to the *interpretation* that Jesus had been raised from the dead."[93] Marxsen refrains from talking about the resurrection of Jesus as an event and rather calls it an "interpretative statement." Similarly, Herbert Braun (1903-92) claims that "the belief in the Resurrection is an early Christian form of expression, a form of expression conditioned by its environment, for the authority Jesus had attained over these people."[94] Though we may no longer share this form of expression, Jesus' authority expressed with it can still be binding for us today.

The significant point, as Marxsen explains, is not the resurrection but the coming to faith of the first Christians.[95] The coming to faith was a reality which the first Christians experienced in a miraculous way and from which they concluded that they owed this to God's action. This activity of God was expressed by them with the help of the assertion that Jesus had been resurrected. Going beyond the older psychological interpretation, Marxsen vehemently rejects the notion that faith creates the resurrection of Jesus.[96] The seeing of Jesus cannot be isolated from the reality of faith. One cannot talk about the resurrection of Jesus without the coming to faith. Isolated talk about the reality of the resurrection of Jesus would no longer be a miraculous event but an everyday occurrence which would be accessible to historical research. Similar to Braun, Marxsen calls the confession of the reality of the experienced

92. Hans Conzelmann, *An Outline of the Theology of the New Testament,* trans. John Bowden (New York: Harper & Row, 1969), xviii.

93. Marxsen, *Resurrection of Jesus as a Historical and Theological Problem,* 31.

94. Herbert Braun, *Jesus of Nazareth: The Man and His Time,* trans. Everett R. Kalin (Philadelphia: Fortress, 1979), 122-23.

95. See for the following Willi Marxsen, *The Resurrection of Jesus of Nazareth,* trans. Margaret Kohl (Philadelphia: Fortress, 1970), 139.

96. Marxsen, *Resurrection of Jesus,* 143.

faith the constant, while the variables are the concepts which this confession employs.[97]

Both Marxsen and Braun maintain that there would have been no Christian faith without the resurrection. But they are less sure that insistence on the resurrection needs to be continued. Perhaps other means can also generate that faith today. John Macquarrie (1919-) brought this kind of reasoning to its logical conclusion when he presented two endings to his christology, "the happy ending" that includes the resurrection and "the austere ending" omitting it. He asks: "Suppose we omitted the 'joyful mysteries' that traditionally came after the cross? Would that destroy the whole fabric of faith in Christ? I do not think so, for the two great distinctive Christian affirmations would remain untouched — God is love, and God is revealed in Jesus Christ. These two affirmations would stand even if there were no mysteries beyond Calvary."[98] Having asked himself the question of whether the resurrection is primarily an event in the disciples rather than in Jesus, he answers with a yes and a no: "Resurrection is an event in the believers, it is indeed the event of the church, which is Christ's living body, and which in its preaching and sacraments and community continues his life and work. But the meaning of the resurrection is originally in Jesus himself — in the possession and mediation by him of true life, eternal life, which he brought to its highest pitch on the cross."[99]

Macquarrie is correct that the church has traditionally been understood as Christ's living body. On the other hand, it would be difficult to restrict the original meaning of the resurrection to Jesus himself while later Christ found his true, living expression in the church. The resur-

---

97. Marxsen, *Resurrection of Jesus*, 147. In a later publication Marxsen squarely addressed the issue of the resurrection. But again the resurrection does not become a means by which the resurrected one calls people to faith in him. It is the other way around. The experience of faith, i.e., that we are "reconciled with God," is subsequently expressed in this way: "He whose faith we live, him God has raised from the dead." This statement is then only true "for the person whose faith is confessed this way." See for these quotations Willi Marxsen, *Jesus and Easter: Did God Raise the Historical Jesus from the Dead?* trans. Victor Paul Furnish (Nashville, Tenn.: Abingdon, 1990), 77. Marxsen seems to have abandoned the Judeo-Christian conviction that faith is always grounded in God's mighty acts in history and not just in the interpretation of history and its subsequent existential appropriation.

98. John Macquarrie, *Jesus Christ in Modern Thought* (London: SCM, 1990), 412.

99. Macquarrie, *Jesus Christ in Modern Thought*, 414.

rection had immediate implications beyond Jesus for his followers. We should not forget that Christ is not confined to the church, as present universalists emphasize and as the Orthodox symbol of the pantocrator reminds us every time we visit an Orthodox sanctuary. The exalted Christ is the Christ not just of the church but also of the universe. Moreover, one wonders how Macquarrie knows that the two distinctive Christian affirmations, God is love and God is revealed in Jesus Christ, would have remained untouched without the resurrection. All we know from the Gospels is that after Calvary the disciples went into hiding and for all intents and purposes at that point in time the Jesus movement was finished. We should not overlook the fact that, for Paul at least, the Christian hope is primarily founded in Jesus' death and resurrection.[100] God's salvational activity in Jesus is the presupposition for allowing the deceased ones to participate in the hoped-for future communion with Christ. It is difficult to understand how God could be a God of love without the resurrection.

It is hardly an overstatement to say that the conviction that in Jesus Christ the resurrection has already occurred is the starting point of all Christian life and thought.[101] Ulrich Wilckens (1928-) is right when he emphasizes that what was central for the first Christian community and has endured for many centuries of Christian history can hardly become meaningless for us today.[102] Without the resurrection the meaning of the cross as a salvational act of God cannot be clearly elaborated. Cross and resurrection are related to each other like question and answer, enigma and interpretation.[103] While the cross is the presupposition for the resurrection of Jesus, since without the cross no resurrection would have been necessary, the latter gives the cross its true significance. A theology of the cross cannot rest on itself but must be founded in the

100. Paul Hoffmann, "Auferstehung I/3: Neues Testament," in *TRE* 4:453.

101. So also Oscar Cullmann, "Immortality of the Soul or Resurrection of the Dead," in *Immortality and Resurrection,* ed. Krister Stendahl (New York: Macmillan, 1965), 33.

102. Ulrich Wilckens, *Resurrection: Biblical Testimony to the Resurrection: An Historical Examination and Explanation,* trans. A. M. Stewart (Atlanta: John Knox, 1978), V, in his preface.

103. See Walter Künneth, *The Theology of the Resurrection,* trans. James W. Leitch (St. Louis: Concordia, 1965), 151ff., who correctly points to the interrelatedness of cross and resurrection and sees in the latter the theological presupposition of the former.

resurrection. It is a self-deception to talk about the death of Christ alone and still claim that it has kerygmatic significance. The same must be said for the proclamation of Jesus.

Jesus' authoritative proclamation through which he put himself in the place of God was verified through the resurrection. God's yes to Jesus beyond his death implied a yes to his authority which he had claimed already during his earthly ministry.[104] While his initial authority was proleptic, through his resurrection it gained final credibility, and the call for decision for or against him and his message could then be issued in his name by the Christian community. The New Testament writings associate the resurrection of Jesus with and hold it decisive for God's saving action.[105] In a nearly set formula Paul talks about Jesus Christ, "who was handed over to death for our trespasses and raised for our justification" (Rom. 4:25). Without resurrection there is no atonement through Jesus' death. While the death of Jesus shows human depravity, of what sinful humanity is capable, the resurrection of Jesus as the Christ demonstrates that God will not abandon humanity on account of its abominable sinfulness. God gives new life and continues to show his solidarity with humanity.

The situation of the followers of Jesus must also be considered. Through the shameful death of their Messianic master they had become completely discouraged and disoriented in their thinking. Once they experienced him as the resurrected one, they were assured that his death had not been in vain. He had been accepted by God as a prophetic martyr and an innocent sufferer.[106] His actions did not result in his demise but in his exaltation. The encounters with the resurrected Lord confirmed the Messianic claim of Jesus which had brought him to the cross. By his resurrection God had proved him to be the sole innocent one "who knew no sin" (2 Cor. 5:21). The disciples could reintroduce baptism, but not just for the forgiveness of sin, as John the Baptist had done. The disciples connected it to Jesus' death and resurrection; baptism signified death to

104. See Pannenberg, *Jesus — God and Man,* 66-67, who persuasively claims that a christology cannot be based solely on the earthly ministry of Jesus but needs the verification of this authority through the resurrection.

105. Delling, "The Significance of the Resurrection of Jesus for Faith in Jesus Christ," 93-94.

106. See Martin Hengel, *The Atonement: The Origins of the Doctrine in the New Testament,* trans. John Bowden (Philadelphia: Fortress, 1981), 65-66.

the old way of life and hope for and a guarantee of new life. Within the apocalyptic context, Jesus' resurrection was understood as the beginning of the general resurrection of the dead. Paul called Jesus "the first fruits of those who have died" (1 Cor. 15:20).

While the hope of the early Christian community for an end-time resurrection of the dead corresponds by and large to the Jewish hope, there is one significant modification.[107] In Judaism the resurrection of the righteous was hoped for as a consequence of their righteous activities. In Christianity the resurrection is expected as a consequence of the salvific efficacy of Christ's resurrection. The Christian faith in something beyond death focuses on Christ and his resurrection, not on some kind of common idea which was already present in Judaism. The resurrection of Jesus simply cannot be derived from some kind of Jewish expectation. While some Jewish concepts are present which correspond to the inauguration of Jesus as the end-time mediator of salvation and as judge, there is no notion of the resurrection of the Messiah. Occasionally we find the understanding of a revivification, such as with Lazarus or with the son of the widow who was brought back to life by Elijah (1 Kings 17:22). But "there is nothing comparable to the resurrection of Jesus anywhere in Jewish literature."[108]

Nowhere in late Judaism is there the expectation of a resurrection to glory as an event in history. Resurrection to glory means the beginning of God's new creation. The disciples interpreted the resurrection upon their encounter with the resurrected one as this kind of end-time event, the beginning of the new aeon, of the new world. The resurrection of Jesus as the Christ signifies the intersection between God's realm and our space-time continuum. The narratives of the encounter with the resurrected one amply demonstrate that the resurrected one was not a phantom, a vision, or the result of a hallucination. He was a being who was as concrete as any earthly human being. He could talk, eat, and be touched. He could be recognized as the crucified one and as the former Jesus of Nazareth. The resurrected one maintained historic continuity with the former Jesus. Yet the resurrected one is no longer confined to space and time, to the necessities of this life, such as sleep, food, and even death. No bones of the resurrected one were ever found, in contrast

107. So also Wilckens, *Resurrection*, 109-10.
108. So Jeremias, *New Testament Theology*, 1:309.

273

to the claim that the bones of Peter had been discovered underneath St. Peter's Basilica in Rome. Jesus Christ was no longer a being confined to space and time. As the first-born of the new creation, he has new possibilities which stand in contrast to the possibilities of our space and time-bound existence. He was resurrected to new and eternal life, to an imperishable existence in continuous community with God as the source of life. The resurrection is then only partially and in a limited sense an event in history. That which resulted in the resurrection transcends the boundaries of space and time and therewith of history.

It is significant that the resurrected one did not just seek union with God but visited his people, summoning them to a new task and a new mission and thus showing that his destiny was both exemplary and proleptic. In Jesus of Nazareth the new creation reached down into the old one. Through this divine intervention hope was inaugurated and strengthened in life within this aeon which is both preliminary and transitory. The resurrection of Jesus as the Christ served both as a catalyst for hope and as a verification that such hope is not unfounded. The rapidly expanding movement which ensued in the Christian church owes its existence to the resurrection. Through Christ's resurrection the true turning point occurred from the pre-Christian to the Christian existence, from the wavering and questioning disciples prior to Easter to the dedicated apostles of the Christian age. The resurrection is not a demonstration of the historical correctness of the Christian faith. It is rather the historic/transhistoric hinge which allowed history to open its gate to a new vision and a new reality. The resurrection of Jesus as the Christ is not one theological truth among many, but is the central and pivotal Christian tenet and an object matter of theological reflection in its own right.[109] Since the resurrection of Jesus as the Christ is a divine act of exaltation and glorification of Jesus, the question needs to be addressed how it is to be correlated to the ascension of Christ.

Ascension of Jesus Christ: The ascension of Jesus Christ is mentioned only three times in the New Testament (Mark 16:19, Luke 24:51, and Acts 1:9-10). Each time a spatial image is used: Christ was "taken up," "lifted up," or "carried up" into heaven. Since such spatial imagery associated with heaven is hardly tenable today, the ascension thus per-

---

109. See also Leo Scheffczyk, *Auferstehung: Prinzip des christlichen Glaubens* (Einsiedeln: Johannes Verlag, 1976), 9, in his preface.

ceived has even been subjected to ridicule, saying that Jesus was taken up like a rocket lifts up from earth and accelerates as it is propelled into space. An only slightly different position was assumed by Rudolf Bultmann when he claimed that since the three-story universe represents an outdated cosmology, "the story of Christ's descent into hell and of his Ascension into heaven is done with."[110] Such reactions are too quick and do not do justice to the biblical narratives.

In Acts 1:9-10 we read that Jesus "was lifted up, and a cloud took him out of their sight," and then the disciples are informed by angels that Jesus will return (at the final judgment). The disciples are told that Jesus has not just temporarily left, as he had disappeared out of their midst several times after his resurrection, but that they will no longer see him until he returns on the final day.[111] The ascension signifies the end of the resurrection appearances. As such it holds validity, but it does not play a significant role in the christology of the New Testament.[112] Correspondingly, the apostolic fathers hardly mention it. The only exception is the *Epistle of Barnabas* (15:9), in which the day of the resurrection and the ascension are mentioned almost in one breath, indicating that they belong closely together.

In the creedal formulations, starting with Justin Martyr and finding their climax in the Apostles' Creed, the ascension receives more attention. Justin Martyr mentions in his *First Apology* that Jesus Christ, our teacher, "was crucified and died, and rose again, and ascended into heaven."[113] Similarly we read in Tertullian that Jesus Christ, "having been crucified, . . . rose again the third day; [then] having ascended into the heavens, . . . sat at the right hand of the Father."[114] Finally, we read in the Apostles' Creed that Jesus Christ "was crucified, died, and was buried. He descended into hell. On the third day he rose again. He ascended into heaven, and is seated at the right hand of the Father." Unlike in the Gospel according to Luke and in Acts, the ascension was no longer seen as the cut-off point of the appearances of the resurrected

110. Rudolf Bultmann, "New Testament and Mythology," in *Kerygma and Myth*, ed. Hans-Werner Bartsch, trans. Reginald Fuller (New York: Harper & Row, 1961), 4.

111. So correctly Goppelt, *Theology of the New Testament*, 1:244-45.

112. So also Horst G. Pöhlmann, "Himmelfahrt Christi II: Kirchengeschichtlich," in *TRE* 15:334.

113. Justin Martyr, *The First Apology* 21, in *ANF* 1:170.

114. Tertullian, *On Prescription against Heretics* 13, in *ANF* 3:249.

one of which Paul's Damascus experience was the only exception. It was now interpreted as part of the salvific activity or rather salvific journey of Jesus Christ. We encounter an early precedent for this in Mark, where it says that "he was taken up into heaven and sat down at the right hand of God" (Mark 16:19). Here the visible event of the ascension was joined to the invisible event of Christ's enthronement at the right hand of the Father.

A translation from this life to an otherworldly sphere is occasionally mentioned in the Old Testament, for instance with Enoch and Elijah, and more often in classical antiquity.[115] But the exaltation motif is from the very beginning primarily associated with the resurrection. Only in the subsequent Christian tradition was it conjoined with the ascension. Ulrich Wilckens reminds us that "the faith in Jesus as the Lord raised on high, who sits in heaven on the right hand of God and is Lord over all powers, formed part of the faith in the risen Christ right from the beginning throughout the whole extent of primitive Christianity. Christ's being raised from the dead and his being lifted up on high belong together."[116] Paul mentions in Romans 8:34 that Christ "was raised, who is at the right hand of God, who indeed intercedes for us." In the famous hymn in Philippians 2:6-11 we read about the exaltation of Christ without his resurrection even being mentioned. "It is a common Christian view that the resurrection of Jesus was bound up with his taking place at the right hand of God and the beginning of the kingly reign of Christ."[117] Since the present world did not visibly change with Christ's resurrection, post-New Testament Christianity perhaps associated the exaltation with the ascension to indicate that with his visible removal from the presence of his disciples, Jesus had indeed entered the divine sphere.

A highly emotional dispute over the interpretation of the ascension erupted between Martin Luther and Huldreich Zwingli during the Reformation. Zwingli understood the sitting of Christ at the right hand of the Father in a locally descriptive way which excluded Christ from being also present in the Lord's Supper. Luther, however, was not inhibited by such cosmological strictures. Since Christ had entered a divine sphere,

---

115. Alfons Weiser, "Himmelfahrt Christi I: Neues Testament," in *TRE* 15:332.
116. Wilckens, *Resurrection*, 67.
117. So Jeremias, *New Testament Theology*, 1:310.

Luther argued, Christ was as omnipresent as God himself and was therefore also present in the Lord's Supper. Indeed, this kind of understanding of the ascension, as an event closely associated and even expressive of Christ's exaltation, can yield significant meaning for us today. Through Christ's resurrection, God vindicated the claim expressed during Jesus' earthly sojourn that he stood in the place of God. The ascension as the visible removal from this earth underscored this vindication, showing in spatio-temporal imagery that Jesus as the Christ was now indeed with God. Yet he was not with God in the same sense that any believer would wish to be with God. He was at the right hand, meaning that he had assumed an authoritative and executive position. Therefore Paul could associate the sitting at the right hand of God with Christ's intercessory function (Rom. 8:34).

God had reversed the self-sacrifice of Christ and had brought him back to God's self, not just in a new form of life, but in a position which, because of our association with Christ, will prove to be eminently beneficial for all of humanity. Exaltation leads to the possibility of salvation for humanity. Shy of his second coming in glory the salvific significance of Jesus the Christ has found its conclusion. Because of his double affinity, with us through his earthly sojourn and with God through his sitting at the right hand, he can now mediate us to God and God to us. Human alienation can be reversed, and the ugly, broad ditch between us and God can be bridged. Because Christ has been exalted, as visibly expressed in the ascension narrative, he has enduring salvific significance for us. The question, however, now emerges of whether this will be an actual possibility for all of us or just for part of humanity.

5. Christus or Christa?

Mary Daly (1928-) squarely addressed the problem of confessing Christ when she claimed: "The idea of a unique male savior may be seen as one more legitimation of male superiority."[118] Rosemary Radford Ruether (1936-) has also addressed the issue of whether a male savior can save women. She sees a threefold move in the patriarchalization of

118. Mary Daly, *Beyond God the Father: Toward a Philosophy of Women's Liberation* (Boston: Beacon, 1973), 71.

277

christology. First there was the development of an institutional ministry which dampened the prophetic vision of Jesus.[119] Then came the de-eschatologisation of christology, through which Jesus was understood as a timeless revelation of the divine perfection: "Access to Christ is now through the official line of apostolic teaching. Only males can occupy the apostolic teaching office and thus represent Christ. Women are to keep silent." After that came the final step with the establishment of the Christian church as the imperial religion of a Christian-Roman Empire under Constantine: "The Christian emperor, with the Christian Patriarch on his right hand, now represents the establishment of Christ's reign upon the earth."[120] Women can still be humble members of the Christian body, but they cannot represent Christ as the head and bridegroom of the church: "Women can represent only the creaturely (female) side, never the divine (male) side."[121]

There are alternatives to the classical christologies, such as an androgynous christology, found particularly in the mystical tradition. Behind these, however, is often buried the myth of an original androgyne.[122] According to this myth there was originally a person who contained both male and female characteristics. Then the female split off from the male, which brought with it the downfall of humanity and the advent of sex and sin. Christ as the new androgynous Adam enables the redeemed to transcend this split and regain spiritual harmony. But normative again is the male in which the female will merge to attain wholeness. Women are never permitted to represent the full human potential.

Even a spirit christology, as present in early Christian Gnosticism and again in mysticism, is not without problems, according to Ruether. Since salvation has so far rested only on the "male line," it is incomplete, and a female line in the form of a new Eve or of holy wisdom will bring final salvation to all humanity. Ruether realizes that "the splitting of the past revelation of Christ as the historical Jesus from the ongoing Spirit leads eventually to a revolt against Christ encapsulated in the past."[123] The tendency in this radical form lies in emancipation from Jesus as

---

119. See for the following, including the quotations, Rosemary Radford Ruether, *Sexism and God-Talk: Toward a Feminist Theology* (Boston: Beacon Press, 1983), 124.

120. Ruether, *Sexism and God-Talk*, 125.

121. Ruether, *Sexism and God-Talk*, 126.

122. For the following see Ruether, *Sexism and God-Talk*, 127-28.

123. Ruether, *Sexism and God-Talk*, 135, for this and the following quotation.

redeemer and in seeking a new redemptive disclosure of God and of human possibilities in female form beyond Jesus. Yet Ruether does not want to go that far.

Ruether prefers to return to the Jesus of the Synoptic Gospels and realizes that once he is stripped of later masculinization, he "can be recognized as a figure remarkably compatible with feminism." This would not turn Jesus into a feminist, but it would recapture his criticism of the existing social and religious hierarchy and his speaking out on behalf of the marginalized and despised groups of society. It would also show that women play an important role in the gospel. It is important to realize that the role played by women of marginalized groups is an intrinsic part of the iconoclastic, Messianic vision portrayed by Jesus. Ruether can even venture to say "that the maleness of Jesus has no ultimate significance."[124] Yet she also cautions that Christ is not necessarily male, nor is the redeemed community only made up of women, but is a new humanity, composed of female and male. In order to be effective today, Christ as redemptive Word and Word of God cannot be encapsulated once and for all in a historical Jesus. "Christ, the liberated humanity, is not confined to a static perfection of one person two thousand years ago. Rather redemptive humanity goes ahead of us, calling us to yet incompleted dimensions of human liberation."[125] Christ is more the critic than the vindicator "of the present hierarchical social order."[126] The victory he has achieved still needs to be inaugurated and completed on a global human scale. He still needs, so to speak, to be liberated so that he can become a liberating person for others.

Since the beginning of the feminist movement, Jesus as a male redeemer has always contained enough conflict for women frustrated with Christianity.[127] Hurt in their self-esteem and their self-affirmation, many women have decided that the church is unable to be a redemptive community for them. They have abandoned the Christian faith and joined feminist communities of spirituality to find the divine in the goddess symbol and in themselves. Many others, however, have dis-

---

124. Ruether, *Sexism and God-Talk*, 137.

125. Ruether, *Sexism and God-Talk*, 138.

126. Rosemary Radford Ruether, *To Change the World: Christology and Cultural Criticism* (New York: Crossroad, 1981), 55.

127. So Elisabeth Moltmann-Wendel, *A Land Flowing with Milk and Honey: Perspectives on Feminist Theology*, trans. John Bowden (New York: Crossroad, 1986), 117.

covered that alongside the androcentric teachings in the tradition there are empowering messages as well.[128] Elisabeth Moltmann-Wendel (1926-) claims that a huge dynamic issues forth from Jesus' history with women once we overlook statements that Jesus is the savior, the Son of man, the Son of God, or the Messiah.[129] Hierarchical structures are leveled, and there is a dynamic in many of these stories concerning women. She notices that women gain something from him: wholeness, health, life, wine, humanness. At the same time, they give something to him: meaning, tasks, a goal in life, and a community without which our tasks and goals would be abstract. "They get strength to live and invest in him hope, trust, visions that transcend him. They make him what he is by going with him on his way: the human being for all human beings, the solitary one who can be a comforting image for all who are solitary, the one who trusts in himself and can give self-confidence to all, a person who goes to death and yet is not alone."[130]

Sallie McFague (1933-), to name a prominent representative from the United States, sees in the biblical Jesus a destabilizing, inclusive, nonhierarchical vision of fulfillment for all of creation.[131] Three aspects are characteristic of the story of Jesus: his speaking in parables, his table fellowship with outcasts, and his death on a cross. According to McFague, the parables suggest "a radically egalitarian, non-dualistic way of being in the world" that goes beyond the dualism of rich and poor, male and female, Christian and non-Christian. It presents a destabilization of all dualisms. This approach to the prevailing social reality becomes even more explicit in Jesus' table fellowship. "The destabilization of the parables becomes an 'enacted parable' as Jesus invites the outcasts of society to eat with him."[132] Jesus disrupts the conventional

---

128. So Barbara Darling-Smith, "A Feminist Christological Exploration," in *One Faith, Many Cultures: Inculturation, Indigenization, and Contextualization,* ed. O. Costa (Mary-knoll, N.Y.: Orbis, 1988), 72. See also Rosemary Radford Ruether, *Womanguides: Readings toward a Feminist Theology* (Boston: Beacon, 1985), 112.

129. Moltmann-Wendel, *A Land Flowing with Milk and Honey,* 121.

130. Moltmann-Wendel, *A Land Flowing with Milk and Honey,* 123.

131. Sallie McFague, *Models of God: Theology for an Ecological, Nuclear Age* (Philadelphia: Fortress, 1987), 49. Darling-Smith, "A Feminist Christological Exploration," 79, correctly observes that McFague and Ruether "are most closely drawn to the Jesus of the synoptic gospels — the Jesus who told parables, who related warmly to other human beings."

132. McFague, *Models of God,* 51, for this and the preceding quotation.

dualisms, for as a friend of the outcasts, he epitomizes the scandal of inclusiveness for his time. Not the holiness of the elect but the whole-ness of all is the central vision of Jesus. The cross, then, "epitomizes the retribution that comes to those who give up controlling and tri-umphalistic postures in order to relate to others in mutual love."[133] McFague rejects a triumphalistic christology and the atonement for the sins of the world, because with this she sees connected "salvation with one individual and in one past act."[134] It furthermore supports an escapist mythology of the worst sort, which suggests that sin is against God and not against other people. On the cross Jesus does something not on our behalf, but he manifests in his own life and death that "the heart of the universe is unqualified love working to befriend the needy, the outcast, the oppressed."[135] The cross is a paradigm of God's way with the world. God in Jesus is not a king but a servant, self-sacrificing, forgiving, nurturing, and supporting. Since feminist theologians are apprehensive of metaphors that may lend themselves to domination and oppression, such as king, savior, or victor, such metaphors, if as-sociated with Jesus' life, work, and destiny, must be replaced with images that imply mutuality, empathy, and egalitarianism.

Carter Heyward (1945-) even goes so far to say that "*a christology of passion has no place for atonement.* There is nothing inherently liberating or salvific about suffering."[136] According to Heyward such terminology smacks of patriarchy and abuse. But still the Jesus story is important for Heyward, since it provides "windows through which we may glimpse part of life, wholly, or all of life, partially. To the extent that the story serves to empower women as well as historically or socially disem-powered men, it participates in a redemptive process that is at once political, spiritual, psychological, intellectual, and material."[137] She calls for an erotic christology that takes delight in "the struggle for justice, aware that what we are doing in this struggle is to help generate condi-tions for each and all of us to enjoy our life together on this planet."[138]

133. McFague, *Models of God,* 53.

134. McFague, *Models of God,* 54.

135. McFague, *Models of God,* 55.

136. Carter Heyward, "Suffering, Redemption, and Christ: Shifting the Grounds of Feminist Christology," *Christianity and Crisis* 49 (11 Dec. 1989): 384.

137. Heyward, "Suffering, Redemption, and Christ," 385.

138. Heyward, "Suffering, Redemption, and Christ," 386.

It is no longer through Jesus as person that something is accomplished, but from this person issues forth a dynamic power which empowers others in the process of socio-political as well as spiritual redemption.

Rita Nakashima Brock moves even further away from the person of Jesus by developing a christology "not centered in Jesus, but in relationship and community as the whole-making, healing center of Christianity. In that sense, Christ is . . . Christa/Community."[139] Brock objects that the old and new quests of the historical Jesus presuppose the primary importance of the individual.[140] Yet individuals only make sense in the larger context of events embedded in particular historical structures. Brock also objects to Ruether's focus on Jesus the individual rather than on "the crucial presence of members of Jesus' community as embodying God/dess and having a transforming impact on him."[141] "If Jesus is reported to have been capable of profound love and concern for others, he was first loved and respected by the concrete persons of his life." There is a mutuality of Jesus' relationships in which he receives support and nurturing as well as enjoying conversation and physical comfort. Jesus should not be misconstrued as a heroic figure, since he encounters and interacts with the real presence of people who then co-create liberation and heal from brokenheartedness. Jesus participates centrally in a Christa/Community, is brought into being through it, and participates in a co-creation of it.

> Christa/Community is a lived reality expressed in relational images. Hence Christa/Community as described in the images of events in which erotic power is made manifest. A reality of erotic power within connectedness means it cannot be located in a single individual. Hence what is truly christological, that is, truly revealing of divine incarnation and salvific power in human life, must reside in connectedness and not in single individuals.[142]

Brock does not base her christology largely on the historical Jesus, but rather on the community's experience of Jesus whose experience then

---

139. Rita Nakashima Brock, *Journeys by Heart: A Christology of Erotic Power* (New York: Crossroad, 1988), 52.

140. Brock, *Journeys by Heart*, 68.

141. Brock, *Journeys by Heart*, 66, for this and the following quotation.

142. Brock, *Journeys by Heart*, 52.

generates erotic power, meaning the feminist eros which encompasses the "life force," the unique human energy which springs from the desire for existence with meaning and integrates the sensual and the rational, the spiritual and the political.[143] Brock admits her indebtedness to process thought in overcoming a dualistic christology and also to the feminist community that gave her a sense of interconnectedness and empowerment. In terms of christology Brock hardly speaks of divine incarnation in one individual, Jesus of Nazareth, but rather of incarnation in the whole human race.

The British feminist Julie Hopkins is as critical as Carter Heyward of the atonement theories, yet for different reasons. She categorically states "that atonement and sacrificial doctrines are unacceptable."[144] One reason for her rejection of the atonement is that she does not believe that "it is possible to encapsulate in a dogma what happens salvifically or within the Trinity when Jesus died on Calvary."[145] She questions the necessity to speculate upon the inner dynamics of the Trinity in order to meditate on the sufferings of Jesus on the cross. Underlying her criticism is the conviction that these ideas are based on the great philosophical presupposition that God cannot suffer, because he is eternal and unchanging. Moreover, what would inspire Christians to self-sacrifice and hope "if love, death and the future salvation of the world is an internal matter between God the Father and God the Son?"[146] Atonement therefore is something that is neither inspiring for humanity nor are we existentially drawn into it.

The other reason for rejecting atonement theories lies for Hopkins in her feminist approach. She argues that her "particular criticism of a sacrificial interpretation of the death of Jesus is colored by its historical effect on women."[147] Since sin had been inextricably associated with sex, women, through virtue of their gender, were considered guilty of the death of Christ. To make satisfaction for their guilt, they had two reme-

---

143. Brock, *Journeys by Heart*, 25, where she explains "erotic power" and her dependence on Haunani-Kay Trask, *Eros and Power: The Promise of Feminist Theory* (Philadelphia: University of Pennsylvania, 1986), 92-93, for her own definition.

144. Julie M. Hopkins, *Toward a Feminist Christology: Jesus of Nazareth, European Women and the Christological Crisis* (Kampen, Netherlands: Kok Pharos, n.d.), 54.

145. Hopkins, *Toward a Feminist Christology*, 54.

146. Hopkins, *Toward a Feminist Christology*, 51.

147. Hopkins, *Toward a Feminist Christology*, 51.

dies, either to assume a spirit of passivity and obedience to bear the pain of childbearing and to submit to their husbands, or to transcend their gender and become like men through celibacy and asceticism. In pursuing the latter option many women assumed masochistic practices through self-flagellation and other "virtues" to identify with the death of Jesus. Therefore Julie Hopkins raises the question whether "it is possible to preach 'Christ crucified' without evoking destructive forms of guilt and masochism?"[148] In seeking an answer she looks at the Gospels, where she discovers that "Jesus never proclaimed the necessity of suffering. His ministry was life-affirming; he sought to eradicate pain and social distress and preach Good News to the poor and heavy-hearted. That he could not finally avoid suffering and an early death is a tragedy and a prophetic exposure of the nihilistic tendencies of those who idolize power."[149] It may well have been, she surmises, that Jesus believed that his action of directly confronting the Roman political and Jewish sacerdotal powers in Jerusalem would inaugurate an apocalyptic crisis in which God would overthrow the corrupted human power structures and come to reign directly.

Whatever happened in the events that led to Jesus' passion and death, one thing is clear for Hopkins. His followers firmly believed that God was present at the crucifixion, not as an impassive transcendental observer, but as actively sharing with the victim in a solidarity of suffering in grief. Therefore we are confronted with a God who suffered with Jesus. This means that we should recover "the central theological insight of the Christian proclamation of the cross that God is present and in loving solidarity with those who suffer unjustly at the hands of corrupt and violent people."[150] Yet such an insight does not require a doctrine of atonement. Jesus was not sacrificed as a guilt offering to pay for human sin, nor do we have continue to repay our debt to Jesus by sacrificing ourselves.

The deity of Jesus, as it was expressed in the later christological dogma, does not explain what happened on the cross. Therefore it is possible to believe that God was in Jesus, reconciling believers to God's self on the cross, without claiming that Jesus was uniquely divine or that a blood price was paid. Hopkins feels that with this she is rejecting the

---

148. Hopkins, *Toward a Feminist Christology*, 52.
149. Hopkins, *Toward a Feminist Christology*, 56.
150. Hopkins, *Toward a Feminist Christology*, 58 for this and the following quotation.

Greek conception of the impassible nature of God and conversely affirms that God did and does suffer. The God whom she affirms "is the source of birth, life and death (which is the process of the transformation of energy and matter into another state). This God is also the power of love and justice which is released in human relationships."

The German theologian Dorothee Sölle seems to pursue a similar line to Hopkins, when she claims that the cross symbolizes both the suffering of the disadvantaged and the peculiar option of God for the poor.[151] The starting point of the christological issue is not atonement or a ransom which Christ paid to God. It is the radical passion for justice and engagement for the disenfranchised which leads to passion and suffering. There is no heroic picture of Jesus, who as a singular and solitary figure saved the world. Such a concept of salvation would be imperialistic. In the cross we do not see a God who wants pain and suffering, but a God who has a special preference for the disadvantaged. The cross is not the triumph of salvation; instead, we still wait with all the nations for another justice and another peace. Insofar as Jesus helps us in that waiting and searching, he is our teacher of the longing for salvation. To love Christ means that we do not sleep while he is hanging on the cross. Without following him, without participating in his salvational work, there is no salvation. Christ then teaches and works through us and empowers us to shy away from a christological or any other imperialism and to embody a new humanity of mutual service and mutual respect.

In our brief overview it is clear that there is no single feminist christology but rather a plurality of interpretations of Jesus from the feminist perspective.[152] Yet in all its diversity feminist criticism of traditional christology focuses predominantly on three points: a patriarchal Christ, excessive transcendence of Jesus the Christ, and exclusiveness of salvation in and through Jesus Christ. It is certainly true that the maleness of Jesus of Nazareth is incidental to and not constitutive of salvation. We may speculate that within the patriarchal context of Jesus' time a

---

151. For the following description cf. Dorothee Sölle, "Der Erstgeborene aus dem Tod — Dekonstruktion und Rekonstruktion von Christologie," in *Tutzinger Blätter* (4/1995), 17ff.

152. So Doris Strahm, "Jesus Christus," in *Wörterbuch der feministischen Theologie*, ed. Elisabeth Gössmann (Gütersloh: Gerd Mohn, 1991), 204.

female savior figure may not have proven as effective as the male Jesus. Yet the significant point is that salvation came through Jesus and not that Jesus was male. Feminist christology rightly points out that up to now the maleness of Jesus has led to a predominance of maleness in the ecclesiastical hierarchy and consequently to a relegation of women to inferior roles within the church. There can be no legitimate inference from the maleness of Jesus to a predominance of males within the ecclesiastical hierarchy or in any churchly office. If Paul is correct that in Christ there is neither male nor female, then no preference in the church can be given to males or to females solely on the basis of gender. Here the church has often neither preached nor taught nor acted in a Christ-like spirit, and women are rightly asking for redress.

Certainly it is a very healthy situation that feminist christologies point to the Jesus of the Gospels instead of the Christ of Nicea or Chalcedon. Throughout most of the history of Christendom christology has suffered from a predominance of the divine. While Jesus is the human face of God, Jesus Christ was so exclusively relegated to the divine realm that other, more human mediator figures had to be introduced. Initially Mary assumed this function. Eventually ever more divine attributes were conferred upon her. Finally the saints had to bridge the gap between humanity and God. To counteract this neglect of humanity, the emphasis on the human side of Jesus, his interrelatedness with other human beings, his suffering, and simply on his humanity are very much in order. As many feminist theologians show, even from the humanity of Jesus a strong liberating power emanates. Nonetheless we should not go so far as to abandon the Chalcedonian emphasis on the truly divine and truly human aspect of Jesus Christ. Only because Jesus was the human face of God and not simply a human being can he bridge the gap between humanity and God. Any notion that by Jesus' inspiration alone we can create truly liberated and egalitarian communities is opting for utopia instead of salvation. Utopian communities, regardless of how inspiring their leaders were, have always ended in failure. They disregard the intrinsic sinfulness of humanity. Of course, in the face of today's universal self-aggrandizement it is not opportune to point out humanity's self-centeredness and finitude. Yet in facing today's often unjust and oppressive political and social realities perhaps such an inopportune move is still not shy of the truth.

Some feminist christologies are dissatisfied that Jesus is the sole and unique redeemer figure. Perhaps they fear that Jesus' unique position might again lead to an oppressive figure and not to the suffering servant whom the Gospels portray. As we will note in the following chapter, Jesus is unique, but salvation through him is not exclusive.[153] Of course, the emphasis on Jesus as *the* savior has led to Christian imperialism and the disqualification of other religions. Yet such an inappropriate, arrogant spirit is not the sole prerogative of the Christian faith. It can also be found in many other world religions. Humbleness, and not self-assuredness and arrogance, would be much more in tune with Jesus' own posture. Yet to assume that there is a continual incarnation of God which leads to liberating and life-engendering relations not only abandons the uniqueness of Jesus but instead opts for philosophical speculation of a Hegelian or a Whiteheadian kind. I conclude that some valuable corrections in feminist christologies can be detected, but so also can some dangers that are quite frequently part and parcel of corrective movements.

153. Hans Schwarz, *The Search for God: Christianity — Atheism — Secularism — World Religions* (Minneapolis: Augsburg, 1975), 152.

287

7. Christ's Presence and Future

The notion that God is the first and the last, the Alpha and the Omega, has a rich and deep tradition in both the New Testament and the prophets. At the outset of the book of Revelation we read: "'I am the Alpha and the Omega,' says the Lord God, who is and who was and who is to come, the Almighty [Greek: *pantocratōr*]" (Rev. 1:8). This statement about God is reiterated at the end of this last book of the Bible: "I am the Alpha and the Omega, the beginning and the end" (Rev. 21:6). This image is also found in the Old Testament prophets: "I am the first and I am the last; besides me there is no god" (Isa. 44:6). This same phrase, this same image, is used for Christ: "I am the Alpha and the Omega, the first and the last, the beginning and the end" (Rev. 22:13). Alpha and omega were the first and last letters of the Greek alphabet and were used to signify the beginning and the end, the first and the last.

The early Christian author of Revelation found it permissible to use the terms *alpha* and *omega* as predicates of divine majesty for both God and Christ. Significant is not only the identification of Christ with God, but also the explication of God as "who is and who was and who is to come." Here the Old Testament understanding of God as "I am who I am" (Exod. 3:14) is expanded with reference to his coming. This indication of the parousia gives the notion of the Godhead "a dynamic quantity peculiar to the early Christian conception of God and Christ."[1] Ever since Jesus, the proclaimer, became the proclaimed Christ, the believer did not simply remember Jesus' words and deeds, but was convinced that he had significance for the present and future existence of Christians

1. Gerhard Kittel, "Alpha and Omega," in *TDNT* 1:1.

and beyond them for the whole world. This cosmic dimension of Christ becomes especially noticeable in the descent and ascension of Christ.

1. Descent and Ascension of Christ

Descent of Christ: Ernst Koch (1930-) concludes his article on the descent of Christ into hell with the telling statement: "In the present creedal formulations it has no noticeable significance."[2] Jürgen Moltmann (1926-), who devotes considerable attention in his christology to the cosmic Christ and the parousia of Christ, makes no mention of Christ's descent.[3] Friedrich Schleiermacher also omitted the descent of Christ into hell from his theological considerations, though he at least gives a reason for this omission. He claims that the descent into hell "according to its dominant idea — would certainly belong to His redemptive activities if only we could regard it as a fact. It would then have to be regarded as an exercise of his prophetic and high-priestly office towards those who had died before His appearance."[4] Schleiermacher omitted the descent since it cannot be based on a fact. He finds it problematic to limit Christ's saving activity to those who had died before his appearance, "for all those also who had died since His appearance without having heard the preaching of the Gospel have the same claims as the others." Christ's saving activity cannot be confined only to those before his life here on earth. It must also be extended into the present and future to all those who have never explicitly heard his voice while they were alive on earth.

As the history of religion shows, the motif of a descent is not peculiar to Christian thought. It is present throughout the Judeo-Christian environment, in Egypt, Babylonia, India, Iran, with the Mandeans and the Manicheans, and in Judaism. Josef Kroll in his comprehensive investigation on "God and hell" claims that descent means myth; this notion initially resulted only from the idea of the disappearance of the sun during the day and in the darker seasons of the year and its renewed

---

2. Ernst Koch, "Höllenfahrt Christi," in *TRE* 15:459.

3. See passim Jürgen Moltmann, *The Way of Jesus Christ: Christology in Messianic Dimensions,* trans. Margaret Kohl (San Francisco: Harper, 1990), 274-341.

4. Friedrich Schleiermacher, *The Christian Faith* §99, Engl. trans. of the 2nd German ed., ed. H. R. Mackintosh and J. S. Stewart (New York: Harper & Row, 1963), 2:419.

rising.[5] Perhaps it originated also in connection with the death and rejuvenation of vegetation. Of more significance was the idea that the realm in which the sun fought with hostile powers was at the same time the abode of the dead. As the Christians realized that their savior had died, that he went to the netherworld and arose again, it was clear that here a descent had to be assumed. "When the evangelist Matthew uses the motif of the earthshaking participation of the whole nature in the death of Jesus (27:51f.), then this Jesus cannot have entered Sheol as a weak captive. When the sun has darkened, the earth shakes, the dead come up, then the *sōtēr* [savior] has also overcome the netherworld."[6]

The scriptural evidence for Christ's descent into hell is very weak. There is basically only one source, 1 Peter 3:18-20 and 4:6. Both texts are very difficult to explain and have led to various speculations.[7] Norbert Brox (1935-) suggests that "the spirits in prison" mentioned in 1 Peter 3:19 refers to the sons of God who went to the daughters of humans who bore children to them (Gen. 6:4). This reference would then express the conviction that even in this most remote place and time Christ is present with his salvific activity.[8] Moreover, 1 Peter 4:6 contains the hope "that even the dead are confronted with a decision through proclamation and therefore can be judged like everybody else so that there is a universal judgment for all people without exception."[9] Leonhard Goppelt (1911-73) concludes in his *Commentary on I Peter:* "'The spirits in prison' are, therefore, the souls of the flood generation preserved in a place of punishment after death. . . . 1 Pet. declares: Even to this most lost part of humanity Christ, the One who died and rose, offers salvation. The saving effectiveness of his suffering unto death extends even to those mortals who in earthly life do not come to a conscious encounter with him, even to the most lost among them."[10] Goppelt also cites Martin Luther's rather straightforward statement concerning

5. See for the following Josef Kroll, *Gott und Hölle: Der Mythos vom Descensuskampfe* (Darmstadt: Wissenschaftliche Buchgesellschaft, 1963), 526-27.

6. Kroll, *Gott and Hölle,* 527.

7. Norbert Brox, *Der erste Petrusbrief* (Zürich: Benziger, 1979), 196-97, in his explanation of 1 Peter 4:6.

8. Brox, *Der erste Petrusbrief,* 181.

9. So Brox, *Der erste Petrusbrief,* 199.

10. Leonhard Goppelt, *A Commentary on I Peter,* ed. Ferdinand Hahn, trans. John E. Alsup (Grand Rapids: Eerdmans, 1993), 259.

1 Peter 3:19-22: "This is a strange text and certainly a more obscure passage than any other passage in the New Testament. I still do not know for sure what the apostle means."[11] Indeed, the details may remain unclear. But the intention of these lines is evident. First Peter is concerned with the salvific activity of Christ, and he wants to assure us that not even the realm of the dead is excluded from that activity.

All parallels in the history of religion to a descent notwithstanding, Christ's descent to the dead can be simply explained by the common Jewish notion that everyone who dies goes down to *Sheol.* Tertullian refers to Jesus' death and burial: "With the same law of His being He fully complied, by remaining in Hades in the form and condition of a dead man; nor did He ascend into the heights of heaven before descending into the lower parts of the earth, that He might there make the patriarchs and prophets partakers of Himself."[12] But as Tertullian also points out, this going to the dead did not simply lead to a neutral resting. It is not without significance that in connection with the descent 1 Peter is quoted for the first time by Clement of Alexandria (ca. 145–ca. 213) at the close of the second century.[13] Clement expands on 1 Peter, saying that "he should bring to repentance those belonging to the Hebrews, and they [i.e., his disciples] the Gentiles."[14] The salvific significance of Jesus' descent through his apostles is extended even to non-Jewish people.

There is no unanimity among the church fathers as to who is to be included in the salvific domain of Christ's power. Some church fathers thought that Jesus had redeemed all the dead with the exception of the most wicked.[15] This was the argument of Melito of Sardis (d. ca. 190), Marcion (d. ca. 160), and Ephraem (ca. 306-73). Others, such as the Alexandrian theologians (the most notable of whom was Origen), thought that even those who had died before the flood had been saved. We must ask here whether the church fathers indulged in

11. Martin Luther, *Sermons on the First Epistle of St. Peter* (1522), in *LW* 30:113; and Goppelt, *Commentary of I Peter,* 255.

12. Tertullian, *A Treatise on the Soul* 55, in *ANF* 3:231.

13. According to Brox, *Der erste Petrusbrief,* 186.

14. Clement of Alexandria, *The Stromata* 6.6, in *ANF* 2:490.

15. For the following see Hans Schwarz, *Jenseits von Utopie und Resignation: Einführung in die christliche Eschatologie* (Wuppertal: R. Brockhaus, 1991), 197-98; and Brox, *Der erste Petrusbrief,* 184.

speculation or dwelled on an uncertain biblical text. To sharpen the issue we must mention that explicit reference to Christ's descent into hell is made only in extracanonical literature, such as the *Gospel of Nicodemus* and the *Odes of Solomon*.[16] It is noteworthy that the descent narrative in the *Gospel of Nicodemus* makes immediate reference to Matthew 27:52-53: "The tombs also were opened, and many bodies of the saints who had fallen asleep were raised. After his resurrection they came out of the tombs and entered the holy city and appeared to many." The whole descent narrative is told from that angle, namely that some who had been brought back to life declared how Christ had come to them while they were in Hades. In Ode 42 of the *Odes of Solomon* the descent is prefaced by Jesus' speaking: "I was not rejected although also I was considered to be so, and I did not perish although they thought it of me" (42:10).[17] The descent, together with Christ's saving activity connected with it, is already seen as a vindication of Christ. He is vindicated as the one who he claimed to be. We may conclude, contrary to Kroll's opinion, that "the influence of pagan myths of descent to the underworld on Christian ideas of Christ's descent to Hades was probably minimal."[18]

Even if 1 Peter 3:19 has nothing to do with Christ's descent to Hades, the theological significance of the descent to the dead would not rest on this passage.[19] It is also not derived from pious Christian folklore. It is based on the conviction of the human face of God, whose earthly sojourn was vindicated so, as the risen one, he could say: "Do not be afraid; I am the first and the last, and the living one. I was dead, and see, I am alive forever and ever; and I have the keys of Death and of Hades" (Rev. 1:17-18). Under that aspect it was incorporated into the Apostles' Creed no earlier than 370. "The descent into hell then assumed the function that the Greek fathers had assigned to the death and resurrection, the triumph

---

16. For the text of the *Gospel of Nicodemus* see Wilhelm Hennecke-Schneemelcher, ed., *New Testament Apocrypha* (Philadelphia: Westminster, 1963), 1:470-76.

17. As printed in *The Old Testament Pseudepigrapha*, ed. James H. Charlesworth (Garden City, N.Y.: Doubleday, 1985), 2:771.

18. So correctly Richard Bauckham, "Descent to the Underworld," in *The Anchor Bible Dictionary*, 2:157, who first presents an extensive survey of possible parallels from the history of religion.

19. This is the conclusion of William Joseph Dalton, *Christ's Proclamation to the Spirits: A Study of 1 Peter 3:18–4:6* (Rome: Pontifical Biblical Institute, 1965), 8.

celebrated by Christ over the devil and his legions."[20] The phrase "he descended into hell," or, as it is now more adequately translated, "he went to the dead," has nothing to do with celestial topography or ancient mythology. It expresses first of all the conviction that Jesus was indeed dead once he had died on the cross. The descent is mentioned after Jesus' death and burial as the last of a triad. In this way it is also closely associated with the resurrection and ascension. It is no surprise that discussion and controversy erupted over whether the going to the dead was the last point of Jesus' humiliation or the first point of Christ's exaltation. Yet picking up on the New Testament conviction that Christ has the keys of death and of Hades, since through Christ's resurrection "death has been swallowed up in victory" as Paul reminded the congregation in Corinth (1 Cor. 15:54), early Christianity felt that this descent was an expression of divine compassion. Jesus, as the human face of God, was not simply a temporary and fleeting vision on this earth. He was the divine attempt to bridge the primordial alienation between God and humanity. All people everywhere, regardless of their respective location in space and time, had through him the opportunity to be confronted with the gospel, God's word of salvation. When the church decided to include this phrase in the Apostles' Creed, its intent was not only to indicate that Christ has triumphed over all possible dimensions, even over that dimension where death usually reigns, but also to express something of the divine compassion. That which in every respect looked like an accidental act of history, that Jesus lived, worked, and died at a specific point in space and time, was now perceived as having axiomatic significance. Through Christ salvation has been made possible for everyone. Schleiermacher's reservation that the descent is only relevant to the destiny of those prior to Christ's coming is only half of the truth. While this was indeed the conviction of the early church fathers, already some of them extended the salvific reach beyond the old covenant. Christ's going to the dead could be seen as an expression of God's unbounding love which still today reaches those who during their lifetime had no opportunity to have a genuine encounter with Christ. The descent must be connected with Christ's ascension to power. Only the one who ascended can bring salvation beyond his immediate physical sphere of influence.

20. Jaroslav Pelikan, *The Christian Tradition: A History of the Development of Doctrine* (Chicago: University of Chicago Press, 1974), 1:151.

Ascension of Christ: In chapter 5 we already briefly dealt with Christ's ascension. But now we must consider it in the larger context of his complete vindication and ascension to power. As the hymn in Philippians 2:6-11 announces, "by way of vindication and approval of Jesus' total self-humbling, the Father has magnificently exalted his Son to the highest station and graciously bestowed on him the name above all other names, that is, his own name, Lord, along with all that gives substance and meaning to the name. In this exalted state Jesus now exercises universal lordship."[21] In the Gospel of John, God is glorified through Jesus' total submission and then the Son is glorified through his death, resurrection, and ascension.[22] He who had been faithful to the very end of his earthly life now experiences the faithfulness of God when the divine name is applied to him. God acknowledges Jesus not as a son but as the Son. It is a commonplace in the New Testament that Jesus as the Christ was "taken up in glory" (1 Tim. 3:16) and that "he who descended is the same one who ascended far above all the heavens, so that he might fill all things" (Eph. 4:10). In the latter reference the assertion is significant that Christ fills all things. This phrase may be understood analogously to the omnipresence of God, which has graciously beneficial as well as punishing effects.[23] In the same way as God fills and permeates everything through his power and might, Christ has subjected to himself all anti-Godly forces. Jesus the Christ is in the position of highest honor and supreme power. This conviction has been underscored by the church in the Apostles' Creed with the reference to Christ "sitting at the right hand of the Father." In the hymn in Philippians 2 the exaltation is explained as giving Jesus the Christ "the name that is above every name." This "unmentionable" name is none other than God's own name, Yahweh. In light of Isaiah 42:8: "I am the LORD, that is my name; my glory I give to no other," such a bestowal by God is indeed the rarest of all honors. "In his exalted state Jesus has a new rank involving the exercise of universal lordship."[24] Jesus became known as none other than

---

21. So Peter T. O'Brien, *The Epistle to the Philippians: A Commentary on the Greek Text* (Grand Rapids: Eerdmans, 1991), 233, in his exegesis of Phil. 2:9.

22. See for the following Raymond E. Brown, *The Gospel according to John (I–XII)* (Garden City, N.Y.: Doubleday, 1966), 475-76, in his exegesis of John 12:27-30.

23. Cf. Rudolf Schnackenburg, *Der Brief an die Epheser* (Zürich: Benziger, 1982), 182, in his exegesis of Eph. 4:10, who suggests this interpretation in analogy to Philo's concept of God's omnipresence.

24. O'Brien, *Epistle to the Philippians,* 238, in his exegesis of Phil. 2:9.

he was from the very beginning. Yet it is made clear that the authority he is claiming in heaven and on earth is not his own but given by God. Yet the fulfillment of the divine intention "that at the name of Jesus every knee should bend, in heaven and on earth and under the earth, and every tongue should confess that Jesus Christ is Lord" (Phil. 2:10-11) will take place at the parousia. Then the universal scope of adoration and confession of Jesus as Lord will be complete.

Some cautions have been raised against such an authoritative redeemer figure. Alfred North Whitehead (1861-1947) claimed that the Galilean origin of Christianity "does not emphasize the ruling Caesar, or the ruthless moralist, or the unmoved mover. It dwells upon the tender elements in the world, which slowly and in quietness operate by love; and it finds purpose in the present immediacy of a kingdom not of this world. Love neither rules, nor is it unmoved; also it is a little oblivious as to morals."[25] As we have seen, a similar sentiment has also been advanced by some representatives of feminist christology. Enthronement, the kingly office, and even Jesus as judge are patterned too much after models of male dominance to have persuasive value for women. Indeed, the notion of a Christ who judges and holds us accountable for everything we have done and left undone drove Luther into the monastery and almost into spiritual and emotional despair.

We began these reflections by considering Jesus' descent, an expression both of divine compassion and of sovereignty. Here we should remember what Martin Luther said about God. In his comments on the First Commandment in the *Large Catechism* he wrote: "As I have often said, the trust and faith of the heart alone make both God and an idol. If your faith and trust are right, then your God is the true God. On the other hand, if your trust is false and wrong, then you have not the true God."[26] And further he writes: "A god is that to which we look for all good and in which we find refuge in every time of need." If we were to apply this kind of reasoning to Jesus, then a compassionate Jesus alone would certainly be a very comforting concept. No threat could ever emerge from him. Yet could we truly find refuge in him in time of need, if he is just compassion without having any authority? In God, as well

---

25. Alfred North Whitehead, *Process and Reality,* corrected ed., David R. Griffin and Donald W. Sherburne (New York: Free Press, 1978), 343.
26. *BC,* 365.

as in Christ, authority and compassion belong together, since a Christ without authority can never implement his compassion. His limits would be similar to those that we encounter. He would be a Christ of our world, but not the human face of God. Exaltation and power belong to Christ so that he can be ultimately trustworthy.

The cosmic dimension of Christ has been particularly emphasized in the Eastern Church. While in the West the work of Christ is considered primarily to be one of restoration, in the East it is one of reunification. The Eastern *pantocrator*, who looks down on the faithful as they are assembled in an Eastern sanctuary, manifests "the passionless visage of absolute serenity."[27] Yet he is not staring at us as an innocent Western Christian might surmise, but a strong energy and motion issues from him. The fundamental dualities of creation, which because of sin have become elements of disintegration and corruption, have been overcome by him. Through his virginal birth he overcame the opposition of the sexes, and by his death and resurrection he destroyed the separation between paradise and the universe that existed since the Fall.[28] Through his ascension he unites heaven and earth, since his human body is co-natural and consubstantial with ours. He establishes the harmony of the whole creation and finally even unites humanity to God. As Maximus the Confessor (ca. 580-662) stated:

> The ultimate aim of the divine plan is man's deification: That whole people might participate in the whole God, and that in the same way in which the soul and body are united, God should become partakable of by the soul, and, by the soul's intermediary, by the body, in order that the soul might receive an unchanging character and the body, immortality; and finally, that the whole man should become God, deified, by the grace of God become man, becoming whole man, soul and body, by nature, and becoming whole God, soul and body, by grace.[29]

We notice here a twofold movement, a divine movement toward humanity through which God participates in creation and a human movement toward God which was intended by the creator from the

27. Joseph Sittler, *Essays on Nature and Grace* (Philadelphia: Fortress, 1972), 53.
28. Maximus Confessor, *Ambiguorum Liber*, in *PG* 91:1308d-1309b.
29. Maximus Confessor, *Ambiguorum Liber*, in *PG* 91:1088c.

beginning and is finally restored through Christ. The two natures, the human and the divine, eventually meet each other and form a divine union.

While for the Eastern church fathers the notion of deification is primarily reserved for humanity, being received up to and into Christ, Pierre Teilhard de Chardin (1881-1955) extended that idea to the whole cosmos. For him Christ is the "organic center of the entire universe."[30] Christ is truly the alpha and the omega, the beginning and the end of all creation. This does not belittle humanity, since human action "can be related to Christ, and can co-operate in fulfillment of Christ, not only by the intention, the fidelity, and the obedience in which — as an addition — it is clothed, but also by the actual material content of the work done. All progress, whether in organic life or in scientific knowledge, in aesthetic faculties or in social consciousness, can therefore be made Christian even in its object."[31] Christians can cooperate with Christ insofar as they make the world more Christ-like. If Christ is indeed not just the alpha but also the omega point, and if he fills all things, then nothing in this world is "outside the directing flood he pours into them."[32] Christ is the one who animates and gathers up all the biological and spiritual energies developed by the universe.

According to Teilhard, the universal Christ is a synthesis of Christ and the universe made possible through the mystery of the incarnation. "By disclosing a world-peak, evolution makes Christ possible, just as Christ, by giving meaning and direction to the world, makes evolution possible."[33] The fullness of time will be reached when the whole of creation is in union with Christ. Then the parousia will take place when Christ's presence is manifested in all things. Teilhard attempts to present a modern-day interpretation of what it means that through Christ "God was pleased to reconcile to himself all things, whether on earth or in heaven" (Col. 1:20). He is looking forward to a christification of the whole cosmos. Whatever happens in the cosmos is not insignificant for Christ and his eternal purpose. Similarly, whatever happened to Christ is of significance to the

30. Pierre Teilhard de Chardin, *Science and Christ*, trans. René Hague (New York: Harper & Row, 1968), 14.

31. Teilhard de Chardin, *Science and Christ*, 17.

32. Teilhard de Chardin, *Science and Christ*, 166.

33. Pierre Teilhard de Chardin, *How I Believe*, trans. René Hague (New York: Harper & Row, 1969), 80.

cosmos. Of course Teilhard is aware of the ontological difference between the created and the creator. Yet he also endeavors to show that Christ is not simply concerned with the inner life of Christians, but with their whole lives and beyond them with the whole of humanity, with the whole earth, and with the whole cosmos. Christ reaches to the uttermost regions of the world through his ascension (in a way not unlike that of his descent), filling everything with his power so that eventually everything will be permeated through him and attain union with God. While it was still clear for Teilhard that only Christ can carry out the function of consolidation and universal animation, this claim of Christ's uniqueness and exclusiveness does not remain unchallenged.

2. No Other Name?

Visser 't Hooft, the former general secretary of the World Council of Churches, presented in 1962 at the theological seminaries of the former American Lutheran Church the C. C. Hein Lectures, which were subsequently published under the title *No Other Name*. He claims:

> The New Testament is not unmindful of the fact that this concentration of the whole history of salvation in one single individual does not fit into the accepted categories of Jews and Greeks, of religion and philosophy. But it considers this central truth so essential that it cannot be stated too often or too emphatically. In every part of the New Testament, in every stage of the early tradition, we find that the coming of Jesus has completely transformed the human situation. Man's eternal destiny depends on his decision concerning the relation to this one Jesus of Nazareth.[34]

Since Christ died for all, all have died, the old humanity is past and the time of the new creation of a new humanity has come. The church universal has a double function: to manifest in its own life that which characterizes the new reconciled humanity and also to be the messenger of God's universal offer of reconciliation.[35] As Visser 't Hooft points out,

---

34. W. A. Visser 't Hooft, *No Other Name: The Choice between Syncretism and Christian Universalism* (Philadelphia: Westminster, 1963), 96.
    35. Visser 't Hooft, *No Other Name*, 100-101.

the Christian faith did not grow up in isolated surroundings. There were many other competing religions, and some of them were quite established. Nevertheless the Christian faith claimed the uniqueness of Jesus Christ as Savior. This was not understood in terms of excluding the rest of humanity from salvation. On the contrary, others were to be invited to be members of the benefits of Christ's salvific activity. The question that is raised with more and more urgency today is whether such uniqueness does not have the implicit claim of arrogance.

Barely twenty years after Visser 't Hooft's publication, Paul Knitter (1939-) published a book with the title *No Other Name? A Critical Survey of Christian Attitudes toward the World Religions*.[36] For Knitter the name of Jesus Christ implies a language of personal commitment rather than ultimate truth. He proposes a theocentric model of christology and asserts a relational uniqueness for Jesus in which Jesus is unique in his relationship with us and is not exclusive or even normative.[37] Knitter finds this theocentric christology justified, since Jesus' original message was theocentric too. After his death and resurrection the focus shifted from a theocentric to a christocentric approach, since the proclaimer became the proclaimed. Yet "Jesus gave us no christology."[38] He seemed to feel and claim a special intimacy with God, a special sonship, and he had a deep awareness of God as his father which was in line with the Jewish tradition. There was initially a diversity of New Testament christologies through which the early church sought to express its understanding of Jesus and his special relationship with God.

When the New Testament writers expressed their conviction that Jesus is exclusive or at least normative, saying that there is "no other name" by which one can be saved (Acts 4:12) or that Jesus is the "only begotten Son of God" (John 1:14), then one has to understand these claims, according to Knitter, in their historical and cultural context. In the classicist culture of that time, something had to have certain unchanging and normative qualities in order to be true and reliable.[39] Moreover, given the prevailing Jewish eschatological and apocalyptic

---

36. Paul Knitter, *No Other Name? A Critical Survey of Christian Attitudes toward the World Religions* (Maryknoll: Orbis, 1985).

37. Knitter, *No Other Name?* 171-72.

38. Knitter, *No Other Name?* 174.

39. For the following see Knitter, *No Other Name?* 182-83.

thought patterns, it was natural that as a Christian one should interpret one's experience of God in Jesus as final and unsurpassable. Furthermore, we must consider the minority status of the Christians within the larger Jewish community and within the vast Roman Empire. To defend itself the community needed clear identity and total commitment. The doctrinal language that we encounter in the New Testament and which sets forth an exclusive and normative christology should therefore be called "survival language"; it was necessary for the survival of the community. By defining Jesus Christ in absolute terms, by announcing him as the one and only savior, the early Christians cut out for themselves an identity different from that of all their opponents or competitors. Such language also evoked a total commitment that would seal them in the face of persecutional ridicule.[40] Since this context is not the same as our contemporary context, Knitter concludes, we can return to a theocentric christology that is nonnormative and nonexclusive.

We must certainly agree with Paul Knitter that early Christian theology, like any other, was contextual. Yet does that mean that it was accidental? Knitter seems to imply that. If the development of christology from the New Testament to the early church were consistent and consequential, one could also argue that it was providential. We are confronted here again with the classical question of why the accidental truth of history should have the same "normative" status as the eternal truth of reason. When Knitter refers here to a "survival language," then the argument could just as well be made that this kind of survival language is needed today because of the onslaught of religious pluralism and syncretism, and the resurgence of old established world religions. One may also question whether this nonnormative christology will further the dialogue with firm believers of other religious traditions, or whether they will surmise that one should not bother to dialogue with someone who is not absolutely sure of his or her own conviction but has relativized it prior to entering into a dialogue.

Though Knitter's publication prompted considerable discussion, his position was not accidental. Already his doctoral dissertation of 1972 at the University of Marburg was concerned with a theology of religions in which he urged dialogue and study of other religions in order to overcome the negative attitude concerning the possibility of salvation in

---

40. Knitter, *No Other Name?* 184.

or through these religions that he discovered in most Protestant continental theologians.[41] Knitter's publication *No Other Name?* is only indicative of a larger movement that urges the reconsideration of the claim of Christ's uniqueness. Even evangelicals are concerned about this sentiment, since they have admittedly "made it ridiculously easy for liberals to attack classical theology (in particular, its christology). Scholars such as John Hick have been making mincemeat of us, arguing all too convincingly that Evangelicals have nothing to contribute to the discussion of religious pluralism."[42]

The standpoint of the evangelicals is not as uniform as one might think. First, there is the restrictive view that all the unevangelized will be damned. Then there is the more inclusive position that salvation is universally accessible. This view is held by most evangelicals, but, as John P. Sanders (1956-) in his comprehensive study *No Other Name* has shown, it can be further broken down into three positions.[43] One group affirms that God will send the message to any person who seeks him out, and they maintain that "only those who hear about and accept Christ from a human agent before death will be saved." A second group affirms that "all people have an encounter with Jesus at the moment of death." Finally, there are proponents of eschatological evangelism, who "maintain that death is not final and that the unevangelized encounter Christ after death." If salvation is no longer contingent upon accepting Christ as one's savior during one's life here on earth, then, the argument often goes, this effectively undercuts "the urgency of proclaiming the gospel of salvation through faith in Jesus Christ."[44] Sanders has thought through the issue of the necessity for evangelism and gives four cogent reasons in favor of it:[45]

1. The first and most obvious reason is that Jesus commanded us to go and preach the gospel to all people. . . . 2. Motivation for missions also

41. Paul Knitter, *Towards a Protestant Theology of Religions: A Case Study of Paul Althaus and Contemporary Attitudes* (Marburg: N. G. Elwert, 1974), 209.

42. So Clark H. Pinnock, foreword to John P. Sanders, *No Other Name: An Investigation into the Destiny of the Unevangelized* (Grand Rapids: Eerdmans, 1992), xiv.

43. See for the following, including the quotations from Sanders, *No Other Name,* 282.

44. This even seems to be implied in the position of James A. Scherer, "Missiological Naming: 'Who Shall I Say Sent Me?'" in *Our Naming of God: Problems and Prospects of God-Talk Today,* ed. Carl E. Braaten (Minneapolis: Fortress, 1989), 111, who also pointed out the juxtaposition of Visser 't Hooft's and Knitter's publications.

45. Sanders, *No Other Name,* 284-85.

arises from the desire to share what we cannot hold inside ourselves, to share with others the blessings we have received. . . . 3. The Bible indicates that God wants to bring the fullness of eternal life into the lives of all people *now*. . . . 4. Finally, proponents of the wider-hope perspective are motivated to missions by the fact that the spiritual warfare that the prophets, apostles, and our Lord engaged in is not finished. The forces of evil still affect human affairs horribly.

Indeed, it would be a strange idea that the salvation of other people depends on our effectiveness, on our spreading the gospel. As Sanders has pointed out, we proclaim salvation in and through Christ not in order to be a helpmate in God's salvational activity but because of the impact the gospel of Jesus Christ has upon us. Evangelicals still insist that Christ in one way or other is the source of salvation, whether in this life, at death, or beyond death.

The philosopher of religion John Hick (1922-) stated very clearly that "it seems arbitrary and unrealistic to go on insisting that the Christ-event is the sole and exclusive source of human salvation."[46] Hick suggests that we have to make a Copernican transition, from the old Ptolemaic worldview in which "Christianity is seen as the center of the universe of faiths, and all the other religions are regarded as revolving round it and as being graded in value according to their distance from it."[47] We have to realize that the universe of faith centers upon God and not upon Christianity or upon any other religion. God then is the sun from whom all light and life originates and whom all the religions reflect in their own ways. Hick hypothesizes that God, the ultimate divine reality, revealed in what Karl Jaspers (1883-1969) called the axial period (ca. B.C. 800–B.C. 500) his presence and his will to humanity through a number of specially sensitive and responsive persons, who in turn gave rise to different world religions according to the history, culture, language, and climate of their particular time and place.[48]

Hick feels it is unlikely that Jesus thought of himself as God

46. John Hick, *Disputed Questions in Theology and the Philosophy of Religion* (New Haven: Yale University Press, 1993), 85.

47. John Hick, "Whatever Path Men Choose Is Mine," in *Christianity and Other Religions, Selected Readings,* ed. John Hick and Brian Hebblethwaite (Philadelphia: Fortress, 1980), 181.

48. Hick, "Whatever Path Men Choose," 182-83.

incarnate and therefore says that the statement that Jesus is the Son of God cannot be taken as a literal fact.[49] The notion that a special human being is the "Son of God," Hick claims, "is a metaphorical idea which belongs to the imaginative language of a number of ancient cultures."[50] The Christian tradition turned this metaphor into a metaphysical term pronouncing that Jesus is the second person of a divine Trinity. This resulted in the doctrine of the unique divine incarnation, which has led to a Christian imperialism and poisoned relationships with other religions. Today we see the Christian tradition as one of a plurality of contexts of salvation within which the transformation of human existence from self-centeredness to God-centeredness is occurring. It can no longer be claimed, since the empirical evidence stands against it, that Christianity constitutes a more favorable setting for this transformation than other traditions.[51] We must be much more modest in our claims today. As Christians "we can revere Christ as the one through whom we had found salvation, without having to deny other points of reported saving contact between God and man. We can commend the way of Christian faith without having to discommend other ways of faith. We can say that there is salvation in Christ without having to say that there is no salvation other than in Christ."[52] Apparently Christ is just one voice among many.

How does Hick arrive at such a positive evaluation of the world religions? The answer is that he believes that each religion is a mixture of the influence of the divine spirit and of specific human traditions.[53] The divine spirit or the divine logos has been at work as long as there has been humanity and is still at work today as the various religious traditions increasingly interact with each other. Hick does not see himself as being unfaithful to the revelation of God's limitless love in Jesus when he conceives of this as only one particular disclosure of a universal reality. On the contrary, he feels he is taking "the universal reality of God's love seriously," since that love is extended to humanity in a

---

49. Hick, "Whatever Path Men Choose," 184-85.

50. For the quotation and the following see John Hick, *God Has Many Names* (Philadelphia: Westminster, 1982), 8.

51. So Hick, *Disputed Questions*, 85.

52. Hick, "Whatever Path Men Choose," 186.

53. See for the following John Hick, *The Second Christianity* (London: SCM, 1983), 88-89.

multitude of ways.[54] Hick understands a Christian not as someone who conceives of Christ as the one in whom God disclosed himself in an unsurpassable way, but "as one who affirms one's religious identity within the continuing tradition that originated with Jesus."[55] There is no longer an ontological truth-claim to be affirmed in terms of exclusivity, but a relational one in terms of affinity. There is no singular revelation, but a plural one, and the world's religions "are culturally-conditioned human responses to God's revelation."[56] Jesus is not *the* human face of God as if there were no others, but *a* human face alongside but not in competition with others.

In evaluating John Hick's position, we must be appreciative that as a philosopher of religion he does not want to be reductionistic. There is indeed a divine agent behind the religious phenomena which we encounter, though this divine attribute is intermixed with human elaborations. While Hick is convinced that the religious phenomena are human responses to the divine, he shies away from classifying any one as a more appropriate response than another. On principle he cannot assert the superiority of the Christian faith or of any other religion. He also has to disclaim two other tenets central to the Christian understanding of Jesus. First, he denies that Jesus was the human face of God.[57] Second, he does not deal adequately with the resurrection of Jesus.[58] "He claims that resurrection experiences were common to the era of religious development in the ancient Middle East, and that the gospels themselves give witness to this in the Christian tradition."[59] Hick does not distinguish between the resurrection of Jesus Christ through which he broke the bond of death forever and did not experience a second death, and the resuscitations through which Jesus called dead people back to life, as we see in the stories of Lazarus (John 11:38-44) and of the daughter of Jairus (Mark

54. Hick, *The Second Christianity*, 92.

55. Hick, *Disputed Questions*, 55.

56. So correctly Gregory H. Carruthers, *The Uniqueness of Jesus Christ in the Theocentric Model of the Christian Theology of World Religions: An Elaboration and Evaluation of the Position of John Hick* (Lanham, Md.: University Press of America, 1990), 41.

57. We must remember that John Hick was one of the authors of the book *The Myth of God Incarnate*.

58. Hick, *Disputed Questions*, 41ff.

59. Chester Gilles, *A Question of Final Belief: John Hick's Pluralistic Theory of Salvation* (New York: St. Martin's, 1989), 92.

5:35-43), both of whom later again experienced death. Of course such nondifferentiation is not accidental. He cannot admit the resurrection event as something unique, as the validation of the life and ministry of Jesus as someone who stood in God's place. If he were to do that, he would concede the uniqueness of Jesus. Since he cannot admit the ontological status of Jesus as the Son of God, he stays with his preselected chosen option: neither Jesus nor the Christian faith is absolute.

There is still another way to affirm Christ's universality without jeopardizing his uniqueness. This has been advanced by Karl Rahner (1904-84), whose position is evident in some of the statements of Vatican II. The *Dogmatic Constitution on the Church* states:

> But the plan of salvation also includes those who acknowledge the Creator, in the first place amongst whom are the Moslems: they profess to hold the faith of Abraham, and together with us they adore the one, merciful God, mankind's judge on the last day. Nor is God remote from those who in shadows and images see the unknown God, since he gives to all men life and breath and all things (cf. Acts 17:25-28), and since the Savior wills all men to be saved (cf. 1 Tim. 2:4). Those who, through no fault of their own, do not know the Gospel of Christ or his Church, but who nevertheless seek God with a sincere heart, and, moved by grace, try in their actions to do his will as they know it through the dictates of their conscience — those too may achieve eternal salvation.[60]

Here salvation is explicitly conceded for the Moslems, but also for others who seek God with a sincere heart and who are moved by grace and try in their actions to do his will. God is present with his saving grace even among those who are not Christians.

Starting with Paul's insight that non-Christians do not know God and yet worship him (Acts 17:23), Rahner is free to admit that God is more comprehensive than the church.[61] Though Christians should be firm toward non-Christians, they should at the same time be humble and tolerant.[62] There is no doubt for Rahner that Christianity is the absolute

---

60. "Dogmatic Constitution on the Church" 16, in *Vatican Council II: The Conciliar and Post-Conciliar Documents*, Austin Flannery, gen. ed., new rev. ed. (Collegeville, Ind.: Liturgical Press, 1992), 367.

61. Karl Rahner, "Christianity and the Non-Christian Religions," in *Theological Investigations*, vol. 5: *Later Writings*, trans. K. H. Krüger (Baltimore: Helicon, 1966), 115-34.

62. Rahner, "Christianity and the Non-Christian Religions," 134.

religion intended for all people. He claims that "Christ and his continuing historical presence in the world (which we call 'Church') is *the* religion which binds man to God."[63] Yet he affirms that non-Christian religions contain supernatural elements arising out of the grace which is given to all people as a gratuitous gift on account of Christ. Without denying the error and depravity contained in it, "a non-Christian religion can be recognized as a *lawful* religion."[64] Such a concession to the validity of non-Christian religions would witness to the fact that God is present outside the limits of the visible church. It would also suggest that every human being is truly exposed to the influence of the divine, supernatural grace which offers an interior union with God and which demands a decision toward this grace which is reflected in the non-Christian attitude toward his or her "lawful" religion.

Rahner understands by lawful religion "an institutional religion whose 'use' by man at a certain period can be regarded on the whole as a positive means of gaining the right relationship to God and thus for the attaining of salvation, a means which is therefore positively included in God's plan of salvation."[65] Religions outside and prior to Christianity are not regarded as illegitimate from the very start, but as quite capable of having positive significance. A member of a non-Christian religion is not simply labeled a non-Christian, but someone "who can and must already be regarded in this or that respect as an anonymous Christian."[66] Such a person already has some knowledge, however distorted, of God's grace and truth. We are reminded here of the distinction by the church fathers between the seminal logos that is present throughout the world and the incarnate logos, present through Jesus Christ.[67] Justin Martyr could claim that Christ "was partially known even by Socrates."[68] Yet while the early church fathers attributed to the power of the universal logos only special insight, here salvific grace is mediated.

Rahner's view was opposed by both conservatives and liberals. The

---

63. Rahner, "Christianity and the Non-Christian Religions," 118.
64. Rahner, "Christianity and the Non-Christian Religions," 121.
65. Rahner, "Christianity and the Non-Christian Religions," 125.
66. Rahner, "Christianity and the Non-Christian Religions," 131.
67. Justin Martyr, *The Second Apology* 8, in *ANF* 1:191, who distinguishes here between "the seed of reason [the Logos] implanted in every race of men" and "the whole Word, which is Christ."
68. Justin Martyr, *Second Apology* 10, in *ANF* 1:191.

conservatives judged that it would undercut the necessity for mission, and the liberals argued that the claim of absolute superiority was still not relinquished. "Non-Christians can be saved because, unknown to them, Christ is secretly 'in a way united' with them."[69]

Indeed, the term "anonymous Christian" is suggestive of Christian imperialism. It is also misleading, because a Buddhist or a Hindu is by no stretch of the imagination a Christian, whether anonymous or explicit. Such anonymity would stand in stark contrast to the biblical admonition that whoever is not with me is against me (Matt. 12:30). While we can have memberships in different clubs, we cannot pledge allegiance to different religions, since each of these allegiances requires a faith structure compatible with that religion. In later writings Rahner abandoned the unfortunate term "anonymous Christian" and returned to the language of Vatican II that "a universal and supernatural salvific will of God . . . is really operative in the world."[70] He sees this salvific will present through Christ's spirit: "Insofar as this Spirit always and everywhere brings justifying faith, this faith is always and everywhere and from the outset faith which comes to be in the Spirit of Jesus Christ. In this Spirit of his he is present and operative in all faith."[71] Rahner here makes explicit mention of the logos of God who was incarnate in Jesus Christ. The spirit who is operative in an incarnate way in Jesus Christ is also operative in a universal way throughout the world. The Christian faith and Christ need no longer be juxtaposed to other religions or other savior figures. "Savior figures in the history of religion can readily be regarded as an indication of the fact that mankind, moved always and everywhere by grace, anticipates and looks for that event in which its absolute hope becomes irreversible in history, and becomes manifest in its irreversibility."[72] Rahner states here explicitly that grace is operative in the world even outside the Christian realm, and he is looking forward and hoping for the manifestation of this hope for all of humanity. Rahner opens the door for other believers without stating who can and who cannot be included. He stays very close to the hope which the creedal

69. Hick, *Disputed Questions,* 84.

70. Karl Rahner, *Foundations of Christian Faith: An Introduction to the Idea of Christianity,* trans. William V. Dych (New York: Seabury, 1978), 313.

71. Rahner, *Foundations of Christian Faith,* 318.

72. Rahner, *Foundations of Christian Faith,* 321.

phrase expresses that Christ descended to the dead. The Christian faith implies a dimension of hope, but it refuses to spell out in detail the extent of that dimension.

The inclusiveness of Christ as the salvific aim for all people has also been promulgated by some representatives of process thought. David Griffin's (1939-) christology sounds initially rather traditional. Jesus is considered as "God's supreme act."[73] In his message of word and deed a deep vision of reality is expressed which contains a view of God's character and purpose. Not only did he have special insight into the nature of things, but his special activity was based on the impulses given to him by God. *"The aims given to Jesus and actualized by him during his active ministry were such that the basic vision of reality contained in his message of word and deed was the supreme expression of God's eternal character and purpose."*[74] Since Jesus as the Christ is God's supreme act of self-expression, it is appropriate to receive him as God's decisive revelation.[75] If Jesus' life provides the decisive revelation of God, then we should find here the supreme exemplification of the mode of God's activity in relation to the world. Indeed, Griffin is convinced that "God supremely expressed his character and purpose, and concomitantly his mode of activity, in the event of Jesus' ministry."[76] This Johannine notion that "who sees me, sees the Father" is expressive of the sufficiency of God's self-disclosure in Jesus the Christ, yet it is not an expression of Jesus' exclusivity.

It is exactly at this point that John Cobb's (1925-) christology enters in. He proposes "that for us Christ is the Way that excludes no Ways."[77] Cobb brings together the notion of the logos and of Christ in claiming "'Christ' is therefore a name for the Logos. No statement can be made about Christ that is not true of the Logos. But 'Christ' does not simply designate the Logos as God as the principle of order and novelty. It refers to the logos as incarnate, hence as the process of creative transformation in and of the world."[78] While in the classical Greek understanding, the logos stood for the world order, through Christ the logos

---

73. David R. Griffin, *A Process Christology* (Philadelphia: Westminster, 1973), 216.
74. Griffin, *A Process Christology,* 218.
75. Griffin, *A Process Christology,* 221.
76. Griffin, *A Process Christology,* 227.
77. John B. Cobb Jr., *Christ in a Pluralistic Age* (Philadelphia: Westminster, 1975), 22.
78. Cobb, *Christ in a Pluralistic Age,* 76, for this and the following quotation.

for Cobb has become immanent or incarnate in the world of living things and especially of human beings. Since God as logos is present in the world, he is present and felt in all events. This divine immanence is the creative transformation of the world, urging on to maximum incorporation of elements from the past into a new synthesis. "To what extent the new aim is successful, to that extent there is creative transformation. This creative transformation is Christ."

According to Cobb, Christ as the power of creative transformation can be discerned in Jesus. This does not mean that Jesus is immediately named the Christ, because it leaves open "the possibility that Jesus is to be seen alongside hundreds of other creative transformers who have fashioned our history."[79] If Jesus is in a more significant sense the Christ, then he must have advanced creative transformation more than these others. While the structure of existence is far from what Jesus had in view, his words do indeed contribute to creative transformation in the hearer. One can see that "they are the occasion for the realization of Christ within the hearer."[80] For those who did not hear him, so the conclusion would go, Jesus is not the Christ. Since Christ is at work throughout the world, the eventual goals must be similar. Cobb shows this in trying to wed together the Buddhist notion of a post-personal existence and the Christian goal that goes beyond a fully developed personal individualization. "That Christianity and Buddhism could each be so transformed by the internalization of each other as to move toward a future unity is an image of hope in a time of fragmentation."[81]

Cobb goes even beyond that in trying to wed together Paolo Soleri's vision for the city of God, Whitehead's understanding of the kingdom of heaven, and Pannenberg's affirmation of the biblical doctrine of the resurrection. All these images of hope point toward a transcendence of separate individuality in full community with other people and with all things. "In this community the tensions between self and Christ decline, and in a final consummation they would disappear. This is the movement of incarnation."[82] Christ is the way that excludes no other ways, since he is intrinsic to all ways.

79. Cobb, *Christ in a Pluralistic Age*, 107.
80. Cobb, *Christ in a Pluralistic Age*, 110.
81. Cobb, *Christ in a Pluralistic Age*, 220.
82. Cobb, *Christ in a Pluralistic Age*, 258.

Cobb seems to have answered the question of whether there is another name with a resolute "No." Christ is the only name. Yet it is interesting that both Griffin and Cobb hardly make any mention of Jesus' resurrection. Griffin stays with Jesus as God's supreme act of self-expression, and Cobb claims Christ as "creative transformation." Yet the answer given by Paul was that "if you confess with your lips that Jesus is Lord and believe in your heart that God raised him from the dead, you will be saved" (Rom. 10:9). The affirmation that Jesus is the Lord or the Christ being concomitant with that God who raised Jesus from the dead answers the question of who Jesus was for the Christian community and who he still is. Jesus is the Christ. As Karl Rahner claimed: The resurrection of Jesus "was the confirmation and appearance of what was given with Jesus' person and message. It was the historically visible victory of God's promise of himself to mankind."[83] Only through Jesus' resurrection as the Christ do we obtain the affirmation of the impotence of death. The resurrection of Christ is the affirmation of life and of grace. Because God acted decisively in Jesus as the Christ, we can have hope as we follow his way and may plead and hope that others also may be sharers in that hope. Any Christian triumphalism would be equal to un-Christian self-glorification. The only glory Christians have is to rejoice in their Lord as they follow his way, while hoping and praying that he will also include the ways of others. The recognition of Jesus Christ as God's decisive revelation never dares to degenerate into a theory about others but in rejoicing in the Lord.

3. The Kingdom and the Church

Jesus announced the coming of the kingdom but what came was the church. Of course, everyone knows that the church is not the kingdom. Yet the real question is whether the church, as it has evolved, is congruent with Jesus' intention.[84] After all, without Jesus there would be

---

83. Karl Rahner, in Karl Rahner and Wilhelm Thüsing, *A New Christology*, trans. David Smith and Verdant Green (New York: Seabury, 1980), 10.

84. Cf. the questions posed by James D. G. Dunn, *Jesus' Call to Discipleship* (Cambridge: Cambridge University Press, 1992), 93. One could bypass this issue altogether and immediately deal with "the church of the kingdom of God." So Jürgen Moltmann,

no Christian church. If Jesus intended something completely different, then the church usurped his name in vain. To decide this question, we first must understand how Jesus used the term "kingdom of God." There is no doubt that the kingly reign of God formed "the central theme of the public proclamation of Jesus."[85] As Mark tells us: "Jesus came to Galilee, proclaiming the good news of God, and saying, 'The time is fulfilled, and the kingdom of God has come near; repent, and believe in the good news'" (Mark 1:15). Yet what does this kingdom of God entail?

In the Old Testament the term "kingdom of God" indicates that God intends to show himself by enabling and demanding a certain arrangement of the sociopolitical life of his people and ultimately in the universal salvational dimension of his kingly rule.[86] The prophet Isaiah is filled with anxiety and despair upon his encounter with God as King and exclaims: "Woe is me! I am lost, for I am a man of unclean lips, and I live among a people of unclean lips; yet my eyes have seen the King, the LORD of hosts!" (Isa. 6:5). In Deutero-Isaiah the mention of the kingly rule of Yahweh left behind this fear-causing dimension for individuals and for the people. As a demonstration of his kingly rule Yahweh himself announces that his people will be rescued and live: "Thus says the LORD, the King of Israel, and his Redeemer, the LORD of hosts: I am the first and I am the last; besides me there is no god. . . . Do not fear, or be afraid" (Isa. 44:6-8). As King, Yahweh is the Lord of all powers, and his rule comprises the whole course of world history. Similarly we read in Obadiah of a new time of salvation which will begin at Mount Zion and which will result in the kingly rule of Yahweh: "Those who have been saved shall go up to Mount Zion to rule Mount Esau; and the kingdom shall be the LORD's" (Obad. 21).

When Jesus used the term "kingdom of God" (or the "kingdom of heaven," in order to avoid the sacred word "God"), he affirmed its Old Testament understanding and envisioned primarily the inauguration of

---

The Church in the Power of the Spirit: A Contribution to Messianic Ecclesiology, trans. Margaret Kohl (New York: Harper & Row, 1977), 133-96. But then one simply skirts this issue, which is ultimately decisive for the church's self-understanding.

85. Joachim Jeremias, *New Testament Theology: The Proclamation of Jesus,* trans. John Bowden (New York: Charles Scribner's, 1971), 1:96.

86. Erich Zenger, "Herrschaft Gottes/Reich Gottes II," in *TRE* 15:173.

God's rule. Of course, there was always a specifically associated realm in which this rule was to be inaugurated. Usually the term was to be understood in an eschatological way, that this rule was to be expected in the future or that it had already started. But in either case it was always thought to be the final rule of God, the rule of the end time.[87] As the kingdom parables show, the kingly rule can only be expressed in metaphoric language. There is no direct way possible to depict this rule. Nevertheless we can discern several moments contained within it: at present the rule of God is still hidden; the future glory of God's rule will be unrestrained; the rule of God will most certainly come; the future rule is already active; its coming cannot be influenced by humanity.[88] Future and present are intimately connected in the rule of God. It is already present but it is not yet manifested. In that light it is difficult to decide what distance Jesus saw between himself and the realization of God's rule. He certainly saw it as a future entity, the coming of which in power was yet to take place. Yet he also emphasized the immediacy of its coming.

Most certainly Jesus announced in "missionary fashion" a temporal nearness of God's eschatological rule. "Jesus developed a concentrated, future eschatology: the reign of God and the judgment of God are incalculably near at hand."[89] This nearness was also taught in his own Jewish environment. But in Judaism it was hoped that through the announcement of the nearness of the kingdom, people would make their own decision to obey the law. Jesus, however, expected more than a decision regarding his demands and promises. For him the rule of God primarily implied not judgment, but salvation. There are already signs of salvation present. The signs of the time of salvation announced in the Old Testament are being fulfilled: "But if it is by the finger of God that I cast out the demons, then the kingdom of God has come to you" (Luke 11:20). In response to the disciples sent by John Jesus answered: "Go and tell John what you hear and see: the blind receive their sight, the lame walk, the lepers are cleansed, the deaf hear, the dead are raised, and the poor have the good news brought to them" (Matt. 11:4-5). Yet this

---

87. Andreas Lindemann, "Herrschaft Gottes/Reich Gottes IV," in *TRE* 15:200.
88. Cf. Lindemann, "Herrschaft Gottes/Reich Gottes IV," 202, with reference to Matt. 13:33 (parable of the leaven) and Mark 4:26-29 (parable of the self-growing seed).
89. Goppelt, *Theology of the New Testament*, 1:61.

inbreaking is not yet the future reign.[90] In the future rule of God the poor will have a share too, since all suffering will be banished. This rule will come through the initiative of God and on behalf of the people. God will comfort them and satisfy those who hunger. The coming of the kingdom is seen foremost "theocentrically as the personalized activity of God among people. The kingdom comes as God encounters people and draws them into his fellowship."[91]

We see that eschatological rule announced in the Beatitudes (Matt. 5:3-12) and in the Lord's Prayer in the first two petitions: "Hallowed be your name" and "Your kingdom come" (Matt. 6:9-10). The two petitions are not only parallel in structure but also correspond to one another in content. They plead for the revelation of God's eschatological kingdom. "They seek the hour in which God's profaned and misused name will be glorified and his reign revealed, in accordance with the promise, 'I will vindicate the holiness of my great name, which has been profaned among the nations, and which you have profaned among them; and the nations will know that I am the LORD, says the LORD God, when through you I vindicate my holiness before their eyes" (Ezek. 36:23).[92]

They are not simply a cry out of the depth of distress over a world which is enslaved to the rule of evil but they are also an expression of absolute certainty. The one who prays takes seriously God's promise that in spite of present world conditions God will fulfill his promises. In contrast to apocalypticism and rabbinic Judaism, "Jesus made no attempt at an objective portrayal of the world to come, the world shaped by God's reign."[93] The only thing we hear is that it will be different (cf. Mark 12:25) and that it can be compared with the communal meal of blessing (cf. Mark 14:25: "Truly I tell you, I will never again drink of the fruit of the vine until the day when I drink it anew in the kingdom of God"). The rule of God in its eschatological completion will not be a nirvana or a paradisal condition of tranquillity, but rather "it is fellowship with Jesus, God's eschatological table of sharing."

90. Goppelt, *Theology of the New Testament,* 1:61, emphasizes this and sees his position in contrast to both Bultmann's "projection of the kingdom into the present" and the notion of the inbreaking of the kingdom by the Pharisees.

91. Goppelt, *Theology of the New Testament,* 1:69.

92. Joachim Jeremias, *The Lord's Prayer,* trans. John Reumann (Philadelphia: Fortress, 1964), 22.

93. Goppelt, *Theology of the New Testament,* 1:72, for this and the following quotation.

Of course, we must ask ourselves whether this kingdom language is applicable today as we live in societies that are either democratically governed or long for democracy. Sallie McFague (1933-) cautions against patriarchal as well as imperialistic and triumphalist metaphors for God. "This language is not only idolatrous and irrelevant—besides being oppressive to many who do not identify with it—but it may also work against the continuation of life on our planet."[94] Similarly, Jürgen Moltmann claims that "by overcoming the notion of a universal monarchy of the one God" through the expansion of the doctrine of the Trinity in the concept of God, the transposition of the religious into political monotheism and the translation of political monotheism into absolutism can be overcome.[95] Only if we unite the almighty Father with Jesus the Son and with the life-giving Spirit in the Trinity can we escape from the threats of an omnipotent universal monarch who is reflected in earthly rulers.

One may wonder whether today's dictators do indeed receive their oppressive inspirations from a monarchical model of God and not rather from their own evil instincts and obsessions. Furthermore, one wonders why often those who have little experience with monarchy are so apprehensive about the allegedly disastrous consequences of the monarchical model. In my home state of Bavaria, Germany, we lived for eight hundred years under one dynasty and, all things considered, fared rather well with the rule of the Wittelsbachers. Even today this dynasty is held in high esteem, and we even have a small "anachronistic" royal party. Yet one must concede that for most people today a kingdom is a foreign concept, since kings and queens usually only live in fairy tales. But then again, most of our theologically cherished metaphors and concepts are foreign to everyday usage. We continuously have to define and explain the words and metaphors that we use. Often we use them since they are given with our biblical or ecclesial heritage. The same is true for the kingdom of God concept. "It is a biblical theme and, therefore, an inherent part of the Christian tradition."[96] We should not too quickly discard it. Before we imply with the kingdom concept the notion of dominance and subservi-

94. Sallie McFague, *Models of God: Theology for an Ecological, Nuclear Age* (Philadelphia: Fortress, 1987), ix.

95. Jürgen Moltmann, *The Trinity and the Kingdom: The Doctrine of God*, trans. Margaret Kohl (Minneapolis: Fortress, 1993), 197.

96. So rightly Howard A. Snyder, *Models of the Kingdom* (Nashville: Abingdon, 1991), 22. See Snyder also for the following arguments.

ence we should first ask what kind of king our God is. Is he a retributive God or a loving, caring, long-suffering and faithful one? Psalm 8:9 concludes with these words of praise, "O LORD, our Sovereign, how majestic is your name in all the earth!" Yet this majestic and sovereign God has turned to small and unimportant human beings, elevated them to a position "a little lower than God" (Ps. 8:5), and entrusted the earth to their care.[97] God's sovereignty is needed to make his kingdom triumph over all adversity and against all wrongdoings. Especially with Jesus as the interpreter of God's rule who embodied God's human face and who carried out his solidarity with humanity up to his bitter earthly end, there need be little apprehension that God's kingly rule will degenerate to some kind of primordial tyranny. Moltmann's caution is still in order; God's rule should never be used as a pretense for imposing our rule. But now we must come back to the crucial question of whether church and kingdom of God can be seen within the same intentionality.

We remember that Jesus had no interest in a political kingdom or in one that could be established by military force or rebellion against Rome's rule. This nonpolitical kingdom was quite often interpreted as nonnationalistic, which meant nonethnic and non-Jewish.[98] The kingdom notion was also spiritualized and universalized. This kingdom is then combined with the idea of millennialism and at the same time with the church. We see this, for instance, in Irenaeus, who views the church as the realm of the Spirit, the thousand-year realm of peace as the realm of the Son, and the final transcendental perfection as the kingdom of the Father.[99] The kingdom is seen as an innerworldly entity, and it is to some extent equated with the church. A few centuries later, Augustine in *The City of God* again mentions in the same breath the city of God and the church, connecting the latter with the kingdom of God.[100] While the

97. Zenger, "Herrschaft Gottes/Reich Gottes II," 179-80.

98. See the insightful comments by J. Ramsey Michaels, "The Kingdom of God and the Historical Jesus," in *The Kingdom of God in Twentieth-Century Interpretation,* ed. Wendell Willis (Peabody, Mass.: Hendrickson, 1987), 114.

99. Irenaeus, "Against Heresies" 5.35-36, in *ANF* 1:566-67. See for further elaboration Carl Andresen, "Die Anfänge christlicher Lehrentwicklung," in *Handbuch der Dogmen- und Theologiegeschichte,* ed. Carl Andresen (Göttingen: Vandenhoeck & Ruprecht, 1982), 1:92-93.

100. See Hans Schwarz, *Evil: A Historical and Theological Perspective* (Minneapolis: Fortress, 1995), 142.

visible church is not an ideal community for Augustine, he nevertheless feels that there is a close affinity between the church and the kingdom. Irenaeus portrayed a theocentric view of the kingdom, and Augustine connected it with its temporal approximation in the church.

But Joachim of Fiore (ca. 1134-1202), Cistercian abbot of Calabria, Italy, fostered the spiritualization of the kingdom.[101] According to him there was first the kingdom of the Father, characterized by the creation and preservation of the world in which God rules over all things through his power and providence. Then there is the kingdom of the Son, in which God rules through the proclamation of the gospel and the administration of the sacraments in the church. Here the fear of God, characteristic for the first stage of the kingdom, is transformed into trust. Finally comes the kingdom of the Spirit, in which man and woman are reborn through the energies of the Spirit. Here God rules through direct revelation and knowledge. Joachim was also not hesitant to date each of these three epochs. The first one lasted until the coming of Christ, whereas the second stretched to A.D. 1230 (safely dated beyond his own life expectancy so that he could not be blamed for any failure of his predictions), and the third one was then inaugurated by Saint Benedict. Since each of these periods overlapped somewhat with the next and since each is an exact recapitulation of the former on a higher level, he was able to make certain general predictions concerning the future. In the first period learning prevails, in the second there is partly completed wisdom, and in the third the fullness of knowledge. Joachim thought of himself as still belonging to the second stage and did not draw revolutionary conclusions from his historical and theological constructions. Later followers of his were less patient. The Franciscan Spirituals in the thirteenth and fourteenth century thought of themselves as leaders of the new order, with Saint Francis as their new messianic head. Since knowledge of God could now in the third age be obtained immediately through contemplation, they rejected the sacraments and preaching. Since they even rejected the clerical hierarchy, including the pope, and replaced Scripture and theology with the order of Saint Francis, it is no

101. For Joachim and his influence up to Adolf Hitler, including documentation, see Hans Schwarz, *On the Way to the Future: A Christian View of Eschatology in the Light of Current Trends in Religion, Philosophy, and Science*, rev. ed. (Minneapolis: Augsburg, 1979), 183ff.

surprise that church and state authorities persecuted them. Yet the fire once kindled in the hope for a spiritual and yet quite earthly kingdom of freedom and egalitarianism could not be so easily extinguished.

The neo-Marxist philosopher Ernst Bloch (1885-1977) called Joachim the most influential social utopian of the Middle Ages, because he envisioned that there would be no class distinctions in the third age. It was to be an age of monks, an age of universal monastic communism, a communism of consumption. Bloch sees the fundamental principle of Joachimism in the fact that revelation is open-ended. He appreciates the active fight of Joachimism against the social principles of Christianity, which ever since Paul had associated itself with a class-conscious society and consequently had compromised its message a thousand times. Bloch saw this third period of history, as prophesied by Joachim, emerge in the Soviet Union and, quite naturally, finds its archenemy in the clerical domination of the second period. As the ruthless suppression and exploitation of the Soviet peoples comes more and more into the open, we see the inherent danger of a this-worldly kingdom.[102]

For centuries Joachim's writings were propagated, and pamphlets were written in his spirit and under his name. Even Thomas Müntzer (ca. 1490-1525), the apocalyptic utopian and "new Daniel" who wanted to enforce God's will rigorously in this eschatological end time, refers to Joachim. In a letter attached to his discourse *Von dem gedichteten Glauben* ("Concerning the Invented Faith") Müntzer mentioned Joachim's external gospel against which the "carnal scribes" extol themselves in mockery. Müntzer held Joachim in high esteem, though he claimed he relied not on Joachim but on the word of God. The Lutheran Reformation categorically rejected any utopian ideas, as can be seen in the following statement in the *Augsburg Confession:* "Rejected, too, are certain Jewish opinions which are even now making an appearance and which teach that, before the resurrection of the dead, saints and godly men will possess a worldly kingdom and annihilate all the godless."[103] The utopian

---

102. Jürgen Moltmann, *The Trinity and the Kingdom,* 204ff., is very appreciative of Joachim's ideas, especially since Joachim connected the Sabbath of world history with the kingdom of the Spirit. Indeed, Joachim's ideas had tremendous impact on Western thought. Yet Moltmann makes no mention that, especially in their secularized form, they did not bring freedom, as Joachim had claimed, but countless cases of oppression, slavery, and destruction both of peoples and the environment.

103. *The Augsburg Confession* 17, in *BC,* 38-39.

communities in the city of Münster were a far cry from what was to be expected as the kingdom: instead of the promised freedom there was new oppression.

The nineteenth century, with its industrial progress and rapid social change, gave the notion of the kingdom new impetus albeit mostly in a secularized form. The kingdom of God was seen as the aim of world history, that which assures its meaningfulness.[104] Hegel interpreted history as a comprehensive process in which reason, incarnate in this world, comes to its concrete embodiment and the world spirit comes to its own.[105] Yet it was of much more far-reaching consequences that even Friedrich Engels (1820-89), Marx's collaborator in the *Communist Manifesto,* declared in 1842: "The self-consciousness of humanity, the new Grail, around whose throne the nations rejoicingly assemble, . . . that is our profession, that we become knights of this Grail, to put the sword around our waists for this Grail and joyfully venture our life in the last holy war which will be followed by the Thousand Years Reich of freedom."[106] Here again we see the claim of an empire of freedom connected with millennial thoughts. In the context of secularized versions of the kingdom notion one must also think of the kingdom of God in America, a country which was not just called the "New World" because it was discovered relatively late.[107] Finally, one notes the attempt in Germanic Europe to establish a "Thousand-Year Reich" or a "Third Reich." The messianic intent of this short-lived and disastrous utopia can be seen from the fact that Adolf Hitler (1889-1945) was called the "leader" of this Reich and was greeted by millions with "Heil!" It can only be considered as one of the bizarre and cruel tragedies of history that this "messianic" leader saw as one of his main goals to exterminate the same Jewish people in whose midst the kingdom idea first originated.

In conclusion we can say that Jesus would have been perhaps as unhappy with the kingdom notion as it evolved through the centuries as with some of the features of the church that saw itself in continuity with

---

104. Michael Beintker, "Herrschaft Gottes/Reich Gottes VI," in *TRE* 15:226.

105. Joachim Mehlhausen, "Geschichte/Geschichtsschreibung/Geschichtsphilosophie VII/2," in *TRE* 12:647.

106. Friedrich Engels, *Schelling und die Offenbarung* (1842), in Karl Marx und Friedrich Engels, *Historisch-Kritische Gesamtausgabe* (Berlin: Marx-Engels-Verlag, 1930), I/2:226-27.

107. H. Richard Niebuhr, *The Kingdom of God in America* (New York: Harper Torchbook, 1959).

Jesus' own intentions. In order to attempt to correlate the intentionality of Jesus' kingdom of God and the church we cannot but return to Jesus' own message. The kingdom which Jesus proclaimed was a future kingdom and could only latently be regarded as present.[108] Nevertheless through his person, through the act of his proclamation together with his healing ministry, there were signs that this essentially future kingdom was already present to his contemporaries. It is significant that Jesus never announced the kingdom to individuals, but to groups, such as sinners or the poor. If the kingdom was in their midst, it must have a corporate dimension.[109] This can also be gleaned from the meal fellowship that Jesus had with other people and which he used as a paradigm for mutual relations among his disciples as well as between him and sinners.

We should also not be too quick to denationalize or universalize the kingdom notion. There are strong indications that, at least in part, Jesus saw it as his task to recall Israel as a whole to its role as the eschatological people of God. To that end the Twelve were chosen to represent the twelve tribes of Israel. The metaphor of the twelve is still present at the close of the first century in the book of Revelation (Rev. 7:4-8). As Matthew tells us, Jesus saw his mission "only to the lost sheep of the house of Israel" (Matt. 15:24), and he restricted the mission of his disciples to the same ethnic and religious entity (10:6). He understood his mission and that of his disciples as gathering the scattered sheep of Israel, implementing Old Testament hopes and fulfilling the expectations for Israel in a new age. To that effect he was even willing to sacrifice his own life (23:37-38). He interpreted his forthcoming death as the point of institution of a new covenant between God and God's people (1 Cor. 11:25), thereby evoking the promise of a new covenant made by God with the house of Israel (Jer. 31:31-34), a covenant more appropriate to this new age. Through his disciples the twelve tribes of Israel were represented, constituting the Israel of the new covenant.

Even if we assume that Jesus spoke of the church and made Peter the rock on which he would build his church (Matt. 16:18), we are still left with an Israelite assembly of the new covenant. Similar to someone

---

108. Michaels, "The Kingdom of God and the Historical Jesus," 110.

109. For the following see the enlightening comments by Dunn, *Jesus' Call to Discipleship*, 92ff., under the rubric "Would Jesus Have Been Disappointed with the Church?"

setting his affairs in order in preparation for death, Jesus entrusted his followers to Peter. This is not an action of concern about the survival of the movement he has initiated. The promise that the powers of death will not prevail against the church made clear that survival will never be at stake. Jesus' promise that he will give to Peter "the keys of the kingdom of heaven" (16:19) indicates that Jesus is not simply talking about a worldly organization but about the new people of God.[110] Their ultimate destiny is their entrance into the kingdom of God. There seems to be a historical connection, if not with Jesus at least with the Evangelists, between the kingdom of God which Jesus announced and the church. Yet what kind of church corresponds to that kingdom?

It is significant that in Paul's letter to the Romans he does not mention the term "church," since he is convinced that the final community of salvation will consist of an enlarged Israel (Rom. 11:17-18).[111] But already in the Synoptics we realize that God's salvific activity goes beyond the original tenants of the vineyard (cf. Mark 12:9). Yet the enlargement does not diminish the conditions for admission. Whether it is God's rule or the church, conformity to God's will is demanded (1 Cor. 6:9). Church and kingdom are not identical, because the church denotes more the present aspect of salvation, while the kingdom points to the future. The church is not just something preliminary, but something which ought to be completed (Eph. 4:13). Important is the integrative function of the church. Paul compares the church to a body in which every member has a distinct but equally important function (1 Cor. 12:23). Even the ethnic differences disappear (Gal. 3:28), and there is no administrative hierarchy, since all "are God's servants, working together" (1 Cor. 3:9). Decisive is the "being in Christ," through which all the separating differences lose their divisive character; otherwise Christ himself would be divided. Those who are in Christ are the church, the saints, the elected, the temple of God, the body of Christ, or those who see and experience salvation in and through Christ. Church and Christ belong closely together since only through Christ can there be a church.

---

110. For a more extensive discussion of the office of the keys see Hans Schwarz, *The Christian Church: Biblical Origin, Historical Transformation and Potential for the Future* (Minneapolis: Augsburg, 1982), 36.

111. See for the following the perceptive comments by Klaus Berger, "Kirche II," in *TRE* 18:213.

Similarly to the followers of Jesus, among whom there was a wider circle, an inner circle, and finally Peter as the spokesperson of the Twelve, the church, too, has developed certain structures. There were prophetic offices consisting of prophets and teachers, a symbolic office of the Twelve, and functional offices with presbyters, bishops, and deacons.[112] The church was always considered to be the church in a certain place and also the church as a whole. Gradually the church came to be understood not just as a community of salvation, but as an institution of salvation. Representative is Cyprian's (d. 258) statement: "There is no salvation outside the Church."[113] But this statement was made in a certain context. Cyprian is dealing here with those who have abandoned the Christian faith. For him the church is not an institution that mediates salvation — such a thought would have been impossible for him — but that the church is in intentional unity with Christ and therefore safeguards his saving truth. Cyprian had not yet considered that a tension could exist between Christ's salvific proclamation and the church as an institution. Yet, as many people have experienced, the church has often strayed away from being in intentional continuity with Christ and his message. In this respect the church has not fared much better than the kingdom notion.

Perhaps it is good to remember that in the Apostles' Creed the church is mentioned in the third article, bracketed on the one hand by the affirmation of faith in the Holy Spirit and on the other hand by the affirmation of the forgiveness of sins. Only in that kind of tension, empowered by the Holy Spirit and simultaneously in need of forgiveness of sins, does the church live up to the headship of Christ. It is noteworthy in this context that the Lutheran confessions contain two brief statements about the church. In the first one, from the *Augsburg Confession,* the institutional aspect of the church is emphasized: "The church is the assembly of saints in which the Gospel is taught purely and the sacraments are administered rightly."[114] The second reference stems directly from Mar-

---

112. Berger, "Kirche II," 214, who rightly points out that the traditional dualistic separation between institutional office and charismatic functions is invalid. Therefore it is also difficult to assume that the charismatic functions eventually died out and only the "rigid" office survived. Instead there is a threefold distinction which, to some extent, can still be seen in today's churches.

113. Cyprian, "Letter 73" 21.2, in *ACW* 47:66. See also Gerhard May, "Kirche III," in *TRE* 18:218, who comments on this statement.

114. *The Augsburg Confession* 7, in *BC,* 32.

tin Luther in the *Smalkald Articles*, where he wrote: "A seven-year-old child knows what the church is, namely, holy believers and sheep who hear the voice of their Shepherd."[115] Here the New Testament direction is preserved. The church is made up of people who are sanctified by God, trust in him, and hear the voice of their Lord.

While the institutional aspect mentioned in the *Augsburg Confession* needs to be maintained, direction today for the church must be derived from its New Testament intentionality and interconnectedness with the kingdom. The church is first of all a community gathered around Jesus as the Christ. He is present and operative in their words and through their ministries. The church is not gathered around a hierarchy or around buildings, but around their risen Lord. While some may be closer to him, speaking on his behalf, none is higher in rank, since they all have peculiar and important functions. If we take our cue from the original community of Jesus' disciples, we can even detect different circles, an inner circle with Peter, James, and John, a wider circle with the Twelve, and still a wider one with the poor, the sinners, and the outcast.[116] As we see with Mary Magdalene, the circles can even overlap. There are no separating barriers between them, but they are open, since Jesus' call is the same for all people. It is important to note that to follow Jesus is to be engaged in a missionary enterprise. While not all are called to be evangelists, some in the community of followers will support missionaries who reach out to others to bring them the good news of God's saving activity. But what does this all mean in terms of the envisioned rule of God?

First of all it means that we should never identify a particular ideology, social and political system, or religious program or structure with the reign of God. The results of such identifications have been disastrous. "What is realized is not the reign of God Jesus preached but the religious oppression and the political dictatorship Jesus would have denounced most vehemently."[117] The reign of God in its completion is an eschatological phenomenon and cannot be identified with either church or society. Nevertheless "the reign of God is manifest when change occurs for the better in relationships that involve human beings,

---

115. Martin Luther, *The Smalkald Articles* 3.12, in *BC*, 315.

116. For the following see Dunn, *Jesus' Call to Discipleship*, 108-15.

117. So very correctly C. S. Song, *Jesus and the Reign of God* (Minneapolis: Fortress, 1993), 18.

the world, and God."[118] The church as a community of believers who listen to the word of their Lord does make a difference in today's world. If it did not, it would not be the church. This difference does not just consist in winning the world for Christ, or feeding the poor, or being a model congregation. The intentionality of the kingdom is the rule of God plain and clear. Being the church today necessitates putting that rule first and not one's own person, interests, or preferences. It means being molded and molding our lives, those of others, and the world around us ever more clearly according to the God-intended mutuality of all creatures and into glorifying God. This implies the transformation of the world into the primordially envisioned garden or, to use another metaphor, into the hoped-for heavenly city. The church employs itself for the proleptic anticipation of the expected goal and in so doing expresses something of the reign of God already in the present. At the conclusion of any christology stands not the kingdom or the church, but Christ alone.

4. The Return of Christ

The return of Christ seems to be a very difficult subject. The *parousia*, literally translated as presence (1 Cor. 15:23, and inadequately translated as "second coming," suggests the repetition of something that has already occurred once.[119] Yet just as there is no second coming there is no second parousia. "The parousia of Christ is first and foremost the completion of the way of Jesus: 'the Christ on the way' arrives at his goal. His saving work is completed. In his eschatological person he is perfected and is universally manifested in the glory of God."[120] Paul uses the term "parousia" for Christ's coming in Messianic glory, whereas in the Synoptics and in John the older term "day of the Lord" or "those days" is used (Mark 13:20).[121] The term "day of the Lord" can be traced back to

---

118. Song, *Jesus and the Reign of God,* 285.

119. See Thomas C. Oden, *Life in the Spirit: Systematic Theology,* vol. 3 (San Francisco: Harper, 1992), 410.

120. So perceptively Jürgen Moltmann, *The Way of Jesus Christ: Christology in Messianic Dimensions,* trans. Margaret Kohl (San Francisco: Harper, 1990), 314.

121. Albrecht Oepke, *"parousia, pareimi,"* in *TDNT* 5:865.

the Old Testament and is shaped by apocalyptic ideas. There was popular longing for the great day of salvation, and in Amos 5:18, the *locus classicus* for the notion of the "day of the LORD," the prophet cautions his listeners: "Alas for you who desire the day of the LORD! Why do you want the day of the LORD? It is darkness, not light."[122] We notice here that this concept included cosmic changes. But historical and political advents are admixed. This concept was then taken over by Jesus, and in Luke 17:24, for instance, Jesus describes it as the day of the Son of man, rather than the day of the Lord, when the Son of man shall appear in the glory of the kingdom.

The apocalyptic environment of Jesus is saturated by an expectation of the end which is near. There is a strong political Messianism, an expectation of the Son of man and the hope for another aeon.[123] The early Christian faithful awaited an imminent coming of the exalted Lord in messianic glory. Of course, this was grounded in Jesus' own attitude, since "the whole thinking of Jesus is permeated by ideas of parousia. This is true in all strata of the Synoptic tradition."[124] But this is exactly where the problem lies, since the parousia is the definite manifestation of what has been effected already as an eschatological reality, and this reality still has not taken place. Since Jesus probably thought of his parousia as being imminent, the question arises of what to do with the so-called delay of the parousia. Perhaps the best thing to do is to abandon this notion, which defies clear systematization, and in so doing leave "the way clear for the wildly proliferating fantasies surrounding the expectation of the parousia which we come across in many Christian sects."[125]

Wolfhart Pannenberg, in his significant christology *Jesus — God and Man,* pays very little attention to the parousia. After the truism: "Only the eschaton will ultimately disclose what really happened in Jesus' resurrection from the dead," he closes his christology with the affirmation: "Until then we must speak favorably in thoroughly legitimate, but still only metaphorical and symbolic, form about Jesus' resurrection and the significance inherent in it."[126] Edward Schillebeeckx (1914-), in his

---

122. See regarding this passage Gerhard Delling, *"hēmera,"* in *TDNT* 2:945.

123. Oepke, *"parousia, pareimi,"* 5:863.

124. Oepke, *"parousia, pareimi,"* 5:866.

125. So Moltmann, *The Way of Jesus Christ,* 313.

126. Wolfhart Pannenberg, *Jesus — God and Man,* trans. Lewis L. Wilkins and Duane A. Priebe, 2nd ed. (Philadelphia: Westminster, 1988), 397.

massive volume *Christ: The Experience of Jesus as Lord,* shies completely away from mentioning the parousia. Salvation in Jesus exists for him in "being at the disposal of others, losing oneself to others . . . and . . . also working through anonymous structures for the happiness, the goodness and the truth of mankind."[127] One must honestly ask Schillebeeckx whether that kind of salvation actually deserves its name when we remember that John Hick demanded that we adduce hard facts to substantiate the claim that Christ is the preferable option over other savior figures. If salvation is attained in the way Schillebeeckx describes it, then the world is indeed becoming a better place in which to live. Indeed, there seems to be a global sensitizing to the plight of humanity and beyond to the plight of all creation. Modern dictators no longer boast about their atrocities but try to conceal them through off-limits torture chambers and paid terrorists. At the same time millions of people are fleeing their countries because of ethnic cleansing, tribal warfare, and other instruments of oppression. Thousands are starving every day, and ten thousand potential human beings are conveniently aborted. No, this earth does not look more redeemed than it did two thousand years ago. It looks more crowded.

If Jesus was a great ethical teacher or even the greatest, or just an exemplary person, we can pick and choose which of his ideas we happen to like.[128] We can then dispose of his eschatological teachings as products of a naive Jewish mind of two thousand years ago. Inspiring as Jesus has been throughout the centuries, he will add his imprint to all other ideas, as he certainly has done, but he will not bring about an actual and decisive change. World history will continue as before. Rudolf Bultmann posed the implications very clearly when he wrote: "*The mythical eschatology* is untenable for the simple reason that the parousia of Christ never took place as the New Testament expected. History did not come to an end, and, as every schoolboy knows, it will continue to run its course. Even if we believe that the world as we know it will come to an end in time,

---

127. Edward Schillebeeckx, *Christ: The Experience of Jesus as Lord,* trans. John Bowden (New York: Seabury, 1980), 838.

128. Our reasoning follows very closely that of Dale Aukerman, *Reckoning with Apocalypse: Terminal Politics and Christian Hope* (New York: Crossroad, 1993), 211, in which he posed very clearly *the* alternative: if Jesus was just a human being, then we can choose what we want to learn from him, but if he was not just a human being, then he can decisively affect world history.

we expect the end to take the form of a natural catastrophe, not of a mythical event such as the New Testament expects."[129] History will continue indefinitely and the polarity of good and evil will remain undecided. Then we will not only have the poor always with us but also misery, injustice, and chaos. Regardless how high we jump or how optimistic we get, we will always fall back onto our self-centered humanness. Yet people always try to inaugurate changes for the better, and optimism even in the face of death never dies out. Life, whether human or nonhuman, does not simply give up but seems to resist annihilation to its last breath. This unceasing struggle indicates that humanity and nature are not satisfied with an undecided status quo. They are yearning for, perhaps even forshadowing, an overcoming of negativity (Rom. 8:22-23).

We must also face the fact that Jesus was not just a superlative human being. Consistent with his own self-understanding Jesus left the overall impression that he was God's embodiment, the human face of God that on this earth lived out and proclaimed God's saving truth. He was an act of God that has become decisive for all history. Since the beginning of this century theology has struggled with the discovery that the whole New Testament outlook must be seen in eschatological terms. This means that it is shaped by the expectation of the eschaton, the end. Concurrent with this, the belief in the parousia or the presence of Christ in glory is firmly rooted in all strands of the New Testament. This parousia idea was not something that belongs to the theology of the Evangelists or of Paul, but is a form of the parousia hope which "does probably go back to the historical Jesus and represents part of that set of convictions most clearly represented in Mt. 19:28 and par. in which Jesus uses eschatological imagery to speak of the future reign with his disciples in the kingdom of God."[130] This parousia was not seen as being thousands of years away, but it was expected to be "imminent." Since this imminent hope was not realized, most theologians claimed that Jesus was mistaken. Albert Schweitzer even demanded that we abandon the notion of a parousia altogether, while most other exegetes tried in one way or other to cope with its so-called

---

129. Rudolf Bultmann, "New Testament and Mythology," in *Kerygma and Myth*, ed. Hans-Werner Bartsch, trans. Reginald Fuller (New York: Harper & Row, 1961), 5.
130. Christopher Rowland, "parousia," in *The Anchor Bible Dictionary*, 5:166.

delay. Small wonder that systematicians by and large did not want to touch this sticky topic. A notable exception in recent years has been Jürgen Moltmann, who in his christology, *The Way of Jesus Christ*, devotes one whole chapter to "the parousia of Christ."[131]

Since the passages that deal with the imminence of parousia can also be convincingly interpreted in other ways rather than pointing to Jesus' immediate coming in glory, we should try to enlighten the concept of the parousia through the historical context.[132] For Jesus two contexts are decisive: the apocalyptic and the prophetic. The apocalyptists believed that they stood so close to the end of the world that they were able to take in the whole of history at one glance and declare its meaning in terms of the divine purpose. From their vantage point they assumed that they could see past, present, and future in one continuous progression preordained by God. They believed that in this age all evil tendencies will grow until they culminate in their domination of the political powers of this world. Then the end of this age will be near. The symptoms of the coming end are unchecked evil, unrest and wars, and disturbance in nature and especially in the stellar courses. At the same time these travails indicate the birth of the new aeon. The new aeon will be the complete opposite of the old. It will be the unlimited dominion of the kingdom of God.

The apocalyptists were predominantly literary persons. They "wrote the content of alleged revelations using an artificial literary form, often employing pseudonymity, and writing as pseudo-prophets."[133] Yet we have not one line which Jesus wrote. He devoted little time to speculating on eschatological conditions. He also was not interested in apocalyptic instructions or timetables. As the people realized, he stood in the line of the prophetic tradition (Matt. 21:11). Yet "the characteristic feature of the prophet's message is its actuality, its expectation of something soon

---

131. Moltmann, *The Way of Jesus Christ*, 313-41.

132. For different interpretations of these passages (Mark 9:1; 13:30, and Matt. 10:23) not entailing an imminent return cf. Anthony Hoekema, *The Bible and the Future* (Grand Rapids: Eerdmans, 1979), 112-19; and George Eldon Ladd, *The Presence of the Future*, rev. ed. (Grand Rapids: Eerdmans, 1974), 311ff. For the whole topic of eschatology see also Hans Schwarz, *On the Way to the Future*; idem, *Jenseits von Utopie und Resignation* (Wuppertal: R. Brockhaus, 1991); and idem, "Eschatology," in *Christian Dogmatics*, vol. 2, ed. Carl E. Braaten und Robert W. Jenson (Philadelphia: Fortress, 1984).

133. Ladd, *Presence of the Future*, 316.

to happen."[134] This prophetic thrust then gives eschatology its immediacy and relevance for the present. One of the distinctive messages of the prophets was the announcement of the day of Yahweh, the day of the Lord. As we noted, this is the prevalent term used in the Gospels to denote that which Paul called the parousia. Since God was the God of the covenant, he was not a distant God but a God who was near to his people. Therefore it was Israel's hope that God would soon intervene. There is also "something peculiar about the expectation of the Day of Yahweh, for wherever it occurs in prophecy, the statements culminate in allusion to Yahweh's coming in person."[135]

Since Jesus regarded himself as the one who stood in God's place, there was no doubt that he would come to bring ultimate deliverance (cf. Mark 14:62). We remember that at the trial the high priest concluded that Jesus had committed blasphemy. Jesus declared himself to be God's representative, to be standing in God's place. Assuming himself to be God's appearance, he also saw himself in the line of the Old Testament prophetic tradition. But the prophetic vision of Yahweh's intervention on behalf of his people against those who threaten them (and indeed Yahweh himself) had become greatly intensified; by the time of the apocalyptic, intertestamental period, the idea prevailed that the war was "to affect all nations, even the fixed orders of creation, and even Israel herself. The event had been expanded into a phenomenon of cosmic significance."[136] Again we remember that Jesus' mission from beginning to end was a battle against the anti-Godly powers. At the day of the Lord, this was Jesus' announcement, this battle would climax, God would finally vindicate his people and himself. His glory would be undiminished.

We have noticed that in picking up the Old Testament tradition and gleaning from his apocalyptic environment Jesus was announcing the imminent reign of God. In so doing there was no self-deception but a prophetic realism that is sadly missing today. It is clear from the Synoptics that Jesus did not set a date for his return. Therefore he cannot have been mistaken. Of course, given the apocalyptic climate of his time,

---

134. Gerhard von Rad, *Old Testament Theology*, vol. 2: *The Theology of Israel's Prophetic Traditions*, trans. D. M. G. Stalker (New York: Harper & Row, 1965), 115.

135. von Rad, *Old Testament Theology*, 2:119.

136. von Rad, *Old Testament Theology*, 2:124.

it is quite possible that "some of his disciples or followers mistakenly understood him to have set a date for the Parousia."[137] When he was asked to lay out a timetable, he steadfastly refused (Matt. 24:3). There must have been a curiosity among his followers and perhaps even speculations about the date of his return. Yet Jesus emphasized only the imminence of the parousia and called for unceasing vigilance and service to God and neighbor. The parousia comes at a time when we do not expect it. That does not mean that we should be watchful for his coming, trying to discern the times and second-guess when he will actually come. The parable of the ten bridesmaids goes in another direction (cf. Matt. 25:1-13). Regardless when the Lord comes, we are to be prepared. Christian faithfulness is the order of the day; the Lord is not to be outguessed. The latter attempt has unfortunately been demonstrated often enough in the history of the church, from the Montanists in the early church to the followers of Joachim of Fiore in the High Middle Ages and the Jehovah Witnesses in our own time. Each of these attempts was mistaken, and any further attempts will also be mistaken.

The advent of the Lord in glory to gather his elect "is pictured in the Old Testament language of a theophany."[138] It will shake the natural order (Mark 13:24-27), and result in the judgment of all of humanity (Matt. 11:22) and the establishment of the kingdom of God. Even more briefly, the return of Christ "is nothing other than the final fulfillment of the promise of the coming of the kingdom of God, when God will be all in all (1 Cor. 15:28)."[139] This parousia will be visible, sudden, cosmic, and glorious.[140] Within these boundaries we may talk about Christ's return. When Jesus of Nazareth dwelled on earth as the human face of God, his humanity was so often overwhelming that people lost sight of who he actually was. Now, however, all ambiguity will be gone. As the Synoptics picturesquely describe: All people "will see 'the Son of Man coming in clouds' with great power and glory" (Mark 13:26).

---

137. Hoekema, *The Bible and the Future*, 122.

138. Ladd, *Presence of the Future*, 309.

139. So rightly Adrio König, *The Eclipse of Christ in Eschatology: Toward a Christ-Centered Approach* (Grand Rapids: Eerdmans, 1989), 201. Yet it is somewhat strange that König talks here about "Jesus" and not more appropriately about "Christ" or "Jesus Christ" who is returning. It is no longer the earthly Jesus but the heavenly Christ whom we expect.

140. So König, 202.

"We will see him as he is" (1 John 3:2). The one who has thus far been with us through the Spirit is now present in his divine glory. The next parameter, the sudden or unexpected advent of Christ, does not need much elaboration. He comes like a thief in the night (Matt. 24:43-44). It is not a slow evolutionary process through which the divine glory will be brought into this world. It is also not a line of progress that will lead us to ever new heights. The cosmic aspect is usually described in metaphors of the apocalyptic. But more importantly there will be "new heavens and a new earth, where righteousness is at home" (2 Pet. 3:13). There will not just be a dissolution of the old world or a creation of a new one, but an actual new world order, directed according to God's precepts. This will necessitate that God comes in glory and that which has been reserved for Christ's return will now be actualized, "that at the name of Jesus every knee should bend, in heaven and on earth and under the earth, and every tongue should confess that Jesus Christ is Lord, to the glory of God the Father" (Phil. 2:10-11).

The ultimate triumph of Christ also necessitates the judgment of those who do not voluntarily accept him as Lord and savior. The announcement that the Son of man will sit on the throne of his glory "and he will separate people one from another as a shepherd separates the sheep from the goats" (Matt. 25:32) has left a deep imprint on the Christian tradition and on the minds of many people. We remember that this fear of Christ as judge drove Martin Luther into the monastery because he was certain that he could not face his Lord and survive. He would surely be condemned. Yet by studying the same New Testament that inspired such a horrific figure Luther recaptured confidence in the face of judgment when, contrary to the mood of the Middle Ages, he no longer conceived of this day as a day of wrath, but as a day of the glory of God, a day he was looking forward to when he said in many of his letters: "Come, dear last day."[141] How did this change in Luther come about? Perhaps he remembered that the return of Christ is an act of God for the salvation of the world and not for its condemnation. It is Christ the savior who is the judge. With all the surprises it may entail (Matt. 25:37), the saving aspect reigns supreme.

---

141. See Paul Althaus, *The Theology of Martin Luther*, trans. Robert C. Schultz (Philadelphia: Fortress, 1966), 420-21, in his treatment of Luther's interpretation of eschatology.

331

There are curious minds that would like to decide whether there will be a universal reconciliation at the end and even a redemption of the devil, or whether there is a strict twofold outcome of history. Yet "if the parousia represents the climactic intervention of God in Christ, let us acknowledge with candor that the representations of the event do not permit us to describe it."[142] It is not our business to outguess God. Whatever the outcome of Christ's judgment of the living and the dead, whether all will be saved or only a few, it is ultimately Jesus' judgment and not ours; "Christians can wait for it only in the light of the gospel of Jesus Christ which they know and believe."[143] Even more restraint must be exhibited with regard to the expectation of the millennium. The idea of a Messianic earthly reign of a thousand years is present already before the time of Jesus in late Judaic apocalyptic literature. Revelation 20 (a highly symbolic text) contains the only mention of a millennium in the New Testament. There have been various interpretations, those, for instance, of a realized millennialism (meaning that the millennium has really occurred or is occurring), of a postmillennialism (meaning that the return will occur after the millennium), and finally of a premillennialism (meaning that the return will occur before the millennium).[144] This has also been correlated with the so-called rapture, meaning that both those who have died in the Lord and the living saints will be caught up to meet the Lord in the air (1 Thess. 4:15ff.). All of these notions, especially if they are brought to the center of the expectation of Christ's return, seem to miss the point. As Karl Barth (1886-1968) cautions, the parousia of Jesus Christ is "the miracle of the divine 'Yes.'"[145] It is a miracle, because it is surprising and because it does indeed come. It is not a timetable or a travel brochure that Jesus Christ must follow on his return.

When we return from the book of Revelation to the Synoptic Gospels, from the periphery to the center of the New Testament, we notice that very little attempt is made there to sketch out the character of the liberation which the parousia entails. There are no details about

142. So correctly G. R. Beasley-Murray, *Jesus and the Kingdom of God* (Grand Rapids: Eerdmans, 1986), 341.

143. Moltmann, *The Way of Jesus Christ,* 338.

144. For more details see Oden, *Life in the Spirit,* 421-30.

145. Karl Barth, *The Epistle to the Romans,* trans. Edwyn C. Hoskyns from the 6th ed. (London: Oxford University Press, 1953), 417, in his comments on Rom. 11:27.

an ideal society or an ideal world, and we read nothing about a political manifesto.[146] Yet the direction nevertheless is clear: That which Jesus was and stood for and which was vindicated in his resurrection will be publicly disclosed and drawn out on a universal scale. Perhaps the Second Assembly of the World Council of Churches (1954) in Evanston, Illinois, captured this major thrust of the New Testament very appropriately when it stated: "God does not leave any of us to stand alone. . . . We do not know what is coming to us. But we know Who is coming. It is He who meets us every day and who will meet us at the end — Jesus Christ our Lord. Therefore we say to you, rejoice in hope."[147]

We are not interested in the return of Christ for the return's sake, but because of its impact on the present.[148] The anticipation of the parousia affects our quality of life. It makes a difference to know whether we are, so to speak, treading water and that nothing essentially will change, whether there will be nothing new under the sun, just new configurations of present cosmic possibilities, or to know that indeed a decisive change will occur, something new will come that will bring an end to all polarities, divisions, and imperfections. If the latter is the case, we will not just gain new hope to live confidently in the present, but the expectation of the Lord's return will be a constant incentive to live for Christ and for his kingdom, to be ambassadors and witnesses of that from which and toward which we live, Christ the Alpha and the Omega. The return of Christ is neither a pie-in-the-sky utopia nor a horror vision. It is the universal implementation of that which started in the womb of the virgin, was vindicated through an unprecedented resurrection, and will find its cosmic completion to the glory of God Almighty. Pierre Teilhard de Chardin phrased that hope and conviction in his own meta-phoric language with the following words:

> One day, the Gospel tells us, the tension gradually accumulating be-
> tween humanity and God will touch the limits prescribed by the possi-
> bilities of the world. And then will come the end. Then the presence
> of Christ, which has been silently accruing in things, will suddenly be

---

146. Rowland, "parousia," 5:169.

147. "A Message from the Second Assembly of the World Council of Churches, Evanston," *The Ecumenical Review* (October 1954), 7:65.

148. See also Ladd, *Presence of the Future*, 327; and Hoekema, *The Bible and the Future*, 128, who reach a similar conclusion.

revealed — like a flash of light from pole to pole. Breaking through all the barriers within which the veil of matter and the water-tightness of souls have seemingly kept it confined, it will invade the face of the earth. And, under the final liberated action of the true affinities of being, the spiritual atoms of the world will be borne along by a force generated by the powers of cohesion proper to the universe itself and will occupy, whether within Christ or without Christ (but always under the influence of Christ), the place of happiness or pain designated for them by the living structure of the Pleroma. . . . Like lightning, like a conflagration, like a flood, the attraction exerted by the Son of Man will lay hold of all the whirling elements in the universe so as to reunite them or subject them to His body. . . . Such will be the consummation of the divine milieu.[149]

We have concluded our long journey through christology which began with the search for the historical Jesus, we have listened to the biblical testimony and its assessment throughout history, and finally we have asked what relevance Jesus Christ has for us today. Yet a christology can never be finished. As the Gospel of John concludes: "But there are also many other things that Jesus did; if everyone of them were written down, I suppose that the world itself could not contain the books that would be written" (John 21:25). In this vein one should also rejoice about the resurgence of interest in the historical Jesus. Each of these endeavors contributes one little facet to the "historic Christ of the Bible," to use a phrase of Martin Kähler.[150]

While we agree with Kähler that that which can be unearthed about the historical Jesus who stands behind the Gospels will always be less than the Christ of the apostolic preaching of the whole New Testament, it should have become clear that we affirm that there exists a continuity between the two. But this means also the obligation for scholarship to stay in tune with the New Testament and not to reconstruct a contextual Jesus who stands contrary to the biblical message. There must be a fidelity to the biblical documents, not just because they happened to be received in the canon, but because the church decided that qualitatively

149. Pierre Teilhard de Chardin, *The Divine Milieu: An Essay on the Interior Life* (New York: Harper, 1960), 133-34.

150. Kähler distinguishes between the "so-called historical Jesus" and the "historic, biblical Christ." For more, see Martin Kähler, *The So-Called Historical Jesus and the Historic, Biblical Christ,* trans. Carl E. Braaten (Philadelphia: Fortress, 1964), 65.

there was more to be gained from them than from extracanonical literature. Fidelity to the New Testament also implies an acceptance of its truthfulness. Therefore the main cues for discerning who Jesus was and what he intended will come from the Gospels and not from Qumran or Jewish apocalyptic literature or Near Eastern sociology, valuable as the insights may be which we glean from these sources.

Since the central claim of New Testament christology is that Jesus was the human face of God, there arises the issue of rational intelligibility. This is not a new issue, but it first emerged at the beginning of Jesus' ministry (Luke 4:24). Even if we point to Christ's resurrection, the issue of rational intelligibility of Jesus as the Christ is not solved but only heightened (Acts 17:32). The claim that Jesus is the human face of God involves therefore an initial decision of faith. Once that is made in favor of Jesus indeed being the one who he claimed to be, then many other points of contention will also be solved. Jesus is not a Christ but the Christ, he is not a word from God but the Word, he does not stand for the principle of liberation but for the fact of liberation. As Bultmann aptly reminded us, God has decisively acted in Jesus Christ. Whether God also acts decisively in other figures remains God's business.

Christology never dares to degenerate into a theory about everything or about others, but always involves an existential dimension. It includes the recognition that only through Christ am I offered a new perspective on life, a new vision of the world, and a new hope for the efficacy of God's salvific power in the whole universe. Yet this existential comfort also implies a hope beyond one's individual sphere. Since God has shown himself in Jesus Christ as a God of mercy, compassion, and salvific power, we dare to hope that redemption will also be effective where, according to our perception, Christ has not been officially recognized. But this kind of universal vision is neither a doctrine nor a proclamation but a hope.

For us, who are encountered by the human face of God, the consequences are much simpler: "Follow me. . . . Immediately they left the boat and their father, and followed him" (Matt. 4:19, 22). Following the way of Jesus does not just mean leading a life of humility and service to other people, perhaps even a life of suffering, though that may be entailed too. It means foremost leading a life of joy as expressed by John and Peter when they responded to the Jewish council in Jerusalem: "We cannot keep from speaking about what we have seen and heard" (Acts 4:20). Christians do not live just by the tradition of Christ or by the hope

335

for Christ's return, but they live by the vision of a new heaven and a new earth in which righteousness will rule. Since they are confident that such a vision will take on reality through God's power and promise, they are free to face the trials and problems of the day with the full assurance that some of that vision is already inaugurated in the present.

Subject Index

Abba, 225
Absolute Paradox, 190
accommodation, theory of, 16
adoptionism, 149, 161-62, 234, 238
Alpha and Omega, 289, 333
Anabaptists, 175-76
anthropology, 67
anti-Godly powers, 124, 133, 260, 295,
    329
anti-Judaism, 213
antitrinitarian movement, 175-76
apocalypticism, 16, 21, 39, 53, 65, 91,
    108, 115-16, 204, 207, 229, 263, 284,
    300, 314, 318, 325, 328, 329, 331, 335
apostles, 55
Apostles' Creed, 144, 169, 179, 209, 275,
    293, 294, 295, 322
Aramaic, 56, 108, 229
ascension, 12, 20, 22; of Christ, 274-77,
    295-99
atonement, 168, 191, 250, 281; doctrine
    of, 255-60; "Happy Exchange"
    theory (also "Joyful Exchange"), 170,
    178, 195; Latin (Western) type, 255-
    56; ransom theory, 162-64; satisfac-
    tion (theory of), 165-67, 168, 169,
    189; theory of, 165, 192, 221, 252, 283
Augsburg Confession (1530), 168, 318,
    322, 323
Auschwitz, 212

baptism, 11, 88-89, 134-35; of Jesus, 18-
    19, 66, 89, 120
Beatitudes, 314
Bethlehem, 77, 80-81
Bible, 70
blasphemy, 207, 216
Buddhism, 1, 113, 230, 308, 310

Chalcedon, Council of, 147, 156-58,
    168, 286
children of God, 126
Christian community, 47, 49, 63-64, 83
Christian Jews, 215
christology: Chalcedonian, 184;
    Ebionite, 149, 195; erotic, 281-82;
    feminist, 277-87, 296; from above,
    191, 196, 199; from below, 181-82,
    187, 191, 193, 200, 219; high, 234;
    Logos, 150-55, 233-34; low, 234; ret-
    roactive, 234, 235; theocentric, 300-
    302; triumphalistic, 281
church, 25, 36, 38, 45, 48-49, 55, 89-90,
    120-21, 122, 147, 270-71, 274, 306-7,
    311-24; catholic (universal), 168, 299-
    300; early, 137-60
communicatio idiomatum, 170
confessional Lutheran theology, 205
Constantinople: Council of (Fifth Ecu-
    menical Council, 553), 158-59; Coun-
    cil of (Sixth Ecumenical Council,

681), 159; Ecumenical Council of (381), 147, 153

covenant, 215, 247-48

creation account (priestly), 126

crucifixion, 132, 284

cultic purity, 215

David (also Davidic), 81, 109, 120, 207

Davidic descent, 82-84, 121, 232, 237

Dead Sea Scrolls, 61, 66

death of Christ, 20, 25, 27, 132, 214

deification, 188, 297-99

descent of Christ, 290-94

devil, 76, 162-64, 177, 254, 255, 256-57, 294, 332

dialectical theology, 192

Didache, 52

dissimilarity, criterion of, 52, 75

divine pluralism, 140

docetism, 149-50, 195, 231, 234, 240, 253

dogma, 240

dualism, 149-50, 154, 280

dyotheletism, 159

Easter, 97-98

egō eimi, 110-12, 127

election, 179, 195

empty tomb, 97-98, 267

Enlightenment, 175, 177, 180-82, 183-84, 187

Enthusiasts, 175-76

Ephesus (Third Ecumenical Council, 431), 156

ethics, 176; interim, 32-34; of Jesus, 32, 99; of the kingdom, 121

eschatological expectations, 33, 90, 300, 318

eschatological Jesus, 63-64, 324

eschatological kingdom (also people of God), 123, 320

eschatology, 20, 24, 30, 31, 32-34, 64-65, 94-95, 102, 103, 110, 132, 133-35, 208, 215, 228-29, 246, 248-49, 251, 313-14, 327, 328-29

essence, 148

Eucharist, 11, 130. *See also* Lord's Supper

Evangelicals, 204, 302-3

extracanonical literature, 66

faith, 33, 40, 70, 75, 204, 206, 269

filioque clause, 160-62

form criticism, 42-44, 46-47, 48, 53, 55-58

gnosticism, 126, 149-50, 225, 235, 253, 261, 278

Good Friday, 261

good news, 90

gospel, 47

grace, 90, 167, 308

Greco-Roman, 76

Greek mythology, 250

Greek philosophy, 150, 252

Hades, 292-93

halakah (the way), 100-101

Heidelberg Disputation (1518), 168

Hellenism (also Hellenistic), 55, 85, 101, 128, 138, 147, 214, 218, 221, 225, 243, 249, 253

Hinduism, 230, 308

historical criticism, 58

historical facts, 56

historical Jesus, 48-71, 197, 222

historical knowledge, 32

historical research, 40-42, 49-51, 68, 221, 222, 268

history, 13, 14, 18, 33, 38, 75-76, 84, 104, 110, 121, 122, 123-24, 133, 185, 187, 203-9, 221-23, 259, 274, 327

Holy Spirit, 11, 14, 26, 84, 124, 125, 128, 146, 147, 154, 161-62, 172, 176, 193, 205, 207, 237, 239, 322

homoousia (also *homoousios*), 143, 144-45, 147

hope, 308-9

hypostases, 142

iconoclastic controversies, 159-60
idealism, 221
incarnation, 22, 152, 166-67, 190-96, 198, 230-32, 298, 304, 308, 310
Intertestamental literature, 67
ipsissima vox, 52, 60
Islam, 1, 113, 159, 201, 209, 224
Israel, history of, 204-5

Jehovah's Witnesses, 330
Jesus Seminar, 61-62
Jewish authorities (also leaders), 31, 95, 284; Christians, 149; context, 249; cynic, Jesus as, 68-69; law, 97, 242; sources (literature), 51, 53, 64, 332, 335; teachers, 55; thought, 90, 318
Jews, 88, 97, 103-4, 126, 127, 184, 206, 246
Johannine Comma, 138-39
John the Baptist, 86-91
Judaism, 46, 54, 75-76, 85, 126, 186, 204, 207, 209-18, 226, 230, 231, 233, 239, 243, 260-61, 264, 273, 290, 313, 314
judgment, 88

kerygma, 40-41, 44-45, 48-51, 52, 55, 58-59, 60, 272
kerygmatic theology, 205
kingdom, 16, 20, 21, 24, 89, 90, 94; of God, 16, 19, 21, 24, 26-27, 30, 34-39, 52, 62-63, 65, 69, 102-5, 106, 125, 187-89, 311-24; of heaven, 10, 121, 132, 177, 310, 312-13
kyrios (Lord), 122, 135

Last Supper, 11, 93-95, 149, 241-49, 251, 259
Law, 99-102, 112, 171, 224, 258
Leo's *Tome,* 156-57
liberal Protestantism, 29, 33
liberal theology, 34, 268
literary criticism, 58
Loci communes, 172

logos, 99, 126, 151-55, 159-60, 167, 195, 198, 221-22, 234, 236, 304, 307, 308, 309-10. *See also* Word
Lord's Prayer, 66, 210, 224-25, 314
Lord's Supper, 170-71, 249-50, 277. *See also* Eucharist
love, 25

magi, 79
Magnificat, 123
martyrs, 250, 253
Marxist theory, 209
Messiah, 29, 30-31, 67, 83, 95, 105-12, 115-17, 122-23, 131-32, 193, 210-18, 233, 251
Messianic secret, 31, 111, 119-20, 227
Messianism, 230, 279, 325, 332
millennialism, 316, 319, 332
ministry of Jesus, 91-92, 123
miracles, 12, 19, 24, 28-29, 68-69, 92, 184, 185
mishna (tradition), 100
missionary preaching, 57
mission, 147, 308; of Jesus, 24, 90, 126, 230, 329
modalism, 139-40
monarchianism, 139-40
monotheletism, 159
monophysitism, 158-59, 219
monotheism, 138, 140, 142, 149
Montanists, 330
Moravians (Brethren Community), 178
Moslems, 306
mystery religions, 135
mysticism, 135, 178-80, 278

narrative criticism, 47-8
neo-Reformation theology, 192
new covenant, 94
new creation, 273-74
New Testament theology, 2
Nicea, Council of (325), 218, 286
Nicene Creed, 144-45, 147, 162
Niceno-Constantinopolitan Creed, 147

Old Testament, 104-5, 105, 110, 117, 122-23, 128, 131, 146, 205, 226, 243, 289, 312, 320, 329

Palestine, 55, 57
pantocrator, 219, 271, 289, 297
parables, 43, 50, 52, 55, 62, 65, 68-69
Paraclete, 128-29
paradox, 193. *See also* Absolute Paradox
parousia, 12, 14, 16, 54, 64, 94, 121, 132, 212, 289, 290, 296, 298, 324-34
passion of Jesus, 92-97
Passover, 12, 91-92, 93-94, 244-46
Passover lamb, 93, 244-45, 247-48
Pelagianism, 168
Pentecost, 125
people of God, 147, 229
person, 148
Pharisees, 92, 95, 105, 115, 215, 216-17, 261
Pietism, 175, 177-80
Platonism, 221
polytheism, 138, 139, 141, 142
predestination, 195
preexistence of Jesus, 233-36
priesthood of Christ, 188-89
process theology, 309-11
proclamation of Jesus, 3, 10, 16, 27, 33, 99-112, 124, 272
proleptic, 117, 134, 204, 244, 272, 324
prophetic tradition, 88

Q source, 68, 89, 104, 106, 123, 222, 226, 233
quest for the historical Jesus, viii, 3, 7-71
Qumran, 51, 53, 61, 67, 83, 87, 88, 110, 335
Qur'an, 113

rabbi, Jesus as, 54-55, 92, 99-102, 105, 216
rabbinic law, 210; thought, 132; tradition, 99
rapture, 332

rational inquiry, 39-42
rationalism, 9, 84, 230
real presence, 171
reason, 8, 15, 182, 203-9
recapitulation, theory of, 254-55
redaction criticism, 44-47
Redeemer, 278-79
redemption, 164; of Christ, 163; of humanity, 165
religious pluralism, 302
repentance, 88
resurrection, 196, 333
resurrection of Christ, 12, 13, 14, 20, 21-22, 27, 97-98, 114-18, 131-34, 189, 260-77, 311
resuscitation, 115, 117-18
revelation (see also self-disclosure, self-revelation), 38, 54, 65, 111-12, 183, 188, 193, 194, 204-6, 208, 304-5, 309, 318; general, 181-82; special, 181
righteousness of Jesus, 250

Sabbath, 101-2, 215
Sabellianism, 162
sacraments, 11, 14
sacrifice of Christ, 165-67, 177, 250, 256-57, 277
sacrificial death, 132
Sadducees, 92, 95, 115, 206, 215, 261
salvation, 102-5, 148-49, 154, 167, 192, 198-99, 254, 301-2, 304, 307, 313, 322, 326
salvation history, 45, 168, 237
Sanhedrin, 12, 95-96
Satan, 124, 252
scholastic theology (scholasticism), 168, 172
scribes, 92
self-disclosure (also self-revelation), 49, 110, 127, 193, 206, 233, 234, 240, 253-54
Septuagint, 122
Sermon on the Mount, 101-2, 210
Sheol, 263, 290-91

Sitz im Leben, 42, 43, 45-46, 54
Smalkald Articles, 323
Small Catechism, 169
Social Gospel, 34-39
sociology, 67
sola scriptura (Scripture alone), 168, 171
Son of God, 11, 122, 125, 131, 135, 150,
    186, 187, 189, 190, 234-35, 236-37,
    304, 306
Son of man, 11, 21, 62-64, 65-66, 107-
    10, 127, 135, 214, 228-30, 325, 331,
    334
sophia (wisdom), 234, 236
Spirit, 45, 128-29, 130, 180, 186, 278,
    304, 308, 316
Spiritualists, 175-76
structural criticism, 47-48
subordinationism, 140, 142
substance, 140
suffering servant, 229, 251, 287
Synod of Frankfurt (794), 162
Synoptic gospels, 42, 49-50, 53-54, 56-
    57, 89, 107, 113, 118-25, 244, 279,
    321, 324, 329, 330, 332
synoptic tradition, 224, 325

table fellowship, 94, 105, 149, 243-44,
    280, 320
teaching of Jesus, 65
theology of the cross, 168-69, 179, 271-
    72
theotokos ("mother of God"), 154-55, 157
Third Wave, 60-71
tradition, 137
Transfiguration, 120
trinitarian controversy, 138-60
Trinity (triune God), 11, 14, 26, 146-49,
    168-69, 171-72, 193-94, 236, 283, 304
tritheism, 146, 148

understanding, 1

Virgin Birth (also virginal conception),
    18, 83-86, 194-95, 236-40, 297
vocation of Jesus, 187, 189

wisdom, 233, 278. *See also sophia*
Word, 41, 224
word of God, 193, 194, 196, 279, 318
World Council of Churches, 333

Name Index

Aalen, Leiv, 179
Aaron (High Priest), 167
Abelard, Peter, 167
Akiba (Rabbi), 217
Alexamenos, 207
Alexander of Alexandria, 143
Allison, Dale C., 79
Althaus, Paul, 331
Ambrose of Milan, 164
Andresen, Carl, 253
Anselm of Canterbury, 164-66, 257
Apollinaris of Laodicea, 152
Apollonius of Tyana, 69
Archelaus, 80
Arius, 142, 143
Armbruster, Carl J., 197-98
Athanasius, 145, 151-52
Augustine, 148, 161, 163
Augustus, 77, 79
Aukerman, Dale, 326
Aulén, Gustav, 255

Baigent, Michael, 61
Bar Kochba, 83, 211, 217
Barnabas, 252
Barth, Karl, 41, 193, 195, 33
Barth, Markus, 209
Basil the Great, 146
Bauckham, Richard, 293
Bauer, Bruno, 26

Beasley-Murray, G. R., 332
Becker, Jürgen, 90
Behm, Johannes, 128
Beintker, Michael, 319
Ben-Chorin, Shalom, 210, 216-17
Benedict of Nursia, 317
Berger, Klaus, 321-22
Bernhard of Clairvaux, 168
Betz, Otto, 61
Billerbeck, Paul, 100, 108
Blancy, Alain, 47
Blinzler, Josef, 95
Bloch, Ernst, 258
Bonhoeffer, Dietrich, 258
Borg, Marcus J., 61, 42, 63-64, 68
Bornkamm, Günther, 121, 227
Braaten, Carl E., 39
Braun, Herbert, 51, 269
Brock, Rita Nakashima, 282-83
Brown, Raymond E., 66, 78-82, 83-86, 89, 223, 238-40, 295
Brown, Schuyler, 76
Brox, Norbert, 291-92
Buber, Martin, 210
Büchsel, Friedrich, 130
Buddha, 188
Bultmann, Rudolf, 2, 40, 42-43, 48, 50, 55, 60, 76, 85, 103-4, 107, 113, 204, 222, 223, 227, 229, 236, 275, 326, 335
Burkitt, F. C., 33

Calvin, John, 173, 174
Campenhausen, Hans Freiherr von, 267
Carruthers, Gregory H., 305
Cassidy, Richard, 123
Celsus, 53, 239
Charlemagne, 162
Charlesworth, James H., 61, 66-67, 70, 115, 293
Chrysostom, Saint John, 164
Clement of Alexandria, 292
Clopas, 82
Cobb, John B., Jr., 309-10
Colleran, Joseph M., 162
Collins, Anthony, 8
Collins, Roger John Howard, 161
Conzelmann, Hans, 44, 45, 81, 91, 119, 120, 122, 124, 126, 223, 269
Crossan, John Dominic, 68, 69
Cullmann, Oscar, 271
Cyprian, 32
Cyril of Alexandria, 155

Dalton, William Joseph, 293
Daly, Mary, 277
Daniélou, Jean, 141
Darling-Smith, Barbara, 280
Darwin, Charles, 23
Davies, William D., 58-60, 79
Deissmann, Adolf, 79
Delling, Gerhard, 243, 249, 262, 272, 325
Dewey, Bradley R., 190
Dibelius, Martin, 42, 43, 119
Diodorus of Tarsus, 153
Dodd, Charles H., 56, 96
Domitian, 82
Draina, C., 139
Duncan, John, 230
Dunn, James D. G., 311, 320, 323
Dupré, Louis, 190, 192

Eisenmann, Robert H., 61
Engels, Friedrich, 319
Ephraem, 292

Epiphanius, 246
Epstein, I., 82
Eusebius, 82, 140
Exiguus, Dionysius, 77

Fedotow, George P., 167
Feuerbach, Ludwig, 182
Fichte, Johann Gottlieb, 203
Finegan, Jack, 78
Fitzmyer, Joseph, 87
Flack, E. E., 7
Fohrer, Georg, 226
Frank, K. Suso, 240
Friedrich, Gerhard, 235
Fuchs, Ernst, 50, 102, 112, 222
Funk, Robert W., 64
Furnish, Victor Paul, 130, 133, 134

Gaius Vibius Maximus, 79, 80
Geismar, Eduard, 130
Gentile, Valentino, 175
Gerhardsson, Birger, 55
Gilles, Chester, 305
Gladden, Washington, 36
Goldstein, Morris, 86
Goppelt, Leonhard, 93, 94, 96, 98, 100, 101, 105, 108-9, 224, 227-29, 242-43, 245, 248-49, 257, 262-64, 267-68, 275, 291, 313-14
Goulder, Michael, 231
Graham, Holt H., 139
Grant, Robert M., 139
Green, Michael, 232
Greer, Rowan A., 153
Gregory of Nazianzen, 146-47, 152-53
Gregory of Nyssa, 163
Griffin, David R., 309
Grillmeier, Aloys, 143-44
Grundmann, Walter, 79, 87
Grünewald, Matthias, 29

Haardt, Robert, 149
Hahn, Ferdinand, 106
Hanson, John S., 67

Harnack, Adolf von, 28-30
Harner, Philip, 111
Hebblethwaite, Brian, 232
Hegel, Georg Wilhelm Friedrich, 23-25, 184-87, 319
Hegesippus, 82
Hempelmann, Heinzpeter, 260
Hengel, Martin, 233, 250-51, 272
Hennecke, Edgar, 262
Hennecke-Schneemelcher, Wilhelm, 293
Herod (Antipas), 216-17
Herod (the Great), 80, 232
Heyward, Carter, 281
Hick, John, 231, 303-5, 308
Hilary of Poitiers, 171, 175
Hillel, 69
Hirsch, Emmanuel, 171
Hitler, Adolf, 319
Hoehner, Harold W., 96
Hoekema, Anthony, 328, 330
Hoffmann, Paul, 263, 271
Hong, Edna H., 191
Hong, Howard V., 191
Hopkins, Julie M., 283-84
Hornig, Gottfried, 16
Horsley, Richard A., 67
Hunter, Archibald M., 225-26, 230, 238, 240

Irenaeus, 140, 253, 254, 316

Jeremias, Joachim, 52, 82, 93-94, 104, 108, 109, 115, 226, 242-44, 246, 265, 267, 273, 276, 312, 314
Joachim of Fiore, 317
John of Damascus, 159-60, 163
Josephus, 78-79, 87, 107
Judas the Galilean, 79, 94
Justin Martyr, 76, 139, 150, 238, 243, 275, 307

Kähler, Martin, 39, 40, 221, 334
Kant, Immanuel, 27

Käsemann, Ernst, 49-50
Keck, Leander, 59
Kelber, Werner H., 111
Kelly, J. N. D., 144, 147
Kepler, Johannes, 78
Kessler, Hans, 252, 255, 257
Kierkegaard, Søren, 191-92
King, Henry Churchill, 36
Kingsbury, Jack Dean, 120, 122
Kittel, Gerhard, 289
Klausner, Joseph, 107
Knitter, Paul, 300-302
Koch, Ernst, 290
König, Adrio, 330
Kroll, Josef, 291
Kümmel, Werner Georg, 15, 102, 127-28, 130, 135
Künneth, Walter, 271
Kuschel, Karl-Josef, 237

Ladd, George Eldon, 328, 330, 333
Lapide, Pinchas, 211-15, 261-62, 264, 265-66, 268
Leibniz, Gottfried Wilhelm von, 177
Leigh, Richard, 61
Leo I (the Great), 156
Leo III, 182
Lessing, Gotthold Ephraim, 9, 14-15, 180-81, 203
Lindemann, Andreas, 313
Lohse, Bernhard, 142, 156, 158
Lohse, Eduard, 245, 247
Luther, Martin, 7, 168-73, 259, 291, 323, 331
Luz, Ulrich, 211-15

McFague, Sallie, 280-81, 315
McKelway, Alexander J., 199
McKnight, Edgar V., 47
Macquarrie, John, 182, 194, 219-21, 223, 232, 270
Manson, Thomas W., 57
Marcion, 14, 292
Marshall, I. Howard, 248, 249

Marxsen, Willi, 46-47, 262, 267, 269-70
Mathews, Shailer, 34-36
Maximus Confessor, 297
May, Gerhard, 322
Mehlhausen, Joachim, 319
Meier, John P., 69-70
Melanchthon, Philip, 172-73, 205
Melito of Sardis, 292
Metzger, Bruce M., 265
Michaels, J. Ramsey, 316, 320
Michalson, Gordon E., Jr., 14
Mohammed, 188
Mollegen, A. T., 197
Möller, Christian, 268
Moltmann, Jürgen, 252, 258, 265, 290,
    311, 315, 318, 324-25, 328, 332
Moltmann-Wendel, Elisabeth, 279-80
Moses, 110
Moule, C. F. D., 252, 259, 263
Mueller, David L., 189, 196
Mühlen, Karl-Heinz zur, 174, 175
Müntzer, Thomas, 318

Neill, Stephen, 104
Nero, 78
Nestorius, 154
Nicodemus, 216
Niebuhr, H. Richard, 319
Norris, Richard A., 152

O'Brien, Peter T., 295
Oden, Thomas C., 324, 332
Oepke, Albrecht, 324-25
Origen, 81, 141, 150, 163, 256, 257
Osiander, 173

Pannenberg, Wolfhart, 110, 158, 200,
    204, 206, 208, 218, 220, 229, 236, 258,
    272, 325
Peabody, Francis Greenwood, 37
Pelikan, Jaroslav, 160, 162, 165, 169,
    175, 294
Perrin, Norman, 111
Philo, 126

Pilate, 87, 95, 96
Pinnock, Clark H., 302
Pobee, John, 96
Pöhlmann, Horst G., 275
Praxeas, 140
Pugh, Jeffrey C., 193

Quirinius, Publius Sulpicius, 80

Rad, Gerhard von, 329
Rahner, Karl, 237, 306-8, 311
Räisänen, Heikki, 237
Rauschenbusch, Walter, 38
Reardon, Bernard M. G., 23, 185
Reimarus, Hermann Samuel, 8-14, 97
Renan, Ernst, 26
Riches, John, 218
Richmond, James, 26-27
Riesenfeld, Harald, 54, 99
Riesner, Rainer, 61
Ritschl, Albrecht, 26, 187-89
Ritter, Adolf Martin, 143
Robinson, James M., 51, 53
Robinson, John A. T., 57, 233-34
Roloff, Jürgen, 229
Rowland, Christopher, 327, 333
Ruether, Rosemary Radford, 277, 278
Rusch, William G., 142

Sanday, William, 33
Sanders, E. P., 261, 302
Saturinus, Sentius, 80
Schäfer, Rolf, 27-28
Scheffczyk, Leo, 273
Scherer, James A., 302
Schillebeeckx, Edward, 264, 326
Schleiermacher, Friedrich, 17-21, 182,
    183, 219-20, 290
Schmidt, Karl Ludwig, 42-43
Schnackenburg, Rudolf, 295
Schoeps, Hans-Joachim, 149
Schwarz, Hans, 132, 287, 292, 316-17,
    321, 328

Schweitzer, Albert, 3, 17, 20-21, 31-34, 103, 327
Schweizer, Eduard, 78
Scobie, Charles H. H., 87-88, 91
Seeberg, Reinhold, 162
Semler, Johann Salomon, 8, 15-16
Servetus, Michael, 175
Sharp, Douglas R., 195
Shimei, 216
Sikes, Jeffrey G., 167
Silver, Abba Hillel, 106
Sittler, Joseph, 297
Snyder, Howard A., 315
Sölle, Dorothee, 258, 285
Song, C. S., 323-24
Sozzini, Fausto, 176
Sparn, Walter, 176
Spener, Philipp Jacob, 178
Sponheim, Paul, 191
Stauffer, Ethelbert, 53, 76, 80, 85-86, 93, 110
Stein, Robert H., 228
Stemberger, Günter, 260
Stendahl, Krister, 44-46
Strack, Hermann L., 100, 108
Strahm, Doris, 285
Strauss, David Friedrich, 21-23, 187
Swing, Albert Temple, 27
Sykes, Stephen W., 192
Symeon, 82

Talbert, Charles H., 9
Tannehill, Robert, 133-34
Taylor, Vincent, 58-59, 106, 248, 252
Teilhard de Chardin, Pierre, 298, 334
Tertullian, 80, 86, 97, 140, 150, 165, 255-56, 275, 292
Theissen, Gerd, 67, 68
Theodore of Mopsuestia, 153-55
Thiering, Barbara, 61

Thüsing, Wilhelm, 311
Tillich, Paul, 196-200
Tiridates, 78
Tolland, John, 8
Torrance, Thomas F., 232
Trajan, 82
Trask, Haunani-Kay, 283
Trigg, Joseph Wilson, 141
Troeltsch, Ernst, 39

Verheyden, Jack, 17, 19-20
Vermes, Geza, 216-17
Vespasian, 82
Visser 't Hooft, W. A., 299

Waldorp, Charles T., 193
Weber, Otto, 194
Weiser, Alfons, 276
Weiss, Hans-Friedrich, 205
Weiss, Johannes, 104
Whitehead, Alfred North, 296
Wilckens, Ulrich, 116-17, 123, 264, 266, 271, 273, 276
Williams, Sam K., 250
Wink, Walter, 89, 90
Wise, Michael O., 61
Wissmann, Hans, 261
Witherington, Ben III, 64-65
Woolston, Thomas, 8, 97
Wrede, William, 32, 227
Wright, Tom, 104

Yerkes, James, 185
Young, Frances, 231

Zenger, Erich, 312, 316
Zinzendorf, Nicholaus Ludwig von, 179
Zoroaster, 188
Zwingli, Huldreich, 173

Scripture Reference Index

OLD TESTAMENT

Genesis

1:1	126
6:4	291
12:7	263
18:18	121
22:4	265

Exodus

3:14	289
12:13	248
19:16	265
24:8	249

Leviticus

16:24	250
17:11	247
19:18	105

Numbers

24:17	78

Deuteronomy

6:4-5	105
14:1	226
32:6	226
32:39	110, 263

1 Kings

17:22	273

Job

16:19-22	128

Psalms

1:3-4	149
2	149
2:7	149
8:5	316
8:9	316
22	259
22:1	259
22:24	259
25:15-20	122
47:1-2	122
113–118	94

Isaiah

6:5	312
7:14	120, 239
9:1	266
9:1-10	120
35:5-6	102
40:3	88
41:4	110
42:8	296
43:10	110
44:6	289
44:6-8	312
45:21	122
46:4	110
53	109, 251
53:4	120
53:12	247, 251
61:1	125
61:1-2	125

Jeremiah

31:31	247
31:31-34	320

Ezekiel

36:23	314
47:8	266

Daniel

7	66, 229
7:13	108
7:13-14	214
12:2-3	260

Hosea

6:2	265

Amos

5:18	325

Obadiah

21	312

Jonah

2:1	265

Micah

5:2	81, 120

Zechariah

1:12	128
9:9	92

Malachi

2:14	84

NEW TESTAMENT

Matthew

1	81
1:1	2
1:17	121
1:18	84, 121
1:18-22	237
1:19	84
1:20	84, 158
1:22-23	120
1:23	239
2:1	77
2:2	77
2:5-6	120
2:6	81
2:15	121
2:16	77
2:16-18	77
3:1-2	121
3:2	10
3:4	88
3:7-10	88
3:16-17	89
4:12-15	120
4:16	121
4:19, 22	335

5–7	121
5:3-12	314
5:14	104
5:17	101
5:17-18	120
5:18	102
5:19	100
5:20	102
5:21-49	101
6:9	225
6:9-10	314
7:12	216
8:11	120
8:15-20	121
8:17	120
8:20	103, 108, 228
8:22	103
9	226
9:17	103
10	121
10:5	121
10:6	320
10:7	99
10:15	226
10:16	121
11:3	91
11:4-5	102, 313
11:6	104
11:10	91
11:18-19	90
11:19	105, 228
11:22	330
11:25-26	227
11:27	225
12:28	124, 125
12:30	308
12:41	224
12:42	224
13	121
13:16-17	102
13:30	121
13:40-43	121
13:47-50	121
13:55	84

14:12	90
15:24	320
16:14-16	113
16:16	211
16:18	320
16:19	321
16:23	114
18	121
18:15-20	121
18.23-35	105
19:28	327
21:11	328
22:11	105
23:3	216
23:15	92
23:37-38	320
24–25	121
24	121
24:3	330
24:5	111
24:27	108
24:37	108
24:43-44	331
25:1-13	84, 330
25:31-46	109
25:32	331
25:37	331
26:13	121
26:26-29	93, 242
26:64	111
27:51-52	291
27:52-53	116
28:7-10	98
28:13	97
28:15	267
28:16	264
28:16-17	265
28:16-20	98
28:17	264
28:18-20	98, 121
28:19	125, 138
28:23-35	105

Mark					
1:1	2, 119	9:17	99, 224	16:8	97
1:7-8	89	9:31	95, 242, 251	16:14	264
1:9-10	89	9:32	119	16:15-18	185
1:10	125	10:29	226	16:19	274, 276
1:11	120	10:38	229		
1:13	124, 125	10:45	109, 125, 251	**Luke**	
1:14	90	10:46-52	120	1:2	46
1:15	312	11:1-10	92	1:3	2
1:16	81	12:9	321	1:4	2
1:21	99	12:14	224	1:5-6	122
1:22	92, 100, 104	12:25	314	1:31-33	122
1:24	124	12:28	105	1:35	125
2:9	99	12:35-37	83	1:47	123
2:10	228	12:41	224	2:1-4	122
2:17	105	12:42	224	2:1-5	79
2:22	104	13	226	2:1-7	77
2:23	91	13:6	111	2:4	81
2:28	228	13:20	324	2:4-11	81
3:4	101	13:21	119	2:5	84
3:7	99, 101	13:24-27	330	2:11	122, 123
3:21	114	13:26	330	3:1-3	87, 217
3:21, 31	85	13:27	109	3:3	88
3:27	103	13:28	109	3:21-22	89
3:31-35	85	13:32	119	3:23-38	46, 81
4:11	227	14	93	4:16	81
4:11-12	119	14:12	91, 93, 244	4:18	125
4:38	224	14:12-14	93	4:18-19	123
5:17-18	120	14:18	94	4:22	85
5:35-43	306	14:22	247	4:24	335
6:1	81	14:22-25	94, 242	4:41	122
6:3	84	14:24	247, 251	6:20	123
6:50	111	14:25	94, 245, 314	6:21	123
6:52	119	14:26	110	7:34	123
7:5	100	14:32-42	124, 225	9:62	103
7:8	100	14:36	225	11:2	225
7:9	100	14:38	67	11:20	101, 102, 313
7:27	92, 105	14:48	67	11:31	233
8:27	92	14:61	110, 120	11:37	216
8:29	244	14:62	110-12, 329	12:8-9	65
8:31	99, 125	15:27	67	13:31	216
9:1	226	15:34	217	15	105
9:5	99	15:39	120	15:2	112
9:7	120	16:1	266	16:16	91, 101, 122
		16:7	98, 266	17:18	245

17:24	325	3:22-23	89	15:14	125
19:7	243	3:26	90	15:16	224
20:27	115	4:25-26	112	15:26	128, 129
22	93	4:35	104	16:7-11	128
22:15	93, 244	5:1	92	16:8-11	129
22:15-19a	242	5:7-8	138	17:5	127
22:15-20	93, 242	5:24	126	17:19	246
22:18	245	5:26	127	17:24	127, 325
22:19	94, 244	5:27	127	18:20	214
22:20	242	6:5	92	18:28	91, 93, 244
22:47-53	95	6:27	127	19:12	96
22:69	109, 198	6:35	128	19:19	96
22:70	111	6:53-36	83, 93	19:22	96
23:2	95	7:5	85, 114	19:31	91
24:6	98	7:11-13	213	20:8	97
24:11	264	8:12	128	20:14-15	264
24:21	96, 107	8:37-43	126	20:15	267
24:30-31	98	8:51	126	20:17	264
24:31	115	8:58	127	20:19	115
24:34	114	9:11	236	20:20	114
24:39	98, 114	9:38	127	20:24-29	264
24:41	114, 115	10:9	128	20:31	129
24:41-43	114	10:11	128	20:31-32	58
24:43	98	10:14	225	21	98, 267
24:46-49	98	10:24-25	227	21:4	115
24:51	274	10:24-29	264	21:25	334
		10:30	11	25	226
John		10:33	127	26	128
1:1-3	126	10:36	236		
1:11	212	10:38	127	**Acts**	
1:12	213	10:38-44	305	1:3	265
1:14	126, 127, 221,	11:25	128	1:4	266
	300	11:38-44	305	1:9-10	274, 275
1:1-18	126	11:50	217	2:32	98
1:30	236	11:55	92	2:36	122
1:32-34	128	13—15	128	2:46-47	244
2:1	128	13:26	94	3:15	98
2:3-4	85	14—16	128	4:10	98
2:13, 23	92	14:6	128	4:12	300
3:1-2	217	14:9	127, 205	4:20	335
3:2	331	14:16-17	128	7:56	107
3:13	127	14:17	128	9:3	114
3:16	128	14:26	128	17:23	306
3:17	105, 236	15:1	128	17:25-28	306

17:32	335	6:20	132	**Galatians**	
		7:10-11	130	1:4	132
Romans		8:6	135	1:11-12	131
1:1	131	9:14	130	1:13	114
1:1-6	131	9:20	16	2:20	133
1:3	83, 234	10:4	135	3:28	321
1:3-4	116, 149	11	93	4:4	84, 235, 238
2:20	168	11:1	82	6:12	132
3:24-25	250	11:23	130	6:14	131, 133
4:25	132, 251, 272	11:23-25	93, 242		
5:6	132	11:24	245	**Ephesians**	
5:8	251	11:24-25	94	1:10	254
6:4	134	11:25	249, 320	4:10	296
6:5	134	11:26	212, 245	4:13	321
6:9	130	11:29	249		
6:18-19	135	12:3	261	**Philippians**	
7:6	135	12:23	321	2	295
8:3	132	15	117	2:5-11	235
8:4	134	15:3-8	130	2:6-11	233, 276, 295
8:11	130	15:4	262, 267	2:8	132, 256
8:15	225	15:5-8	97	2:9	133
8:18-25	118	15:7	114	2:9-11	117, 132
8:19	135	15:8	131, 263	2:10-11	296, 331
8:22-23	327	15:9	129	3:10	133
8:32	132	15:12	263	3:10-11	133
8:34	276	15:13-14	117	3:5	82
10:9	133, 311	15:17-18	117	15	117
10:14	212	15:20	273		
11:1	82	15:21	117	**Colossians**	
11:17-18	321	15:23	118, 324	1:15	135
12:14	130	15:24	133	1:20	135, 298
16:25-26	206	15:28	330	2:3	233
		15:3-5	130	2:9	135
1 Corinthians		15:4	267		
1:21	132	15:4-5	262	**1 Thessalonians**	
1:23	130, 214	15:54	294	4:15-17	332
1:23-25	242	15:54-57	133	5:21	ix
1:24	234				
2:8	132	**2 Corinthians**		**1 Timothy**	
3:9	321	5:14	132, 133	2:4	306
5:7	249	5:17	118	3:16	296
5:17	118	5:21	132, 272		
6:9	321	11:4	130	**Hebrews**	
6:14	133	13:13	138	1:1-2	204

1:2	234	7:4-8	320	*2 Clement*	
1:3	234	20	332	1:1-2	139
2:17	234	21:6	289		
5:8-9	234	22:13	289	**Ignatius**	
				To the Ephesians	
1 Peter				7:2	139
3:18	291	**EXTRACANONICAL**			
3:18-20	291	**WRITINGS**		*To the Magnesians*	
3:19	291, 293			9	253
3:19-22	292	**2 Maccabees**		9:12	252
4:6	291	12:43-45	261		
				To the Smyrnaeans	
2 Peter		*1 Enoch*		1	253
3:13	331	51:1-5	115	2	253
1 John		*Odes of Solomon*		*To the Trallians*	
3:2	331	42:10	293	2	253
5:7-8	138				
		Barnabas		**Polycarp**	
Revelation		2	252, 253	*Phil.* 9	253
1:17-18	293	14:9	252		
1:8	289	15:9	275		